MOSQUITO MISSIONS

RAF AND COMMONWEALTH DE HAVILLAND MOSQUITOES

MARTIN W. BOWMAN

Pen & Sword
AVIATION

First published in Great Britain in 2012 by
PEN & SWORD AVIATION
An imprint of
Pen & Sword Books Ltd
47 Church Street
Barnsley
South Yorkshire
S70 2AS

Copyright © Martin W. Bowman, 2012

ISBN 978 1 78159 167 3

A CIP catalogue record for this book is
available from the British Library

Printed and bound in India
By Replika Press Pvt. Ltd.

Pen & Sword Books Ltd incorporates the Imprints of Pen & Sword Aviation,
Pen & Sword Family History, Pen & Sword Maritime, Pen & Sword Military,
Pen & Sword Discovery, Pen & Sword Politics, Pen & Sword Atlas,
Pen & Sword Archaeology, Wharncliffe Local History, Wharncliffe True Crime,
Wharncliffe Transport, Pen & Sword Select, Pen & Sword Military Classics,
Leo Cooper, The Praetorian Press, Claymore Press, Remember When,
Seaforth Publishing and Frontline Publishing

For a complete list of Pen & Sword titles please contact
PEN & SWORD BOOKS LIMITED
47 Church Street, Barnsley, South Yorkshire, S70 2AS, England
E-mail: enquiries@pen-and-sword.co.uk
Website: www.pen-and-sword.co.uk

Contents

Acknowledgements

I am enormously grateful to the following people for their time and effort and kind loan of photos etc, not least to my fellow Mosquito author, friend and colleague, Graham Simons, for getting the book to press-ready standard: Eric Atkins DFC* KW*, Chairman MAA; Michael H. A. T. Bayon DFC; Andy Bird; Philip J. Birtles; Barry Blunt BA Hons; Dr. Theo Boiten; Bill Bridgeman; Tommy Broom DFC**; Derek Carter; George Cash; Peter Celis; Johnny Claxton; Bob Collis; Squadron Leader Joe Cooper AFC FC; Hank Cooper DSO DFC; Patrick Corness; Luc Cox; Des Curtis; Tom Cushing; Grenville Eaton; Reg Everson; Leslie Fletcher; Stephen M. Fochuk; J. D. S. Garratt DFC*; Rev Nigel Gilson; Air Vice Marshal L. W. G. 'Bill' Gill DSO; Ted Gomersall; Richard T. Goucher; Terry Groves; Cato Guhnfeldt; Alan Hague, Leo Hall; Vic Hester; Leslie 'Dutch' Holland; G. Horsfield; Richard Howard; Squadron Leader Stephen J. Howard; M. Howland; Dennis Hudson; Harry Jeffries; Bernard M. Job; Lawrence 'Kev' Kevan DFC; Ian McPherson; Norman McPherson DFC; Nigel McTeer; W. H. Miller DFC; Denis Moore; Eric Mombeek; Wing Commander A. P. Morgan; F. G. Morris; Mosquito Aircrew Association; Wing Commander George Newby; Wing Commander George Parry DSO DFC; Simon Parry, Air Research Publications; Derek Patfield; Squadron Leader Charles Patterson DSO DFC; John Rayner; Alf Rogers; Jerry Scutts; James Maunder Taylor; Henk Van Baaren; Colin 'Ginger' Walsh; Peter Waxham; Alan B. Webb; Brian Williams.

Introduction

In September 1939 Robert K. Shorter had just left school and had started work at a bakery. When he heard the news he went to the local police station to volunteer for the Army. He was told to go back to his job and grow up a bit more and then try again. He stopped at the bakery for a few more months when one day he heard of a job at the local dairy for a roundsman. As he had always wanted to drive a horse and cart he applied for the job and was taken on. As it turned out he never got to drive a horse and cart but delivered the milk by bicycle round the villages of East and West Hanney in Oxfordshire. One day he had just finished his round and was cycling back to his base when he saw a lot of activity at an old flour mill known as Dandridges and being nosy (like all fifteen year olds) he stopped and asked what was going on. The reply was that the building was being converted into a factory to help the war effort. He was intrigued and when he was told that there were vacancies he rushed back to the dairy and gave in his notice. He did not know what he had let himself in for. Firstly, he had to cycle four and a half miles to get to the mill and after a 12 hour day do it again to get home. His first job was to clean the cobwebs off all the walls and ceilings but he kept at it when he was told it would help the war effort. After the mill had been cleaned three centre lathes and three milling machines, a dozen bench drills and a grindstone arrived. Most of the power used to operate the machines was produced by a water turbine. The biggest shock of all came when the workers were told that they were going to make the hydraulic parts for the Mosquito aircraft and they had to learn how to operate the machines as they went along. 'Bob' Shorter recalled that 'as it turned out, we must have learnt quickly and well because the Mosquito was one of the most successful planes of all times. I worked twelve hour shifts on week days and one week on nights for four and a half years. However, during the last year we were only allowed to make 50 components a shift [which were secretly transported to an underground assembly plant near Maidenhead], so on the night shift we used to play a lot of cards. Some weeks I lost most of my pay!'

Four hundred sub-contractors worked on the various units for the Mosquito. Because the aircraft was built almost entirely of wood many were well known furniture companies such as Harris Lebus at Tottenham and E. Gomme Ltd and Dancer and Hearne Ltd in High Wycombe, who were making spars and wings and Vanden Plas in Hendon who were making wing coverings, as well as members of the exhibition stand and coach building industries. Detail parts were being manufactured by numerous other small companies including bicycle manufacturers and a firm of craftsmen used to making ecclesiastical ironwork, while in homes, garages and church halls the length and breadth of the country, women ranging from 'duchesses to charladies' made everything from simple parts to small components. The London bus refurbishment facility at Aldenham became a major Mosquito subcontractor, ESA in Stevenage produced complete wings and the smallest contractor was located in a garden shed in Welwyn!

The concept of a bomber built almost entirely of wood with two crew and no gun armament and relying on speed as the bomber's only defence was not new. In World War I the de Havilland D.H.4 unarmed bomber was faster than the fighters of the day. Throughout the 1930s de Havillands concentrated on civil aircraft of many types from Moths to airliners, ending with the Flamingo, the first all-metal airliner they had built. But as the clouds developed over Europe in 1937 and 1938 and war with Germany became almost inevitable, thoughts turned very reluctantly towards military aircraft. There was every confidence that the high-speed bomber that could out-fly most enemy fighters would be as novel and as vitally needed as it had been before. If officialdom did not stifle him Geoffrey de Havilland was convinced that his company could do better still the second time. 'DH', as he was universally known, was born the son of a clergyman in 1883 who had joined the Aircraft Manufacturing Co at Hendon in 1914 as designer and chief pilot. Meanwhile he had been commissioned in the Royal Flying Corps (RFC) but his true brilliance was at the drawing board. In 1920 DH had formed his own company, at Stag Lane in North London. Ten years on Stag Lane was needed for redevelopment, so he moved his operation to the green fields of Hatfield in Hertfordshire, but not before three DH.88 Comet racers had been built, amid great secrecy, before final assembly and testing at the new factory at Hatfield[1.]

One day in 1937 Geoffrey de Havilland and John E. Walker, Chief Engine Installation Designer went to the Air Ministry to put forward their project 'with hope and some pride' in their hearts. 'Our scheme was to discard every item of equipment that was not essential, design for a two-man crew and no rear armament, relying on high speed for defence. We proposed using two Rolls-Royce Merlin engines, the best in the world. A specification and general arrangement drawings were therefore prepared and we got ready for the next stage. We knew it was not going to be an easy one. We outlined our scheme and showed the drawings' says Geoffrey de Havilland. 'They were barely glanced at. Then the bolder of the two officials, addressed us like a schoolmaster and waving a hand towards our cherished plans, he said: 'Forget it. You people haven't produced a war machine for years and if you want to do so now you must start on something quite simple - perhaps design a wing for an experimental plane.'[2] DH was a rare of mixture of reserve, defiance and technical genius and would not be dissuaded. Being confident of the final decision he ensured that work on the design continued. If the design had been accepted, six months of precious time could have been saved but it was estimated that a year could be saved in production due to the simplicity of wood construction as compared with metal. All members of the technical staff were enthusiastic about the project. Ronald E. Bishop had been chief designer for some years and was in charge of the team ably assisted by C. Tim Wilkins, now a director and Chief Designer, Richard M. Clarkson, head of the aerodynamics section and Robert Harper head of the stress section. Bishop had been raised in the de Havilland tradition of wooden structures and had seen how, in the 1930s, the DH.88 Comet Racers had made use of innovative diagonal planking to achieve a thin wing of high aspect ratio without external bracing. This form of construction had also been adopted in 1937 for the DH.91

1   The streamlined low-wing monoplane ultimately was to play a significant role in the development of the Mosquito just as the Supermarine S6B influenced the design of the Spitfire, after the seaplane's success in the Schneider Trophy races. In 1934 Grosvenor House, one of the three Comets entered in the Mildenhall to Melbourne race, won first place.
2   *Sky Fever: The Autobiography of Sir Geoffrey de Havilland.* (Airlife 1979)

Albatross airliner - probably the largest airliner of high performance to be made of wood and its lines too were extremely clean and attractive, everything possible being done to reduce 'drag'. The Albatross was powered by four of the newly designed DH Gipsy 12 engines with a new scheme of ducted air cooling and was used by Imperial Airways on the London-Paris service for a short time, but production and development of this airliner and also of the Flamingo and Moth Minor, were ended by the onset of war.

In September 1939 the Air Ministry remained unconvinced that an unarmed high speed bomber was realistic but Geoffrey de Havilland found an ally in Air Marshal Sir Wilfrid Freeman, the Air Council's member for Research and development. Geoffrey de Havilland had known Freeman since the early days of the 1914 war and had always liked him. 'He had technical knowledge much above the average and in discussion was helpful and without bias. I had stayed a short time at his headquarters in France in 1916 when he was in charge of a squadron of D.H.4s and I felt he would appreciate our wish to build a modern version of that successful machine. It needed only one meeting with this wise and far-sighted man to discuss our plans and to get his full approval and blessing for the Mosquito.' Sir Wilfred was in favour of having no armament but he doubted that the unarmed wooden bomber could carry a 1,000lb bomb load for 1,500 miles and at a speed faster than the Spitfire. The Mosquito would do both.[3]

On 1 January 1940 DH received an order for a single prototype of the unarmed bomber variant with a level speed of 397 mph at 23,700 feet and a 1,480 mile range at 24,900 feet on full tanks. The final design and building of the prototype which was referred to originally as 'E-0234', was moved from Hatfield to Salisbury Hall, an old country mansion surrounded by a moat about five miles away, for safety during air raids.[4] Of historical and romantic interest, Salisbury Hall was the home of Sir Nigel Gresley who designed the Mallard steam locomotive and Jennie Lady Churchill who lived at the house with her second husband and was visited by her son Winston. Amongst many Salisbury Hall traditions was one that claimed that a smaller building on the side of the moat had been the temporary home of Nell Gwynne.[5] The team of nine designers led by Ronald Bishop worked in the house and sheds were erected in the grounds for assembling the prototype in strict secrecy.

The Mosquito embodied several new design features. The radiators for the Merlin engines were placed in the wings on both sides between the engine and fuselage. The exit of the air was under the wing. This considerably reduced resistance as compared with an external radiator. Experiments were made with the exit shape of the engine exhausts and led to appreciable forward thrust being obtained. The fuselage was formed

3   On 16 January 1941 W4050 outpaced a Spitfire in tests at 6,000 feet. In July the Mosquito became the world's fastest operational aircraft, a distinction it would enjoy for the next 2½ years. Over a period of a few days in early February 1941 W4050 made a number of level speed trials, during which it reached a maximum speed of 390 mph at 22,000 feet and with Merlin 61 engines, reached 433 mph at 28,500 feet. Multiple ejector exhausts were a contributory factor. On 20 October W4050 achieved a speed of 437mph in level flight. Using two-stage Merlin 77s, W4050, which made its last flight around December 1943 - shaded this with a maximum speed of 439 mph in level flight.

4   Bombs fell within a mile of Hatfield one day in every five and when a low flying Ju 88A of KG77 dropped four bombs on the Hatfield factory on 3 October 1940 21 people were killed and 70 injured. Among the bomb wreckage was 80% of the Mosquito work in progress.

5   Salisbury Hall is now the site of the DH Heritage Centre, formerly the Mosquito Aircraft Museum.

by a balsa wood filling between an inner and outer skin of plywood. This made a light, stiff and stable structure with no need for further stiffening. A feature that helped greatly in construction was the division of the fuselage into two half sections down the top and bottom lines of the whole length. This allowed nearly all the equipment, controls, wiring, instruments, etc, to be installed with much greater ease. Two spars with tip-to-tip top and bottom booms of the laminated spruce, boxed with plywood webs, were finally chosen. Canadian spruce was selected for construction of the 50 feet spars, although only one in ten trees met the required standard laid down in the Air Ministry Specification. Some of the Mosquito materials were home grown - approximately 6 million cubic feet of beech on Lord Bathurst's estate near Cirencester, for example, was extracted from three forests in three years to be made into plywood at Lydney, Gloucestershire. The fixed tail surfaces were all wood and plywood-covered while the rudder and elevators were made of aluminium and the elevators fabric-covered though in 1943 metal skinning of the elevators was introduced to give better performance in high speed dives. The wing structure had to be designed so that 500-odd gallons of fuel could be carried in tanks in the space between structure members. The top and bottom wing skins were each formed by two layers of three-ply separated by long stiffening 'stringers' running the whole span of the wings.

The gluing operation was critical. In fact, a well glued laminated spar could be stronger than a solid spar. Laminations also obviated the shrinkage and warping which single beams might suffer. The glue was at first casein, a milk-based adhesive with which de Havilland and other wooden aircraft manufacturers had had long experience, but which proved unsatisfactory because of fungal growth.[6] Later, casein was replaced by synthetic 'Beetle', introduced in Britain in about 1942, made by Dr N. A. de Bruyne's Aero Research Company at Duxford (now Ciba-Geigy).

The first order for DH.98 (Mosquito) aircraft was received on 1 March 1940. It was for fifty bombers to be built 'off the drawing board'. But in May DH were instructed

6   The Air Ministry decided in January 1944 to equip 22 bomber and strike squadrons in India with FB.VIs but all Mosquito operations came to an abrupt end on 12 November, when, following a series of accidents, a signal to all units required Mosquito aircraft to be grounded pending inspection. In March 1944 production of the first batch of Mosquitoes in Australia had been disrupted when it was discovered that components in the wing failed to 'mate'. Consequently, gaps occurred in the glued joints between the main spar and the plywood stressed-skin of the wings (under load the plywood upper wing surface could become detached and the box-section spar assembly could collapse). The wings for the first 20 Australian-built aircraft were scrapped. In the UK a series of fatal flying accidents on Mosquitoes of various marks was attributed to failure of the wing structure. DH still maintained that the failures in India resulted from climatic conditions and ordered the destruction of all parts made with casein glue. At first it seemed that the defects were restricted to the FB.VIs built at Canley by Standard Motors Ltd. Of 24 such aircraft inspected by 8 November, 23 had defects 6 feet from the wingtips. But Hatfield found similar faults in 16 Mosquitoes produced. An investigating team led by Major Hereward de Havilland in India in November reported that the accidents were caused by extensive shrinkage of airframes during the monsoon season. However, Mr F. G. Myers, DH technical representative in India signalled: 'Defects not due to climatic conditions. The standard of glueing...leaves much to be desired.' Meanwhile, an inspection team at the Ministry of Aircraft Production at Defford found that six different marks of Mosquito, all built at Hatfield and Leavesden showed signs of similar defects. Yet none of the aircraft had been exposed to monsoon conditions, nor had termites attacked them! A meeting at the AM on 1 January 1945 decided that the accidents in India were caused by 'faults largely due to climate'. To cure the problem, a plywood strip was inserted along the span of the wing to seal the whole length of the skin joint along the main spar. The modification was applied to all Mosquitoes in production in Australia, but few, if any, sets were sent to India, where defective Mosquitoes were simply SOC. In India the large scale re-equipping of squadrons never took place.

to stop work on the order and concentrate all its resources on repairing Hurricanes and Merlin engines. By persistently worrying the officials who stopped Mosquito work DH eventually got it reinstated in July. The company had never stopped work entirely and not much time was lost. E-0234 was completed at Salisbury Hall and moved by road on two Queen Mary trailers to Hatfield on 3 November 1940. In a hangar there it was assembled and the two Merlin 21s engines with two-speed single-stage superchargers installed. The aircraft emerged on 19 November for engine runs and on 24 November taxiing trials began with Geoffrey de Havilland Jr., Chief Test Pilot at the controls. Next day, just four days short of 11 months from the start of detailed design work, Geoffrey de Havilland Jr. and John Walker made the maiden flight. Take-off, de Havilland was to recall, was 'straightforward and easy'. The undercarriage was not retracted until considerable height had been gained and this was observed by John Walker through the nose windows. The aircraft reached a speed of 220 mph and the only real problem encountered was the inability of the undercarriage doors to fully close and their opening, by 12 inches, as speed was increased. In November on the third flight the undercarriage would not come down and had to be pumped down by hand.[7]

On 30 December 1940 de Havillands received a contract for 150 Mosquitoes, although it was not specified how many would be fighters and how many would be bombers and no firm figure was given on the number required as photo-reconnaissance versions. This indecision would cause problems in production because wings for the bomber and fighter versions were different (the fighter version needed strengthened wing spars for stronger manoeuvre load factors) and bomber noses too were not the same as fighter noses since accommodation had to be provided in the fighters for four machine guns and four 20mm Hispano cannon. Fortunately, de Havillands recognized this and had arranged space under the floor to house these weapons if and when required. Even so, 28 completed bomber fuselages later had to have the nose replaced.

While the Ministry deliberated, W4052, the night fighter prototype, was also completed at Salisbury Hall. It differed from the bomber prototype in having up rated Merlin 21s, each capable of producing 1,460hp, a flat bullet-proof windscreen and the then secret AI.Mk.IV radar. Entry was by a door in the starboard side of the cockpit instead of through a trapdoor in the floor as on the bomber version. To save a month of dismantling, transport and reassembly, W4052 was flown out of a field adjacent to the assembly hangar on 15 May 1941 by Geoffrey de Havilland Jr with Fred Plumb, who was in charge of construction, in the second seat. W4050 was used to help eliminate problems on W4052, not least of which concerned armament and exhaust systems. (Flash eliminators later had to be fitted to the machine guns on the NF.II to prevent the crew being dazzled when they were fired at night.) The cooling intake shrouds for the 'Saxophone' type exhausts tended to overheat and even burn through after prolonged use. Flame-dampers prevented the giveaway exhaust-glow at night but they inhibited performance. The problems became so great that Frank B. Halford, head of de Havilland Engine Division, felt moved to say that 'next time it would be better to design the aircraft around the exhaust system!' Multiple ejector-open-ended exhaust stubs solved the

---

7   Tail buffeting experienced at speeds of 240-255mph was virtually eliminated in February 1941 after the
    engine nacelles were redesigned and finally extended beyond the trailing edge of the wing (although as
    a consequence, the flaps had to be split).

problem and were fitted to PR.VIII, B.IX and B.XVI models with a resulting quantum leap in performance, the B.IV, for instance, gaining an additional 10-13 mph as a result. Official trials, which began at the A&AEE Boscombe Down on 19 February 1941 confirmed de Havilland's faith in the design and on 20 April the prototype was demonstrated to Lord Beaverbrook, Minister of Aircraft Production and Major General 'Hap' Arnold, Chief of the USAAF and other senior officers. W4050, in the hands of Geoffrey de Havilland Jr., gave a dazzling performance, making rolling climbs on one engine. Major Elwood Quesada, General Arnold's aide and later to control IX Fighter Command in England said, 'An airplane that looks fast usually is fast and the Mosquito was, by the standards of the time, an extremely well streamlined airplane and it was highly regarded, highly respected'.[8]

W4051, the photo-reconnaissance prototype, was the third Mosquito to fly, on 10 June 1941. Though it was the second Mosquito completed at Salisbury Hall, construction had been delayed when the fuselage originally intended for W4051 was used to replace W4050's fuselage, which had fractured at Boscombe in a tail wheel incident. W4051 received a production fuselage instead, a factor which enabled this prototype to fly later on operations. On 21 June the Air Ministry finally decided that apart from five prototypes (one bomber, one PR and three fighter), nineteen aircraft were to be PR models (the last ten aircraft (W4064-72) were converted to B.IV Series I bombers) and 176 fighters. At this time the further fifty Mosquitoes ordered were unspecified. In July the Air Ministry finally confirmed that these would be unarmed bombers and they wanted de Havillands to produce 150 Mosquitoes a month. Eighty would have to be built at Hatfield, while 30 would be built by Second Aircraft Group (SAG) and 40 in Canada.[9]

8   Arnold asked for and received, plans data and photos of the Mosquito and engineers from Curtiss-Wright spent nearly a month visiting the de Havilland factory, but the Material Division of the AAC expected that P-38 Lightnings would soon be available and capable of handling American PR needs. Reports from Britain emphasized only technical problems or 'teething' problems but if the Americans were not to use the Mosquito Arnold felt that there was much to learn from the design. A request was sent to Britain for one airframe to evaluate at Wright Field, but this request was only three days old before the US declaration of war and the US entered WWII without a single combat worthy photo-plane.

9   A widely-dispersed shadow scheme was first conceived in 1940 when de Havillands had considered building Armstrong Whitworth Albermarles and so, while Hatfield geared up for mass production of Mosquito aircraft, a second Mosquito line was planned for a new factory at Leavesden and Standard Motors at Cowley near Oxford were approached with the idea of producing more Mosquitoes there. By September 1941 it was anticipated that by 1942 Mosquitoes would be coming off the production lines at the rate of 200 (90 fighters and with Canadian production included 110 bombers) a month. By the end of January 1942 contracts totalled 1,378 Mosquitoes of all variants, including 20 T.III trainer versions and 334 FB.VI bombers by the SAG at Leavesden. Additionally, 400 more were planned to be built by DH Canada. Drawings and schedules - there were 10,000 to make a complete set - were sent to the Canadian and Australian factories. Canadian production was to suffer as a result of the climate. The wooden jigs used to make the fuselage varied considerably. Heating the glue used in the half shells of the fuselage to make it set fast and the humidity of Toronto, which is on the Great Lakes, caused the 40 feet long wooden moulds to vary so much that concrete moulds finally had to be used. At peak production and including sub-contractors, a total of 75,000 people worked on DH wartime products. All told, 3,326 Mosquitoes were built at Hatfield. Leavesden produced 1,476 Mosquitoes and Standard Motors built 1,066 examples. Others were built by Percival at Luton and by Airspeed at Portsmouth and at Chester. The 6,439th and last Mosquito to be built in the UK left the Chester factory in November 1950. Total Mosquito production throughout the world (including 1,076 in Canada and 212 in Australia) was 7,781.

W4072, the prototype B.IV bomber, flew for the first time on 8 September 1941. The fifty B.IV Series II bombers differed from the Series I in having a larger bomb bay to carry four 500lb bombs instead of the Series I's four 250 pounders. This was made possible by C. Tim Wilkins, R. E. Bishop's Assistant Chief Designer, who shortened the tail stabilizer of the 500lb bomb so that four of these larger weapons could be carried. Twenty-seven B.IV Series II (W4066 was the only PR.IV Series I) were later converted to PR.IV reconnaissance aircraft, with three additional fuel tanks in the bomb bay, while twenty B.IVs were modified by DH, Vickers-Armstrong and Marshalls to carry a 4,000lb bomb.

On 4 December 1941, three days before America declared war on Japan, a request was sent to Britain for one airframe, this to be evaluated at Wright Field. In the summer of 1942, Colonel Elliott Roosevelt brought two squadrons of F-4 Lightnings and a squadron of B-17F 'mapping Fortresses' to Britain. The President's son was preparing his group for the invasion of North Africa and was to work with the RAF until ready. Given a Mosquito B.IV for combat evaluation, Roosevelt discovered that the aircraft outperformed his F-4s and had five times the range. The first of the Canadian-built Mosquitoes had already given demonstrations at Wright Field. It was so good that General Arnold ordered that no US aircraft were to be raced against the Mosquito, to avoid embarrassing American pilots! Arnold asked that Mosquitoes be obtained to equip all American photo-reconnaissance squadrons in Europe - almost 200 aircraft for 1943 alone! In 1943 30 Mosquitoes were diverted from British production after the Canadian allocation of 120 for the Americans had been reduced to just 60 B.XXs because of RAF demands. These, plus eleven Canadian-built F-8 models, were delivered to the 802nd (later, 25th) Bomb Group at Watton who operated the Mosquitoes on all manner of operations such as 'Chaff' ('Window')-dispensing sorties, 'Bluestocking' weather reconnaissance flights, night 'Mickey' night radar-mapping missions using the H_2S radar and 'Redstocking' agent-dropping missions as well as on Project 'Aphrodite' and 'Anvil' pilotless drone operations when war-weary B-17s and PB4Y-1 Liberators packed with 18,000lb of nitro-glycerine were flown against V-weapons sites. Initially, most of the American pilots were drawn from the 50th Fighter Squadron in Iceland who were used to the P-38 Lightning's contra-rotating propellers and had never experienced the take-off and landing characteristics of the Mosquito; especially its high landing speed and tendency to swing on take-off. They had also to remember to open the radiator shutters just prior to take-off to prevent the engines overheating.

1st Officer Peter George of 6 Ferry Pool, Ratcliffe recalled an occasion when he and another pilot delivered two Mosquitoes to the USAAF at Watton. 'On the way we flew in open formation across the flat land of East Anglia. Shortly after landing I was greeted by a smiling US pilot (probably from the Deep South) and he said to me - 'Buddy, they say these little babes (pointing to the Mossie) swing like a fly on a shit house door!' I replied, 'Matey, they sure will if you let 'em.'

By mid-1944 pin-point bombing by high speed Mosquitoes, hedge-hopping their way over enemy-occupied Europe in broad daylight, had become a common practice. Often, the sheer speed of the aircraft and the élan of their crews got them home again through flak and fighters. The Mosquito gained such a deserved reputation for achieving the impossible that at one stage the British press claimed that when one was shot down the Luftwaffe crew could count it as two victories. Apocryphal this may be but during four years of war the 'Wooden Wonder' was to prove the scourge of the Axis throughout Europe, the Mediterranean and the Far East. Such was the incisive contribution made by this remarkable aircraft, built largely of beech, spruce and ply and the shattering effect it had on the Germans as a whole, that its very presence eventually caused *Moskitopanik* throughout the *Reich* territory. One RAF officer summed up the success of the aircraft, saying: 'The Mosquito represents all that is finest in aeronautical design. It is an aeroplane that could only have been conceived in this country and combines the British genius for building a practical and straightforward machine with the typical de Havilland flair for producing a first-rate aeroplane that looks right and *is* right.'

Chapter 1

Photo-Reconnaissance

In July 1941 W4051 and W4054 became the first Mosquitoes to be taken on charge by the RAF when these unarmed PR.1 examples were delivered to No.1 Photographic Reconnaissance Unit (PRU) at Benson, Oxfordshire. Hereward de Havilland DSO, Geoffrey's brother, who had taken an engineering degree before the First World War and had flown with the RFC, would travel to every country where Mosquito squadrons were operating and send reports back to Hatfield. A first-class engineer, he never showed any desire to become a designer, except in connection with one of his main hobbies, which was designing and making particularly fine furniture. After visiting Benson Hereward de Havilland recalled that 'Wing Commander Geoffrey Tuttle and all flying personnel accepted the aircraft as being something quite outstanding; in my experience it is one of the only aircraft which, initially, has not been branded by pilots as a death trap in one way or another. On the other hand, the engineering and maintenance personnel, especially the younger generation, were definitely biased against it, mainly on account of wood construction'.

W4055, which arrived on 8 August made the first operational Mosquito flight on 17 September when Squadron Leader Rupert Clerke and Sergeant Sowerbutts made a daylight photo-reconnaissance (PR) of Brest, La Pallice and Bordeaux. They were pursued by three Bf 109s but the PR.1 easily outpaced them at 23,000 feet and the 25-year Old Etonian and 32-year old former Margate barber returned safely. A second photo-reconnaissance was made in W4055 three days later, when Flight Lieutenant Alastair 'Ice' Taylor DFC and Sergeant Sidney Horsfall successfully photographed Bordeaux, Pauillac, Le Verdon and La Pallice. The third flight was made when Taylor and Horsfall covered Heligoland and Sylt. In October the three Mosquitoes carried out sixteen successful sorties, all of them to Norway. By spring 1942 the PRU at Benson was in need of additional PR.1s, only nine having been built. During April to June 1942 four NF.IIs - DD615, 620, 659 and W4089, all without long-range tanks - were diverted to the PRU and in December, two B.IV bomber variants - DZ411 and DZ419 - arrived. Ground crew at Benson installed the three vertical and one oblique camera aboard each of the machines and they were pressed into service. On 7 May Flight Lieutenant Victor Ricketts and Sergeant Boris Lukhmanoff his Russian born navigator flew the furthest flight over enemy territory so far when he used DK284, a modified Mk.IV to photograph Dresden, Pilzen and Regensburg, returning after six hours. On 10 June a 7¾ hour sortie was flown from Benson to La Spezia, Lyons and Marseilles.

On 14 May, meanwhile, Wing Commander Spencer Ring RCAF the CO used DD615, the first of the modified NF.IIs, to photograph Alderney. On 25 May Victor Ricketts used it to photograph Billancourt, Poissy and Le Bourget.[10] On on the 27th Flight Lieutenant Gerry R. Wooll RCAF used DD615 to successfully photograph Saarbrücken and Amiens. On 24 August he and Sergeant John 'Maxie' Fielden were dispatched on a PR sortie in

10 On 11 July Ricketts and Lukhmanoff and W4089 were lost on a sortie to Strasbourg and Ingolstadt.

DK310 to confirm a report that Italian warships were putting to sea. They were to obtain photos of Venice, Trieste, Fiume and perhaps Pola, if conditions were right. DK310 took off from Benson and stopped at Ford to top off its tanks before proceeding uneventfully to Venice. However, as Wooll departed the area the glycol pump on the starboard engine began malfunctioning. The shaft had become slightly elliptical and fluid began escaping. Within a few seconds, the engine seized. Wooll found the aircraft too heavy and unbalanced to attempt to continue on one engine and his problems were compounded a few minutes later when the port engine began overheating. Wooll headed for Switzerland and managed to put down safely at Belp airfield near Berne. After landing, Fielden tried unsuccessfully to set the aircraft on fire before the two men were marched off to a small village camp at Yen. After four months Wooll and Fielden were repatriated as part of an exchange deal which allowed two interned Bf 109 pilots to leave for Germany. (The Mosquito was retained by the Swiss, who later used it as a turbine test bed aircraft). Wooll returned to flying, as a test pilot for de Havilland in Canada.

On 19 October 1942 'H' and 'L' Flights of the Photographic Reconnaissance Unit at Leuchars were merged to form 540 Squadron. That same day, 544 Squadron formed at Benson, equipped with Ansons, Wellington IVs and Spitfire PR.IVs. In the main, 540 Squadron were used to photograph German capital ships in Baltic waters and North Germany, later the Mediterranean also.

James MacEwan an Intelligence Officer at Leuchars recalled: 'The Norwegian coast was no less than 400 miles distant from Leuchars and the major concern of the station was marine reconnaissance and convoy escort, the sector in which it operated having its centre at Leuchars and subtending an arc which stretched from Bergen down to Kap Lindisness at the south west tip of the Norwegian coast. This comparatively short section of coast was of particular significance in the prosecution of the naval war against the enemy, for here the long barrier of skerries which protected the shipping channels all the way south from the North Cape finally petered out, forcing vessels to take to the open sea. Iron-ore ships from Narvik constituted an obvious target; but what, at this stage, was of more significance to the Admiralty were German raiders, either pocket battleships or heavy cruisers, trying to slink out undetected into the North Atlantic, there to prey on merchant shipping. The Admiralty seemed to be concerned even more about these than about U-boats.

'My very first night on duty in the Ops Room shocked me into realisation of what these night-flights to the Norwegian coast, undertaken in all kinds of foul weather, meant to the crews. Just at dusk, before setting out, they had swarmed into the Ops Room, laughing, clear eyed and alert. Five hours later saw their return, when they came into the Intelligence Officer for interrogation, grey and gaunt, their cheeks sunken, men nearing the limits of endurance. Like the men who flew them, our aircraft also operated on the frontiers of endurance. Added to the hazards to be encountered was the fine, modern aerodrome of Sola, near Stavanger, where the Germans had stationed fighters and night-fighters. Anyone of our pilots, straying into this danger zone was liable to be set upon; and even if he was not shot down, he would have to expend so much fuel in evasive tactics as to place his return to base in jeopardy. Further strains upon our men were imposed by the very nature of the operations, since they were subject to sudden calls for a sortie at any time without prior warning or notice. Roused from bed, their resources drained by an earlier sortie, they would, after a hurried briefing, be dispatched out over the bleak and lonely waste of the North Sea to a rendezvous that was as vague as it was hazardous. Most of these long, tense flights by night over the dark dangerous waters of the North Sea were, in the nature of things fruitless. At first it was decreed that any sightings by our crews of hostile vessels should be reported to Bomber Command, whose aircraft would deliver an attack. But as often as not, by the time that the bombers reached their target, the enemy had escaped.

'There was another activity at Leuchars, which was so secret that no one simply ever mentioned it. Specially adapted fighter-planes, unarmed and flying by night, maintained a regular ferry service with Stockholm. So cloaked in secrecy was the whole operation that it was next to impossible to find out what was the purpose of the flight, though it was whispered that the carriage of ball bearings was involved. I remember being summoned from the Ops Room early one morning to inspect a secret small aircraft that had just landed on the runway. Built of plywood it could fly, we were told, at 350 mph - almost as fast as a Spitfire - and was called a Mosquito. No mention, of course, was made of why it had suddenly appeared at Leuchars, but we had our suspicions. There were certain other things which were not so easy to conceal. In the dead of night strange men would appear from nowhere, often tall, muscular and flaxen-haired and wearing reindeer-decorated sweaters. They stayed beside us in the Ops Room, until they were whisked off secretly to London. One or two of them, coming into the Intelligence Room, did permit us a guarded word about what they were up to. In Odda one of them gravely assured us, the Germans were engaged in some very secret operations which might well have a profound effect on the outcome of the war. When an attack was on the point of being launched against the electric power station and aluminium factory near Odda an urgent telegram arrived from Group HQ - the raid was called off! Across the fjord at Odda between the vast rock walls, the Germans had just strung a series of steel hawsers; and had the attack gone as planned, the leading flights at least, having no warning of their presence would have been cut to pieces and their crews lost.' [11]

The Mosquito's high speed made it ideal for use as a courier aircraft and a number were operated and crewed by the British Overseas Airways Corporation (BOAC) between Leuchars and Stockholm from 1942 to 1945. During 520 round trips from 3 February 1943 to 17 May 1945 these carried diplomatic mail and personnel in a pressurized bomb bay. Downed airmen and VIPs such as Professor Nields Baks, the Danish 'heavy-water' atomic physicist and Dr Nils Bohr, who was flown to England in a Mosquito on 7 October 1943 and various others including Marshal Timoshenko, were brought back successfully from Sweden, as were cargoes of precious ball-bearings, as John F. McDonald a Senior Technical Officer at Leuchars from 1942 until the end of the war, recalls: 'One of the Government appointed tasks was to bring Swedish SKEFKO ball-bearings and ball races to aid the critical shortage of such stuff for military aircraft manufacture in the UK. Our BOAC pilots informed us how, if the Air Ministry would peel off a few of the beautiful, very fast and efficient Mosquitoes, they could fly through the straits of the Skagerrak between Sweden and the north tip of Denmark so cutting hours off the elapsed flying time. After some 'proving flights' we were allocated six FB.VI fighter-bombers. These aircraft were quickly modified with a sort of pannier to hoist and carry 3,000lb of ball-bearings which, of course, could be compactly loaded. Then came the famous air raids on the principle German ball-bearing works at

11   *The Mossie* No.28 May 2001.

Schweinfurt, very effectively performed but sadly destructive to the USAAF 8th Air Force (daylight raids). Not very long afterwards British military intelligence warned that the Germans were putting together a 'commission' to purchase the entire output of the Swedish SKEFKO manufactory and BOAC received a request (spell that 'demand') from the Air Ministry to somehow or other fly two high ranking men with unlimited purchasing authority to Sweden to beat the Germans to it. We were given 48 hours to modify two of our FB.VIs to carry a single passenger in the bomb bay, or somehow, to countermand the German effort. We had cleared out the area forward of the 'bomb basket' which had formerly housed four .303 Browning guns and now we were to reinforce the plywood doors and metal hinges to bear the weight of the passenger and to provide him with oxygen, a small light, a crude intercom and the slightest modicum of heat to survive the winter cold at 26,000 feet. The operational plan was to attain that sort of altitude and put the aircraft into a dive through the Skagerrak so that the FW 190s couldn't shoot us down.' [12]

On 8 March 1943 meanwhile, the CO of 540 Squadron, Wing Commander M. J. B. Young DFC in Mk.VIII DZ364, became the first Mosquito pilot to photograph Berlin. The Squadron also carried out battle-damage assessment and target reconnaissance at such places as the German rocket research site at Peenemünde on the Baltic coast. It was on 12 June 1943 when Flight Lieutenant Reggie A. Lenton in a Mosquito took photos of a V-2 rocket lying horizontally on a trailer at Peenemünde that the attention of RAF intelligence at Medmenham was aroused. On 23 June Flight Sergeant E. P. H. Peek brought back such clear photos of rockets on road vehicles that news was relayed immediately to Prime Minister Winston Churchill. In all, six Mosquito pilots on 540 Squadron at Leuchars photographed Peenemünde and in August 1943 rocket research site was bombed by the RAF and USAAF. In November, 540 Squadron became the first to take photographs of V-1 flying bombs.

544 Squadron, meanwhile, continued to use Ansons, Wellingtons and Spitfire PR.IVs in the PR and night photography roles over Europe, until in April 1943 Mosquito PR.IVs replaced the Wellingtons. In October, PR.IXs completed 544 Squadron's re-equipment. One of the crews who joined 544 in November 1943 was Pilot Officer John R. Myles DFC RCAF and his navigator, Flying Officer Hugh R. Cawker, a fellow Canadian. The RCAF had interrupted Myles' tour with 541 Squadron and posted him to 410 Squadron RCAF at Colby Grange where the Canadians wanted him to form another PRU for them, but it fell through. He recalls: 'PRU was a very interesting job and we knew in advance of many occurrences such as the Dams raid, V-2 rockets and the like. It was also one of the few jobs where one had the opportunity for independent action. We operated singly and although we were briefed for definite targets, how and when we got there was largely up to us. We also had authority to divert to photograph any convoys, or other unusual targets spotted. We covered the whole of Europe in daylight from Norway to Gibraltar and inland as far as Danzig and Vienna. On one trip we landed at a detachment at San Severo just north of the Foggia Plain in Italy. From there we did a sortie over Yugoslavia.'

In March 1944 544 Squadron received PR.XVI aircraft, while 540 had to wait until

12 'BOAC Mosquitoes flew 520 round trips from Bromma (Sweden) to Leuchars (Scotland) over the period February 1943 to May 1945 for a total of 783,680 miles. Several Mosquitoes made three single trips in one night when conditions were optimum. The average was around nine single (one way) trips per week for 2½ years. Several aircraft were lost together with their crews in this gallant and dangerous service.' *The Mossie* No.32 September 2002.

July 1944. G. W. E. 'Bill' Newby, a navigator from 544 Squadron, flew in the prototype PR.XVI Mosquito (MM258, a converted B.XVI), the first aircraft in the world (apart from the pre-war Bristol Type 138A) to be fitted with a pressurized cabin. He recalls: 'I had the privilege of flying on cabin tests with my squadron commander, Wing Commander D. W. Steventon DSO DFC and Geoffrey de Havilland. We were having trouble with 'misting up' of windows and I was the smallest navigator on the two squadrons, so we flew '3-up' for short periods to carry out tests. Crews from Benson covered the Dams project, keeping an eye on how full they were in readiness for the raid, May 1943 and photographing the after-damage and the chaos the Dam Busters caused locally. Our job on 544 Squadron was to take photographs before and after air attacks, by both RAF night- and USAAF day-bombers (high-tailing it back and overtaking the USAAF on the way home) - we photographed Wiener Neustadt, north of Vienna before the USAAF arrived, then we cleared off to Lake Constance to take the Zeppelin sheds at Friedrichshafen before returning to take the after-damage shots. We also took strategic photos of the coastal defences prior to the invasion of Europe; U-boat pens; pocket-battleships holed up in various French, German and Danish ports; oil-plants and aircraft factories deep in Germany; V-1 launching sites in the Pas de Calais; and even secret underground manufacturing sites in the Hartz mountains; and fields etc, which were to be used for dropping zones in France for SOE agents. For all of this, the Mosquito was ideal.

'Most PR flights, in cinematograph terms were routine. Occasionally, they were spiced up with 'one-offs', like rushing to Copenhagen late on Whit Sunday afternoon, 1944, because one of our 'informers', sitting on a hillside in Sweden, was sure that the pocket-battleship *Deutschland* [renamed *Lützow*] had disappeared from its moorings overnight and was thought to be free in the North Sea. We did a square search up the Kattegat and Skagerrak but could find no trace. So with light fading, we swept low over the Tivoli gardens and Hans Christian Andersen's Mermaid to the dockyard, only to find that the ship had been moved to a new berth and was disguised overnight to look like a tanker.

'Other flights were more exciting: long hauls up the Baltic as far as Gdynia, equally long trips to Austria and on over the Alps, to Venice and Yugoslavia, stopping overnight at Foggia (San Severo), after the landings in Italy; returning via Ajaccio, Corsica, or Gibraltar, to refuel, on one occasion taking photographs of Vesuvius in eruption. Another operation which took pride of place in the national press was a visit to the Gnome et Rhône aircraft engine works at Limoges on the morning of 9 February 1944 after it had been a special target of 617 Squadron - the Dam Busters - the night before. The place had been utterly devastated and we could easily see the damage from 30,000+ but we had been authorized to 'go low-level', so we could not pass up the chance to scream across at tree-top height to take really close 'close-ups', which later appeared in the press. My operational life on Mossies came to an abrupt end on 18 July, when we met four 'squirts' and they blew our nose off, hit both engines, put cannon shells in the cabin behind the pilot's armour-plate and we had to evacuate in quick time. We became guests of the Luftwaffe.'

The only Mosquito PR squadron in the Middle East theatre in 1943 was 683 Squadron, which formed at Luqa, Malta on 8 February. It was equipped initially with Spitfires before adding Mosquito IIs and VIs in May 1943 for a month of operations over Italy and Sicily.[13] In the Far East in 1943 the aerial reconnaissance of Burma and Malaya from bases in Ceylon and India proved one of the most difficult tasks facing South East Asia Command (SEAC). The success of the Mosquito in the PR role in Europe was viewed with envy in India where strike photographs were taken from obsolescent Blenheim bombers and the only two camera-fitted B-25Cs on 681 Squadron at Dum Dum, Calcutta. These were the only aircraft that possessed the range and speed for long-range PR over the Bay of Bengal and the Rangoon area. At the beginning of April 1943 three Mosquito F.II Series Is and three FB.VIs were allotted to 27 Squadron at Agartala. Three were for performance tests and familiarization and three were to be used in weathering trials during the coming rainy season under the supervision of Mr F. G. Myers, de Havilland's technical representative, However, late in the month, it was decided that the aircraft should supplement the unit's 'initial equipment' of Beaufighters for 'Intruder' operations. It is reported that Major Hereward de Havilland, visiting 27 Squadron, was horrified to find that the Mk.IIs were put to operational use and attempted to have them grounded because he considered that the casein glue with which they were bonded was unlikely to withstand insect attack and the tropical weather (the FB.VIs, still awaited, were supposedly bonded with 'waterproof' formaldehyde adhesive). It was rumoured that Major de Havilland attempted to damage the wing of one Mk.II to ensure that it could not be flown. In the event, 27 Squadron flew the first Mosquito operation, a reconnaissance over Burma on 14 May and then used the Mk.IIs again on only one occasion; one crashed and the other was damaged by ground fire on 5 June.

In August, when the aircraft situation in 681 Squadron became so bad, (the two B-25Cs had been in use for over 12 months) the Air Ministry agreed that Mosquitoes could be converted to PR aircraft at No.1 CMU (Central Maintenance Unit), Kanchrapara. Two Mosquitoes and their flight crews were transferred to the twin-engined Flight on 681 Squadron and these were followed by three newly arrived Mk.VIs. All five had been fitted with a camera, but not the four cameras of the 'PRU type', nor did they have additional fuel tanks, or in the case of the Mk IIs, provision for fitting under wing fuel tanks. During September 681 Squadron flew eight PR sorties over vast areas of Burma. On 29 September 1943 684 Squadron formed at Dum Dum from the twin-engined Flights on 681 Squadron with Mk IIs, VIs and IXs and a few Mitchell IIIs and continued operations with the early aircraft until they were replaced with nine pressurized PR.XVIs in February 1944. [14]

In Europe on 19 February 1944 a PR.XVI brought back photos of Berlin, despite the appearance of German fighters sighted at 42,000 feet! Production of PR.XVIs had begun in November 1943 and 435 were eventually built. With 100-gallon drop tanks, the PR.XVI had a range of 2,000 miles. The first PR.XVI production examples were urgently despatched to 140 Squadron at Hartford Bridge where they supplemented PR.IXs on

13 In early February 1944 6 Squadron at Matariya added Mk IX and XVIs to its strength for photo-reconnaissance operations in the Mediterranean, Eventually, the Mosquitoes and Spitfire XIs became the standard equipment and in August 1944 680 Squadron moved to San Severo to range over the Balkan an Hungary, finishing the war mapping Italy.

14 684 Squadron operated long-range PR sorties during the Burma campaign, regularly going to the Andaman Islands, Rangoon and the Burma-Thailand railway. Survey flying using IXs and XVIs from Calcutta took place before the squadron moved to Alipore for the remainder of the war. In June 1945 the PR.34, a VLR (Very Long Range) version of the XVI, entered service and based on the recently completed airfield at Cocos Island, made reconnaissance missions to Kuala Lumpur and Port Swettenham. By the end of July 25 sorties had been carried out by PR.34s from Cocos and 13 more by VJ-Day.

reconnaissance and mapping duties as part of the build up to D-Day.[15] Russell Cunningham, a navigator, crewed up at 8 OTU Dyce for Mosquito High Level Photographic Reconnaissance training with Pilot Officer 'Polly' Pollett, an ex-Army major, ex BEF, who transferred to the RAF as a to protect his feet from marching. Polly had done a tour on Army Co-operation and Typhoons and was sent to Dyce for Spitfire PR training. As the Spitfire course was full he was given a couple of hours on a dual Mosquito and off they started on a Mosquito IX.

'On conclusion we were posted to 140 Squadron, 34 Wing 2nd TAF at RAF Northolt. The aim of the Wing of Mosquito (140), Spitfire (16) and Wellington (69) squadrons was in support of the Army, initially mapping the European coastal area. Our accommodation was a tent on the Mess lawn, but at least we used the same dining room as Churchill. The time came when we were issued with camp kit and khaki battledress for flying (in case we were shot down and had to pretend to be lost soldiers - bit odd if shot down in the middle of Germany). We were then sent to A12 Lingerolles in the Cherbourg Peninsula. As we did not have our own aircraft we were asked to take an Auster across. Immediately the Army saw us in France and with Polly's Army Co-op experience, we were asked to do some spotting at Rouen and Le Havre. A week later we moved to Amiens, again in the Auster, to prepare the advance camp. Not wishing to taxi all the way round the airfield Polly decided we should take a short cut across the grass to the waving personnel. I walked in front to keep the aircraft clear of potholes and spikes. It was not a friendly wave - it was to tell us the grass area had not been cleared of mines. We all lived in a large Mess tent, including the escaped aircrew who had been hiding out in a brothel in Amiens. We fed them hard biscuits and whisky and made a bed for them out of three camp chairs. Next day they left for the UK.'

'After operating out of Amiens/Glisy we moved to B58 (Melsbroek), Brussels at the beginning of September 1944. We had an enterprising Adjutant, Jock Richmond, one time observer with Marshal of the RAF Hugh Trenchard, who unhooked a German wagon in the siding adjacent to the airfield. It was full of wines and liqueurs which were sold in the Mess for one franc a glass (174 francs to the pound).

'Our high level PR was carried out by single unarmed Mk.XVI flying at around 30,000 feet and where possible, avoiding tell-tale vapour trails. The target area had to be cloudless obviously and the navigator, when not down the nose on photo runs, navigated by reverse map reading from the cockpit blister, keeping an eye out for German fighters, mainly FW190s who had a nasty habit of arriving in pairs and interrupting our flying. To be a success a PR aircraft had to return to base, a tenet to which we happily subscribed.

'My first op was six straight runs to map the Scheldt Delta. My runs were curved, as a 20 year old suffering from the 'trauma' of a first op. I was called in to see the Wing Commander Flying for 'counselling' - short and sweet 'Go out tomorrow and get the runs straight'. We did then and thereafter. Targets were in support of the Army, troop movements etc, e.g. Bremen-Hamburg main road, the Friesian Islands and in and around the Ruhr. One time from Stendhal we returned mating each engine a few times because of coolant problems, losing 25,000 feet in the process. Another time, near Magdeburg, we were bounced by two FW190s; luckily there was cloud at around 8,000 feet. In the almost

15 The first PR.XVI to reach the Middle East was MM292 at the end of January 1944 and on 17 February the first of nine PR.XVIs for 680 Squadron arrived at Matariya, Cairo. Twenty-four hours earlier, the unit had received its first PR.IX (LR444). On 7 May 680 flew its first Mosquito PR sortie when MM333 and Flight Lieutenant A. M. Yelland, covered ports and airfields in Crete and the Cyclades.

vertical dive to reach it, off came the cockpit cover, the maps all shredded as a snowstorm in the cockpit. Navigation then became easy, keep the sun on your left until we reach the Rhine, if missed then the North Sea and up the Thames to Oxford (for Benson). We made Brussels. As a result of the dive Polly was hospitalised and became restricted to less than 10,000 feet. As the Squadron had a night flight I was returned to Hartford Bridge (Blackbushe) for 'Rebecca/H' and night photography training which was carried out at 6,000 feet with 18 photo flashes, dropped in sixes. My first night ops were with Charlie Butt mainly over the Ruhr area.'

'When Polly returned to the Squadron he was converted to night flying by degrees, day take-off-dusk landing, through to full night flying via Air Tests. In the middle of training, following a dusk landing, all aircraft were required for ops, ours included. On coming back to base I asked Polly about his previous night flying experience - yes, 12 hours in a Tiger Moth in 1940! This became obvious when over the airfield he could not make out the airfield lights. I guided the aircraft round the Drem lights, through the approach lights, until he eventually picked up the runway lights. What are the two red lights at either side of the runway for? Apart from night ops using R/H, one of which was Münster car park (for tanks), life was reasonably civilised. We lived in barracks - the Mess was fine; it had glass windows all down one side of the dining room. One breakfast a flying bomb engine stopped - that room was cleared in one second flat. During the Battle of the Bulge we emptied our kit bags to find our rusty revolvers! After Christmas you always went to Brussels with a Jeep motor arm in your pocket. This enabled you to return by American Jeep! Otherwise it was the Nivelles tramcar.

'From Brussels we moved to Eindhoven in April 1945. Ops became low-level recce of German shipping. Bremerhaven, Cuxhaven, Kiel Canal etc. On our last trip we were nearly shot down by our own guns when crossing the Rhine. They were celebrating the surrender on 4 May of which we had not been advised. Our arrival at base, hardly a vehicle was left, most had headed for Brussels. We followed in a 15 cwt truck.'

Squadron Leader (later Air Marshal, Sir) Alfred H. W. 'Freddie Ball DSO DFC, one of the war's foremost Spitfire and Mosquito PR pilots was of the opinion that perhaps the most important operational requirement for survival on PR operations was the ability of the pilot to keep a really effective look-out for enemy activity during the whole course of a sortie. 'No matter how good his aircraft, if the enemy saw him first the pilot was a sitting duck. Unfortunately, seeing before you were seen came with experience which was why so many PR losses were amongst relatively new pilots even though they had been introduced to operational flying as gently and carefully as possible. On one occasion I had to fly eight overlapping runs, each about 25 miles, from 25,000 feet on the northern outskirts of Berlin. Two enemy fighters appeared at the halfway stage but I managed to lose them as there was some cirrus cloud about and although they came in sight again, they seemed to be badly controlled and never got really close. I saw nothing saw anything further and had an unusually uneventful trip - I must have been either badly anoxic or blind, perhaps even both! But I like to think there was an Angel on my wingtip.' 16

An Angel must certainly have been on his Mosquito's wingtip on 29 September 1944 when 'Freddie' Ball and Flight Lieutenant Ronnie Knight the 540 Squadron Navigation Officer, flew a bomb-damage assessment trip at low level which came up unexpectedly

16   *Above All Unseen: The Royal Air Force's Photographic Reconnaissance Units 1939-1945* by Edward Leaf (PSL 1997)

as the weather was hopeless for high-level photography. Ronnie Knight considered this probably his most 'exciting' trip. The target was the Kembs Dam on the Rhine 50 miles north of Basle. Wing Commander Ball, who had taken command of 540 Squadron that same month, recalled: 'We flew to the target at 200 feet and all went well en route. Just as we were approaching the river and looking for the dam at about 1,500 feet, we suddenly ran into intense flak and whilst trying to avoid it we were attacked by three or four FW 190s. We dived to ground level and weaved around the woods and hills on the eastern side of the river with the fighters pressing us very hard. We held our own to begin with, but soon things became a bit tricky and I decided that, as we could not shake them off, the only thing was to try and get clear and start again. Our target had been bombed the night before[17] and undoubtedly they had been expecting us - at high level we would have been all right - but on the deck there was little room to manoeuvre and their performance was superior to that of a Mosquito.

'All things being fair in love and war, I decided that the best thing to do was to disappear into the Swiss mountains whatever the rules, whilst Ronnie continued watching the FW 190s and giving me highly successful evasion instructions. It seemed to work and we eventually lost them. When we felt the time was ripe to try again we swung out of Switzerland and headed back towards the target, but they were circling around waiting for us and quickly gave chase. It became very unpleasant and although they never managed to actually hit us we were forced back into Switzerland. I then thought we might be able to get round them by coming in from a different direction. We headed west as though we were going home, keeping on the deck and thereby being invisible, as far as possible. However, when we turned north and re-entered Germany there they were, having apparently flown parallel with us and obviously under some form of control. We were duly chased back once again. At times like that it would have been nice to have had guns but it was probably just as well we didn't, for I don't suppose we would have survived in that role against experienced fighter pilots!'

Apart from three PR.IXs detached from 540 Squadron to the Mediterranean in the summer of 1943, only a few PR Mosquitoes operated in this theatre. 'B' Flight on 680 Squadron mostly covered Greece and the Balkans and later, central and southern Europe, whilst 'B' Flight on 60 SAAF Squadron made deep penetration sorties over southern Europe and Poland. Navigation was crucial on operations, especially over the mountainous regions in Italy. Captain Charles H. H. Barry, senior flight commander of 60 (PR) Squadron at San Severo (opposite the spur in Italy) who flew sorties with his trusty navigator, Lieutenant G. R. Jeffreys, recalls one that stands out, a mapping sortie in the Po Valley in a Mosquito XVI. 'It was one of those days when your instinct told you it wasn't going to be healthy flying. Something in the air. No enemy aircraft or flak. The weather at base looked unpromising but met assured us it wouldn't deteriorate. So Geoff Jeffreys and I took off for the Po Valley. The target

---

17 The only raid on the Kembs Dam mentioned in *The Bomber Command War Diaries* by Martin Middlebrook and Chris Everitt (Midland, 1985, 1990, 1995) was on 7 October 1944 after it was feared that the Germans would release the vast quantity of water to flood the Rhine Valley near Mulhouse should the American and French troops in that area attempt to advance. Thirteen Lancasters on 617 Squadron were tasked with destroying the lock gates of the dam. Seven aircraft bombed from 8,000 ft and drew the flak, while the other six came in below 1,000 ft and placed their 'Tallboys', with delayed fuses, alongside the gates, which were destroyed. Two Lancasters were shot down by flak.

weather was good, Geoff's guidance on the runs was excellent, as usual and we turned for home an hour or so later, confident of a successful job. At 27,000 feet over the Adriatic, just east of Ancona, we entered thick cloud and began descending. I called up 'Commander', the superbly efficient area control unit near Termoli and asked for a plotted return to base. 'Geoff and I relaxed. All seemed well, as a check every five minutes revealed. We just stooged on in the murk, losing height as directed, flying the plotted course, warned that the cloud stretched down to ground level. Then the VHF went dead...

'I had levelled out at 500 feet above the sea, but we hadn't the foggiest - apt word, that - idea of exactly where we were. If we turned to starboard we would cross the coast and fly into the Apennines; if we stayed on our present course, we would fly into the spur of Italy. 'We'll have to take a chance,' said Geoff after we had examined all switches and channels to confirm the VHF was powerless. 'Turn on to 240 degrees and pray.' We did both... 'After about half a minute the cloud suddenly broke. About 500 feet below us was the choppy surface of the sea with the coastline coming up. On our port side, so close you could have touched it, was the Gargano Peninsula, the spur of Italy. Another half-minute on our former course and we would have flown straight into it...' [18]

Flight Sergeant Lawrence 'Kev' Kevan, a navigator who had crewed up at 8 OTU in December 1943 with Pilot Officer Ron Watson (who had already completed a PR tour on Spitfires), recalls that there were many 'highlights' and some 'hairy do's' during their tour on 680 Squadron: 'On 26 September 1944 I flew a five-and-a-half-hour operation in MM348 with Squadron Leader Law over Greece, the Aegean and Crete from our forward base at Tocra, near Benghazi. I experienced my first flak (about twenty-five bursts) while on the photographic run up the Corinth Canal to Pireaus (Athens). It was a strange feeling lying on one's belly in the nose, giving instructions of 'left-left-right-steady' etc to the pilot with those harmless looking black puff balls appearing alongside.

'On 16 October I flew another Greece-Aegean-Crete operation from Tocra with Pilot Officer Ron Watson, again in MM348. On along, curving photo run over Salonika town-harbour-railway yards, we attracted about 100 bursts, again when I was on my belly in the nose giving directions and camera operation. On landing back at Tocra we discovered that we had sustained shrapnel hits in the forward area of the bomb-bay doors in the belly - and near mine! Four days later, in another operation to Greece and the Aegean in MM330, we flew in 10/10ths cloud with lightning for about one-and-a-half hours until, at 23,000 feet Ron decided that it was mission impossible and he was beginning to disbelieve his instruments. He dived immediately and we finally broke cloud at about 1,000 feet above the Corinth Canal. We remained at almost sea level back across the Med to Tocra. I think that we were extremely lucky.

'On 29 October it was off again in MM330 from Tocra to Greece-Salonika-Crete, which we had to abandon when, south of Athens, Ron had to feather the starboard engine after he could not control the revs. We made an emergency landing at Hassani (Athens), where the ground crew found that a nut on the CSU had stripped. After a good night in Athens (the Greeks treated us as though we were Gods descended from Mount Olympus!), we returned to Tocra on 30 October and on 1 November, in MM330 again, we set out on the operation we had abandoned. However, we only got as far as

18 *Out of the Blue: The Role of Luck in Air Warfare 1917-1966*, edited by 'Laddie' Lucas (Hutchinson & Co 1985)

Crete when we had to feather the starboard engine yet again! We went on to IFF and made a successful S/E landing at Tocra. All went well on 22 November in MM297, to Rhodes-Dodeconese-Melos-Crete, but we attracted 50 accurate flak bursts on a run over Soda Bay. September, October and November 1944 had been quite an exciting time for Ron and myself.'

In 1944 540 Squadron went over totally to reconnaissance of the German rail transportation system in preparation for D-Day. Mosquitoes in 4, 140 and 400 Squadrons in 2nd TAF were also used to carry out reconnaissance over the continent for a limited period. 'B' Flight in 4 Squadron and 'A' Flight in 400 Squadron (their other flights were equipped with Spitfires) operated Mosquitoes from January until mid-May 1944 when both converted to the Spitfire XI. At Northolt 140 Squadron continued to operate its Mosquito PR.IXs on long-range photo reconnaissance from France after the invasion and in 1945 PR.XVIs equipped with 'Gee' and 'Rebecca' were used on blind night photography operations.

PR operations to northern Norway, meanwhile, especially those concerned with maintaining a watchful eye on the 41,000 ton German battleship *Tirpitz*, were not being neglected, for the 544 Squadron detachment at Leuchars was kept constantly busy. Built to be the most powerful warship of the western world, it radiated menacing competence in every aspect of design from the water line to its eight 15-inch guns and radar masts. In March 1944 *Tirpitz* with a crew of 1,500 men had left its anchorage in Alten Fjord and later that month it was found in Kaa Fjord by a PRU Spitfire on 542 Squadron operating from Russia. On 3 April *Tirpitz* was damaged by 14 hits with 1,600lb armour piercing bombs in an attack by Royal Navy Fairey Barracudas from Victorious and Furious. Bad weather conditions prevented a damage assessment being made until 7 April. Even then it remained impossible as the battleship lay at anchor in the deep shadow of the fiord wall. On 9 July Flight Lieutenant Frank Dodd and Flight Sergeant Eric Hill on 544 Squadron carried out a visual and PR of the west coast of Norway, flying as far north as fuel permitted and certainly beyond the Lofoten Islands, paying attention to any fiords likely to provide suitable anchorage for the *Tirpitz*. Dodd and Hill flew at heights ranging from between 6,000 and 24,000 feet over the Norwegian shipping lanes from Stattlandet to the Lofoten Islands, including Narvik. Their Mosquito was hit by flak in the starboard wing whilst photographing Bodø at 15,000 feet. Nevertheless, valuable negative information was obtained from this sortie, the Mosquito having been airborne 7 hours 44 minutes when it landed back at Leuchars with less than ten gallons of petrol remaining.

On 12 July Dodd and Hill flew to Sumburgh to top up their tanks for another sortie in search of the *Tirpitz*. Fifteen miles west of Bodø they were greeted by a perfect box-barrage of flak at their precise height but came through unscathed. With no sign of the *Tirpitz* they pressed on to Alten Fjord, which intelligence thought might be a possible lair. They gentled up the coast and started to sneak into the many fjords past the Lofotens until they came to Alten. At an uncomfortable 8,000 feet under the cloud they saw the *Tirpitz* 'looking oddly menacing and peaceful at the same time'. There was a little flak as Frank Dodd did a steep turn on to a short photographic run on the ship. Almost immediately there was a huge explosion and maps, Q codes, escape kits, Horlicks tablets, hopes and fears flew wildly around the cabin and Eric Hill remembered thinking, 'God, these Germans are bloody good'. They weren't. The top of the cabin had just flown off into the fjord'. They did the run and then discussed feathering one engine as the fuel situation was getting desperate. At long, long last they saw a gap in the cloud just after ETA, dived anxiously through it and saw land. Soon it became Wick and with all fuel gauges reading zero, Frank Dodd landed safely. They had spent 9 hours 25 minutes in the air.

An unsuccessful attack on the *Tirpitz* followed on 17 July and four more attacks were made between the 22nd to 29th August which resulted in only two hits. In October information from Norwegian Resistance was that the *Tirpitz* had left Kaa Fiord in tow on its way south for Ofot Fiord, four miles east of Tromsö, where it was to be used as a heavy artillery battery. *Tirpitz* lay motionless in the fiord 215 miles inside the Arctic Circle restrained by tidal anchors wedged into the rocky sea-bed under her. Around her for protection were floating booms hung with anti-submarine/torpedo nets which hung deep into the water down towards the sea bed. Protection against air attack was provided by the *Harald Haarfagre,* an anti-aircraft vessel stationed to the north-east and several land based AA batteries. The crew of a PR Mosquito were soon to photograph her. Flight Sergeant Joe Townshend was a quiet man in his early twenties, whose powers of concentration and general abilities provided the necessary intellect to operate efficiently against the enemy. Flight Lieutenant Hubert 'Sandy' Powell his pilot, three years older, tended to be absent minded and somewhat odd, taking most of any aggressive enemy action as an interesting experience, but not in a very serious manner. He had a tendency to sing parts of very old ballads in an unusual monotone when gaps occurred in any action which he felt needed filling. His airmanship had doubtful qualities even to himself. He was always mildly surprised when he found himself walking away from his aircraft completely unscathed after a complicated landing. 'Sandy' had learned on that day, 13 October, that his wife had given birth to a daughter, Jennifer Francis, in a nursing home at Edgware, London. On the 14th he sneaked a day off from 540 Squadron at Benson to hitch-hike home to see them. Next day 'Sandy' and Joe Townshend carried out aerial photography in East Germany. Light flak greeted them over the rocket ranges at Peenemünde. Their final target was Stettin and they returned to base after a five hour flight in the usual adrenalin induced high spirited exuberance. The 16th October was passed quietly in playing Mah Jong in the crew room and four crews were advised that they were to go to Dyce, near Aberdeen, the following day. The prospect of operating for a while over Norway came as welcome news as 'Sandy' and Joe liked the mountainous scenery which was quieter and far more picturesque than the heavy industrial centres of Germany. On 17 October the four crews were transported North in a Hudson aircraft. Shortly after arriving at Dyce 'Sandy' Powell checked out orders for the next day. Their details called for an early start and they were aroused at 04.45. After breakfast they arrived in the Operations Room at 05.45 where a middle aged Scottish Intelligence officer briefed them that their job was to locate the *Tirpitz*. Norwegian Underground sources had provided information of its locality and this required confirmation. The position to be searched was beyond the usual range of their aircraft so they were to refuel at Scatsta, an outlaying airfield in the Shetland Islands opposite St. Magnus Bay. Met briefing, navigational planning and recognition signals data were completed and they reached the hangars at 06.50. The prospect of the long flight ahead, their 25th Op over enemy territory, made a visit to the toilet an essential part of their preparations. The only facility on the aircraft was a urine relief tube which was invariably iced up.

After changing into flying gear they carried parachutes and other equipment to Mosquito NS641. This aircraft was fitted with drop tanks and had a fuel load of 850 gallons. Powell walked around the aircraft to assure himself all salient appendages looked properly attached and the pitot head cover had been removed. He did not like flying with an unserviceable ASI; even with one, difficulties occurred! He then strapped on his parachute harness with the personal dingy built in as a seat cushion and clambered awkwardly up the short ladder into the open hatch on the underside of the fuselage. Joe Townshend followed to fit into the small remaining space. The ladder was removed and the outer hatch closed by one of the two ground crew. They were airborne at 07.46 and climbed to 8,000 feet on a NE heading. There was a comfortable tail wind of 35 knots to speed them along the way on a scenic route over the hills of the Highlands and seascapes of the Atlantic Ocean reaches separating the Orkney and Shetland Islands from the North Coast of Scotland. The 55 minutes taken travelling this 270 miles first leg was enjoyable. Shadows of outlaying rocks and promontories dappled the sea breakers, visually distorting the shorelines. Muckle Roe in St. Magnus Bay was easily identified while they continued to descend to 1,000 feet over Scatsta runway. The landing was made without incident at 08.41.

The Mosquito again became airborne at 09.38, the fuel tanks having been refilled. They crossed out from the Shetlands ten minutes' later and climbed to 25,000 feet in just over half an hour, the external air temperature at that height being -30°F. A course of 050T was kept for a further hour during which time it was discovered that the starboard drop tank could not be made to feed its 97 gallons to the engines. They assumed the fault was merely due to icing up, but this was later found not to be the case. A course alteration was made to seek a land position fix. White foaming seas breaking over rocks were sighted at 11.30 but it was not until 11.50 that they saw land. The coastline was followed northward and every fiord was searched. Shortly after this the town of Bodø was identified SE at 11.52. Townshend again tried to get fuel from the starboard drop tank. This proved to be abortive and the loss of over 10% of the original total fuel capacity now became a serious consideration. The calculated margin of safety for the return flight was gone and so the drop tanks were immediately jettisoned to reduce drag and weight of the inaccessible petrol. At this time they were 200 miles from the probable location of the *Tirpitz*.

Large cloud banks had been assembling from the west over the Lofotens and ahead to the north. This meant flying lower in order to keep visual contact with the coastline. About 12.28 when flying at 18,000 feet Townshend sighted the *Tirpitz* anchored in Ofot Fiord. Powell adjusted course on the navigator's continuing instructions to either 'left' or 'right' and finally 'steady'. He also put the aircraft into a slight dive to get below the cloud and increase speed and change height for the run over the *Tirpitz*. They were then down to 15,000 feet and hoping the changes would mislead and Gunnery Predictor's operator while they were on their photographic run over the battleship.

Flak appeared in the form of greyish black blobs dotting the air. It had no real pattern in the way it appeared about their track and it was only light and inaccurate. The run completed Townshend then edged his way back into the cockpit. Powell put the aircraft into a medium rate turn to port while climbing away from the target, settling down on a westerly heading out over the sea with the Lofotens over to port. Powell suggested that they should now make some decisions on future actions. It was agreed the fuel left in the tanks severely limited flying time. Also the water looked unpleasantly uninviting for bathing if they were forced to ditch. There was a suggestion they could try for Sweden, the food reported to be good there. However, finally taking account of all relevant factors it was decided to 'go for home'. No small part of this decision came from the pilot who was sure that if his wife heard he was 'living it up' somewhere in Scandinavia with her and their new daughter left in food rationed UK, he would probably never hear the last of it.

Townshend settled down to consulting his chart. Flying now below the cloud base at 15,000 feet into the wind, the temperature had risen to -20°F. He gave Powell a new course which was set for Scatsta at an assessed ground speed of 224 knots and allowing for a headwind of 34 knots. Wind lanes and white horses on the sea indicated that the wind had changed little and at 13.55 he tried to get a long range fix. The position was ignored as it was well to the west of their course and probably came from a German station in Norway. At 14.23 a bearing (QTE) came from Sumburgh confirming that we were on course and at 15.00 a Medium Frequency fix confirmed their position. Townshend adjusted their course accordingly. A further 40 minutes elapsed when a new fix caused them to increase the westerly heading. Twenty minutes' later a QDM (course to steer) from Sumburgh confirmed their heading. At 15.58 the white capped waves breaking around the outlaying promontories and rocks NE of Shetland could be seen. Ten minutes' later two tired crew landed at Scatsta with 15 minutes' fuel left in the tanks. The flight from Scatsta and back was more than 1,600 miles and they were airborne continuously for 6 hours 35 minutes. During the return flight the engines had been nursed to extend the distance each gallon of fuel would carry them. Keeping the course heading accurate was an act of intense concentration. When the first fix was confirmed, a comparison of the range they would get with the remaining fuel and the distance to run made it evident the situation was precarious. Some nervous strain eased when the out laying rocks of Shetland were sighted but the fuel gauges showed how near they were to the end.

'Sandy' Powell telephoned Dyce on a scrambled line from the Scatsta control tower. He spoke to the Intelligence Officer who had briefed them that morning. His words were simple but precise, 'Named Target spot on! Operation DCO! Return to base shortly'. They had confirmed the locality of the *Tirpitz*, which was now in range of UK-based bombers. Refuelling and flight back to Dyce were without incident. They landed at 18.00 in good time for dinner and went into Aberdeen that night for a drink to celebrate. They covered the 2,150 miles in an overall 8 hours 35 minutes flying time. Even though the Mosquito completed this remarkable flight from Scatsta at reduced speed it still managed to average nearly 245 mph.[19]

Meanwhile, in addition to the detachment at Yagodnik, in the USSR covering the 5 Group operations against the *Tirpitz* a 540 Squadron detachment had also been established at Gibraltar in September in preparation for a survey of the Canary Islands. Further trips to the USSR commenced on 9 October with courier flights for Operation Frugal. 544 Squadron's Mosquitoes transited to the Soviet Union, via Memel to

19   Their outstanding feat earned 'Sandy' Powell a DFC and Townshend the DFM. They went on to complete a further 25 sorties together. During this later period Joe's parachute harness and trousers were holed by a piece of shrapnel and they had an exciting 10 minutes being chased around the sky by an enemy fighter which jumped them from the rear starboard quarter. The *Tirpitz* was sunk by Lancasters on 617 Squadron flying from Scotland on 12 November.

Ramenskoye for eventual operations over eastern Germany and Poland. These flights lasted six hours and when Moscow (Vnukovo) was used they became 4 hour 30 minute trips for the crews involved. Others were flown to Yalta, via San Severn in Italy and Saki in the Crimea or via Malta and Cairo. In December some Mosquitoes were stripped of their cameras and used to carry diplomatic mail to Hassani, in Greece. This run, which was known as Operation Haycock was extended to Italy and Egypt in connection with the Cairo Conference. A similar service was performed by the PR Mosquitoes during the Potsdam Conference.

Flight Lieutenant 'Lofty' South and his pilot, Flying Officer R. M. Hays had a harrowing flight on 16 March 1945 when, over Leipzig, they were intercepted by three Me 163 rocket-powered fighters. Hays managed to throw them off by putting the Mosquito into a 480 mph dive, during which the starboard engine caught fire. After feathering the propeller the ore went out, so they decided to set course for the Allied lines. Flying through violent frontal conditions, they were then jumped by a Bf 109, which Hays threw off once again by putting the nose down and diving for He ground, before pulling up. NS795 eventually landed at Lille, still on one engine. For this exploit, Hays was awarded an immediate DFC. Two weeks later, on 30 March Hays and South were killed when they lost an engine on take-off from Benson.

On 30 April, five days before the war in Europe ended, Warrant Officer Lawrence 'Kev' Kevan on 680 Squadron at Deversoir in the Egyptian Canal Zone, endured an even more harrowing experience. British Intelligence learned that the German general commanding the island of Rhodes was determined to fight on and Wing Commander J. C. Paish, commanding 680 Squadron was immediately ordered to mount a PR sortie of the island. Flying Officer Ron Watson and 'Kev' Kevan were set for an operation which would complete their tour. Just before take-off time, the original flight plan was scrubbed because HQ ME wanted an urgent low level visual recce of a suspected radar site on Rhodes. Kevan recalls: 'After a visual recce of the islands of Allinia and Calchi (off the western coast of Rhodes) at about 1,000 feet we headed for the radar site somewhere near Kattavia airfield, on the southern tip of Rhodes. We came down to 200 feet and in a small clearing among trees was a radar mast. Ron took the plane down to about 30 feet so that I could get as much detail as possible. There appeared to be no Germans around, so Ron decided to repeat the run at 30 feet to make sure that we had not missed anything. Suddenly, as we approached head-on, soldiers firing automatic guns appeared. The aircraft was badly hit and so were we. Ron hauled back the controls and up we zoomed. I thought, 'Good, he's OK'. At level-off at about 1,500 feet however, Ron suddenly said 'Take the controls, Kev', which I did, but thought he would take back control. However, when he tried to he could not. His next words shook me. 'Take it home Kev and prang it! I can't move'. He left me holding the control column. I had never had a flying lesson! Furthermore, in the confirmed space of a Mossie cockpit, there was no way in which we could change seats, especially with an unconscious and wounded pilot. Thoughts were racing through my head and I decided to lift Ron's feet off the rudder bar, hold the aircraft at about 1,500 feet and head towards the sun, which should fetch me up on the Egyptian coast (i.e., southwards).

'After a while Ron came to and asked, 'Why are we heading south - go for Crete, it's nearer'. I said no, we would not stand any chance in the mountains. He drifted into unconsciousness again and I struggled on for another half an hour or so, when he again came to and quietly said, 'Kev, I'm going - say goodbye to my folks for me'. I told him not to talk like that. We would get through somehow. However, Ron was sure he was dying and he told me to shake hands and say goodbye. To comfort him, I did and he sank back into an unconscious state.'

Incredibly, 'Kev' Kevan made it to Lydda in Palestine, where, despite having no rudder control and trimmed for flying at 250-300 mph he got the Mosquito down after three circuits. The impact took most of the propellers and gears off before the Mosquito took off again and rose several hundred feet before landing in fields beyond. Kevan saw a peasant with his donkey standing transfixed right in his path. He yanked the column to port and the aircraft turned through 90° and stopped. Great red clouds shot up all round. 'God!' he thought, 'we are on fire' but it was the red earth that had been disturbed. Later that evening 'Kev' Kevan was told that Ron had died on the flight home. We had been hit by dum-dum bullets and Ran had been hit in the stomach and would never have survived. [20]

Eric Hill on 544 Squadron concludes. 'Flying solitary sorties over heavily-defended enemy territory in unarmed wooden aircraft I suppose needed special qualities. I had the best luck of all. I had Frank Dodd as a pilot, whose brilliant airmanship, calm appreciations and simple courage got us through. Perhaps many other navigators will say the same of their pilots and just to end this tribute to them all, I hope that many who have forgotten the part PRU played in the victory, will perhaps pause and reconsider.'

---

20   'Kev' Kevan had flown the Mosquito for two hours 40 minutes. The next day Ron Watson was buried in Ramla cemetery and his funeral was attended by 680 Squadron officers. After the burial, with the RAF guard of honour formed up, AM Sir Charles Medhurst (Air Officer Commander in Chief, Middle East) awarded 'Kev' Kevan an immediate DFC at Ron Watson's graveside.

Chapter 2

Defensive and Offensive Night Fighting

Existence of the 'Wooden Wonder' would not be public knowledge in Britain until the night of 25 September 1942 when listeners to the BBC Home Service heard that this revolutionary new aircraft had made a daring roof-top raid on the Gestapo HQ in Oslo. Norway had fallen to the Wehrmacht on 9 April 1940 when Weserübung Nord - the German invasion of the country began. The same day a 64-strong British contingent who had volunteered to fight in the Finnish war with the Soviet Union, which had attacked Finland in November 1939, had arrived in the Norwegian capital after the so-called 'Winter War' ended on 13 March 1940. One of the volunteers was Neil Munro, a well-educated 18-year-old, six foot tall 'devil-may-care' student from London who had played rugby for the Saracens and was training to become a dentist. In 1938 he had tried to join the RAF but was refused. Munro's sister Muriel had tried to dissuade him from going to Finland but he was not to be deterred. 'The fun began when our train was nearing Oslo' Munro said. 'We heard a great roaring of aeroplane engines and looking out of the windows we saw a flock of bombers. 'Great Scot!' I yelled, 'they're German!' The train went on and ran into Oslo station. Talk about excitement! The place was in ferment. We saw the first 400 Germans march into the town. They looked to us a rather weedy lot and dull-looking.'

The British contingent was billeted in the City Hotel in the Norwegian capital. There were some Americans at the hotel; the USA at that time was neutral. The officer-in-charge of the British contingent advised that it was now a case of every man for himself and the American Consulate had said that a train was expected to leave for Stockholm in neutral Sweden. Forty escaped by train to Sweden and 20 were caught by the Germans; only four decided to make a dash for it themselves. Neil Munro and his friend, 17-year old Jack Smith, a clerk from Norwich who had worked for a bus company and L. R. Thompson, a Londoner from Camden Town and W. H. Tosh, a 40 year old Scot living in Devon. Munro told his friend to burn their passports and follow him downstairs, say nothing and look as if everything was normal. As they entered the lobby Munro stole two American coats and they then walked calmly through, Munro putting on an American accent, which he was good at mimicking. The Germans did not stop them and Munro and Smith walked away, intending to try and make contact with the Resistance.

'We couldn't muster a word of Norwegian between us' recalled Munro 'but we had an inspiration. As we went along we laughed and gesticulated and cried out the names on shops and any word that was big enough to catch our eye without our having to look about. You can guess how we startled the Norwegians for our pronunciation must have sounded absolutely crazy. After about three miles we hailed a chap who was driving a large car and I pretended to be an American. He didn't understand my

American though but he said he knew English! I said, 'Will you give us a lift, to Honefoss, which was about 60 miles away?' Certainly he said. 'Jump in'.

'A mile or two out we found the road blocked by German guards. We left the talking to our Norwegian friend and jabbered our own kind of Norwegian in the back of the car. Thank goodness those Nazis didn't know much more Norwegian than we did. We were lucky enough to get several good lifts on the way to Trondheim on the coast but we had to tramp about 150 miles before we reached a spot where we could get on board a British warship.'

Half way there a group of children were gathered in a fork in the road and waved them to the right; a German patrol as only two miles away and down the other fork. They had to cross a quiet sentry post, manned only by one soldier who they killed with a knife. In Honefoss the local Norwegian Police took charge of them but were not sure what to do. The next day the police put them on the right road to Trondheim. At Jaren a bus driver tried to give them 20 Kroner and the passengers also insisted on a collection. They spent the night in a wood cutter's hut and went on to Gjoevik. It was 0615 hours on Saturday morning - four days after they started - that they reached the coast and saw two British warships in the fiord. They met Mr Michael Gawthrop the British vice-consul for Arendal in the South and they found a hotel for breakfast. At 0800 hours they boarded a Royal Navy destroyer and soon afterwards the town was 'violently bombed'. For five days the warship dodged German bombs as it searched inlets up and down the coast. Eventually they met some troopships, including the C.P.R. liner *Empress of Australia*, which carried them back to England. The troopship docked in Scotland and Neil Munro arrived in Victoria in London on the night of 23 April and a joyful reunion with the family who had not known whether or not he was alive. They only knew what they had read in the newspapers. In a short while Neil Munro tried again to join the RAF and this time he was accepted and by 1942 he was a fully fledged Mosquito NF.II fighter pilot on 157 Squadron at Castle Camps.

In October Air Chief Marshal Arthur 'Bomber' Harris, the Air Officer Commanding RAF Bomber Command, advocated that Mosquito fighters - 'a lethal brute with no vices' - should be used in the bomber stream for raids on Germany. ACM Sir W. Sholto Douglas, AOC Fighter Command argued that the few available Mosquitoes were needed for home defence should the Luftwaffe renew its attacks on Britain that had begun in the spring of 1942 when following an attack by 234 RAF bombers on the old Hanseatic city of Lübeck Hitler had ordered a series of Terrorangriff (terror attacks) on England, mainly against cities of historic or aesthetic importance, but little strategic value. In Britain they became known as the Baedeker raids, after the German guidebooks of the same name. The only effective salvation from Luftwaffe attacks was AI (Airborne Interception) radar equipped fighters such as the Beaufighter and the Mosquito but both were in short supply At the time of the first Baedeker raid on Norwich on the night of 27/28 April only nine Beaufighters, ten Spitfires and three AI.Mk.V radar-equipped Mosquito NF.IIs on 157 Squadron at Castle Camps were able to meet the 28 Luftwaffe raiders and the Mosquitoes suffered particularly from problems with cannon flash and exhaust manifold and cowling burning.

RAF bombers also began to suffer increasing losses due to Nachtjagd night fighter interceptions and it was decided that RAF 'Intruder' aircraft roving over enemy airfields in France and the Low Countries could alleviate some of the attacks on the bomber streams. The value of 'Intruding' was not so much that enemy night fighters were destroyed but rather that they were persuaded to stay on the ground. The first major support of bombers by night fighter squadrons was on the night of 30/31 May 1942 during the 1,000-bomber raid on Cologne when Blenheims and Havocs and Boston IIIs intruded over Holland. Raids on Britain's towns and cities were still being met by small numbers of albeit determined young men in Beaufighters and Mosquito IIs, which were operated largely by 85, 157, 151 and 25 Squadrons. [21]

Neil Munro was one of the determined young men on 157 Squadron and was now a flight sergeant pilot on the Mosquito NF.II. On the night of 19 October he and Warrant Officer Eastwood his radar operator took off at 0705 hours and while under Sector Control off Southwold, at 0839 hours they were advised of a contact - 'Cheery 27' - one mile ahead. Munro recalled: 'We sighted this momentarily just in cloud at a half a mile range and closed to 500-600 yards when it was sighted again. I gave 'Tally Ho' when the enemy aircraft (a Ju 88A-4 of KG 6) turned on his back and dived straight down. Then we sighted a Beaufighter coming head on, which we at first took for the enemy aircraft but Sector asked if we had fired because the enemy aircraft had crashed. I replied that I had not fired but that the enemy aircraft had seen me and gone straight down. At no time during this interception was any AA fire observed. We were turned on to 180° after a second enemy aircraft. After five minutes we sighted it one mile ahead just in cloud at 2,000 feet crossing from port to starboard. We turned in behind and were given several vectors by Trimley Heath GCI (Squadron Leader Kidd). After a further 5 to 10 minutes vectoring we sighted a Do 217 crossing starboard to port on a north westerly course 500 yards ahead. I fired a second burst of cannon only, closing in all the time. Both the observer and I saw strikes on the port side of the fuselage near the wing root. The Dornier dived very steeply and was never sighted again. Several vectors were given and 'throttle right back' as the Dornier had slowed down from 280 to 190 IAS. On the last vector, heading east, information was lost. We stooged around for a bit but ground control could give no further information.

Early in 1943 the Luftwaffe began to employ specially-equipped Junkers Ju 52 aircraft for mine-sweeping in certain coastal areas around Europe, usually from first light on days following any suspected Bomber Command 'Gardening' (mine-laying) sorties. These Ju 52s were known colloquially as 'Mausi' aircraft. 'Ranger' and 'Intruder' Mosquitoes were soon called upon to combat the 'Mausi' Junkers, 605 Squadron being the first unit to be so employed after May 1943. While a Junkers 52 was no match for a Mosquito fighter, the real dangers of a 'Distil' sortie as they were known, lay in the fact that it took place off the enemy-occupied coastline, in broad daylight and a Mosquito crew could often expect the 'Mausi' aircraft to be escorted by German fighters.

21　In July 1942 23 Squadron began conversion to the NF.II at Ford but for a time had only one aircraft until eventually 25 modified NF.IIs were made available. In April 1943 604 Squadron at Scorton converted to the NF.XIII and 256 Squadron began equipping with the NF.XII and 29 Squadron who did likewise, followed them in May. In February-March 456 Squadron RAAF, which was largely equipped with Beaufighter VIfs, began to include some NF.II Ranger operations in addition to their day fighting role, first from Middle Wallop and then from Colerne. From late May they were successfully employed on Intruder sorties over France attacking railway rolling stock and intruding on French airfields. In May 1943, 60 OTU at High Ercall was expanded and made responsible for all 'Intruder' training. In June 605 Squadron began small-scale Flower attacks on enemy night fighter airfields.

In early 1943 also, Focke Wulf 190A-4/U8 fighter-bombers, each carrying a 250kg or 500kg bomb on its centreline took part in attacks by Schnelles Kampfgeschwader (SKG) 10 on Eastbourne, Hastings and Ashford and London. To be better sited to meet the threat 85 Squadron moved from Hunsdon to West Malling and 157 moved from Bradwell Bay to take their place. Wing Commander John 'Cats Eyes' Cunningham DSO* DFC* had assumed command of 85 Squadron at the end of January 1943. Cunningham had shot down 16 enemy aircraft while flying Beaufighters. This was due to a combination of flying skill and good shooting and airborne radar operated by his navigator, 39-year old Flight Lieutenant C. F. 'Jimmy' Rawnsley DFC DFM*.[22] Cunningham's miraculous night vision, the propagandists explained, was due to the fact that night-fighter pilots ate lots of carrots because they were good for night vision. This legend had its origins in the half-truth that a deficiency of certain vitamins could cause night blindness. Not unnaturally, the public who knew nothing about airborne radar went along with it, but the Germans were not fooled for a moment and Cunningham was saddled with the nickname 'Cat's Eyes', which he detested. The FW 190's superior speed gave little chance of interception but there were notable successes. On 13 May 85 Squadron claimed five FW 190s destroyed and another 'probably destroyed'. Not as successful were 157 Squadron, which tried sitting over the enemy coast as 20,000 feet under 'Appledore' control and chasing the fighter-bombers on their way to England. Crews shivered at 25,000 feet over the balloons, AA fire and searchlights of London and endeavoured to catch them, or on their way out but with no results. However, a trained few carried out 'Ranger' operations and destroyed enemy aircraft at such places as St-Trond, Twente and Düsseldorf. The mainstay of the Luftwaffe's raids on England at this time remained the Ju 88 and Do 217 and several fell to the Mosquitoes' guns. At the end of May the first Ju 88S-1 with power-boosted BMW 801G-2 engines fitted with the GM-1 N_2O (nitrous oxide) injection system to fall over England was shot down by an 85 Squadron crew. On 13/14 July the first Me 410 Hornisse (Hornet) to be shot down over Britain was also claimed by 85 Squadron.

Mosquitoes were ideal for 'Intruder' operations but few in number and squadrons had to use converted NF.IIs with increased fuel capacity and no radar. No radar-equipped aircraft were used as its operation over enemy territory was still banned and were closely guarded secrets. What few NF.IIs were available made 'Night Rangers' to airfields in France from Trebelzue, Cornwall. 'Rangers' were low level operations on moonlight nights, mainly against railway rolling stock and road transport, although one could shoot down enemy aircraft if they were encountered. 'Ranger' aircraft at night were literally free-lance operators, left to their own devices to cause as much chaos and disruption as possible among the enemy. Whereas 'Intruders' had specific areas or objectives to prowl Mosquitoes usually flew in pairs on 'Day Rangers' when they literally went looking for trouble. 'Flower' was the codename given to the overall role of Bomber Support by fighter Mosquitoes and was intended to cancel out enemy night fighter operations against the Main Force. A 'Flower' operation usually consisted of two phases, the first being bomb-carrying Mosquitoes ahead of a main bomber force to raid Nachtjagd airfields in an attempt to keep the enemy fighters on the ground; while behind them came the long range

22 Rawnsley was awarded the DSO in late 1944.

Mosquitoes who patrolled the known night fighter areas, waiting to pounce on any aircraft taking off or landing.

In August 1943 when it was realised that the Luftwaffe were operating radar equipped night fighters against the 'heavies' of Bomber Command, some AI equipped Beaufighters and Mosquito night fighters were released over enemy territory on 'Mahmoud' operations [23] as bait for enemy night fighters in their known assembly areas. With centimetric AI being used in Mosquitoes it was necessary to fit 'Monica' tail warning devices, as the later Mks of AI did not scan to the rear. Mosquitoes pretending to be bombers were not successful as the enemy soon recognized their speed difference. Nevertheless, there were successful interceptions. Six FB.VIs and six NF.II fighters with AI were available to 410 'Cougar' Squadron RCAF for 'Flower's operations in August in addition to the Squadron's usual defensive commitments.

On the night of 17/18 August, in support of Bomber Command's devastating attack on Peenemünde, Wing Commander Francis Noel Brinsden, a New Zealander from Auckland and his navigator, Flying Officer P. G. Fane-Sewell were patrolling the area near Sylt and decided to bomb the airfield there. Brinsden had fought as a fighter pilot over France and in the Battle of Britain. He had taken command of 3 ADU at High Ercall in mid-August 1942 and was posted to 54 OTU Charter Hall in February 1943 for a night-fighting conversion course and then joined 25 Squadron flying Mosquito 'Intruder' fighter-bombers at Church Fenton.

'We determined to fly out to sea, at about 2,000 feet, as though flying home, then descend gradually, still heading westwards until at sea level, about-face and fly back to Sylt, hoping by these means to outwit the radar screen and carry out a surprise attack. All went well. As we approached Sylt pinpointing was easy for the town was silhouetted against a clear sky and the full moon made the scene as light as day. Over the town then at roof height, a slight turn to port towards the aerodrome hangars shining in the moonlight at about half a mile away, range shortening, coming up to optimum - stand by - bombs gone. Now a vicious turn to starboard to pass between the hangars - and blindness. A searchlight shining right into the cockpit instruments; nothing to help us orientate ourselves and too low to evade vigorously. Then tangerine tracer shells passing too close to be safe. Now something had to be done. Violent evasion-and at sea level-while still heading generally eastwards was the only course open.

'At last the searchlights were lost and the tracer stopped but before vision had fully returned a violent acceleration, a dreadful - shuddering, broken airs crews screaming. We had touched water and bounced. Warning my navigator to prepare for a ditching I meanwhile scanned the cockpit. Rev counter needles were against the stops but other instruments seemed normal. Would it fly us home? Too soon it became evident that it would not and pre-ditching action was taken. The ditching was normal and I had some seconds in which to gather vital papers - before the aircraft sank. Then I swam towards the dinghy and joined my navigator who by this time was sitting in it. A quick survey of our position showed us to be between Sylt and the mainland and south of the railway embankment joining the two.

'Fortunately neither of us was seriously injured. Little could be done to manoeuvre the dinghy. The type we had was a beast of burden, not of navigation and although we rigged

---

23 'Mahmoud' was the code-name for a special kind of operation which was devised after it was realized that the Luftwaffe were operating radar equipped night-fighters against the 'heavies' of Bomber Command.

our seat type dinghy sails and endeavoured to sail out of the bay and westward under a favourable off-shore breeze, dawn brought an inshore one and a change of tide and back we went into the bay. Finally at the mercy of another inshore breeze we were blown inshore at, mid-day on the 18th into an encircling ring of troops, who were impatiently waiting our arrival, having watched us drifting up and down the bay for the last six hours!'

In September 605 Squadron began 'Intruder' sorties over Denmark and Germany. In November 1943 a 307 Squadron detachment at Sumburgh, Scotland carried out 'Rhubarb's'[24] over Norway, destroying two He 177s and a Ju 88. When they returned south they continued intruding and later flew Bomber Support operations until March 1945. During November also 157 Squadron operated under 19 Group Coastal Command at Predannack. British convoys from the Mediterranean were being attacked by U-boats based on the French Biscay coast. Sunderlands, Liberators and Wellingtons were dispatched by Coastal Command to hunt and destroy the U-boats. Ju 88s were sent out to combat the attackers and the Mosquitoes at Predannack with other coastal squadrons of Beaufighters took turns to deal with the Ju 88s. It was even said that the Mosquitoes could be engaged by FW 190s from the Brest peninsular, though none were seen during their stay. A squadron of Typhoons were stationed with the Mosquitoes to counter the FW 190s. During four months at Predannack 157 Squadron destroyed or damaged ten Ju 88s as well as six heavy German reconnaissance aircraft which had been spying on Allied convoys. The prize of these was a Blohm und Voss Bv 222 Viking six-engined flying-boat of 1.(F)/129 which Squadron Leader Herbert 'Tap' Tappin DFC and Flying Officer I. H. Thomas destroyed during a 'Night Ranger' to Biscarosse Lake in France on 8/9 February.

It was with much regret that on 26 March 1944 157 Squadron left Predannack to move to Valley, although the squadron was promised new aircraft, a new mark of AI and a new job. The aircraft however, did not materialise. They continued training and countless air-firing sorties with the aircraft they had, the majority of which had over 600 hours to their credit; and though all navigators passed through the M.X 'Circus', no indication was given of their future role. Not until April, when the CO, Wing Commander Denison, was summoned to a conference at HQ ADGB and the news that they were to become a Bomber Support squadron in 100 Group did the sense of uncertainty and 'unemployment' disappear.[25]

100 (Special Duties) Group (Bomber Support from May 1944) had been formed on 23 November 1943 under the command of Air Commodore (later Air Vice Marshal) E. B. 'Addy' Addison after it became obvious to all that the RAF needed a specialized bomber support force. From stations in Norfolk 100 Group dispatched bomber aircraft on radio countermeasures (RCM) sorties and Mosquito squadrons on 'Day' and 'Night Intruder' operations, which were extended to include loose escort duties for the Main Force. Three

---

24   Offensive operation by fighter aircraft, originally to tie down enemy aircraft in the west to prevent them being sent east to the Russian Front.

25   On 6 May the Squadron moved by road to Swannington in rural Norfolk where with ten borrowed Mosquito aircraft pilots and navigators on both 157 and 85 Squadrons practised intensively under the tutelage of the inimitable Wing Commander Bertie Rex O'Bryen Hoare DSO DFC* who sported a large handlebar moustache, 'six inches, wingtip to wingtip' and was one of the leading *Intruder* pilots of his generation having flown first Blenheims, then Havocs on *intruder* sorties over the Low Countries. Despite losing an eye before the war when a duck shattered the windscreen of his aircraft, Sammy Hoare became one of the foremost Intruder pilots in the RAF. The end of the month produced Mosquito XIXs.

of the squadrons - 141, 239 and 169 - were equipped with 'Serrate', a device designed to home in on German night-fighter radar transmissions; 23 and 515 Squadrons flew 'Intruder' operations by day and by night and 85 and 157 Squadrons joined the Group from Fighter Command in May 1944. Some of these squadrons sent low level fighters to patrol the known German night-fighter airfields. Others provided high level patrols near their assembly points, about 40 miles from the bomber stream, in order to shoot them down before they reached it and a third wave of low level Mosquitoes would arrive at their airfields as they were returning. Very soon the Nachtjagd pilots started to use phrases Moskitopanik! and Ritterkreuzhöhe (literally 'Knights Cross height')! After carrying out their attacks against RAF bombers, they would immediately drop down almost to ground level, i.e. 'Ritterkreuz height' in order to avoid the dreaded Mosquitoes.

In just 18 months 100 Group developed electronic warfare to an almost state-of-the-art technology and its Mosquito force accounted for many valuable German night fighters. On 28/29 January Flying Officer 'Harry' White DFC and Flying Officer Mike Allen DFC on 141 Squadron destroyed their fifth enemy aircraft and their first Mosquito victory of the war when they were one of seven Mosquitoes dispatched from West Raynham as part of the Diversion and Support operations for 677 aircraft attacking Berlin. North of the 'Big City' Allen picked up AI contacts on an enemy aircraft, which turned out to be a single-engined machine, probably, a Bf 109. White dispatched it with a five-second-burst of 20mm cannon fire from astern and below. The enemy aircraft burst into flames and exploded, diving through haze. Harry White and Mike Allen had become known in Bomber Command, as 'The Old Firm' since they had already been a team for more than two years. Experienced as they were in combat, however, both were barely 20 years of age. All told they went night-fighting together either defensively or offensively for four years and they were a brilliantly irreverent pair, collecting three DFCs apiece. Their first four victories were on Beaufighters and nine more were achieved flying the Mosquito. Harry White's graphic account of two victories on the night of the Peenemünde raid reveals the secret of their wartime successes.

'Four lines of yellow tracer streaked over our canopy and almost simultaneously we heard the rattle of cannons. There was a shout from the navigator: 'Some bastard's firing at us.' 'I know,' I said. I had already pushed everything - stick, rudder, throttles - into the 'bottom right-hand corner'. As 'Night Intruders', 141 Squadron's remit that night was for one flight to escort the Lancasters out as far as the limited range of our Beaufighters would allow. Our other flight was, later, to meet the returning bombers as deep into Germany as possible and escort them home. Our targets were the enemy night-fighters which ranged along the bombers' route.

'Mike Allen and I were approaching Hamburg at about 16,000 feet on a clear but very dark night. Mike had picked up a contact on his radar. Normally we would know from the type of contact whether it was hostile or not. This time we did not. I suppose, looking back, that was why I was less alert than I should have been. I presumed it would be 'one of ours'. Using our radar we closed rapidly from two to three miles and had to lose height to put our target slightly above so I could identify it visually against the rather lighter sky. Going 'downhill' we had built up a fair overtaking speed... At 500 feet I realized this shape was a Messerschmitt 110. I swore. I was closing too fast to open fire. I eased back the throttles. I dare not snap them shut. If I did there would be sheets of flame from our exhaust. We would be seen. To help lose speed I turned hard to port and then back to starboard. It was at that precise instant that we became the target. The Me 110 must have seen this Beaufighter slip out from underneath him and then, slowing down, turn to port and starboard in front of him. A gift...

'If it hadn't been for that momentary glimpse of four lines of tracer streaking past, I would not have had that split-second lead which I needed to get the hell out of it. If he hadn't used tracer - and only some German night-fighters did - he would have had time to correct his aim before I knew I was being attacked. He would then, perhaps, have written this story - not me.

'Chastened, breathing deeply, but having evaded, we climbed back to our operating height. Neither Mike nor I was in a mood to let matters rest.

'Twenty minutes later, using our radar, we were closing slowly on a known enemy aircraft. Even at full throttle it took an age. Our opponent was obviously on his way towards our returning stream of bombers. Mike read off the range: '1,500 feet... 1,200 feet... 1,000 feet'. It looked like another Me 110... '900 feet'... It was a Me 110... 'Still 900 feet' ... And again, 'Still 900 feet.'

'Even at full throttle we couldn't close the range further. I took aim. Nine hundred feet is not ideal on a dark night. I opened fire with our four cannons and six machine guns. There were strikes, like fireworks; flecks of flame; flashes; the Messerschmitt dived, steeply... It might have been destroyed, but we couldn't be sure.

'We climbed to our operating height again and reset course to meet our returning bombers. On we went eastwards. Shortly, there was another enemy radar contact. 'It's a Junkers 88, Mike.'

'My navigator grunted and looked up from his radar. 'Fix him properly,' he said. 'Don't bugger about this time.'

'Slowly I closed to 700 feet. I took careful aim and gave him everything... The fire flashed through the fuselage and engulfed the port engine. The Ju 88 was well alight... It spiralled down shedding pieces of burning aircraft. Minutes later, it blew up as it hit the ground...

'With fuel now critical, we set course for base... We had made a hash of one attack and had only survived to make two successful attacks that same night because our attacker had - by chance - been armed with visible tracer ammunition... For Mike and me that tracer had been the difference between life and death...' [26]

The other success on the night of 28/29 January went to Flying Officer Neil Munro, who was now a pilot on 239 Squadron in 100 Group in Norfolk having paired up with Flying Officer A. R. 'Dick' Hurley. Near Berlin they destroyed a Bf 110, possibly Bf 110G-4 of 11./NJG6, which crashed at Celle with the loss of Feldwebel Karl Gunselmann, a pilot with one victory (an Il'yushin Il-4 on the Eastern Front) and his crew (both KIA); Unteroffizier Willi Nagel, radar operator and Gefreiter Günter Sauerhering, air gunner. Munro and Hurley's kill was the first 239 Squadron victory using 'Serrate'.

On 25/26 February ten 'Serrate' patrols were flown as part of the Diversion and Support operations for the raid by 594 aircraft on Augsburg. Neil Munro and 'Dick' Hurley hit a hill in fog on approach to RAF West Raynham and crashed at Manor House, Tittleshall on the return. Munro was killed and Hurley died in No.53 Mobile Field

26 *Out of the Blue: The Role of Luck in Air Warfare 1917-1966,* edited by 'Laddie' Lucas (Hutchinson & Co 1985)

Hospital at Weasenham a few hours later. When the telegram giving the details of Neil Munro's death was received his mother and Rene Chandler his fiancée were shopping for fruit and other items for his birthday cake. They were told the news of his death when they returned home at 4pm. Neil Munro's 22nd birthday would have been 17 March 1944. It was been established that their R/T system had stopped working and fog had descended to within 100 feet of the ground. They were heard flying around trying to get their bearings but apparently they could not see and they crashed three miles from the aerodrome. Squadron Leader Evans told Munro's father that to have gotten back at all without R/T was magnificent work on the part of both pilot and navigator. February had proved a bad month for the three 'Serrate' squadrons and to compound it, seventeen Mosquitoes had returned early with engine failures.

Mosquito night-fighters were in constant action again when in January to May 1944 German bombers headed for London in the first of a series of revenge raids on Britain code-named Operation Steinbock directed by Generalmajor Peltz, Angriffsführer (Attack Leader) England. With characteristic understatement, Britons called the raids the 'Baby Blitz'. Mosquito night fighter crews encountered all manner of German bomber and fighter types, including Do 217s, Me 410s and even the occasional FW 190 and He 177; all of which were no match for the Mosquito.

Bomber Support sorties meanwhile, continued on nights when the Main Force was operating. On the night of 27/28 May when four forces of Halifaxes and Lancasters attacked Bourg-Leopold, Aachen, Nantes and Rennes 28 'Serrate' sorties and ten 'Intruder' patrols were flown by the Mosquitoes. Three Mosquitoes - two 'Intruders' and one 'Serrate' - were lost. Flying from West Raynham Harry White and Mike Allen on 141 Squadron scored their 11th victory and 239 Squadron destroyed a Bf 110. Flying Officer A. C. Gallacher DFC and Warrant Officer G. McClean DFC were one of six other crews on 141 that were airborne this night and they flew a 'Serrate' patrol to Aachen and Bourg Leopold. Gallacher recorded: 'DUTY PATROL. UP 01.10 hours. DOWN 03.40 hours. We crossed in at 01.55. Just after enemy coast at 01.56 hours, 23,000 feet 'Serrate' identification showing port and below. Aircraft turned on to 060 degrees and chased for four minutes, when contact dived off to starboard and switched off 'Serrate'. Immediately a backward AI contact appeared slightly to port at 5,000 feet range, no elevation. Aircraft turned hard starboard but contact did not re-appear. At 02.20 hours, 22,000 feet, 3 separate 'Serrate' contacts showed which appeared to come from Bourg Leopold. Aircraft turned on to contacts; one being singled out. Aircraft chased for 8 minutes, closing range almost to within AI range when starboard engine cut. Just after engine cut and prop feathered forward AI contact was seen and another in backward AI at 2,000 feet range showing slightly to port. AI set now went completely U/S so aircraft peeled off down to 12,000 feet and returned to base on one engine, crossing out at 03.05 hours. Weather, slight haze up to 4,000 feet. Clear above with good visibility. No cloud. Patrol uneventful.' [27]

One of the dozen Mosquitoes dispatched by 141 Squadron on 5/6 June, the eve of D-Day, was a 'Serrate' patrol to Northern France by Wing Commander 'Winnie' Winn DFC, the new CO and his navigator-radar operator, Flight Lieutenant R. A. W. Scott DFC. Winn recorded: 'DUTY PATROL. UP 23.35 hours. DOWN 03.05 hours. Crossed

27 On 8/9 June Gallacher and McClean chased a U/E/A over Northern France into a flak barrage at Rennes where it was brought down with a single burst.

in at 00.12 hours. Uneventful until 01.02 hours, 20 miles North of Paris fleeting AI contact, max range ahead and to port. Mk III G IFF switched on. Condensation trails of presumed Fortress well above seen to NW approx same time 15 miles. S.W. of Paris. At 01.23 hours at 18,000 feet an AI contact max range ahead to port and below chased for 3 mins after Jinking and orbiting target and overshot at 10,000 feet 240 ASI obtaining a fleeting visual on Me 110 going into steep dive to starboard. Backward AI contact seen but lost as enemy aircraft peeled off. Searched for several minutes but contact not regained. No 'Serrate'. Mk III G IFF switched on for half minute until it was decided from its behaviour that contact was hostile. Remainder of flight uneventful and re-crossed out at 02.25 hours. Weather 10/10ths strato cumulus 8,000 feet with one clear patch 30 miles diameter in area 10/10ths cloud above at 24,000 feet. Visibility good. Condensation trails well above, N/E Paris.'

On 7 June Winn and Scott flew another Duty Patrol to Northern France, as Winn recalled: 'Up 00.05 hours. Down 4.10 hours. Crossed in at 01.30 hours. Channel Islands area, many AI contacts on Bombers well below at Rendezvous. Aircraft went into target with bombers getting more contacts and three visuals on four engined aircraft in target area. At 02.20 hours in target area, at 14,000 feet AI contact seen starboard and ahead and slightly below at max range. This was chased for eight minutes with contact fading intermittently in interference and was finally abandoned at 02.35 hours. 20 miles off Southwold at 03.35 hours at 8,000 feet AI contact seen behind and slightly below at 4,000 feet closing rapidly. Aircraft turned steeply to port and contact disappeared in ground returns. After crossing coast, contact was picked up again. Aircraft made a steep turn to port and then starboard and obtained a visual on exhausts of an aircraft but both aircraft now went into cloud at 6,000 feet and contact disappeared in ground returns. Weather clear at base at take off. Low stratus over Channel clearing over Channel Islands and Beach Head, strato cumulus until North Sea where it cleared. Rain and 10/10ths cloud, low cloud on return to base.

In June Squadron Leader Russ Bannock joined 418 (City of Edmonton) Squadron RCAF at Holmsley South airfield after completing a Mosquito OTU course at High Ercall and at Greenwood, Nova Scotia. Prior to training on the Mosquito the Canadian pilot had spent four years in the Joint Air Training Plan in Canada training flying instructors at CFS Trenton, Ontario and No.3 Flying Instructors School at Arnprior, Ontario. While at Greenwood he teamed up with his navigator, Robert Bruce, who went to Canada for navigator training. Bruce recalls: 'The war had been going on a long time when we reached operational flying and we were both 'fully primed'. In 1939 I was a graduate of Edinburgh University with a first in Music, a brilliant outlook and no money. Deeply influenced by the poetry of Wilfred Owen, who was killed in action in November 1918, I joined the Friends Ambulance Unit (as gallant a bunch as any military). But after two and a half years I knew the war was ruinous and I must be part of the ruin. I was accepted for aircrew training. I was almost 28. Russ on the other hand was young in years - 23 - and old in flying experience and leadership. I arrived at Holmsley South about the 10th of June, Russ a few days earlier.

'We wasted no time and after practice trips' on the first three days, set off on the night of 14/15th June on our first 'Intruder', a two-hour patrol off Bourges-Avord airfield. Luck was with us and after some time we spotted the exhaust of a night-fighter as it passed overhead. We picked it up as it turned on final approach but had to break off to the south due to heavy anti-aircraft fire. Fortunately for us the pilot switched on his landing lights. We attacked in a shallow dive and fired a burst of cannon and machine guns. As it exploded and caught fire we recognized it as a Me 110. We were subjected to a barrage of AA fire from the north side of the airfield and we turned sharply to the left to avoid this wall of fire, but Russ was reefing so hard on the elevator we did a high-speed stall just as we almost turned 180 degrees. The aircraft flicked (rolled) to the right and I caught it after we rolled almost 180 degrees. We then exited to the west of the field. At that time I had never heard of a high-speed stall and was blissfully unaware of it. We saw pine trees illuminated by a searchlight just off our right wing tip. Surprisingly I emerged from these manoeuvres with no debilitating sickness and I recall a moment of smug gratification when I had to exert my authority by calling a course for the pinpoint on the river Loire! We were, by the way, still carrying two bombs under the wings and by the time we reached Holmsley South our fuel reserves were getting low. It was a memorable first trip.'

It had been intended that V-1 flying bombs would rain down on Britain as part of the Steinbock offensive but only ten of the 55 launch sites in north-eastern France were ready for the opening of the 'rocket blitz' on the night of 12/13 June 1944.[28] The Vergeltungswaffe 1 (Revenge Weapon No 1), or Fieseler Fi 103 'Kirschkern' ('Cherry Stone'), was a small pilotless aircraft with a 1,870lb high explosive warhead, which detonated on impact. The devilish weapons became known variously as Divers, 'Buzz-bombs' and 'Doodlebugs'. At West Malling a Mosquito XIII on 96 Squadron flown by 21-year old Flight Lieutenant Frank 'Togs' Mellersh DFC was approaching to land when a flying bomb crossed the airfield at 1,500 feet going quite slowly and flashing a yellow light from its tail. Another crossed over the airfield at about the same height and crashed about five miles away. Mellersh, the son of an air vice marshal, destroyed no less than 44 V-1s during the V-1 offensive; more than any other Mosquito pilot. [29] His navigator on 37 of these successful interceptions was 29-year old Flight Lieutenant Michael John Stanley DFC, who had become a student priest in 1932 before abandoning his vocation and becoming a student teacher before joining the RAF. The first V-1 claimed destroyed by a Mosquito was on 14/15 June 1944 and fell to Flight Lieutenant Rayne Schultz DFC who was on a freelance sortie over the sea when he was passed by a 'queer aircraft' flying in the opposite direction.

Squadron Leader Russ Bannock on 418 Squadron continues: 'The Squadron had been engaged in 'Night Intruding' against enemy airfields as well as conducting low level 'Day Rangers' against airfields when operating in pairs. On the night of 16 June Bob Bruce and I were departing on a 'Night Intruder' sortie and while over Beachy Head at about 2,000 feet we spotted what we thought was a burning aircraft flying at high speed below us and going inland. We called Sector Ops to alert them of the aircraft in distress but they replied that we were witnessing Hitler's new secret weapon, the V-1 flying bomb. When we returned from our 'Intruder' sortie there was great excitement in the ops room as several V-1s had been dispatched towards

28 *Diver! Diver! Diver! RAF and American Fighter Pilots Battle the V-1 Assault over South-East England 1944-45* by Brian Cull with Bruce Lander (Grub Street 2008).

29 Squadron Leader Joseph Berry DFC* a Tempest pilot, shot down the most V-1s (61). Flight Lieutenant Remi van Lierde DFC** a Belgian Tempest pilot, was second highest with 47 V-1s. Wing Commander Roland Beamont DSO* DFC* was fifth top score with 32 V-1s destroyed including six shared. *(Diver! Diver! Diver!)*

London and 418 were assigned to patrol a sector of the English Channel from dusk until dawn starting the following night. We were to put up two aircraft for two-hour patrols. This was up to about 60% of the squadron strength for the next month.

'There was V-1 activity two nights later but as we were patrolling a 2-3,000 feet and the V-1s were travelling at about 400 mph between 500-1,000 feet, we were unable to catch up before the V-1s crossed the coast. Our Mk.VI Mosquitoes could only attain about 380 mph at full power. The following day Flight Lieutenant Don MacFadyen and I worked out some tactics of patrolling at 10,000 feet and when we saw V-1s being launched from their launching platforms on the French coast (there was a big flash when it was launched and then it streamed a flame approximately 15 feet long). We headed for an intercept course over the Channel and turned our heading towards London until the V-1 caught up directly below. We then dove on the V-1 from 10,000 feet, achieving a speed of approximately 430 mph which gave us 20-30 seconds within gun range before we decelerated and the V-1 would pull away.'

On 18/19 June Flying Officer Sid Seid and Pilot Officer Dave McIntosh on 418 Squadron were sent out on an 'Anti-Diver' patrol, having had a careful briefing from Russ Bannock and Don MacFadyen. They were advised to climb to 10,000 feet, wait for an incoming flying bomb and then dive flat-out hoping that, at 400 mph, they could catch it. Accordingly they climbed away from Holmsley South, heading for the Channel. Seid decided to remain at 2,000 feet however then followed an hour of 'stooging around' waiting just inshore of Le Havre. Suddenly they caught sight of a red glow below and ahead and Seid rammed the throttles forward, the Mosquito accelerating to 350 mph and the crew watching in frustration as the missile simply ran away from them'.

Dave McIntosh then reminded his pilot of their Flight Commander's advice. Seid pulled up the nose and they ascended to 10,000 feet, with McIntosh getting a sore neck from craning around in the darkness. Suddenly Seid saw another, stood the Mosquito on its nose and down they went, the speed building up fast. With the ASI needle hovering around 400 mph, they found themselves hurtling past it before Seid could line up for a shot. Regretfully, they abandoned this attempt and climbed again to 10,000 feet. Dave McIntosh described what happened next: 'Another hour went by and we were thinking of doing another stooge before heading home, when we spotted a third doodlebug. 'By God, this time,' Sid said.

'The speed went up as we went down. I looked at the clock. It read 350 mph. I looked out along my wing. It was flapping like a seagull working in a hurricane. My stomach gave another wrench. Christ, the wings will come off and we'll go straight in. I didn't take any comfort from what had happened to Tony Barker and Gord Frederick, his navigator. They hit the drink so hard the cannons pulled them through the floorboards of the cockpit and clear of the Mosquito. They got into their dinghies and a rescue plane picked them out of the Channel two miles off the Dieppe beaches. It takes all kinds.

'Down, down, down. We were gaining some because the fire coming out of the ass end of the V-1 was getting bigger. The Mosquito was screaming in every joint. Sid had both big, hairy hands on the stick. When he began to pull back I thought the wings would never stand it. But we began to level out and the clock said 400 mph. Sid pulled and pulled and she kept coming out of the dive. I tore my eyes away from the shaking wing and looked ahead. It was just like looking into a blast furnace.

'We're too close,' I screamed. I shut my eyes as the cannons began banging away. I was thrown against my straps because the cannons going off cut the speed down suddenly. 'When the explosion came I thought I was going to be dead. The goddam thing went off right in our faces. I opened my eyes and caught a glimpse of things whirling around outside the window. Black things and blobs of smoke.

'I can't see,' Sid said.

'OK, boy,' I said. 'Just keep her like that. You can cut your speed, though.' He throttled back. After those hours of darkness, he had been blinded for a few seconds by the flash. Why we hadn't been smashed up by all that flying debris, I don't know. We had flown right through it.'

They returned to base to discover that the entire aircraft was blistered black. Every inch of paint had been burnt. Next day, after the crew had gathered to inspect the blackened aircraft, Seid gave a hilarious account of the encounters, ending by saying: 'I don't know how you are supposed to tell how far away you are. I thought we were about 300 yards away. Jesus, we weren't three yards away. I'm going to wear dark glasses at night after this.' [30]

Russ Bannock and Bob Bruce destroyed their first V-1, on 19/20 June. Bannock recalled: 'Bob Bruce and I vividly recall the occasion we came up behind the first V-1 that we intercepted from directly behind. Its pulse-jet engine streaming a long flame reminded us of looking straight into a blast furnace. After picking up some small debris from the first V-1, we learned to attack from an angle-off of about 30 degrees. Each one that we destroyed exploded with a vivid white flash, which would temporarily blind us until we pulled away from the explosion. There was always a secondary explosion when the V-1 hit the sea, which led us to conclude that only the fuel tanks exploded when hit with cannon and machine-gun fire and the warhead exploded when it hit the sea.'

On the night of 22/23 June Flight Lieutenant 'Stan' Cotterill DFC and 'Pop' McKenna on 418 Squadron RCAF destroyed two V-1s to take the Canadian squadron's score that night to five. Cotterill, who was from Toronto, said in an interview with for a Canadian newspaper: 'We used to stooge around, just out from the launching area in France. We were the first-line night fighter patrol. Sometimes we could see the actual launchings - a launching looks like a great half-moon of brilliant explosion. Then, when the thing came up and it could be spotted by the steady glow from the rear end, we dived down vertically on them at full throttle. Several kites would line up on one bomb and if the first one missed, then the others would go down for a try. After our dive on the thing we would level out and let go with a quick burst and then if you were too close you'd be thrown all over the sky by the explosion, or flying debris would damage the machine. Sometimes, from a distance, we weren't always sure whether there was a Doodlebug or not, so we used to line up the light with a star and then, if it moved, in we went.'

Russ Bannock adds. 'On one occasion we had an amusing experience when we only fired our 4 x .303 mg. (we were out of cannon ammo) and we only seemed to damage the auto pilot. The V-1 did a 180° turn and then the auto pilot righted it and we watched it continue southward and crash on the French coast. As the V-1s often came in salvos of 10 to 20 there was a general free for all with two or three aircraft

30 *Terror in the Starboard Seat* by Dave McIntosh.

diving on the same V-1. There were four Mosquito squadrons on patrol so there were at least eight aircraft around at any time. Fearing collision we agreed that we would turn on our nav' lights when we were in a dive. Although there was a tremendous barrage of anti-aircraft fire along the south English coast we never saw a V-1 shot down by anti-aircraft artillery although we saw several fly through the barrage. I learned after the war that the anti-aircraft had little success until they obtained the proximity fuse towards the end of the V-1 threat from the French coast. 418 continued on V-1 patrols until the launching sites were overrun by the advancing 21st Army in August.'

'By 28 August' recalls Bob Bruce 'we had destroyed 18 over the sea and one whose speed was much reduced by our fire before we ran out of ammo. We were frustrated to watch it limp over the English coast before it exploded on the ground. As navigator, I had little to do but record the time and position of the kills and recover those parts of my body, which had dropped into my boots as we pulled out of the dive. I was a victim of air-sickness. It hit me on my first pre-training trip in a DH Dragon, pursued me through Nav training intermittently and lasted into to ops. I never found the cause; it was sometimes the aerobatics of the camera-gun practice, but I survived the strains of diving on V-1s. It developed in straight and level flight and blew away in the first whiff of action at Parow at sunrise. A real agony of psychology which reality banished in an instant. I always thought it an example of the highest toleration that Russ put up with my failings. Everyone who flew in Mossies will know the benefit to crew co-operation of that close cockpit. Russ tells a story which I am sure (I hope) is apocryphal, of a dive he was making on a ground target, when a left hand appeared to help him pull out! I can only speak for my own case, but crew cooperation was so close that Russ has consistently included me even in actions where my role was simply passive and I am duly gratified.'

The V-1 forced 85 and 157 Squadrons in 100 Group to divert part of their resources to ADGB on 25 June and 'Anti-Diver' patrols were flown off the French and English coasts under the control of the South Eastern GCI stations. This met with considerable success, some pilots destroyed two or three 'Beechcraft' in one night, though the necessary modifications - stub exhausts, 150 octane fuel, 25lbs boost and the strengthening of the Mosquito nose, many of which were cracked by vibration or blast - entailed added work for the servicing crews. The injection of nitrous oxide (better known as 'laughing gas') with petrol gave the added power needed to catch the V-1s. Using the gas for two minutes gave an increase of 41 mph at 27,000 feet. On 18 July the squadrons reached the peak of their versatility, 157 Squadron flying five Diver and two high and three low patrols. It could not last. The V-1 menace increased and they moved to West Malling to combat the 'buzz-bomb'. The disappointment of leaving an interesting job so well begun at Swannington, coupled with diversions and little intelligence of what was happening among the night-fighters of Germany, caused the majority of crews to regard this new job with disfavour. Nevertheless, they practised AI on NFTs whenever possible at night and held weekly conferences on how best to keep in trim for Bomber Support on their return. The saving graces of West Malling lay in the very pleasant mess at Addington, the beauties of the surrounding countryside and pubs and the halcyon off duty afternoons at Hilden Manor. These kept the Squadrons happy in an otherwise monotonous existence.

In July 1944 264 Squadron at Hartford Bridge was taken off the beach-head work to try to tackle the V-1s. 'London was being bombarded and the citizens were beginning to panic' recalls Tom Arden, a FB.VI navigator on the squadron. 'The day fighters could deal with them fairly easily, but a Mossie at night was not a good weapon. You had to fly at about 8,000 feet over Kent and when you saw the light of a 'doodlebug' heading for London you dived down on it, to build up airspeed of about 480 mph. Mostly we went wrong by flying towards the light, whereas it was necessary to work out where it was going and head that way. Again and again we would all finish the dive about half a mile behind with no chance of catching up once the dive speed had dropped off. On 21 July Alan Turner and I judged it right for once. We came down behind the bomb at about 500 feet and 500 mph - fired - saw strikes and flipped over on our back due to a warp in the starboard wing! We knew that HK473 had a tendency to try to roll when flying fast, but this was overdoing it a bit. All the same, it was a very good aircraft and Alan and I did a lot of ops in it.'

On 28 August the V-1s had been to an extent got under control and ADGB allowed 85 and 157 Squadrons to return to Swannington to pick up the threads of their former task. Altogether, Mosquitoes accounted for 471 V-1s with 418 Squadron flying 402 sorties and destroying 83 V-1s; all but seven of them being shot down over the sea. This was 14% of the total V-1s shot down. From July to 21 August, based variously at Hurn, Middle Wallop and Hunsdon, 418 Squadron, during the 'Anti-Diver' offensive, had destroyed no fewer than 123 V-1 pilotless bombs. By September the Allied advance had overrun launching sites in the Pas de Calais. (Thankfully for the troops hitting the beaches all along the Normandy coastline on 'D-Day', 6 June, they had no need to fear bombing by the V-1s.) However, the Allied advance had not wrong-footed the Luftwaffe, who mounted a new terror blitz from the skies by air-launching 'Doodlebugs' from aircraft over the North Sea. In 1943 experiments at the German research establishment at Peenemünde on the Baltic coast where V-2 rockets were being built and tested resulted in several He 111s being modified to H-22 standard to carry a V-1 under its wing. By August 410 V-1s had been air-launched against London, Southampton and Gloucester. All of them were fired from Heinkel He 111s of III/KG3 based at Venlo and Gilze Rijen in Holland. Normally, the Heinkels took off at night, flew low over the North Sea to evade radar and climbed to 1,475 feet before firing their missiles from approximately 50 miles off shore. In September 1944 the Allied advance forced III/KG3 to abandon its bases in Holland and move to airfields in Germany. Only the radar-equipped Mosquito and Tempest V night-fighter were able to counter the new threat.

German revenge weapons aimed at southern England had proved such a menace that in June 1944 some 'Intruder' Mosquitoes from 100 (Special Duties) (Bomber support from May 1944) Group in Norfolk had been detached to West Malling for anti-Diver patrols. On 5/6 June, the eve of 'D-Day', 21 'Serrate' Mosquitoes were dispatched to northern France and ten 515 Squadron Mosquitoes on 'Ranger' patrols patrolled and bombed enemy airfields in France and strafed road, rail and canal traffic. That same night the Mk.X radar-equipped NF.XVIIs of 85 Squadron and 157 Squadron's NF.XIXs at Swannington officially began operations when sixteen sorties were flown. Twelve Mosquitoes in 85 Squadron operated over the Normandy beachhead, while four on 157 Squadron patrolled night-fighter airfields at Deelen, Soesterberg, Eindhoven and Gilze Rijen in Holland. When a Ju 88G-1 night-fighter landed at RAF Woodbridge on 13 July having become lost in thick cloud Scientists at TRE were able to examine the FuG 220 Lichtenstein SN-2, FuG 227/1 and FuG 350 Z Naxos radars, the last two types being previously unknown to the RAF. They confirmed 'Serrate's ineffectiveness and discovered that the Nachtjagd was using the FuG 227/1 equipment to home on to 'Monica' tail-mounted warning device and the FuG 350 Z Naxos to home on to H_2S radar bombsight transmissions. RAF bombers were ordered immediately to restrict the use of H_2S while 'Monica' sets were removed from the Lancasters and Halifaxes. 'Window' was modified to jam the new 'Lichtenstein' radar.

Forward bases usually used for 'Flower' included Bradwell Bay, Ford, West Malling, Coltishall, Manston and Hunsdon. On 17 September 1944 a Mosquito on 29 Squadron took off from Hunsdon at 2015 hours on a free-lance patrol covering the airborne landings on a line running north to south-east of Arnhem. The crew were Lieutenant D. R. O. Price RNVR and Sub-Lieutenant R. E. Armitage RNVR. Crossing out from the English coast at Orfordness at 20.37 hours, they made landfall on the Dutch coast at Westhoofd at 2101 hours and arrived on the patrol line at 2139 hours after some difficulty in pinpointing positions en route due to bad visibility and enemy defences. Commencing their patrol at 6,000 feet, their first radar contact came at 2205 hours.

The pilot's report continued: 'I was flying at 4,500 feet when my navigator obtained a contact at 2 o'clock 10°, range four miles, crossing starboard to port, position 25 miles from Arnhem on bearing 075°. I turned hard to port and contact was held at 12 o'clock, 10°, at 4 miles range. I immediately started to climb hard and followed aircraft which was taking gentle evasive action in height and azimuth. I closed range to 1,800 feet, my height being 11,000 feet and obtained a visual on a very bright single exhaust well above and to starboard. I closed range to 1,000 feet and obtained a silhouette which was identified as an Me 110 carrying long-range tanks slung under the wings, out-board of each engine, at 300 feet range. My navigator also confirmed identification.

'Just before the visual was obtained, the EA started to make hard port and starboard turns also throttling hard back, causing the engines to emit vast showers of sparks. In spite of this evasive action, contact was held and range was opened to 150 yards. 'Waggle your wings or you will burn' was given without response from the EA which also gave no response to IFF interrogation. I fired a 3-second burst on a very bright white exhaust on the starboard engine causing it to explode with debris flying off. The windscreen was covered with oil and as the EA's speed had fallen off considerably, I broke away hard starboard and noticed that the engine had fallen out of the starboard wing of the E/A which dived vertically to the deck with its port engine enveloped in flames.

From 11,000 feet I was unable to follow it down owing to the steepness of the dive. The E/A disappeared through low cloud and thick ground mist. I then orbited at 4,000 feet unable to see the deck and as we were not quite sure of our position, which was later estimated to be 15 miles SSW of Münster, I climbed to 6,000 feet and returned to our patrol area. As we were now overdue on patrol, I set course for home in thick cloud at 22.49 hours. Crossed out Dutch coast at Westhoofd 23.10 hours. In English coast at Orfordness at 23.38 hours and landed base at 23.55 hours: I claim one Me 110 destroyed.'

Defensive and Offensive Night Fighting

During a 157 Squadron patrol while on a High Level Support operation Mosquito XIX on the night of 7/8 October, Warrant Officer Alan 'Penny' Penrose picked up a contact at six miles range west of Neumünster, ten degrees above crossing from port to starboard, doing a slow right hand orbit. Penrose held the DFC and bar for actions during two tours of fighter operations. His first tour began with 125 (Night Fighter) Squadron, which at the time was part of 10 Group of Fighter Command. He was a navigator/radar operator. When he joined 125, in February 1942, they were still operating Boulton Paul Defiants, so he flew as an air gunner. Later in the year the squadron was re-equipped with Beaufighters and he teamed up with John Owen Mathews who had joined 125 in June 1941. Mathews had been a clerk with the Prudential Insurance in 1939 before joining the RAF.

Flight Lieutenant Jimmy Mathews closed climbing from 8,000 feet to 9,000 feet. 'As we got a visual, 1,000 yards away, 40 degrees above' continues Mathews, 'the enemy aircraft straightened out on a course of about 240 degrees, doing 160 ASI. We recognised it as a Me 110 with long range tanks and opened fire with a short burst from 100 yards dead behind. Strikes were seen and a small explosion occurred in the starboard engine. Another burst and the starboard engine caught fire. The colours of the day were fired off and it dived down burning, hitting the ground with a very large explosion lighting the countryside for miles.' It took their score to three aircraft destroyed and three damaged and by August, they had destroyed five flying bombs. One they attacked exploded so close to them that the blast set the Mosquito's rudder and rear fuselage on fire.

On 21 November Pilot Officer Beynon and Pilot Officer Pearcy took off from Hundson on a 'Flower' at 18.45 hours, bound for Sachsenheim aerodrome. The pilot's report reads: 'The English coast was crossed at Manston on way out at 19.05 hours landfall being made on the French coast at Calais, 19.13 hours. The route to target was uneventful, patrol area being reached at 20.32 hours. The weather at the target was 9/10ths stratus base 1,500 feet and visibility was very poor. Through a break in the cloud the airfield was seen lit with red perimeter lights. The patrol was continued on DR with the aid of the aerodrome beacon visually flashing 'VG' and seen occasionally through breaks in the cloud till 20.47 hours when contact was obtained.

I was patrolling Sachsenheim airfield at 4,000 feet on an east-west patrol line on the north side of the visual beacon when my navigator obtained a contact at 2¼ miles range, crossing from starboard to port, slightly above. I immediately turned to port behind the bogey, increasing speed to 270 mph. Giving chase, I gradually closed range to 3,000 feet, when I observed ahead and to port an airfield which was fully lit with V/L and red perimeter lighting, on the west bank of the Rhine. This we later assumed to be Spayer airfield.

'The target flew over the top of the airfield, orbited to port, gradually lost height from 5,500 feet to 2,500 feet. I followed down to 3,000 feet, when my navigator informed me target was making off in a northerly direction. I followed target which flew at varying heights between 3,000 and 6,000 feet and closed range to 600 yards dead astern. Visual was not obtained due to poor visibility, so I lost height placing myself 200 feet below target which was then slightly to starboard, when a faint visual was obtained. I closed still further to 300 feet to positively identify target, continuously calling 'Bogey, Bogey, waggle your wings' and navigator interrogated with IFF. To this there was no response. At 300 feet, I obtained a visual on a Ju 188 and ked navigator to confirm independently.

'We both simultaneously identified target as a Ju 188 which was flying at 4,000 feet with speed of approximately 240 mph. I then increased range to 600 feet and pulling up dead astern opened fire with a 3-second burst, closing in from 600-300 feet. The port engine caught fire enveloping the wing in flames which broke off from the fuselage. At the same time an explosion occurred in the cockpit which set the fuselage blazing. The enemy aircraft rolled over on its back and dived vertically into the ground where it blew up with a violent explosion and burnt at 20.08 hours. I estimated my position to be West of Ludwigshafen at time of combat. I claim one Ju 188 destroyed thanks to persistent work on the part of my navigator.'

Flight Sergeant Alf 'Snogger' Rogers, Flying Officer Frank Bocock's navigator on 515 Squadron recalls: 'It was not all exciting, dramatic action. Indeed there were times when it was remarkable uneventful. I recall what it was like to be prowling over Germany on a dark winter's night. The moon and the stars completely obscured by 10/10ths cloud, the ground below equally invisible. Cocooned in total darkness, sitting silently side by side, the only sound, the regular soporific drone of the engines. It was a strange, lonely feeling as if nothing existed beyond the confines of that tiny cockpit. Then suddenly a voice over the R/T and we knew that we were not, after all, alone in the universe. Somewhere out there was at least one other person. Who was he? Where was he? Why was he flying on such a night? But the moment quickly passed and once again the darkness and silence closed around us and we flew on in solitude. Eventually, as we approached the Norfolk coast on our way home, our call 'Pale Green 23 identifying' was acknowledged. A few minutes later we could see the runway lights at Little Snoring and then we were in contact with 'Ex-King Control' requesting permission to land. After landing, de-briefing, a meal in the Mess and off to bed. We had returned to a world inhabited by people.

'One night in December we were assigned an 'Intruder' target at Giessen in southern Germany. The previous few days had been very wintry and there was good deal of snow on the ground. The snow plough had been busy keeping the runways usable. As we walked out to dispersal the sky was heavy with more snow and as we climbed into our Mossie the snow began to fall heavily. We settled ourselves into the cockpit, started the engines and began to move off. After we had moved just a yard or two Frank said 'Can you see anything at your side?' I said 'No - but I have an uneasy feeling that we are not right.' Frank said 'So have I - we'd better stop.' He put the brakes on and we strained our eyes in an effort to see something through the darkness and the falling snow. We spotted a ground crew coming round in front of us carrying two marshalling torches. He stood with his back towards us, put both torches together and shone them straight ahead. In the light of the torches we were just able to see directly in front of us a petrol bowser. The ground crew pointed us in the right direction and we began to creep around the perimeter track.

'We had not gone far when over the R/T a voice from Control said, 'Aircraft on runway - return to dispersal.' So it seemed that ops were scrubbed. We were about to turn round and return when another voice on the R/T said 'It's all right control, we can cope.' After that silence. We didn't quite know what to make of that so Frank called Control and asked 'Do we go or don't we?' Back came the reply 'You can go if you like.' - Go if you like! - On ops! We decided that having gone so far we might as well continue. So we taxied round and took off along the snow covered runway.

'We always flew over the sea at a maximum of 500 feet so it was no problem to stay below cloud at first. But eventually we had to climb in an effort to get above the weather. Being a low-level squadron our engines had a rated altitude of 2,000 feet. On this occasion we climbed steadily up through the cloud but never quite out of the top. There was a spectacular display of St. Elmo's Fire and serious icing. Icing on the control surfaces prevented any manoeuvring and we had no alternative but to fly straight and level hoping to run into clear skies. When we did eventually run out of the cloud we had passed our target area. There was no possibility of carrying out a low-level 'Intruder' so once we were free of the ice we just had to turn round and come back. In a way that was worse. On the outward flight we had pressed on in the hope of finding better weather. Now we knew exactly what lay ahead - all the way back to base. We had not encountered enemy action, but that was one occasion when we were glad to get back home.'

On 4/5 December during a patrol north of the Ruhr over Dortmund airfield, Jimmy Mathews and 'Penny' Penrose attacked and destroyed a Ju 88. Two nights later on a patrol east of Frankfurt, they first destroyed a Bf 110 and then a Ju 88 was seen and Mathews attacked from fifty yards. The starboard inner petrol tank and the fuselage both caught fire. The night fighter dived steeply downwards, burning fiercely and was seen to crash amidst some houses near Giessen killing the air gunner. On Christmas Eve, a patrol three miles south-west of Cologne gave support to a bomber attack on the marshalling yards and Hangelar airfield near Bonn. A Ju 88 was chased and shot down with a 1½ second burst, the starboard engine bursting into flames. As it turned to port, three parachutes came out in quick succession and the aircraft spun down in flames and crashed. Mathews and Penrose landed back at Swannington at 9.43 pm with more than Christmas to celebrate.

In all, 42 100 Group Mosquitoes were abroad this night and four Bf 110s and the one Ju 88 were claimed destroyed. Also, 37 Mosquitoes of the 2nd TAF patrolled the areas of Aachen, Arnhem and the Dutch Friesian Islands and they flew 'close support' sorties over the front lines. None of these Mosquitoes was lost and they claimed two Ju 87 Stukas, two Ju 188s, one Ju 88 and one Bf 110. Fifty trucks and six locomotives were also destroyed.

A patrol to Karlsruhe on 2/3 January 1945 produced a Ju 88 which Mathews and Penrose then lost, but then a second 88 was found ten miles north-east of Stuttgart. A two-second burst produced strikes and then a fire in the cockpit and central part of the fuselage. The 88 dived to port and exploded on the ground ten miles to the south-west of Crailsheim. Penrose's second award came on 22 January, when he was recommended for a bar to his DFC. All their combats were mentioned and his total ops had now reached 85. Mathews too received a bar to his DFC. Their next action was on 16/17 March. This time they were supporting a bomber attack on Würzburg and a contact was made in the bomber stream in the Stuttgart area. Then a Ju 88 was identified and a burst of fire from 150 feet caused the port side of the fuselage to catch fire. It dived to port and exploded on the ground twenty miles south of Würzburg. Their final awards were put forward on 19 April, a DSO to Mathews who was promoted to Squadron Leader and the Conspicuous Gallantry Medal to Alan Penrose. By this time Penrose had flown 97 sorties covering 350 hours. Fifty-seven of these operations had been in 100 Group on Support and 'Intruder' operations. He had assisted in the destruction of nine enemy aircraft and five flying bombs, plus the damaging of three others.

The large-scale use of the Mosquito late in 1944 and early 1945 had forced the Nachtjagd to re-think their tactics and this seriously reduced their efficiency. One Geschwader with a strength of about 100 crews lost, in just three months, twenty four crews killed, ten missing and fifteen wounded. It was at around this time that the real Moskitopanik started and from then on all the normal run of crashes through natural causes were attributed to the Mosquito. Moskitopanik reached a peak during December 1944 when 36 enemy night fighters were shot down. The Mosquito's increased reputation heightened the German night fighter crews' despondency and their demoralization was complete when they had to resort to throwing out 'Düppel' ('Window') as a routine, to mislead and distract the Mosquito night fighters.

Chapter 3

'Low Levellers' and the 'Shallow Divers'

On 15 November 1941 Blenheim aircrews on 105 Squadron at the 2 (Fighter Bomber) Group grass airfield at Swanton Morley - a hell spot only 15 miles from Norwich but which might have been in deepest Siberia - gathered to see Mosquito W4064 fly over at about 500 feet, at a speed of 300 mph. It approached the Watch Office and hangar from the west and went into a vertical bank at a height of 2-3,000 feet before turning a circle so tight and at such a speed that vapour trails streamed from his wingtips. This was followed by a normal circuit and landing. Compared to the Blenheim IVs 105 Squadron was used to, this performance was quite breathtaking. All crews watched with great enthusiasm the performance in the air. Even the Spitfire pilots on 152 Squadron were impressed. Company Chief Test Pilot Geoffrey de Havilland Jr. emerged from the tiny cockpit; climbed down the ladder and was received like a conquering hero by Group Captain Battle OBE DFC the station commander. Flying anti-shipping operations from Malta, 105 Squadron's losses had been high. The arrival of the 'Wooden Wonder' provided a much needed morale boost but W4064 had to return next day to Hatfield, where the first of just ten B.IV bombers was coming off the production lines, for adjustments. A further 60 Mosquito bombers were on order, but deliveries would not begin until the following February. W4066, the first Mosquito bomber to enter RAF service, arrived at Swanton Morley on 17 November watched by the AOC 2 Group, Air Vice Marshal d'Albiac and his staff. Three other B.IVs - W4064, W4068 and W4071 - were delivered at intervals to Swanton Morley by Geoffrey de Havilland Jr. and Pat Fillingham.

Swanton Morley was unsuitable for Mosquito operations and the 'rumour now to scoff at' recalled Sergeant (later Flight Lieutenant) Michael Carreck, an observer, 'was that 105 Squadron was going to move to a permanent station, central heating, two to a cosy room, hot baths at the turn of a tap. To our amazement this turned out to be 'pukka gen' and on 10 December there we were, with all four of our Mosquitoes, at Horsham St. Faith next door to all the joys of Norwich, mildly puzzled, one must admit, that a tremendously Top Secret aircraft had been put on display on an airfield bound by a busy road, spies galore clicking their cameras. Not for us to worry, warmth and comfort, Mosquitoes to0 fly and Norwich nearby - who could ask for more?

'Euphoria however, came to a shuddering halt and cries of anger rent the air as we learnt that we were to be re-crewed. Three to a crew in a Blenheim, only two in a Mosquito so sadly, some of our navs and WOps were surplus to requirements. Sadder still they were posted to Blenheim squadrons flying in the Sea of Carnage; attacks on North Sea convoys, whose escorting flak flak-ships didn't bother to aim, just fired splash into the sea, a curtain of exploding steel through which the doomed Blenheim crews flew with unmatchable courage. One afternoon one of our pilots had to hop the station Tiger Moth over to one of these squadrons to deliver something bureaucratic. He went to the crew room to ask after an OTU friend. 'Jimmy so-and-so here?' 'There he is' said someone, pointing to a photograph papered to a wall - a head over heels Blenheim somersaulting into the sea. Small wonder they called us 'Poor Bloody Two Group'.

'The Mosquito needed a navigator plus a wireless operator to belt out Morse and cope with the T1145 transmitter and the R1115 receiver - but there was room for only one beside the pilot. So the poor devil in the right hand seat began to train as an overworked one-man band of nav, Warrant Officerp, photographer and bomb-aimer. We navs tapped out squealing Morse until our wrists ached while the WOps grappled with the esoteric mysteries of the triangle of velocities. We practised our new trades in the Blenheim or in the flying classroom of the Squadron Anson, which made us feel as if we were back at Kitty Hawk with Orville and Wilbur. We navs eventually reached a Morse speed of 12 words a minute, a fraction of that of the ground operators. But they were very tolerant when they heard P7F, the Squadron call-sign and answered us at the same speed and never with SWOF - Send With Other Foot, or UCP - Use Carrier Pigeon. Although one or two Mosquitoes were to arrive to join W4064 at agonisingly long intervals there was always a lengthy waiting-list for flights. We were encouraged, however, to familiarise ourselves with the Mosquito cockpit. My original pilot, Pilot Officer Ron Onley - first violinist in the London Philharmonic - and I clambered up the wonky red ladder. While the pilots had nice comfy seats with everything just so we took indignant note that we were expected to sit on the hard wooden spar. Moreover we had to twist ourselves like contortionists, left hand over right shoulder, to reach the Morse key. Yet again, whenever you pulled out the navigator's table it fell to the floor, crash. Eventually we clipped our Mercator to a piece of board; with this on our knees it was like being at the Mad Hatter's tea party, juggling with protractor and Dalton computer instead of cup and saucer and cucumber sandwich. During that spring of 1942 105 had four accidents. Two overshoots, major damage to one Mosquito, minor damage to the other. Then another aircraft collided with Ron Onley's Master - he crashed, was rushed to hospital and I was told he had died. I grieved for my pilot until 25 years later I was delighted to hear that Ron, after two distinguished tours, had ended the war training Mosquito Pathfinder pilots. [31]

'To acquaint us with one of the dangers of stratospheric flying a decompression chamber was fixed up at Horsham St. Faith. They pumped out oxygen and put us in, a few at a time and told us to pick up that pencil and hit the French letter hanging on its string. Whack, whack - you didn't know what you were doing, missed it by miles. What you also didn't know was that the rest of the Squadron were watching you, an object of derision. Bad show, reminiscent of the days when people went to chortle at the lunatics in Bedlam; but when you were a spectator it was the funniest thing you ever saw. Much as we enjoyed ourselves five miles high our greatest thrill was streaking across the countryside balls-out at hedge-top height, the pilots rejoicing in what was otherwise a court-martial sin. Mind you, while navigation in the stratosphere was a piece of cake, a thousand square miles at a glance with everything below laid out like a map, by contrast on-the-deck navigation, a mile every fifteen seconds from the top of a bus, meant that we were in the obligatory phrase of the Navigator's Union, 'temporarily unsure of our exact position'. But it was all the most enormous fun. Pete Rowland, who was a superlative pilot, used to bring us down low, lower, lower still over the tree-tops until we heard twigs scratching our fuselage and

30   Onley was KIA on 11/12 December 1944.

we'd grin at each other, he twenty - me six months his senior.

'By now further thought had been given to the development of the Mosquito. Blisters in the side windows improved view to the rear. Squadron Leader Peter Channer [who as a Blenheim pilot on 18 Squadron had received the DFC for the attack on the Knapsack power station at Cologne] had investigated the effects of veneering the outer surfaces and speed was raised by 5mph. Another attempt was made to arm the Mosquito, this time by fitting a backward firing machine gun beneath each nacelle. This project was abandoned when it was pointed out that we could only pull the triggers when the fighter was sitting on our tail, by which time we'd be dead.

'Suddenly it was goodbye to the life of Riley and we became the pioneer - the guinea pig - operational Mosquito bomber squadron. We now had eight Mosquitoes and 13 crews, five of which were hurriedly summoned for briefing in the early evening of 31 May. And so began Bomber Command's leisurely exploration of how not to use the Mosquito. This we paid for with Russian roulette losses of one in six but we blazed the trail for future Mosquito glory and it is the pride of my life that I flew with what was then 'Poor Bloody One-Oh-Five'.' [32]

On 27 May 2 Group had issued orders for 105 Squadron to prepare four Mosquitoes with bombs (two 250lb and two 500lb) and cameras to harass and obtain photographic evidence in the wake of the 'Thousand Bomber' raid on Cologne, scheduled for the night of 30/31 May. Squadron Leader 'Jesse' Oakeshott DFC, followed later by Pilot Officer 'Ken' Kennard and Pilot Officer 'Johnny' Johnson, took off from Horsham before the 'heavies' had returned. Pilot Officer Edgar Costello-Bowen and Warrant Officer Tommy Broom and Flight Lieutenant Jack Houlston AFC and Flight Sergeant James Armitage followed them, shortly before lunchtime the following day. Oakeshott flew at 24,000 feet over the battered and blasted city and added his four bombs to the devastation; but with smoke reaching to 14,000 feet, which obliterated Cologne entirely his F24 camera was rendered useless. 'Ken' Kennard and 'Johnny' Johnson failed to return, their aircraft (W4064) being hit by anti-aircraft fire. Costello-Bowen and Houlston dropped their bombs from high-level into the smouldering and smoking ruins to prolong the night of misery for the inhabitants and bomb disposal teams and headed back to Norfolk. There was no flak and no fighters. In the late afternoon Peter Channer took off from Horsham to try and get low level photographs in the evening. He crossed the coast as low as possible and after a time the cloud level came down to 1,000 feet. He went up into this for a time and when about sixty miles from Cologne opened up to + 6lb boost and shallow-dived to very near the ground at 380 mph indicated. He noticed that when passing over a large marshalling yard, nobody looked up at him. Cattle in fields took no notice until he was well past them. He told Hereward de Havilland afterwards that this flight impressed him more than any he had ever done before and greatly strengthened his belief in the soundness of low Mosquito attacks on selected targets.

On the evening of 1 June, two Mosquitoes returned to Cologne to bomb and reconnoitre the city. One of the aircraft failed to return. Then, just before dawn on 2 June, 18 hours after a 'Thousand Bomber' raid on Essen, Flight Lieutenant George Parry and his navigator, Flying Officer Victor Robson, flew a lone 2 hour 5 minute round-trip to Cologne. They carried four 500-pounders to stoke up the fires and a camera to

31   *105 Squadron - Mosquito Bomber - The First Days* by Michael Carreck DFC writing in *The Mossie No.37* January 2005.

observe the damage. However, thick smoke made the latter task impossible. (Robson, who had come to 105 Squadron from Coastal Command was, according to his pilot, 'at night [he] was like a homing pigeon. No matter how bad the weather, he always pinpointed exactly.') The Mosquitoes were of course much faster than the 'heavies' were and as Parry recalls, 'We were back having breakfast in the Officers' Mess while the 'heavies' were still overhead, heading for home.'

In June the Mosquitoes on 105 Squadron continued their lone reconnaissance missions over Germany. On 8 June, 139 Squadron was formed at Horsham St. Faith under the command of Wing Commander Peter Shand DFC, using crews and a few Mk.IVs on 105 Squadron. Jack Houlston was promoted to Squadron Leader and transferred to 139, flying that Squadron's first operation on 25/26 June, a low-level raid on the airfield at Stade, near Wilhelmshaven. He returned after dark just as bombers for the third in the series of 'Thousand Bomber' raids were taking off for Bremen. Two of 105 Squadron's Mosquitoes flew reconnaissance over the city after the raid and four more went to reconnoitre other German cities to assess damage and bring back photographs.

On 2 July the first joint attack by 105 and 139 Squadron Mosquitoes took place when four aircraft from 105 Squadron carried out a low-level attack on the submarine yards at Flensburg and two Mosquitoes in 139 Squadron also bombed from high level. Group Captain J. C. MacDonald DFC AFC the Station Commander and Wing Commander 'Jesse' Oakeshott DFC failed to return. MacDonald and his observer, Flight Lieutenant A. E. Skelton, became PoWs. Oakeshott and his observer, Flying Officer Vernon 'Titch' F. E. Treherne DFM were killed. Houlston came off the target pursued by three FW 190s. Two more fighters chased Flight Lieutenant George Pryce Hughes MiD RCAF, who, despite his name, was an Argentinean, after he had been hit by flak over the target. Both pilots made their exits hugging the wave tops and applying plus 12½-lb of boost, they easily outpaced their pursuers.

High-level raids in clear skies were now the order of the day and during July the first 29 'Siren Raids' were flown. These involved high-level dogleg routes across Germany at night and were designed to disrupt the war workers and their families and ensure that they lost at least two hours' sleep before their shifts the following day.

On 11 July Flying Officer Sydney Clayton DFM flew his first Mosquito operation as navigator to Flight Lieutenant Joseph Roy George Ralston DFM. Ralston, a Mancunian from Moss Side, had enlisted in the RAF in 1930 as a technical tradesman. By 1938 he had progressed to become a sergeant pilot on 108 Squadron flying Hawker Hinds and Blenheim IVs on 107 Squadron. Clayton had been an observer on Blenheims on 105 Squadron in 1941 and had flown 72 operational sorties before being 'rested' as an instructor. Clayton recalled: 'On 11 July the aircraft was Mosquito B.IV DK300, our load 4 x 500lb GPs and the target the submarine base at Flensburg, as a diversion for the heavies' hitting Danzig. It was a low-level attack and we met medium flak which damaged our fin and rudder, severed the pipe to the pitot head and further damaged the hydraulic system. We had no trouble getting home but due to the damaged hydraulics, the pilot couldn't drop the wheels or lower flaps. Our air speed indicator was u/s and we had to be led in by another aircraft for a belly landing at around 160 mph - which, thankfully, was safely accomplished. From then on we alternated on high and low-level work. Intelligence did a marvellous job in locating flak batteries, particularly along the coast and consequently a good land-fall was essential on low-level ops. By using the Mk.IX bomb sight to check drift and the wind direction off the sea lanes, this was accomplished[33] without trouble. Sea gulls were a hazard when crossing over the coast and in the early days (before the thick, bullet-proof windscreens were installed) one or two Mossies had windscreens completely shattered.'

High-level raids in clear skies were now the order of the day and during July the first 29 'Siren Raids' were flown. These involved high-level dogleg routes across Germany at night and were designed to disrupt the war workers and their families and ensure that they lost at least two hours' sleep before their shifts the following day.

On 25 August 'George' Parry and 'Robbie' Robson and Roy Ralston and Syd Clayton DFM were detailed to raid two electric power stations. Costello-Bowen and Tommy Broom were given a switching station at Brauweiler near Cologne but they hit a pylon en route and crashed in a wood. Incredibly, both men survived and with the help of the Underground movement they evaded capture and were sent along the escape route to Spain. In October they returned to England aboard the battleship HMS *Malaya*.

In September 1942 Marham was transferred to 2 Group, Bomber Command and on the 13th 105 and 139 Squadrons received orders to vacate Horsham St. Faith by 28 September, as the Americans were due to arrive to base medium bombers there. The Mosquito Conversion Unit also moved to Marham with the two first-line squadrons. 105 Squadron were equipped with Mosquito Mk.IV bombers and 139 were then converting to this type from Blenheim V (Bisleys), while the Mosquito CU flew a mixture of Blenheims and Mosquitoes. (On 18 October the CU was renamed the Mosquito Training Unit). Amid the changeover, on 19 September, six crews on 105 Squadron attempted the first daylight Mosquito raid on Berlin but only one crew succeeded in bombing the 'Big City'.[34] A few days later, on 25 September, the expert low-level raiders in 105 Squadron carried out the longest Mosquito operation thus far when George Parry, now a squadron leader and three other crews attacked the Gestapo HQ in Oslo, a round-trip of 1100 miles with an air time of 4-hours 45 minutes. Hereward de Havilland reported: 'Four Mosquitoes set out from Leuchars. The formation was originally to have been led by Wing Commander Hughie Edwards VC DSO DFC but this arrangement was altered at the last minute by Bomber Command and Squadron Leader Parry took Edwards' place. They attacked in two pairs, Parry leading the first pair, with Pilot Officer Rowland close up on his starboard quarter; then came Flying Officer Bristow, with Sergeant Carter on his right. During the run up

33 Pilot Officer Laston made it home with part of his fin blown away by flak, but Flight Lieutenant George Hughes and his navigator, Flying Officer Thomas A. Gabe were killed when their Mosquito crashed, possibly as a result of flying too low after they attacked a train. Sergeant Peter W. R. Rowland, in DK296, borrowed from George Parry, flew so low that he hit a farmhouse roof and returned to Horsham with pieces of chimney pot lodged in the fuselage. After he had landed Parry barked at Rowland, 'I'm not lending you my aircraft again!'

34 Two pilots - Sergeant Norman Booth (KIA 13.11.42) and Flight Sergeant K. L. Monaghan - were both forced to return early. Flight Lieutenant Roy Ralston and Flying Officer Sydney Clayton bombed Hamburg after finding Berlin covered by cloud. George Parry and 'Robbie' Robson were intercepted on two occasions by FW 190s but managed to evade them. Parry jettisoned his bombs near Hamburg and turned for home, heading back across the north coast of Germany and into Holland. At 1,000 feet just off the Dutch coast, two 109s attacked but although one of them scored hits, Parry dived down to sea level and soon outran them. Squadron Leader Norman Henry Edward Messervy DFC and his navigator Pilot Officer Frank Holland in M-Mother were shot down by a FW 190 piloted by *Schwarmführer* Oberfeldwebel Anton-Rudolf 'Toni' Piffer of *2nd Staffel/JG1*. The Mosquito crashed NNW of Osnabrück with the loss of both crew.

to the target, three FW 190s made a diving attack from the starboard quarter, one going for the leading pair and two for the second. Bristow had to turn a few degrees left to get on to his target and Carter on DK325 was thus left rather farther astern and was hit; one of Rowland's airscrews was hit by a cannon shell which exploded on the spinner. Parry's aiming was good and Rowland actually saw his bombs strike the roof of the Gestapo building. After being hit, Carter turned left and was last seen, still under control, making towards Sweden with one engine apparently on fire and a fighter on his tail.' [35]

The post-mortem and camera pictures taken on the raid revealed that at least four bombs had entered the roof of the Gestapo HQ; one had remained inside and failed to detonate and the other three had crashed through the opposite wall before exploding. A few days later the *Daily Mail* called the Mosquito - or *Anopheles de Havillandus* as military wags liked to call it[36]: the 'grandson of the Comet Racer and a prodigal son of the Albatross' and another writer said '...it is aptly named as it will sting the Nazis time and time again, proving far worse than its namesake and far more dangerous'.

October ushered in new tactics as two distinct types of low-level attack eventually came to be developed by 105 and 139 Squadrons. These were the low level proper and the 'Shallow Dive' and they frequently used together on the same target, starting at Liège on 2 October. Six to eight 'Low Level' raiders went in at the lowest level carrying bombs that exploded eleven seconds after impact and they would be followed by the second formation of 'Shallow Divers' who climbed up to about 2,000 feet just before the target was reached. When over the target they peeled off and dived straight down on the target and releasing their bombs fitted with instantaneous fuses at about 1,500 feet. Only a very restricted number of Mosquitoes could cross the target at low level before the leaders' bombs exploded but a 'Shallow Dive' formation enabled a target to be hit by a far larger number of Mosquitoes. October was a mix of low-level shallow-dive raids at dusk on targets in Belgium and Holland and high-level attacks on German cities. It was also a month when several crews were lost to the 'Butcher Birds' of JG1 and JG 26[37]. The Focke-Wulf 190s put in an appearance on 21 October when Syd Clayton flew his 85th op as he recalls.

'Our Mosquito was DZ343 and the general idea was to bomb four separate targets in different areas so that, apart from bomb damage, production was lost due to the alerts. We made a general nuisance of ourselves for about three hours and then, crossing

---

35 Flight Sergeant Gordon K. Carter and Sergeant William S. Young blew up and crashed in to a lake killing both crew.

36 *Agent ZigZag* by Ben Macintyre (Bloomsbury 2007). Eddie Chapman, the renowned double agent, was tasked by the German secret service to sabotage the Mosquito factory at Hatfield in 1942. Using skilful camouflage and deception, the Germans were fooled into believing that he had carried out his task successfully.

37 On 9 October Wing Commander Edwards and 'Tubby' Cairns and another Mosquito crewed by Warrant Officer Charles R. K. Bools MiD and Sergeant George Jackson set out to bomb Duisburg. Feldwebel Fritz Timm of 12./JG1 shot down Bools and Jackson over Belgium. Oberfeldwebel Timm was KIA on 28 May 1944 flying Bf 109G-6 'Yellow 3'. At dusk on 11 October three pairs of Mosquitoes were despatched to bomb Hannover but two of the Mosquitoes were intercepted by FW 190As of II./JG26 while en route over Holland. Unteroffizier Günter Kirchner of the 5th Staffel took off from Katwijk and intercepted Pilot Officer Jim Lang and Flying Officer Robin P. 'Tommy' Thomas and shot them down. Unteroffizier Kolschek of the 4th Staffel was credited with shooting down Squadron Leader James G. L. 'Jimmy' Knowles DFC and Flight Sergeant Charles Gartside. Lang and Thomas survived to be taken prisoner. No trace was ever found of Knowles and Gartside.

the north Dutch coast, we were jumped by two Focke-Wulf 190s who had obviously been vectored on to us. Cloud was about six-tenths at 3-4,000 feet and on sighting the EA, we entered cloud, turned north and dived for the deck. On breaking cloud cover we had gained some distance, but the 190s were being controlled and soon turned on to us. However with our dive we managed to hold them off, although they chased us for about 15 minutes. The big snag was trying to keep a sight on their position and distance away. The Mossie wasn't fitted with VHF, but we had the Marconi 1154-1155 W/T and the only way one could keep check was to slip your head sideways between the top of the radio and the canopy. Being more or less at sea level and going flat out, it was a very bumpy ride and my head vibrated between radio and canopy. Luckily the Focke-Wulfs finally broke away and we made for base.'

'I found the Mossie very good. With the introduction of VHF and then 'Gee', plus adequate pre-flight planning, it was a doddle. With two average-sized blokes the cockpit was comfortable and practically side-by-side seating ensured that the nav' could grab the control column if necessary. Maybe the difficulty of bailing-out in a rather confined space under any attitude would be a snag, but as I personally never had to, I can't comment. I'm obviously biased regarding the Mossie, but as a pilot I found her a wonderful aircraft which would take a severe hammering and still fly on one engine.'

On 30 October Sergeant Reginald Levy and Sergeant Les Hogan and Flying Officer William 'Bill' Blessing RAAF and Sergeant J. Lawson on 105 Squadron attacked the Luftwaffe night fighter aerodrome at Leeuwarden in Holland. They attacked successfully but Levy was hit by flak from the ground defences coming across the boundary of the airfield. The port engine was set on fire and the instrument panel and windscreen disappeared with the nose of the aircraft. Levy and his observer, Les Hogan, who was wounded in the arm, got back to Marham but the Mosquito was completely demolished on landing. After three weeks in Ely hospital both men were back at Marham and operating again.

In November 139 Squadron ceased all operational work while the squadron was being fully equipped with Mosquitoes and the whole month and the first few days of December was spent in bombing practice and formation flying. On 7 November an operation was mounted at short notice. Squadron Leader Roy Ralston DFM led six Mosquitoes at wave top height across the Bay of Biscay to the Gironde estuary on the French coast, which leads to the port of Bordeaux, to attack two large German blockade-running motor vessels loaded with rubber. The ships' crews were taken completely by surprise as the 500lb bombs fell full on them but Flight Lieutenant Alec Bristow and Pilot Officer Bernard Marshall were shot down by flak. They survived to be taken prisoner. Ralston was to become one of the most accomplished and skilful low-level bomber pilots of the war. A raid on 9 December demonstrates his quick thinking and rapid response to a given situation. He spotted a German troop train about to enter a tunnel on the Paris to Soissons railway line and immediately decided on a plan of action. Unlike the more conventional thinking of the 'average' pilot he did not attack the train itself but decided to create more havoc with an unconventional attack. He dropped down to tree top height behind the train and dropped a bomb into the mouth of the tunnel. He then quickly orbited the tunnel and bombed it at the other end before it emerged, thus effectively entombing the train, its crew and cargo in the tunnel.[38]

---

38 By the end of November 1942 105 Squadron had flown 282 operational sorties and lost 24 aircraft.

On Sunday 6 December ten B.IVs on 105 and 139 Squadrons were part of the force that took part in Operation 'Oyster', the 2 Group daylight raid on the Philips works at Eindhoven. The Mosquitoes carried out a shallow diving attack on the Strijp works and Douglas Bostons and Lockheed Venturas bombed from low level. The Mosquito flown by Pilot Officer John Earl O'Grady, who was on his first trip, was hit by flak and streamed smoke as they left the target area. O'Grady and his navigator Sergeant George Lewis died when their aircraft hit the sea. Nine Venturas and four Bostons also failed to return. The Philips works was devastated, essential supplies destroyed and the rail network disrupted.

After Eindhoven the Mosquitoes' targets were small in number raids on railway lines and yards in France, Belgium and Germany. On 20 December 11 Mosquitoes on 105 and 139 Squadrons led by Squadron Leader Reggie Reynolds with Ted Sismore attacked railway targets in the Oldenburg-Bremen area in northwest Germany. One Mosquito came down so low that the crew read the name *Fritz* on a river-tug. The bombers swept over men working on a new barracks and one pilot reported later that 'They were near the end of the work and we finished it off for them'. Near Delmenhorst Reynolds planed off to attack a gasholder and his four 500lb GP bombs set the gasometer on fire. The Mosquito took a 40mm cannon shell in the port engine, which made the aircraft lurch drunkenly but Reynolds managed to get the Mosquito on an even keel again. However, the anti-freeze mixture was pouring from the radiator and the cockpit filled with cordite fumes. His No.2, Warrant Officer Arthur Raymond Noesda, moved in closer to Reynolds. Together the pilot from Western Australia and his CO re-crossed the German coast over Wilhelmshaven Bay. Coastal batteries opened up on them and the guns of a warship joined in. fountains of water rose on each side of the aircraft which were down on the deck but Reynolds got his crippled Mosquito back to Marham where he landed wheels up. Squadron Leader Jack Houlston DFC AFC and his observer, Warrant Officer James Lloyd Armitage DFC failed to return. They were buried in the Reichswald Forest war cemetery. Luck finally ran out for Noesda, who had flown Blenheims on suicidal anti shipping strikes from Malta and his observer, Sergeant John Watson Urquhart, on 3 January when they were hit and killed by anti aircraft fire in the attack on engine sheds at Rouen.

In January 1943 attacks were maintained on rail targets on the continent. With no armament the Mosquitoes of course relied on speed and hedgehopping tactics. A fortnight's work went into low-level formation training for a raid on the Burmeister and Wain U-boat diesel engine works in Copenhagen in occupied Denmark. Wing Commander Hughie Edwards VC DSO DFC and Flying Officer 'Tubby' Cairns DFC led nine Mosquitoes on 105 and 139 Squadrons in a round trip of more than 1,200 miles to the target on the 27th. The Mosquitoes' war paint of dull silvery grey and green blended well with the cold, grey-green wave-tops and Danish countryside as they flew at low level in close formation to avoid attacks from enemy fighters. If it had been summer visibility would have been impaired by dust and squashed insects splattering their windscreens but Edwards' only concern was that they were too far south and fuel consumption was a vital consideration. When the coast was eventually sighted the lighthouse on Braavardo Point showed up clearly. Edwards said that 'this made it evident that we were 20 miles north of track. Then no sooner were we across the coast than we went straight over the top of Bröndurn aerodrome. This was a bad start, for we had hoped to get well across Denmark before the alarm went up. Near the coast light flak from ships opened up on the formation. Flight Lieutenant John 'Flash' Gordon and

Flying Officer Ralph Gamble Hayes thought their aircraft had been hit when the trailing edge of the starboard wing became enveloped in puffs of blue smoke. Thinking he had been hit by flak Gordon carried out evasive action but he had caught the port wing in telegraph wires and damaged the aileron. This together with the fact that the rest of the formation had gained a considerable lead caused Gordon to decide to abandon and he jettisoned his bombs at 16.09 hours and headed home.

Edwards continues. 'Cairns did a fine piece of work by steering a little north of east until we were across the neck of Denmark. This must have led the Germans to suppose that we were going for a target in the Baltic coast of Germany. We passed just south of the great bridge over Star Strom, then turned slowly north and ran up past Cliff Lighthouse. It was rather a thrill to look away to starboard and see Sweden. By the time we were halfway across Köge Bay we could see the outline of Copenhagen on the horizon. We flew up the east coast of Amagen and could clearly see ships in the canal separating it from the mainland. Then the Wing Commander opened his bomb doors and we packed in tight for the bombing run. The buildings of Burmeister & Wain came up just as we had seen them in the photographs and as we swept low over the roofs the bombs could be seen showering down - skidding, bouncing and crashing into the factory. Then, as we turned away across the spires of the city, the flak came streaming up from the ships in the harbour to the north. Only one aircraft was slightly damaged [Edwards' Mosquito received two holes in the starboard nacelle] but five minutes later a Mosquito went smack into a set of high-tension cables and blew up. [Sergeant James G. Dawson and Sergeant Ronald H. Cox were killed]. This was the worst of misfortune but the rest of us got safely away without further incident.'

The next raid by Mosquitoes produced large headlines in the Britain, as Hereward de Havilland in his report on Mosquito aircraft recalled: 'On January 30th, the tenth anniversary of Hitler's regime, Mosquitoes bombed Berlin twice in daylight. The time of arrival of the first raid was arranged to coincide with the opening of Goering's speech at 11.00 am. Three Mosquitoes on 105 Squadron took part - DZ413, DZ372 and DZ408 - and all arrived on time. They flew low as far as the enemy coast, to fox the RDF [radar], then climbed to 25,000 feet, bombed from 20,000 and came home in a steady power descent from that height. There was very little opposition of any sort at Berlin, but Reynolds got very intense and accurate flak over Bremen on the way back at 20,000 feet. Times (not including warming up and taxiing) and consumptions were as follows: DZ413 - 412 gallons in 4 hours 36 minutes; DZ372 - 450 gallons in 4 hours 42 minutes, DZ408 - 450 gallons in 5 hours 03 minutes. The total track mileage was 1,145.

'The afternoon raid consisted of two aircraft on 105 Squadron and one on 139 (Squadron Leader Darling). They were due to arrive for the opening of Goebbels' speech at 4 pm and much to their surprise, met little opposition. Darling, who was last man to arrive at Berlin, was seen to be getting rather more flak and was shot down over or near the city.[39] One pilot, already in a homeward power descent, saw a fighter a long way behind which eventually disappeared without attacking.'[40]

On the afternoon of 14 February, in what became known as the 'Great Tours Derby'

39 Squadron Leader Donald F. W. Darling DFC and his navigator, Flying Officer William Wright were shot down and killed by flak.

40 Squadron Leader 'Reggie' W. Reynolds DFC was awarded the DSO while all the other officers received the DFC and the sergeants, DFMs.

six Mosquitoes on 139 Squadron and a subsidiary formation of four Mosquitoes led by Squadron Leader Robert Beck 'Bob' Bagguley DFC set out to attack the engine sheds in the French city. 'Unfortunately, the weather marred the complete success of the show,' reported Flying Officer William E. G. 'Bill' Humphrey. 'For though the leader and four aircraft of his formation succeeded in bombing their primary - the engine repair shops - from fifty feet, the rest of the formation was split up by cloud right down to the deck. Three of the remainder turned back but Flying Officer Vernon Pereira carried on by himself and carried out a Shallow Dive attack on the engine round house to the east of the town. He scored direct hits with at least two of his six bombs, one of which hit the turntable in the middle.[41] Flying Officer G. S. W. Rennie RCAF having lost the formation looked around for an alternative target and finally bombed a train with devastating results, hitting the engine with all four bombs in salvo. Everyone returned safely from this operation.'

The following evening, twelve Mosquitoes on 105 Squadron attacked the goods depot from low-level and on the 18th, twelve Mosquitoes made a shallow dive attack. Two aborted and one aircraft failed to return.[42]

On 14 February Hughie Edwards, who had been promoted Group Captain four days earlier, left 105 Squadron to take up a post at HQ Bomber Command prior to taking command of RAF Binbrook on the 18th. Edwards' successor was Wing Commander Geoffrey P. Longfield who on 26 February led an attack by twenty Mosquitoes on the Rennes Naval Arsenal. Longfield his navigator Flight Lieutenant Roderick Milne were killed when Canadian Flying Officers Spencer Kimmel and Harry Kirkland, who were formating on Longfield, sliced into their leader's tail and Longfield went up into a loop and dived straight into the ground west of Rennes St-Jacques. Kimmel lost height and disappeared below the trees at 300 mph.[43] On the way home the 139 Squadron Mosquito flown by Lieutenant Tycho D. C. Moe and his observer 2nd Lieutenant Ottar Smedsaas, both RNAF, crashed and the two Dutchmen were killed.

Pilot Officer G. W. 'Mac' McCormick, a young officer on only his fourth operation did not see the dive-bombers until it was too late and he went in at low level. (139 Squadron were dropping 500lb MC - medium capacity - bombs with instantaneous fuses). He came back with his radiators full of flock from bombed bedding stores. Next day 'Mac' McCormick and visiting Wing Commander John W. Deacon were killed on a training flight when the wing fairing broke up during a dive from 30,000 feet and they crashed a mile to the southeast of Marham.

On Sunday 28 February six on 105 Squadron's Mosquitoes led by Wing Commander Roy Ralston went to the John Cockerill steel and armament works in the centre of Liège. Four more led by Pilot Officer Onslow Thompson DFM RNZAF and Pilot Officer Wallace J. Horne DFC went to the Stork Diesel Engine Works at Hengelo, in what was the eighth raid on the Dutch town by Mosquitoes. At Liège the Mosquitoes bombed at about 200 feet and results were 'good' but at Hengelo very little damage was done to the factories. On 3 March Wing Commander Peter Shand DFC and Flight Sergeant Christopher D.

41 Flying Officer C. Vernon Pereira, a Trinidadian, flew 80 ops on Mosquitoes on 139 and 105 Squadrons and he was awarded the DFC and Bar.
42 Flight Sergeant Frederick Alfred Budden and Sergeant Frank Morris in DZ420/F, which crashed northwest of Tours at Vengeons.
43 On 17 March Acting Wing Commander John 'Jack' de Lacey Wooldridge DFC* DFM RAFVR took command of 105 Squadron. He had joined the RAF in 1938 and he flew two tours (73 operations) on heavy bombers.

Handley DFM led ten Mosquitoes on 139 Squadron to the molybdenum mines at Knaben in South Norway. Molybdenum is a metallic element used in the production of high-speed steels. At the target Shand would lead the six Mosquitoes of the Shallow Dive section while Squadron Leader Bob Bagguley led would lead the four 'Low Level' attack aircraft. The formation set course over Marham at 1210 hours in good formation for Flamborough Head. Shand wrote: 'We were ninety minutes over the sea at low level, during which time the 10/10 cloud gave way to a clear sky and brilliant sunshine. Track was maintained accurately by constant drift reading and a landfall was made within a mile of the appointed place. Visibility was exceptional and the snow capped mountains over which we had to climb presented a striking sight.' Flying Officer William S. D. 'Jock' Sutherland, a Scot from Dollar, whose navigator was Flying Officer George Dean, flew No.2 to Wing Commander Shand. They were very impressed by the scenery over Norway. Sutherland recalled: 'Visibility was about twenty miles and there was no cloud. The snow-covered mountains with lakes dotted about made a very pleasant change after the long sea trip. We reached the target after climbing up and started our attack straight away.'

The six 'Shallow Divers' led by Shand commenced their climb and the remaining four Mosquitoes kept as low as possible on Sirdale Lake and overtaking them. They were seen to pass underneath the 'Shallow Divers' just before reaching the northern end of the lake and then turn east, climbing steeply over the surrounding hills in line astern and stepped down. The Shallow Dive formation then turned east on to course. Bagguley's formation climbed up the rather steep crevice and the much studied pin-point of Risones was picked up. 'From then onwards' said Bagguley, 'it was a piece of cake. The target appeared just as per illustrations and was cleanly silhouetted against the snow of the surrounding mountains. We made a perfect run on and dropped our bobs from roof-top height.' Flight Sergeant Peter McGeehan DFM and Flying Officer Reginald Morris DFC flying at the rear of the 'Low Level' formation were not in a suitable position for an attack so they peeled off and took another run at it. McGeehan remarked. 'During this time we saw the 'Low Level' bombs going off, the 'Shallow Divers' making their attack and Massey attacking the gun positions. It looked good and the stuff was still going off as we ran over, successfully this time.'

As the 'Shallow Divers' approached the target they saw brown and white smoke rising from the 'Low Level' formation's bombs and only the roof of the target building was still visible. They commenced their attack immediately. Sutherland continues. 'I followed the Winco in rather low and the debris from his bombs flew up at least 300 feet above us. After bombing we headed straight for home and could see smoke from the target rising to a very considerable height. Crossing the Norwegian coast going out we saw a Mossie being attacked by two 190s. We didn't wait to see the result. We made a landfall at Hunstanton and landed at base at 1630. Altogether a very enjoyable and satisfactory trip.' Bomb bursts accompanied by orange flashes and a red glow were seen on and around the target, which resulted in the plant being enveloped in clouds of white and brown smoke and debris being blown to a height of 1,000 feet. Air Officer Commanding Air Vice Marshal J. H. d'Albiac sent his congratulations for a 'well planned and splendidly executed attack... Mosquito stings judiciously placed are very painful.'

On 4 March Squadron Leader Reggie Reynolds DSO DFC led a successful attack by six Mosquitoes at low level from 50-200 feet on engine sheds and repair workshops at Le Mans. On 4 and 8 March 139 Squadron made two extremely successful attacks on

Aulnoye. The first of these directed against the railway engine sheds and a bomb manufacturing factory was led by Squadron Leader Bob Bagguley DFC. Three Mosquitoes were employed on the 'Low Level' attack on the railway target and three on the Shallow Dive. Bagguley's navigator, Flight Lieutenant Charles Hayden DFC recalled: 'A most pleasant trip. We made good landfall thanks to J. C. and my pilot and met no opposition the whole way to the target. The bombs made a wizard sight as they went up, making a sheer column of flame about 200 feet high. No opposition was encountered on the way out except some machine-gun tracer, which was seen going up at another Mossie. We landed in semi-daylight.' Sergeant Robert Pace and Pilot Officer George Cook, who were part of the Shallow Dive formation on the bomb factory, were flying their first raid. Cook recalled. 'A most enjoyable first op. good to see bombs from two aircraft in front hitting the roof of the target and 300 foot columns of smoke after leaving target. Our photographs show direct hits from our own bombs.'

On the second raid on Aulnoye on 8 March against the railway repair shops the six Mosquitoes of the 'Shallow Dive' attack was led by Wing Commander Shand and the four in the 'Low Level' section by Squadron Leader Bob Bagguley. One of the 'Shallow Divers' was the Mosquito flown by Flying Officer Jock Sutherland and Flying Officer George Dean. Sutherland recalled. 'We took off in good order, setting course for the enemy coast from North Foreland. Crossing the French coast slight A/A fire came up at the rear part of the formation. At le Cateau we turned on to a northeast heading for the target climbing up to 4,000 feet. The 'Low Level' formation continued at 50 feet. As we were about to attack our target we saw a huge sheet of flame and black smoke where the 'Low Level' boys' bombs were going off. Our target was bombed at 1855. There was no flak from the target area, which was covered with a slight industrial haze. We did not see our own bombs burst for once but got good photographs and saw a very thick cloud of smoke as we left the target. We came out at Termonds. Coming out of the coast there was a great deal of flak aimed in our direction from the shore on one side and ships on the other. I think we caught them with their trousers down, for they were too late. We landed away from base owing to bad weather and returned the following morning.'

Another of the 'Shallow Divers' was the Mosquito flown by Flight Sergeant Peter McGeehan DFM and Flying Officer Reginald Morris DFC. They were so engrossed in looking at the large sheet of flame and quantities of black and brown smoke coming from the engine sheds, which had been bombed with excellent results by the 'Low Level' formation that they overshot. They had to peel off to starboard and come in last before dropping their bombs on the target. Looking back after they had reached ground level again they could see a column of smoke 1,000 feet high. That same day three Mosquitoes on 105 Squadron bombed rail targets at Tergnier, 12 miles south of St-Quentin in France from low-level and Flight Lieutenant 'Flash' Gordon led another pair of Mosquitoes in an attack on the railway shops at Lingen in Germany. The Mosquito flown by Sergeant W. W. Austin and Pilot Officer P. E. Thomas was hit by flak and crashed on the return trip at Den Ham in Holland. Both men survived and they were taken prisoner.

On 9 March the Renault Aero Engine Works at Le Mans was the target for fifteen of Marham's Mosquitoes. The whole formation was led by Squadron Leader Roy Ralston DSO DFM and his navigator, Flight Lieutenant Syd Clayton, DFC DFM at the head of five Mosquitoes on 105 Squadron, who carried out the 'Low Level' attack. A Shallow Dive section was led by Squadron Leader Bob Bagguley DFC at the head of ten aircraft on 139

Squadron. One of the 'Shallow Diver' teams was Flying Officer Sutherland and Flying Officer Dean. Sutherland wrote: 'Rather a ropey take-off. Squadron Leader Bagguley had trouble with his port engine and turned back. I took over the lead but Bob caught us up on the circuit and regained the lead. From then on it was a normal trip. Visibility was bad, but we spotted the target wreathed in smoke from 105's 'Low Level' attack. We were greeted by plenty of accurate flak over the target, but managed to avoid same as we were diving fast. Coming out over the coast, we found an enemy convoy of twenty ships dead ahead. Big moment. We altered course to port and the escort ship challenged us by lamp. We gave her a long series of garbled 'dits' and 'dahs' on our recognition lights and nipped smartly off. 'Base was reached without further incident.' 'Bob' Bagguley and Flight Lieutenant Charles Hayden DFC were seen to bomb the target and when last observed, 'appeared to be sailing home in fine style' but they failed to return. No trace of the crew was ever found.

On 12 March twelve Mosquitoes on 105 and 139 Squadrons led by Squadron Leader Reggie Reynolds and Pilot Officer Ted Sismore were briefed to attack the John Cockerill works at Liège again. The briefing officer stated that two crack fighter units had recently been moved to Woensdrecht, south of Rotterdam and that they had recently been re-equipped with FW 190s. Allowing for several doglegs flight time to target was between 2 and 2½ hours. Attacks of this nature were normally planned for dusk or just before dark so that the Mosquitoes could return to England individually under the cover of half-light or darkness. Bombing had to be carried out very accurately indeed to keep losses to a minimum and this task was given to the shallow dive section led by Squadron Leader John V. Berggren on 139 Squadron with his observer Flying Officer Peter Wright DFC. At 15.40 hours all twelve Mosquitoes took off. They headed south before flying across the Channel to France and up and over the cliffs to the west of Cap Gris Nez then on across the heavily defended Pas de Calais at naught feet. Finally, the Mosquitoes, seldom flying at more than 100 feet and keeping echelon formation on the leader, picked up the River Meuse which led straight in to the target. At around five miles from the target 105 Squadron split from the rest of the formation and went straight in at low level to each drop their four 500lb 11-second delayed action bombs. These burst in the target area as Berggren and his six Mosquitoes hurriedly climbed to 3,000 feet and then dived onto the target to release their four 500lb bombs with instantaneous fuses. Turning away to the north the crews could see a huge mushroom of smoke building up over the main target area. Leaving the target the formation broke into individual aircraft and raced for the Scheldt Estuary at 280 mph in gathering dusk. The Mosquitoes had to climb to 200 feet to avoid HT cables, which criss-crossed Belgium and France. The Mosquito flown by Sergeant Robert Pace and Pilot Officer George Cook was hit by flak and caught fire before it crashed on the runway of Woensdrecht airfield and was smashed to smithereens on impact leaving a stream of burning debris in its wake.[44]

On 16 March sixteen Mosquitoes on 105 and 139 Squadrons led by Squadron Leader John Berggren DFC made low level and shallow dive attacks on roundhouses and engine sheds at Paderborn. Flight Lieutenant Bill Blessing DFC on 105 Squadron led the 'Low Level' section. Berggren's navigator, Flying Officer Peter Wright DFC, recalled:

44 9.8 tons of bombs were dropped on the John Cockerill works. Pace and Cook crashed into the Ooster Schelde off Woensdrecht.

'Paderborn is quite a few miles east of the Ruhr and it looked an alarmingly long way into Germany when we studied the route on the large-scale map in the briefing room. There were to be sixteen aircraft, which by our standards is a big formation. The target consisted of engine sheds and they were to be attacked in two waves, first by six aircraft at low level and then by ten from about 1,300 feet in a Shallow Dive. Apart from the bombing run, we were to fly at low level all the way. We, in our aircraft, were to lead the formation to a point about twenty-five miles short of the target and then to climb to 3,000 feet with nine others behind us, while the last six raced in ahead to bomb first from low level. The rest of us were to dive down to thirteen hundred feet before bombing. It was hoped that our bombs would begin falling just as the last of the low-level aircraft had got clear of the target. It would be too bad for him if we bombed a bit early. You can't see Mosquitoes when you are directly above them; their camouflage is too good. So, good timing would be needed if we were going to make a concentrated attack and yet give that last man a chance.

'All went well till we were over the Zuider Zee, when we were intercepted by a formation of low-flying ducks. They attacked strongly, but inflicted only one casualty. Their leader crashed through the Perspex of Sergeant Cummings' aircraft and landed as a heap of blood and feathers on his observer's stomach. Two others hit his starboard engine nacelle. It was very draughty in that aeroplane (and messy, too), so it turned back for home. The rest of us managed to take the effective evasive action. We are better at avoiding birds than we used to be. We carried on very smoothly over the flat lands of Holland and North-West Germany. Occasionally we would lift a wing to avoid a church steeple. Visibility was just right - enough to map read by and no more. Between Minster and Osnabrück the country became hilly and the formation inevitably got more ragged. But everything was still very quiet. We crossed a big autobahn and began to climb, while the last six Mosquitoes stayed down. It's an uncomfortable feeling to be up at 3,000 feet after a spell of low flying. You feel naked and motionless and a sitting target for the gunners. But it gets better when you dive on to the target and the earth comes close again and you recapture the feeling of speed.

'There was a lot of industrial haze drifting over from the Ruhr and the target was difficult to see. Perhaps it was the haze that made the flak gunners so slow off the mark. They allowed half of us to bomb before they opened up. When they did open up, they were pretty good and the boys at the back had a nasty few minutes. Flight Sergeant McGeehan was hit and did not return. Sergeant Massey came back on one engine and did very well to make a crash landing at an aerodrome close to base. We, personally, were lucky and were out of the target area in time. When we looked back the target was going up into the air and above it the Mosquitoes were bucking like broncos to avoid the streams of orange balls thrown up at them from all angles by the Bofors guns.

'On the way home over Germany the mist got thicker and thicker and we all felt safer and safer. We saw two Junkers 52s and wished we had some guns. Nothing else happened and we sneaked quietly out over the Dutch island, which we thought would give us the least trouble. I doubt if they could have seen us, anyway.'

On 18 March at one of Generalfeldmarschall Milch's fortnightly conferences that he attended personally, Hermann Goering raised the subject of the Mosquito and referred to the raid on Paderborn. '...I could go mad when I think of the Mosquito. I go green and yellow with envy. The British, who can afford more aluminium than we can, build themselves a wooden aeroplane without any trouble, one with a speed that has even just been increased again. The Mosquito that photographed Linz was flying, according to our precise calculation - not that of the British at a speed of 530 kph - and that was a bomber, would you believe it? And that is a machine that any piano factory over there can make! Unfortunately - I could kill myself! - I didn't insist with the Generaloberst, because at that time I gave him the benefit of the doubt when it came to making decisions. When war broke out, I demanded this wooden aeroplane time and time again, because there was no harm in building wooden fighters and bombers as well. But they said that that was impossible; no pilot could imagine such a thing; the whole world would laugh at us - now the whole world can laugh at us because we haven't got it. The day before yesterday Mosquitoes made another low-level attack on Paderborn. They didn't lose any, or perhaps only one. Our fighters didn't see them. The Mosquitoes flew around like mad things and they relied on their speed alone and they were incredibly fast. Even though they were only flying at fifty metres they didn't have any guns, they relied on their speed and they got away with it. Gentlemen, you should have a good look at this aeroplane - perhaps you might learn something. The primitiveness of this aircraft is astounding. And here too I say, 'Why waste time looking?' We should be copying the Mosquito. That's the easiest thing for us to do!'

On the 20th six Mosquitoes on 105 Squadron carried out low-level attacks on the engine sheds and repair shops at Louvain in Belgium. Six Mosquitoes on 139 Squadron led by Flight Lieutenant Mike Wayman DFC and Flying Officer G. S. 'Pops' Clear carried out a 'Low Level' dusk attack on the railway workshops at Malines. This raid was unsuccessful as Flying Officer Jock Sutherland recalled: 'Everything was OK until we reached the enemy coast. [Over Blankenburg] Mike Wayman was hit in the starboard engine. He tried to carry on, but after a couple of miles he peeled off and feathered his airscrew. We took over the lead. Near the target, the visibility closed in to 500 yards and we were unable to locate our exact position in the industrial haze and general filth. We eventually bombed a goods train. We boobed coming out and went slap across Antwerp aerodrome, where we got plenty of accurate flak. There we ran into trouble good and proper in the Flushing estuary, where everything opened up, including a convoy and escort. Fortunately we were not hit and landed OK at base at 20.30 hours.' Wayman made it back to England and he crashed at Martlesham Heath on overshoot, Wayman and 'Pops' Clear were killed. Flying Officer Cussens and Sergeant Munro had also experienced 'intense' flak crossing the coast at Blankenburg, which knocked out their hydraulics. They saw the target momentarily but were unable to open the bomb doors. Coming out they had more flak at Antwerp and an 'incredible amount' at Beveland Island, which shot away their rudder controls and port landing edge, causing the aircraft to stall at 180 mph when eventually landed at Marham. Flying Officer J. H. Brown summed up the operation thus: 'Never has the carefree attitude of some aircrews toward operating been more apparent! We stooged almost over Ostend to make a good landfall, pouncing on the target at thirty seconds' notice. A false alarm of 'snappers' after the target - which we missed - resulted in Mosquitoes pulling the plug in every direction and screaming about like a gaggle of alarmed hens; not to mention some cheery optimist who flew for fifty miles or so over enemy territory with his navigation lights on. The visibility was wicked; we went over Antwerp; we went over the mouth of the Scheldt; and back over this country, we went round from aerodrome to aerodrome with our wireless u/s, before base, which had spent a busy evening changing the flare path about, condescended to receive us. What a life!'

On 23 March ten Mosquitoes on 139 Squadron led by Wing Commander Peter Shand DFC and five on 139 Squadron led by Flight Lieutenant Bill Blessing DFC attacked the Compagnie Gènèrale de Construction des Locomotives Batigniolles-Chatillon at St-Joseph two miles northeast of Nantes at low level. The raid had to be timed to perfection as the French factory workers finished work. Flying Officer J. E. Hay, a South African from Pretoria, who was navigator to Pilot Officer T. M. Mitchell in the 'Shallow Dive' section led by Wing Commander Shand, recalls.

'The Battle Order was issued early on the morning of the 23rd March and my pilot and I were on the list, which was a long one. All this and the very long trainload of bombs being pulled along the tarmac seemed to indicate a big 'do'. We entered the briefing room with more than the usual feeling of excitement that a formation made up of both Squadrons was to attack the St-Joseph Locomotive Works at Nantes - quite a deep penetration into enemy-occupied territory. We were airborne at 1350 and set course across the aerodrome about ten minutes later. The weather was good over base, but it had started to deteriorate before we reached the south coast. People at the seaside that afternoon must have been startled as the large formation went out over the Channel at nought feet. The weather improved for us over the Channel and on schedule the French coast was sighted - a low belt of sand dunes followed by wooded downs. We shot over these in tight formation and for once experienced no flak - we were over the first hurdle. From this point onwards the weather was perfect with excellent visibility and some cloud about 2,000 feet above us.

'Our route across France lay over a series of hills and valleys. We skimmed over the hilltops and flew down through the valleys and across the small towns. On one hilltop we saw three Huns make a dash for their machine-gun; we dived straight at them and they threw themselves flat as we roared over the gun pit. There was nothing very dangerous in this, for we could see the tarpaulin cover still on the gun! Then, after almost thirty minutes of breathless chase across France, we swept into the broad plains of the River Loire to find the sun breaking fitfully through the clouds. At about a quarter to four the town of Nantes appeared ahead and we began to climb up to our bombing height, while Squadron Leader Blessing led 105 Squadron on ahead at low level. As we climbed away from the earth, we seemed at first to hover stationary in mid-air. Then we saw the first black puffs of anti-aircraft fire. As we peeled off for our dive, I saw 105 streaking across the target below us and then the vivid flashes of their bombs exploding. Within a few seconds we were diving fast after them and our bombs were following theirs. Then we went across the town and away to the south. Looking back, I could see the old works covered by an immense pall of smoke and I also caught a glimpse of six enemy fighters circling about twenty miles away to the west in the direction of St-Nazaire. They suddenly formed up and flew off north, apparently not having seen us. As we were racing south with a very pretty turn of speed, they were soon lost to sight. 'The job completed, we flew out over the Bay of Biscay in brilliant sunshine, heading for home. In every direction there seemed to be Mosquitoes just skimming the wave-tops. It was a grand sight! Shortly afterwards we all lost touch in a heavy bank of fog and when we at last emerged from this the Cornish coast lay below us.' This raid was an outstanding success, not one bomb missing the target and no building in the target area failing to be hit. Squadron Leader Berggren added, 'the target…looked a good enough mess even before the second formation dropped their bombs.'

Next day, 24th March, three Mosquitoes on 105 Squadron were sent on a Rover operation to shallow dive-bomb trains and railway lines within specified areas in Germany. On 27 March 139 Squadron dispatched six aircraft on another low level raid on the Stork Diesel Works at Hengelo. The bombing results at de-briefing were described as being uncertain; though photographs showed many near misses. On this occasion serious damage was done to the primary target although nearby houses were hit once again. Henk F. van Baaren attended a funeral for the first time in his young life when a 17-year-old boy from his school and a member of the same gymnastic club that he attended, was killed.[45]

On 28 March seven Mosquitoes led by Flight Lieutenant 'Flash' Gordon were dispatched to attack the railway marshalling yards at Liège but rainstorms reduced the evening visibility to half a mile and instead he led the aircraft in an attack on a factory north of Valbengit Bridge at Liège. They were spotted by Unteroffizier Wilhelm Mayer of *6th Staffel JG26* heading towards Dunkirk at low level and Oberfeldwebel Adolf 'Addi' Glunz and three other FW 190s of *4./JG26* were sent off from Vitry immediately. They intercepted the Mosquitoes after they had bombed. Glunz was credited with shooting down in the space of a minute the Mosquito flown by Flying Officer George Bruce DFM and Flying Officer Dick Reilly about 18 miles east of Etaples and Sergeant George Leighton and Sergeant Thomas Chadwick south of Lille. All four airmen were later buried in Lille Southern Cemetery. (Glunz finished the war with 71 confirmed victories).

On 30 March ten Mosquitoes on 139 Squadron led by Wing Commander Peter Shand DFC set off to bomb the Philips Works at Eindhoven which was about ready to begin full production again. One 139 Squadron Mosquito, which was hit by flak on crossing the enemy coast lost its hydraulics and was unable to open its bomb bay doors to bomb and abandoned the strike, leaving four aircraft to attack from low level and five in a shallow dive. The attackers switched back over Holland, dodging flocks of seagulls over the Zuider Zee and tearing over Eindhoven once more at zero feet. Pilot Officer T. M. Mitchell, who brought up the rear of the formation with his navigator Flying Officer J. E. Hay, recalls.

'We encountered very intense light flak at the coast. This was accurate and followed all the aircraft for about eight miles inland. We saw no further flak until the target was reached. The run-up was beautiful, the building being silhouetted against the sky. On reaching it we found it necessary to climb 50 feet in order to get over that blasted chimney, about which we had been warned. I saw the Wing Commander's bombs, which were timed to go off a short time after impact, fall into the buildings as we skimmed over the rooftops. Then I let our own bombs go right into the middle of the factory. As I circled after the attack I saw the whole building become enveloped in smoke with huge red flashes as the bombs exploded. On the way out the weather was very bumpy but we reached base without further incident. My navigator saw V-signs flashing from Dutch homes in the falling light.' Flying Officer Paney and Sergeant Stimson noticed a Dutchman hoeing in a garden. He glanced up once and then went on hoeing!

Two days later six crews on 105 Squadron and four on 139 Squadron went down to the ops room as usual that morning. Syd Clayton recalled: 'It was 1 April and the RAF had a birthday. 'We didn't know yet where or how we were going to celebrate'. Noisily, most probably. Over Germany for preference. To me it was more than a birthday celebration. My eagerness was personal, for I had done 99 trips. [46] For three weeks now I had waited

---

45 *Bommen Vielen op Hengelo* by Henk F. Van Baaren, translated in *The Mossie* - MAA, Vol. 16, April 1997.
46 His 99th operation was against the Renault Aero works at Le Mans on 9 March.

for the century. I wanted it to be something to remember. It was that, all right.

'It was 09.30 hours and our Group Captain was in deep consultation with Group Met. It all depended on the weather, as it always did. And the weather was going to be just right. The Group Captain laid on a trip to a power station and railway yards at Trier. [The four Mosquitoes on 139 Squadron led by Squadron Leader John Berggren were to hit the engine sheds at Ehrang]. The weather experts forecast low cloud and rain extending right across our target area between 1500 hours and 1700 hours. So we would drop in at 1600 hours. We were to cross the French coast south of Boulogne and after that fly practically due east. The front of bad weather would give us cover all the way to our target; some engine repair sheds on the west side of Trier. When all the intricacies of the operation-which included met, routing, intelligence, bomb load and type, cameras and number of aircraft and crews available-had been dealt with, the crews who were to go on the show were called down for briefing. I was getting my hundredth trip! As navigator in DZ462 to the leading pilot, Roy Ralston. Take-off was to be at 1400 hours, so we lunched in the briefing room. Then, after emptying our pockets, we collected our flying kit, parachutes, Mae Wests, dinghies and emergency rations. The first part of our journey to Trier began-out to the dispersed Mosquitoes.

'At 1410 hours we were airborne, circling the airfield, waiting for the formations to take position behind us. At 1430 hours we set course and flew down to Beachy Head at between 50 and 100 feet. Down there close to the deck, the sensation of speed was exhilarating. Occasionally a flock of white birds would come hurtling towards us and at the last moment, flash away to one side or above us. The weather was good. Too good. Cloud base was about 3,000 feet and visibility was good too. We changed course at Beachy Head. The cloud was still high above us and visibility stayed the way it was. We'd had our orders to turn back if we didn't meet with the right kind of cloud cover and it began to look as if this birthday party was off. Roy decided to carry on a little longer - to within 10 miles of France, anyway. Then, just as I was getting ready to be disappointed, the bad weather the Met men had promised came on to the horizon. Cloud lowered and visibility decreased. We crossed the enemy coast in pouring rain with high spirits and visibility clamped down to 400 yards. It was like this for 230 miles, with cloud covering hills and visibility down to 200 yards or less in places. Nevertheless, the pilots kept good formation.

'All this time my job was with my maps and maybe I was a bit more tense than usual. Not only was this my 100th trip, but it was the last operation for Roy and I as a crew. I kept praying I wouldn't get off course or endanger the success of the trip. We skimmed over several aerodromes on the way - just a fleeting glimpse of them and they were gone. Little French villages deserted and fields empty of peasants. The rain, our ally, had driven them all indoors.

'France slid swiftly beneath our wings; railways, roads, rivers-all pinpoints on which we had to depend to read our way to Trier. The idea of fighter opposition wasn't bothering me for we had the weather on our side, but the clouds giving us protection might also be down on the hills around Trier and might prevent us locating and attacking the target. Ten miles west of Luxembourg, however, the weather cleared. Cloud rose to 2,500 to 3,000 feet and visibility lengthened to about ten miles. For a few moments I had a spot of 'finger' trouble. Looking for parallel railway lines, I could only see one line and it wasn't until I looked at my map for a second time that I realised this 'line' was the Luxembourg border

! South of Luxembourg, over the German frontier and then on to final course for the target - with an inevitable feeling of excitement beginning to possess me. Then I saw the smoke from Trier rising above the hills and I suddenly realised that everything was going to be all right. We opened the bomb doors. In a matter of seconds we had nipped over the hills and were roaring down the valley, heading for the target. The photographs we had studied made target location easy enough. Nearer and nearer, expecting a hail of flak at any moment, we raced on. There was the target, dead ahead. I watched Roy's thumb on the bomb button as the sheds came steadily towards us. He sat dead still-and then suddenly his thumb jerked just once and he laughed.

'Then we were away, up the hillside north-east of the town. Looking back, I could see tall columns of black and white smoke rising from the centre of the target. It had been decided that we should follow the bad weather front out over enemy territory and this sheltered us to within 50 miles of the enemy coastline. There the low cloud broke up and we found ourselves with a canopy of cloud about 4,000 feet above us and good visibility. We decided to go up and as we climbed, I looked back and saw the other Mossies coming up with us, still in perfect formation. This was where we expected trouble and some flak did come up from Merville aerodrome, but it did no damage and we were soon comfortably in cloud.

'When we came down through it and set final course for home, the enemy coast was far behind us and I looked down and out to the quilt of English fields ahead of us. It was over. I'd done my 100th operational sortie, but I'd also done my last trip with my pilot, Roy Ralston. In a few weeks I'd be flying again, but in a Tiger Moth for I should be beginning my training as a pilot.[47]

On 3 April Wing Commander Wooldridge led his first 105 Squadron operation and eight Mosquitoes carried out Rover attacks on railway targets in Belgium and France. All three of 105 Squadron's Mosquitoes returned safely from attacks on locomotive repair sheds shops at Malines and engine sheds at Namur but a Mosquito on 139 Squadron was lost. Flying Officer W. O. Peacock and his observer, Sergeant R. C. Saunders, were shot down by Oberfeldwebel Wilhelm Mackenstedt of 6./JG26 three kilometres south of Beauvais for the German pilot's sixth and final victory.

On 11 April four Mosquitoes on 105 Squadron led by Squadron Leader Bill Blessing DFC and his navigator Flight Sergeant A. J. W. 'Jock' Heggie ventured to Hengelo to bomb the Stork Works. This was the tenth and final low level attack by 2 Group Mosquito IVs on the long-suffering town. Light was failing and visibility about three miles with 10/10ths cloud at 3,000 feet when the formation was intercepted at 50 feet by two formations of three FW 190s before reaching the target. One section of FW 190s fired a burst of two seconds and then they broke off to starboard to attack two of the Mosquitoes. Flying Officer Norman Hull RCAF and

---

47 The attack on Ehrang resulted in a huge explosion and a red flash from a coal container. One bomb was seen to bounce off railway tracks into a house, which was blown to pieces. On leaving the target area smoke was seen rising to about 1,500 feet. No aircraft were lost although Flying Officer Talbot's and Sergeant Sleeman's Mosquito, which was hit by blast from bomb bursts and also by flak, returned on one engine with gyro artificial horizon and turn-and-bank indicator out of action. They crossed the enemy coast one mile south of Boulogne harbour and flak 'of various assortments' followed them up to five miles out. Talbot, who landed safely at Manston concluded, 'Ain't life grand!' In the messes that night crews celebrated Syd Clayton's award of an immediate DSO. After training, Syd Clayton joined 464 Squadron RAAF, a Mosquito unit of 140 Wing, 2nd TAF at Thorney Island and flew the first of 45 more operations on Mosquitoes on 26 August 1944 - a night sortie against rail and road transport.

Sergeant Philip Brown, No.3 in the formation, were intercepted by four FW 190s who came in from starboard and opened fire for about fifteen seconds at a range of 350 yards. The Mosquitoes carried out evasive action by turning into the attack, weaving and gaining and losing height between 150-200 feet and increasing speed. After making one attack, the enemy aircraft broke off and wheeled round to attack Z-Zebra flown by Flying Officer David Polgase RNZAF and his observer Flight Sergeant Leslie Lampen that had been hit by flak at the coast. Z-Zebra had one airscrew feathered and with his speed greatly reduced Polgase and Lampen fell behind the rest the formation. Unteroffizier Gerhard Wiegand of 2./JG1 shot them down. The Mosquito crashed in a wood near Bentheim, Germany and both crew were killed. Flying Officer F. M. 'Bud' Fisher, an American pilot from Pennsylvania and Flight Sergeant Les Hogan were unable to bomb the primary target and attacked a train in the area instead. Blessing pressed home his attack from 50 feet and he dropped his bomb load directly onto the Stork Works causing severe damage to the plant. The Resistance seems to have signalled London that the Stork and Dikkers factories should no longer be considered targets, as production of war machinery had stopped.

On 19/20 April there were no Main Force operations and six Mosquitoes of 2 Group failed to locate rail workshops at Namur in bad visibility returned without loss. On the night of 20/21 April nine Mosquitoes on 105 Squadron and two from 139 Squadron led by Wing Commander Peter Shand DSO DFC carried out a bombing attack on Berlin. This was a diversion for 339 heavy bombers attacking Stettin and 86 Stirlings bombing the Heinkel factory near Rostock. The Mosquito 'night nuisance' operations were also designed to 'celebrate' Hitler's birthday. Over Berlin it was cloudless with bright moonlight and the Mosquitoes dropped their bombs from 15,000-23,000 feet. Flak was moderate and quite accurate but the biggest danger proved to be night-fighters. One of these was Oberleutnant Lothar Linke, Staffelkapitän 12./NJG1 who the night before had claimed to be the second Nachtjagd pilot to destroy a Mosquito whilst flying a standard Bf 110G.[48] Linke, again led by his night fighter controller Eisbär ('Polar Bear'), overtook Shand's Mosquito at high altitude and at high speed in a power dive, shot the Mosquito down over the northern part of the Ijsselmeer at 0210 hours. Shand and his navigator Pilot Officer Christopher Handley DFM were killed.[49]

On 26 April two Mosquitoes on 105 Squadron led by Flight Lieutenant John 'Flash' Gordon DFC and his navigator, Flying Officer R. Hayes DFC were ordered to bomb the railway workshops at Jülich, near Cologne. This had always been looked upon as a particularly difficult target to find, as it had no easily distinguishable landmarks near it to assist the observer. Any errors in navigation would bring the aircraft dangerously near to Cologne to the east or Aachen to the west. Gordon wrote: 'Very shortly after briefing we were airborne and after circling base a couple of times both aircraft set course for the Dutch coast. All the way over the North Sea I did nothing but sweat -' I hope we're not too high. Can any enemy ships see us? Down a bit. Altimeter reads just under nought feet. Hope to Heaven our landfall is OK. Worry! Worry! Worry!'

'At last the enemy coast loomed up, the spires of Gravenhage to the left, the Hook

48   On 28/29 June 1942 Oberleutnant Reinhold Knacke, Staffelkapitän, 1./NJG1 had been the first Nachtjagd pilot to claim a Mosquito kill, when he shot down DD677 of 23 Squadron at Haps, Southern Holland.
49   Shand remains missing while the body of his navigator was washed ashore at Makkum. Linke, with 24 night and 3 day victories was killed on the night of 13/14 May 1943.

of Holland to the right. We were very low. Closer now. A latticed naval beacon went past to the left; we turned four degrees to port and straightened up for our run in. I saw the hummocks on the beach; the white foam breaking on the sands; soldiers running like the Devil for their guns - 'Look out for flak - we're over!' Weaving madly, we shot over the sand-dunes and set a new course, flying as low as we dared over the glass roofs of the bulb nurseries and turning and twisting among the tall thin chimneys of the greenhouses. Soon we left the coastal towns behind us and altering course southwards, roared across the level plains around the River Maas and past the tall smoking chimney of Eindhoven. Soon we could see rich black fields of ploughed earth, teams of chestnut Belgian horses and sleepy red-roofed hamlets. A quick glance behind showed us that Coyle, our No. 2, was just behind our tail.

'Another alteration of twenty degrees to port and we crossed the frontier into Germany, with plenty of dark cloud ahead and green plantations of young Douglas firs below. Then, in the gloom ahead we picked up the gleam of the Roer River, pin-pointed ourselves quickly and made a slight alteration to bring us directly onto the target. A river and a railway crossing appeared immediately ahead - good show, we were dead on track. The little town of Jülich soon showed up and in climbing to clear the buildings we saw the big railway sheds lying in a valley running southwards from the town. As I opened the bomb doors we dived straight for the target and waited until the serrated roofs were just in front of the nose. I got a quick impression of tall chimneys on either side, a small engine snorting and grunting on the sidings, stacks of white wood laid on long wagons and a group of workmen scattering in every direction - 'Look out, you blasted Huns! Here they come! Bombs gone!' My navigator slewed round in his seat and looking back, shouted 'Yes! I can see where they've gone in. Up they go! Number 2's hit it as well!'

'No flak. I turned to starboard onto the next course and throttled back a little. Why all the hurry? Then we ran into a sharp rainstorm. I passed the target to starboard again, as I turned back and grey smoke was drifting slowly away. It began to get really dark on the way home, the dusk obscuring the power cables that raced underneath from time to time. A few lighted windows showed through the trees - it was too dark for a fighter interception now. I relaxed slightly. Everything seemed too easy and there was plenty of cover in this semi-darkness.

'Take care,' came a warning from Hayes. 'We're off track. Keep low - lower still.' Then, before we knew what had happened, we were over the middle of Eindhoven Aerodrome. Everywhere there seemed to be little spurts of fire from machine-guns and great gobs of flame from the Bofors. They all missed. As we sped on into the darkness the Huns lobbed a few long shots after us which fell around us and then suddenly - we were hit. From the port wing, outboard of the engine, a little trail of vapour streamed back and slowly grew less and less until it died away. I checked over the instruments but could find nothing wrong and carried on, going fast. 'Is that the coast? Open up and go like Hell – or is it the coast? No. Just a bank of mist. False alarm - but it can't be far away now!

'Then far in front we saw a flock of white seagulls and knew that the sea was ahead. As we weaved our way across the dunes a feeble spurt of tracer swung lazily up from the left and followed us until we were out of range. It was lighter out to sea. Very pleasant it was to see the sunset in front of us to the west. Throttling back a few miles outside the coast, I climbed a few hundred feet and took things easy. We passed over one of our convoys off Norfolk, were challenged by a destroyer and replied to everyone's satisfaction.

'Far ahead we saw our own coastline and before long our own beacon gave us a friendly wink and our flare path came into view.

'The Germans had dropped a shell into one of our petrol tanks, but by some stroke of luck it had not exploded.'

Late in the evening of 27 May the final large-scale daylight raid by the Mosquito IVs of 2 Group took place when fourteen Mosquitoes were given two targets deep in Southern Germany. The briefing was very long and complicated. It meant flying at low level for well over three hours over enemy territory, of which a good two and a quarter would be in broad daylight. Six aircraft on 139 Squadron led by Wing Commander 'Reggie' W. Reynolds DSO DFC and Flight Lieutenant Ted Sismore DFC set out to attack the Schott glassworks at Jena. A few miles further on eight Mosquitoes on 105 Squadron led by Squadron Leader Bill Blessing DFC and Flying Officer G. K. Muirhead were to bomb the Zeiss Optical factory, which at that time was almost entirely engaged on making periscopes for submarines. At briefing crews saw the red ribbon running right down into SE Germany near Leipzig and the target, the Zeiss optical lens works at Jena. Flight Lieutenant Charles Patterson, a pilot on 105 Squadron recalled: 'It gave a great sense of anticipation and excitement that such a tremendously long trip was going to be undertaken but not undue alarm because it was so deep into Germany, an area that had never seen daylight flying aircraft before. We rather assumed that by going deep down not only could we achieve a great deal of surprise but there might be much light AA fire round this factory and what there was the gunners would be inexperienced.'

Engines were started at 7 o'clock and the Mosquitoes taxied out, formed up and headed across the North Sea in two formations in clear daylight. The Dutch coast was crossed and the route continued on behind the Ruhr and down near Kassel and then on into the Thüringen Mountains. Then suddenly they came across all the floods of the Möhne dam raid which had taken place only ten days before. For twenty minutes there was nothing but floods. The Mosquitoes flew between the Möhne and Eder dams and suddenly came over a mountain ridge and there was the Helminghausen dam beneath them. Flak opened up and an enormous ball of flame rolled down the mountainside. Two Mosquitoes had collided.

Charles Patterson continues: 'The weather closed down about 50 miles short of the target. We had to fly over mountains and then come down into the valley below and fly straight towards the target. We ran into cloud over the mountains, having had glorious sunny weather all the way. I was at the back of the second formation and I, together with two others out of the 14, simply lost formation. We couldn't keep in touch with the aircraft next to us, but carried on, on dead reckoning. When I came down out of the cloud the visibility was still poor and I couldn't find the target at all. I set off to look for it and the cloud base lifted to 1,000 feet. There was a large city spread out to my port side. I thought I would fly round the edge and look for some factory that looked worth bombing. I flew right round the edge of the city at 800 feet but it was all residential, a lot of prosperous-looking houses in the outskirts up in the hills. It turned out that this was Weimar, a university city that does not have an industrial complex. But right in the middle was a big railway station with an enormous goods train stationary in it. I dived down into the centre of the city at 2133 hours and dropped my bombs from 200 feet straight into the railway station and then went down over the rooftops to fly away north-west of the city. Bombs which were dropped in a salvo on the second run over target fell between platforms near two goods trains with steam up. The explosions threw debris 150 feet into the air.

'I had no sooner dropped my bombs than the most horrendous light flak barrage I had ever known opened up. When I got clear of the city and went up the river valley the flak was coming down from both sides of the hills. I was twisting and turning. When you are under light flak you have to throw the aircraft around because they are firing over open sights and trying to aim at you. We did get clear and I set off for home, alone of course. Having come through that and then realising, having looked at the map properly, that we were right down in south-east Germany, all alone, at 50 feet, I did feel a bit daunted, a bit desperate. But there was no alternative but to keep going.

'We flew for a long time north, north-west until we were certain we were clear of Hannover; before turning to port and flying due west back to England. Once we started to fly across the open German plain I knew we'd got away with it. Once we got over the Dutch frontier it was getting dark and the Dutch farmers were amazing. When they heard low-level aircraft around - we would come up from 50 feet to about 300 feet - they would rush to the doors of their cottage or farmhouse and open and shut the door, flashing their lights inside to us as a sign. They risked death by doing that just to give us encouragement. I never forgot it.'

The weather over the target was covered with 10/10 cloud at 1,000 feet and bad light cut visibility to 500-800 yards. Squadron Leader Bill Blessing and Flying Officer G. K. Muirhead in O-Orange and Pilot Officer H. C. 'Gary' Herbert RAAF and Sergeant Jacques in C-Charlie attacked the Zeiss works at just after 2131 hours from 200-300 feet. Bombs were seen to fall in the glass grinding and polishing shops - a sixteen storey building - and a cloud of grey smoke was seen after bombing. C-Charlie was hit in several places on the way out. Flying Officer 'Bud' Fisher and Flight Sergeant Les Hogan in N-Nuts were prevented from attacking the primary by the balloon barrage and bombed the town at 2130 hours from 200 feet and as long delay bombs were used, no results were seen. Flying Officer Don C. Dixon, an Australian from Brisbane and Flying Officer W. A. Christensen from New South Wales attempted three runs on the primary in D-Dog but were also prevented from bombing by the balloons and intense flak. As an alternative the two Australians bombed goods train at Lastrup and although bursts were not seen the tail end of the train was derailed. Sergeant McKelvie and Sergeant 'Jock' Heggie in V-Victor, having also lost formation in cloud and failing to locate the primary, bombed a factory at Lobeda. The bombs were seen to explode in the buildings. Flying Officer Alan Rea and Pilot Officer Kenneth Bush in R-Robert was seen over the target but crashed on landing at Marham, killing the crew. P-Peter with Pilot Officer Ronald Massie and Sergeant George Lister was last seen as the formation entered cloud prior to reaching the target, but failed to return.

The Schott optical glassworks, closely associated with the Zeiss Works, was the target of six on 139 Squadron led by Wing Commander 'Reggie' Reynolds and Flying Officer Ted Sismore in B-Beer. Three Mosquitoes successfully bombed the target between 2131 and 2132 hours from 200 feet. The six-hour delay bombs dropped by the first two were seen to fall into the southern and eastern section of the factory, immediately causing a sheet of flame 100 feet high. Flying Officer 'Smokey Joe' Stovel and Sergeant W. A. Nutter flying K-King believed that their bombs fell in the centre of the SW section of the factory. Flying Officer Vernon Pereira and Flying Officer Gilbert in N-Nuts were forced to abandon the primary owing to an engine defect and bombed a railway bridge over the river Fulda at 2100 hrs with unobserved results. This aircraft returned to base on one engine. Intense light flak was encountered over Jena and there was a barrage of 10-20 balloons around the town flying at about 1,000 feet. Wing Commander Reynolds's aircraft was hit in the port airscrew, part of which came into the cockpit, injuring the pilot in the left hand and knee. The intercom was also rendered useless by flak which narrowly missed hitting the pilot. Flight Lieutenant 'Jock' Sutherland and Pilot Officer George Dean were seen to bomb the target but crashed at Wroxham railway station near RAF Coltishall on their return journey, both crew being killed. The following day the BBC turned up at Marham to record the story of the raid.

On 4 June 105 and 139 Squadrons were taken off daylight operations to begin a new career in 8 (PFF) Group PFF as markers using 'Oboe' and as high-level 'nuisance' raiders flying B.IX Mosquitoes respectively. The Path Finder Force (PFF) had been formed from 3 Group using volunteer crews on 15 August 1942 under the direction of Group Captain D. C. T. 'Don' Bennett and was headquartered at Wyton. The tough talking Australian ex-Imperial Airways and Atlantic Ferry pilot wanted Mosquitoes for PFF and target-marking duties. 'Oboe' was the codename for a high-level blind bombing aid, which took its name from a radar-type pulse which sounded rather like the musical instrument. 'Gee-H' (from 1944, H_2S)-equipped B.IXs on 139 Squadron and 'Oboe' II-equipped B.IXs on 105 Squadron spearheaded the Main Force bombing raids. On 'Spoof' raids 139 Squadron went in with the target-marking Mosquitoes on 105 Squadron, sowing bundles of 'Window', which produced a 'clutter' of blips on German radar screens to give the impression of a large bomber force to attract enemy night fighters anything up to 50 miles away from the Main Force. 109 Squadron's Mosquito IVs and IXs joined those on 105 Squadron as the Mosquito marking force. In addition to its flare marking duties for the heavies, 109 Squadron's Mosquitoes carried bombs.

In April 1942 109 Squadron had been established at Stradishall, Suffolk to bring 'Oboe' into full operational service as a navigation aid for Bomber Command before moving to Wyton in August, where at the end of the year, it received the first 'Oboe' equipped Mosquito B.IVs. Squadron Leader H. E. 'Hal' Bufton DFC AFC recalls: 'It was 109 Squadron's Commanding Officer, Wing Commander C. C. McMullin, who was the man who produced the final gleam of genius to put the four main facets of 'Oboe' together-the principle of a target-finding force, Coxen's target indicator, Dr. A. H. Reeve's 'Oboe' and the Mosquito - and one week before the final decision to begin installation of the Wellington VI on a production basis, he got hold of a Mosquito and installed all four bits into it just in time for the conference, which accordingly rejected the Wellington in favour of the Mosquito. It was a most happy result and one which gave us the thing we needed most - a large degree of immunity on operations. If the Germans had been able to recover an 'Oboe' set from a crashed aircraft, the run of the system would have been very short indeed. As it was, it appears almost certain that they did not capture a set until early 1943. With the successful application of 'Oboe' and the decision to use the Mosquito in the summer of 1942, two flights on 109 Squadron, which had been dealing with investigation of German radar and counter-measures against German beam bombs, were split off and 109 was realigned as purely an 'Oboe' marking squadron.

'We moved to Wyton as the first Path Finder squadron in August 1942, began to equip with Mosquitoes and build up our crew strength from the original three. We should have been ready to start work by about October but ran into a snag with 'Oboe'. Up till that time we had only flown it in Wellingtons at heights of up to 10,000 feet. We found that in the Mosquito one of the radio valves regularly blew up at little over 20,000 feet. After some smart detective work, Reeves and his colleagues from TRE found the trouble lay with a small electric motor (from the Hoover vacuum cleaner) used to drive a cooling fan which speeded-up at altitude and got into resonance with the valve. They cured this problem in time for us to begin operations during December. There were no other fundamental faults with the 'Oboe' sets after that, I believe, but we were always subject to technical failures of up to 30 per cent.'

Six operational crews and eight Mosquito IVs were available when on 20/21 December 1942 Bufton and his navigator, Flight Lieutenant E. Lister 'Ding' Ifould - who had navigated one of the leading Lancasters on the famous Augsburg daylight raid of 17 April 1942 - and two other crews, were sent to bomb a power station at Lutterade in Holland on border with Germany. Bufton and Ifould dropped the first 'Oboe'-aimed bombs. Two other crews bombed on 'Oboe' but the equipment in remaining three Mosquitoes did not function properly and their crews bombed targets of opportunity. All six Mosquitoes returned safely. Bufton recalled: 'It was supposed to be a virgin target, completely clear of bomb holes and we were intending to use it as a calibration target for checking 'Oboe' accuracy. When we got the photographs about three days later we found the attack had been useless as a calibration as the target was smothered with bombs from some earlier attack [on 5/6 October, when the pathfinder mistook Lutterade for Aachen 17 miles away] which had hit this target in error. [In fact nine bombs fell together in open ground two kilometres from the power station]. We subsequently had to set up a further calibration effort which was done on a small German officer cadet school at St-Trond, near Florennes, Belgium on 15 February 1943. This had previously been a Belgian boarding school and appeared to be a medium-sized country house, probably about 30 or 40 yards square. We had four aircraft on this target and apart from photographs which showed that we had some direct hits we received a detailed intelligence report from a man on the ground who gave us the exact location of the bomb hits. We had three or four hits on the school which killed a sentry at the gate and two officers in their rooms. Significantly, it was also reported that two separate bombs from different aircraft had landed a kilometre from the target. We were not sure how authentic this report was and we played down these loose bombs at the time. Which was unfortunate as later on similar results cast doubt on the 'Oboe' system. In the Florennes attack two aircraft had dropped their bombs in salvo. This was our regular practice when marking so that the TIs covered the smallest area possible. At that time we did not know that when bombs were dropped in salvo, frequently two of them hit each other with a high risk of one of them spinning and falling back. We were not aware of this happening during the Ruhr attacks of 1943, probably because the fires started were so intense and the normal drift back of the attack obscured the odd stray marker which might fall short.

'Four more crews were trained by January and by June 1943 we reached about 20 crews. In July 1943 105 Squadron was linked up with 109 as the second 'Oboe' squadron and a few of their existing crews were trained on 'Oboe', while the rest of them joined 139 Squadron and became the first of the Mosquito Light Night Bombing Force. About half of the 20 crews on 109 Squadron moved to 105 and half the ex-105 'Oboe' crews came to 109. By the end of 1943 109 Squadron crew strength had again increased to a full strength of about 20 crews. Only five 109 Squadron crews were lost up to the end of 1943. That is, we only lost one quarter of our force which is a striking tribute to the performance of the aircraft. As I believe it, only one of these was positively identified as going down over Germany, with the possible loss of security to the system.

'We followed up the first 'Oboe' attack on Lutterade by further HE attacks against Ruhr targets for the remainder of December 1942. 'Ding' Ifould and I were one of the crews from 109 on Essen on 23 December and on Hamborn in 24 December. This last one was interesting. Up till that time there had been no damage of any consequence done to Ruhr targets due to the heavy defences and constant smog. On the night of 24 December one of the crews, K. J. 'Slim' Somerville and M. S. Maas, had a small malfunction which resulted in a delayed bomb release of about three seconds (600 yards). On Christmas Day 1942 'Lord Haw Haw' reported that the RAF had carried out a 'terror' attack on Christmas Eve but had only succeeded in hitting a cemetery at Hamborn. We checked the maps and sure enough there was a cemetery 600 yards south of our target - just where we calculated Somerville's bombs had hit. Presumably the rest of us - whose equipment worked correctly - must have hurt quite a bit.

'By the end of December we were ready to mark targets. The weather over Germany, however, was against us and continuous cloud cover prevented the first ground marking until March. Our AOC, Don Bennett,[50] thought up [Wanganui] a skymarking technique[51] which we tried out for the first time, with two Mosquitoes and eight Lancasters of PFF acting as main force bombers, on a raid on Düsseldorf on 31 December. We dropped bundles of coloured parachute flares at some height - say 10,000 feet - above cloud level. The follow-up bombers would approach on a pre-determined heading and aim at the markers. There were big errors in the system, the principal one being the drift down-wind of the marker flare. With a 60 mph wind at flare height, the flare would drift three miles during the time it was burning i.e. it would be between one and one and a half miles off target at start and finish. Despite these limitations 'Oboe' skymarking was spectacularly successful compared with the strictly negative results achieved on the Ruhr prior to this and was used on a number of nights during January-February 1943. Ifould and I did seven sky-marking trips to the Ruhr in January.'

On 16/17 January 1943 Berlin was bombed for the first time in fourteen months by 190 Lancasters and eleven Halifaxes. Air Marshal Sir Arthur Harris, C-in-C Bomber Command sent them on their way with the words. 'Tonight you are going to the Big City. You will have the opportunity to light a fire in the belly of the enemy that will burn his black heart out.' This raid marked the first use of purpose-designed Target Indicators (TIs) instead of modified incendiaries, which had previously been used.[52] Only one Lancaster

50 On 13 January 1943 the Path Finder Force became 8 (PFF) Group. 'Don' Bennett was promoted Air Commodore (later AVM) to command it.
51 In total, three types of marking, using names selected from the hometowns of three of Bennett's staff were employed. Parramatta in New Zealand gave its name to the blind ground marking technique, which used only H2S in bad visibility or broken cloud. Newhaven was ground marking by visual methods when crews simply aimed at the TIs on the ground and Wanganui in Australia lent its name to pure 'sky marking'. The TIs themselves were made in various plain colours and used vivid star-bursts of the same or a different colour to prevent the enemy from copying them at their many decoy sites near major cities.
52 There were eventually several types of TI from 250lb to the 'Pink Pansy' model weighing 2,300lb, which made use of a 4000lb bomb casing. It got its name from the red pyrotechnic added to the basic marker mixture of benzol, rubber and phosphorus. There were also TIs of good ballistic form arranged to eject coloured roman candles either in the air or on impact with or without explosives. A 250lb TI lit up a radius of 100 yards.

was lost but the raid was a disappointment. Thick cloud en route and haze over the target caused problems and the bombing was scattered. The Berlin flak had proved light and ineffective and it was assumed that the greater altitude of the attacking force had surprised the German gunners. Harris repeated the raid on Berlin, sending 170 Lancasters and 17 Halifaxes back to the Big City the following night, when the weather was better.

'An interesting development early in January' continues Hal Bufton 'was an instruction from Bomber Command that 'Oboe' Mosquitoes were to stand by to lead daytime formations of Lancasters against the Ruhr.[53] It was one of those utter stupidities that develop in war from the intense drive to 'get on with it'. We had the potential with 'Oboe' to enable Bomber Command to write-off the Ruhr; but we were operating on a shoe-string; we needed highly trained and experienced crews - we had only 10 or 12 with only one flight of aircraft. 'Oboe' could be jammed within a few days if the Germans captured a set of equipment. Yet the Bomber Command C-in-C's determination was such that he was willing to risk losing use of the system during the whole of 1943 just to get in a few relatively small-scale daylight hits during the bad weather winter months.

'The idea was that the 'Oboe' aircraft would lead the formation at about 23,000 feet and after crossing the coast, would climb above the formation to 28,000 feet to make the bombing run. The Lancasters were supposed to bomb when they saw the bombs leave the Mosquito a mile above them! We had one formation practice with Lancs on 9 January which was a disaster. [That night four PFF Mosquitoes and 55 Lancasters of 1 and 5 Groups attacked Essen. The 'Oboe' equipment of the first Mosquito to arrive failed and the other three Mosquitoes were all late. Because of this many of the Lancasters bombed on dead reckoning].[54]

However, we stood by for this folly for several weeks until our representations to Air Ministry resulted in a clamp-down on the Command which resulted in 'Oboe' Mosquitoes being restricted to night-time marking operations only. This was almost as bad from our angle as the C-in-C's plan as it meant that we could not train our new crews by giving them practice with HE before they were let loose with markers. 'Oboe' Mosquito-led Lancaster formations became practical in late 1944 when the ground stations were based on the Continent and the shorter range allowed attack at 15-20,000 feet.'

On the night of 2/3 February 161 bombers including 116 Lancasters and 35 Halifaxes went to Cologne in another experiment using a four-engined bombing force with various forms of Pathfinder techniques. The night was cloudy and markers were dropped by both the 'Oboe' Mosquitoes and their H_2S heavy marker aircraft. Results were disappointing once again with no clear concentration of markers being achieved and with subsequent bombing well scattered. The 'Oboe' Mosquitoes flew a series of minor operations against enemy targets throughout February sending twos and threes to targets as far afield as Lorient on the French Atlantic coast to eastern Belgium and Essen, Düsseldorf and Rheinhausen in Germany as well as to night fighter airfields in Holland.

53 Starting on the night of 3/4 January 'Oboe' Mosquitoes operated on two successive nights in attacks by the Lancasters of 5 Group on Essen and on 8/9 January against Duisburg. 'Oboe' led operations against Essen were resumed on the night of 7/8th and then again on the nights of 9/10th, 11/12th and 12/13th.

54 On the 13/14th 66 Lancasters and three Mosquitoes visited Essen. Two 'Oboe' Mosquitoes had to return without marking and the sky markers of the third Mossie failed to ignite above the cloud but the city was bathed in light. German aircraft even dropped decoy flares to try to distract the Lancaster crews..

'The first 'Oboe' ground-marking effort' continues Hal Bufton 'was made on St-Nazaire on 28 February, using the experimental ground stations on the South Coast. We had only one 'Oboe' channel so our risk of failure was high. As it happened the first marker aircraft succeeded by the skin of its teeth and the two or three backers-up all failed. The markers were right on target and huge damage to the town's dock area resulted. It was the first time one of the French ports had really been hit despite numerous attacks by Bomber Command and within a few weeks, further 'area' attacks on these targets were prohibited to prevent further damage to the French. St-Nazaire was the first full trial of the 'Oboe' Mosquito in its ground-marking role and proved a resounding success.'

The first time ground-marking was used against a German target was on Essen on the night of 5/6 March 1943 when 442 aircraft, 157 of them Lancasters and 'Oboe'-equipped Mosquitoes, began what has gone into history as the starting point of the Battle of the Ruhr. The cascade that night included no less than 150 4,000 pounders and two-thirds of the bombs carried were incendiaries. For most of the way out the route was cloudy but fifteen miles from the target the weather cleared although pilots reported valley mists were still seeping in from the river. The eight 'Oboe' Mosquitoes marked the centre of the city perfectly with Red TIs and the Pathfinder 'backers up' arrived in good order and dropped their Green TIs blind on the target. Only if there were no reds visible were the Main Force to bomb the 'Greens'. These were followed by the first 'Cookies', which wailed down and then erupted with violence and flame and the raid was well under way. The valley mists and industrial haze did not affect the outcome of the raid, which was bombed in three waves with the Lancasters bombing last, the entire weight of the raid being concentrated into a volcanic forty-five minutes. Fifty-six aircraft turned back early because of technical problems and other causes. Fourteen aircraft were shot down and 38 other bombers returned with damage. Damage was modest but a week afterwards the Air Ministry announced that 450 acres of Essen were a devastated area. Of the Krupps' plant alone, 53 separate large workshops were affected by the bombing. Thirteen of the main buildings in the works were completely demolished or seriously damaged. Over 470 people were killed on the ground and over 3,000 houses were destroyed while over 2,100 were seriously damaged. The havoc was caused by nearly a thousand tons of high explosive dropped by crews without them needing to see the target. 'Essen,' said the special Air Ministry announcement on 12 March 'is now the second most blitzed town in Germany. Only in Cologne is there a greater area of devastation.'

The second time ground-marking was used was on Essen again on 12/13 March, when 457 aircraft, including ten Mosquitoes acting as Pathfinder markers using the 'Oboe' technique of marking the target were dispatched. The role of the other aircraft taking part was that of fire raisers. They were to follow immediately after the first pathfinders had dropped their marker flares and drop incendiaries and 1,000lb bombs to 'stir things up' and light the fires for the following Lancasters to plaster them with their 4,000lb Block Busters. It was estimated that the Krupps' works received 30 per cent more damage on this night than the earlier raid that month. Sir Archibald Sinclair, the Secretary of State for Air, sent Harris an appreciative message. 'Your cunningly planned and brilliantly executed attack on Krupps has destroyed no small part of Germany's biggest war factory. Congratulations to you and all under your command on this achievement in the teeth of Germany's strongest defences.'

On 26/27 March the raid on Duisburg by 455 aircraft was one of the few failures of this series of attacks on Ruhr targets. The night was cloudy and for once accurate 'Oboe' sky marking was lacking because five 'Oboe' Mosquitoes were forced to return early with equipment problems. A sixth was lost when Flight Lieutenant L. J. Ackland RCAF and Warrant Officer F. S. Strouts DFC RCAF were forced to ditch in the North Sea and both men were drowned. This aircraft was the first 'Oboe' Mosquito lost on operations. Beginning on 27/28 March Berlin was attacked for two nights in succession. The first raid by 396 aircraft was a failure. The Pathfinders marked two areas but they were short of their aiming points by five miles. Consequently, none of the bombs came within five miles of the target area in the centre of the city. Nine aircraft were lost. Another 'Oboe' raid, on Bochum on 29/30 March by 149 Wellingtons and eight 'Oboe' Mosquitoes failed also. The night was moonless and cloudy. The Mosquitoes were unable to stick to their timetable and there were long gaps in the sky marking. Essen, the home of Krupps, was bombed by 317 aircraft with marking by ten 'Oboe' Mosquitoes on 3/4 April. The weather forecast had predicted unfavourable conditions and so the Mosquito force had planned for both sky-marking and ground-marking the target. As it turned out there was no cloud over Essen and the Main Force crews were confused to find that two types of marking were employed. Even so, bombing was accurate and over 600 buildings were destroyed and more than 500 seriously damaged. Fourteen Halifaxes and nine Lancasters failed to return. Thick cloud on the night of 8/9 April when the target was Duisburg ruined Pathfinder marking by ten Mosquitoes and the resultant bombing was scattered. On the night of 26/27 April when the target was Duisburg again, 561 aircraft including ten 'Oboe' Mosquitoes and 215 Lancasters, 135 Wellingtons and 119 Halifaxes were dispatched. Seventeen aircraft were lost - ten of them to night fighters over the Netherlands - but all the Mosquitoes returned. The Pathfinders claimed to have marked the target accurately. More than thirty tons of bombs a minute for a space of three-quarters of an hour rained down on the important inland port, the largest in Europe which handled about seventy-five per cent of all the cargoes passing along the Rhine. However, the bombing was not accurate mainly because the Main Force may have bombed too early or dummy fires short of the target may have duped them.

On the last night of April, over 300 bombers headed for Essen again to drop more bombs on its already devastated environs. Cloud had been expected over the target so a pathfinder technique based entirely on 'Oboe' Mosquito sky-markers was planned. This was not expected to give such good results as ground marking but the plan worked well and 238 bomber crews reported that they had bombed the city to take the figure of bombs dropped on the long suffering city to 10,000 tons. At the time this was the heaviest weight of bombs dropped on any town in the world. Twelve aircraft failed to return. Half the losses were inflicted by night-fighters. The World's press took notice of the performance of Bomber Command and the New York Times commented in its leader: 'Germany is apparently reaching the point where she cannot cope, materially or physically, with the effects of bombing. Her enemies did not wait to pummel her cities until the population was strained by years or war and the armies were scraping the bottom of the barrel for men and material. They waited because they were unable to hit sooner. But if Allied strategy had been dictated not by necessity but by a plan to reserve its full striking power until German force was spent, the results would be very much like what there are now.'

The attack on Duisburg-Ruhrort on 12/13 May by over 570 aircraft saw more than fifteen hundred tons of high explosives and incendiaries being dropped. This was more than was dropped on Cologne in the thousand-bomber raid a year earlier. Whereas the Cologne raid had taken 98 minutes, concentration at Duisburg-Ruhrort was so controlled that delivery was made in half that time and the ten 'Oboe' Mosquitoes did their work well. Zero hour was fixed for 2 o'clock. The first flares and bombs went down dead on time. The last aircraft was winging home forty-five minutes later. The night following over 440 bombers and ten 'Oboe' Mosquitoes raided Bochum. The raid began well enough but after 15 minutes what were thought to be German decoy markers drew much of the bombing away from the target.

Raids on Ruhr targets continued with Dortmund, the fourth heavy Bomber Command raid of May, on the night of the 23rd/24th. Of 829 aircraft (including thirteen 'Oboe' Mosquitoes) despatched, 38 bombers failed to return. The Pathfinders marked the target accurately in clear conditions and the bombing which followed went according to plan. More than two thousand tons of bombs, the biggest bomb load ever dropped anywhere in a single night, fell on the luckless city and the great weight fell in less than an hour between one and two in the morning. The next morning came more accolades and another promise from the Commander-in-Chief, addressed to all crews in Bomber Command. 'In 1939 Goering promised that not a single enemy bomb would reach the Ruhr. Congratulations on having delivered the first 100,000 tons on Germany to refute him. The next 100,000, if he waits for them, will be even bigger and better bombs, delivered more accurately and in much shorter time.' On the night of the 25/26th when a dozen Mosquitoes marked for the 759 bombers dispatched to bomb Düsseldorf, 27 bombers were lost - 21 of which, were due to night-fighters. The raid was a failure due to the difficulty of marking in bad weather. Another raid on Essen on 27/28 May saw twelve Mosquitoes mark for over 500 bombers but the weather was cloudy and sky-marking had to be used. The main bombing was scattered with many aircraft undershooting.

By contrast, the raid on Wuppertal on 29/30 May when eleven 'Oboe' Mosquitoes took part was the outstanding success of the Battle of the Ruhr. Both Pathfinder marking and Main Force bombing was very accurate and a large fire area developed in the narrow streets of the old centre of the extended, oblong shaped town, which had a population of almost 360,000. Wuppertal had been formed in 1920 by the union of the adjacent towns of Elberfeld and Barmen in the Upper Wupper Valley. The Barmen half of the town was the target for the 719 aircraft despatched on that Saturday night which was moonless and 292 of them were Lancasters. Sixty-two aircraft turned back early but the remainder, aided by blind-marking systems, devastated about 1,000 acres of Barmen's built up area. Nearly 4,000 dwellings were destroyed and 71 industrial and 1,800 domestic buildings were seriously damaged. Thirty-three bombers, seven of them Lancasters, were lost.

On 11/12 June 783 aircraft including thirteen Mosquitoes attacked Düsseldorf. The Pathfinder marking plan went extremely well until an 'Oboe' Mosquito inadvertently released its load of TIs 14 miles north-east of the city, which caused part of the Main Force to drop their bombs on open country. Even so, in the city itself damage was extensive and 130 acres were claimed destroyed. When over 700 bombers attacked Krefeld on the night of 21/22 June the raid took place in good visibility and the

Pathfinders carried out an almost perfect marking operation. Ground-markers dropped by the dozen 'Oboe' Mosquitoes were well backed up by the Pathfinder heavies and 619 aircraft were reckoned to have bombed these markers, dropping more than 2300 tons of bombs. More than three-quarters of the bombers achieved bombing photographs within three miles of the centre of the city. A large fire ensued, took hold and burned out of control for several hours and 47 per cent of the built up area was laid waste. About 72,000 people lost their homes; the largest figure so far in the war. The night following, 557 aircraft, including a dozen 'Oboe' Mosquitoes, went to Mülheim where the Pathfinders had to mark the target through a thin layer of stratus cloud. The marking proved very accurate and large fires raged throughout the city destroying over 1,100 houses and damaging over 12,600 dwellings. The post-war British Bombing Survey Unit estimated that this single raid destroyed 64 per cent of the town of Mülheim.[55]

On 25/26 June 473 aircraft including twelve 'Oboe' Mosquitoes, were despatched to Gelsenkirchen for the first raid on this city since 1941. Cloud obscured the target and the dozen 'Oboe' Mosquitoes, for once, failed to produce regular and accurate marking since equipment in five of the aircraft was unserviceable. The raid was not a success and bombs fell on many other Ruhr towns. Three nights later only seven of the twelve 'Oboe' Mosquitoes reached the target, Cologne and only six of these were able to drop their markers. The weather forecast had predicted that the city would probably be cloud covered although there might be a break so the Pathfinders had to prepare for both ground marking and the less reliable sky marking. The target turned out to be cloud-covered so sky-marking system was used. This was seven minutes late in starting and proceeded only intermittently, despite all of this, the Main Force of nearly 600 bombers devastated Cologne in the most destructive raid on the city in the entire war. Thousands of buildings were destroyed, over 4,300 people were killed and about 10,000 inhabitants were injured while 230,000 people were forced to leave their damaged dwellings. A follow up raid took place on 3/4 July when 653 bombers aimed their bombs at industrial targets on the east bank of the Rhine. Pathfinder Ground marking by the Mosquito 'Oboe' aircraft and the backers-up was accurate and much devastation was caused.

After July 109 Squadron 'Oboe' Mosquitoes were not called on as frequently as the Ruhr began to receive lower priority. At the same time German jamming became more of a problem since the Mk.I system was still in use.

'With an aircraft of such performance' continues Bufton 'fighters were no great worry, but I believe we lost a few to lucky fighters - they had to be lucky to cope. It was sometimes disconcerting to be following a series of, say, five condensation trails of the aircraft ahead of you and to have an extra trail from a fighter join in for the rest of the trip. Still, so long as the trail was in front, you were safe. We required crews of very high ability to give the responsibility, skills and consistent determination needed. I believe that, above all, the Mosquito gave us those crews. We had a free hand to recruit anyone in Bomber Command during 1942 and probably we could have any willing customer from anywhere in the RAF. We were very lucky in our initial recruiting-later on the Mosquito did the recruiting for us when the news got around. We got Mark IX Mosquitoes about May 1943. I flew LR496 on 29 May. The Mk.IVs were terrific, but the IXs were fantastic. It was a tremendous boost to fly an aeroplane without fear of icing - those winter thunderstorms over the North Sea were

---

55 See *The Bomber Command War Diaries* by Martin Middlebrook and Chris Everitt (Midland 1985).

now below us - and with the certainty you could get back on one engine. Even better, that a minor crash, like hitting a haystack and traction engine at full circuit speed resulted in gentle disintegration of the aircraft, splinter by splinter, with the crew walking safely away (this happened!). While enough can never be said of it as an operational aircraft in 1943-44, it should be said that the Mosquito had a few minor snags. These were its tendency to swing on take-off and landing. These faults were much pronounced on the IXs and XVIs and when the paddle-blade props came along with consequent increase in critical speed, they became a source of some trouble in single-engine landings to us, in our ignorance of those days. We lost a few crews due to these faults, but without them the aeroplane would not have given us the near-immunity we needed on operations. Roundabout trips, most times, easily outweigh a few swings. I never met a Mosquito crew that was not thrilled to bits with its aircraft from 1943 on.

'Despite its ceiling the Mosquito could not fly high enough for longer range targets - we would have needed a satellite. As a solution to this a system of 'Oboe' repeaters was developed, whereby a relay aircraft patrolled a line joining the ground station and the target. This could have increased our range up to about 600 miles. It was a very complicated system and failed to get enough high-level support to ensure its full introduction (by which I mean that the opposition was strong enough to squash it). We had one repeater working at the end of 1943 and did one operational trial against Emden. One 'Oboe' leg was direct from East Anglia and the other, via repeater, from Dover. Squadron Leader Bob Findlater and I flew this trip on 24 October 1943 in a Mk.IX Mosquito, LR499. We were trying out the very complicated system of radar routings and relays through our two aircraft, the repeater and the bomber. For the sake of form we had to have a target and the gate to the dry dock was selected. We heard later that we hit it.

'The individual sortie consisted of a climb to height from base to the English coast. From there we flew at our operational height, 28-30,000 feet, to the start of our bombing run, about 50-60 miles from target. We had 'Gee' over the North Sea so that our navigators could get extraordinarily exact timing. Our bombing runs were 10 minutes long and were along arcs of circles centred on either Dover or Caistor. For most of the Ruhr we used Dover for our tracking station which gave us a north-south run. For Düsseldorf, Cologne and Wuppertal etc, we tracked on Caistor on a North-east bombing run. Whenever possible we chose the north-south run as it was usually down-wind and gave us a ground speed of 400+ mph and sometimes as much as 600 mph. The 10-minute run was straight and level, so we appreciated the speed of the Mosquito. Our biggest trouble was with flak. Since we were straight and level, almost always from the same direction and ahead of the main bomber stream, we were a nice exercise piece for the gunners. They developed an efficient plot system of gun control which frightened us all but did not produce too many losses. For the last three or four minutes of our bombing run, we were the centre of concentrated fire. We could always see it; sometimes from behind reflected in the side blisters - which was good. Sometimes ahead, which was bad. Sometimes we could hear it, which was worse and sometimes smell it as well, which was awful. The usual practice was to put the seat down as low as possible so that you could not see out and do the run on instruments-it was like putting on blinkers. We frequently had flak holes and often lost an engine due-to splinters. The Mosquito did not seem to mind. Flak holes were patched in a few hours with a fabric patch or simple carpentry repair. Engines could be changed in 3-4 hours after the crews got the hang of it. It was easy to get back on one engine even if on some of the landings one went astray.

'We continued to be successful until 19 November 1943 when we had our first complete failure, due to jamming, on Leverkusen. After that we were of little use until the flying-bomb targets came up in January 1944, leading to the pre-invasion interdiction programme on rail yards and the later close support for the army. By this time we were using Mk.II 'Oboe' and also could use Mk.I as we were away from the areas of jamming in central Germany. During the pre-invasion sorties in the spring where the targets were mainly railway yards and only high explosive (HE) bombs were used by the main force, errors stood out. At Tergnier in April 1944 we had one aircraft using the Mk.I 'Oboe' system with reds and one using Mk.II with greens (TIs). The Mk.II system was still experimental at that time-hence the difference in colour and reds were the primary markers. It developed that both aircraft marked at just about the same time. The reds and greens were about 400 yards apart, as we had suspected they might be, but in each case one of the four markers had fallen back by nearly a mile so the result was a rectangle marked by three reds at one corner, three greens at another and a red and a green at the others. Results of this sort tended to destroy confidence in 'Oboe' after that and a master bomber was introduced to assess the accuracy and if necessary, report the TI to attack. If we had only studied the results of the Florennes calibration earlier we would have resolved this gap in the RAF's technical knowledge before the main bomber offensive got under way and saved a lot of grief. As it was it was not until May 1944 that we did the necessary trials ourselves on a bombing range which showed that bombs dropped in salvo might cause trouble.

'On one major attack on flying bomb sites in north France in April, nine targets were marked with 'Oboe' reds only and all attacks were successful. A tenth target - the 5 Group one - was marked by 'Oboe' with yellow proximity markers with the intent that these would be followed up by a 'Newhaven' marking technique of illumination and final identification and marking by the master bomber. Unfortunately, the illuminating flares did not go down on time, the master bomber could not identify the target for a long time and in the end his reds went down about 30 minutes late. There were about 120 Lancasters on the target which was three miles inside the French coast. During that half-hour alone we saw 20 shot down. These were the only aircraft lost out of a thousand-plus operating on flying bomb sites in the area that night. To make it worse, the target was not hit.

'The ten coastal gun sites on the invasion coast were marked with 'Oboe' on 6 June for the follow-up attack by the full Command. Afterwards 'Oboe' Mosquitoes were used for marking in close support of the Army. They came back into their full strategic role against German targets in the autumn, using ground stations in Belgium and France which extended their range to Berlin.

'Our operations were strictly a team effort. Each of the two 'Oboe' channels we normally had available could work only one aircraft every ten minutes. In 1943 a full-scale Command attack of 600-1,000 aircraft took about 40 minutes. Our plan was normally for one channel to mark at H-2 minutes, H+8, H+18 and H+28; the other channel at H, H+10, H+20 and H+30. We had a failure rate of about 30 per cent which gave us, perhaps, an 80 per cent chance of getting one of the two aircraft successfully on target at each 10-minute interval. That is, of the aircraft at H and H+2 which started off the attack, we could only expect 80 per cent success. Since that first mark was the be-all and end-all, we laid on a heavy system of back-up. We put a reserve aircraft on each channel which went in with the leader and stood by (about 7-10 minutes from target) waiting to replace any failures. In addition, the second and subsequent aircraft on each channel went in ten minutes early, so that it could take over the time slot of the aircraft ahead if it and the reserve both failed. This gave us six chances of getting the first mark down on time and until Leverkusen, we did not fail. However, there were a few occasions where we were a minute or so late when the reserve or second back-up was called after failure of the lead aircraft late in the proceedings. Usually, even if the reserves were called in, we managed to keep timing within 30 seconds. With our concentration on getting the mark down at H-hour, we often missed at H+10 or H+20 spots - but never (I think) both of them. Since the TIs lasted only three minutes in the early days (six and 12 minutes later on when a proportion of delayed candles were used), there were big gaps between the Mosquito red markers even when our programme was perfect. These holes were filled up by the Lancaster markers of PFF which covered our reds with green TIs and kept the pot boiling. 'Oboe' by itself would rarely have worked. It needed the follow-up of the rest of PFF.

'Some mention should be made of the Mosquito/Lancaster value ratio. A figure of 3 to 1 is sometimes quoted. The Lancaster cost three times as much as a Mosquito and had a crew over three times as big. It carried three times the bomb load, but for only one-third of the sorties i.e. an average tour of 20 sorties per crew compared with 60 for the Mosquitoes. What is left out of this picture is the experience of the crews. The Lancaster crews had average experience of ten trips at any one time and were thus almost always half-trained. The Mosquito crews had an average experience of about 30+ trips and had a far more satisfactory performance. For an 'Oboe' Mosquito, carrying a 4,000lb bomb, the ratio would be almost 50 to 1.'

Chapter 4

Find, Mark and Strike

'The first thing that struck one about the Mosquito' recalls Frank Ruskell, an 'Oboe' navigator on 109 Squadron 'was the beauty of line of the fuselage, tailplane, fin and engine cow lings. They all went together and made a lovely aeroplane. The cockpit cover also had a sweet line and the simplicity of the undercarriage and the treaded tyres set the whole thing off. The aeroplane sat on the ground looking pert and eager and it was easy to become fond of - which was by no means true of all aeroplanes, the Hampden for example. These were my feelings about the B.IV. The line was marred in the Mk.VI by the flat windscreen and the protruding guns. When the B.IX came along, it looked even better than the B.IV because the engines were larger and the spinners extended forward of the line of the nose (the later Hornet had a similar feature). This gave the line added beauty and also conveyed an air of warlike viciousness which was very apt.

'Inside the cockpit there was just room for the crew to do what they had to do. The pilot sat in the usual sort of seat, with his seat pack and dinghy; the navigator sat on the main spar on his dinghy, but with his parachute pack elsewhere for lack of headroom. In the 'Oboe' version the nose was full of black boxes and the Gee and bomb switches were near his left elbow. I used to push my parachute pack on top of the boxes in the nose, out of the way-you could not leave it on the floor as that was the escape hatch. The navigator in the 'Oboe' version had a little navigation board, made on the squadron, on which was screwed the two parts of a Dalton computer-triangle and Appleyard scale - and on which you pinned your chart. There was also a little box let into the top where you kept the protractor, pencils etc. The plotting chart we used was a 1-million 'Gee' chart. Our routes to and from the English coast were fixed and our range was such that you never went off the printed 'Gee' chart.

''Oboe' attacks were always started from a 'waiting point', ten minutes' flying time from the target. Up to that point you followed a Bailey Beam for track accuracy, monitoring on 'Gee' (once or twice the beams were laid wrong...) and checking the ground speed between 'Gee' fixes. Operating in this rigid pattern, we were able to ensure navigation and timing accuracy of a high order-the record speaks for itself ... For greater range on the 'Oboe', we flew as high as the aircraft would go - which meant climbing on track with consequent complications to the navigation. We were, however, able to reach operating height before we ran out of 'Gee' cover, so we were able to maintain accuracy. As we experienced wind shear in the climb, the pilot could detect it by the change in heading (or 'course' as it was known) to maintain constant direction on the Bailey Beam. Coming back to England from the Ruhr area, we used to do a cruise descent which brought us home at a tremendous speed (for those days). We always went out at Southwold and came in at Orfordness, so that the little tracks from your base to these points used to get smudged with rubbing-out 'Gee' fixes all the time.

'Pathfinder operations were of two kinds - Sky-marking, code-named 'Wanganui';

and ground-marking, known as 'Parramatta'. If the primary marking was to be done by the 'Oboe' Mosquitoes, the operations were known as 'Musical Wanganui' or 'Musical Parramatta'. Because of the characteristics of 'Oboe', the 'musical' operations gave marking accuracy of the highest order (100-200 yards error) and were welcomed by everybody involved. For technical reasons 'Oboe' could only put markers down every five minutes (in the earlier and busier days, anyway), so certain of the 'heavy' Pathfinders used to keep our markers stoked up until the next lot came down. On a 'Musical Parramatta' everybody knew that the red TIs would be spot-on.

'We were also very proud of our timing accuracy, but there were times when individual aircraft failed to drop their markers due to enemy interference with the 'Oboe' signals. These occasions caused us some distress as we knew the 'heavies' down below were taking a pasting on their run-in, expecting the TIs to go off in front of them. Of course, when all went well we had a most marvellous grandstand view of a technical triumph. The first 'Oboe' aircraft in could be heard by the others and they knew when to watch for the TIs bursting. Before that you could follow his progress down the run by the concentration of flak and searchlights, because 'Jerry' knew what was coming. Lower down, the 'heavies' would be battling through and only a couple of minutes after the first TI, the bombs would begin to go off - HE and incendiaries right on the TIs. The back-up green TIs would keep coming down and every five minutes new 'Oboe' reds - spot-on the target as everybody watching knew. As you pulled away for home you could see the whole thing - TIs, bombs, incendiaries, flak searchlights, aircraft in flames, fighter fire - and of course the fires on the ground. On a good clear night, I used to be able to read my wristwatch in the fires - and that is the truth! We used to screech home like bullets and the crew could be back in the Mess quite early.

'When there was no marking for, us to do, we used to go on nuisance raids into the Ruhr and Rhineland, taking off at half-hour intervals from about half an hour before sunset, with a load of four or six 500lb HE bombs. We used to go to different targets all over the Ruhr and Rhineland areas and it was quite possible to see chaps on other targets being pasted by flak - black aircraft in searchlights look silver, anyway. These sorties were rather different from the true marker sorties, as you were on your own and the Jerries knew what you were up to. There was the odd night when nobody fired at you, but they were few and far between. We were laid on pinpoint targets, needless to say. If you were on one of these trips, you might take off just after four on a winter's afternoon, fly the trip, go through interrogation and be back in the Mess before 8 pm. I remember once going into the Mess ante-room in battle dress at about that time and the Padre ('Bish' Bradford) said, 'Are you on tonight, Junior?' and I said 'I've been'. It was quite uncanny.

'We were occupied like this during the winter of 1943-44 when the 'heavies' went further afield and PFF was using H_2S. Before and after D-Day we used the 'Oboe' accuracy to go for flying-bomb (V-1) sites in northern France. Each site would have a couple of 'Oboe' Mosquitoes to mark it and 20-30 'heavies' to bomb it. When we were on a target in the Pas de Calais, we used to start our 'Oboe' runs over the Thames Estuary-quite a change! But we hardly regarded these as 'operations'. I left the squadron in April 1944 and did not take part in D-Day or post D-Day operations. What was it like? There was a feeling of relative immunity given by height and speed. There was also the feeling of great responsibility when you were dropping primary markers. If you were the first aircraft of all, the worry was immense - quite apart from the fact that you knew you were going to get the undivided attention of the defences. One sat up there in the dark with a grandstand or bird's eye view and could see the muzzle flashes of the guns as they opened up at you. You knew you had to wait half a minute or so for the shells to climb up to where you were and all this time the guns kept going off and you knew the shells were climbing up. Mercifully, they mostly went off behind and below, but not always. You sat in your little wooden aeroplane, hanging on to its props, watching the show, with the 'Oboe' signals coming in and everything else silence. The navigator used to have his head-set wired so that he had the pilot's signal (the 'Cat') in one ear and his own (the 'Mouse') in the other. I used to sit on the floor to tune the gear and trim the aerial. Then, when I was satisfied, at say five minutes to target, I used to sit up on my seat again and watch the fireworks. Often you could smell the flak and on alarming occasions, hear it. The searchlights were blinding and pilots used to drop their seats so that they could see the instruments better. I have sometimes been looking at a bit of sky where a shell went off and seen the red-hot bits of metal fly out - this is no exaggeration. The aircraft used to get peppered quite often and I had two bits of flak I picked out of ours one night, which I carried around in my pocket.

'Sometimes the aircraft got knocked off their run at a crucial point by flak bursting under the wings. Of course, you had to recover and press on. Even so, for all the attention we got, you knew it was nothing like what the 'heavies' were getting down below. In the spring and summer of 1943 when the 'Oboe'-led offensive on the Ruhr and Rhineland was at its height, the intensity of effort was enormous and I believe crews did whole tours, or nearly so, on these raids.

'I said the aircraft used to hang on their props. This was true of the Mk.IV, but not the Mk.IX. In the IV the nose was up at a noticeable angle and the coolant vents in the tops of the engine cowlings used to give off vapour at height-you could see it in the moonlight or searchlights and there would be paler streaks across the wings. The IVs battled gallantly on, but the IXs took it in their stride. They had Merlins with two-stage, two-speed superchargers and climbed like the proverbial home-sick angels. We had much more freedom of manoeuvre in IXs and it was a pity we didn't have them for the main offensive. Another feature of the IV was that there was no pressurisation, so that you had difficulty in finding enough breath to speak with. Not knowing any better, we took this in our stride and had a pleasant surprise when we found the Mk.IX was pressurised.

'Early in 1943 when we first flew at 29,000 feet over NW Europe, we occasionally had a rough ride for no apparent reason. You would be flying along towards the target and run into high frequency turbulence. It was like going over a cobbled road on a bicycle with no tyres and was most alarming as there was no apparent cause. We used to fly out of it in the end but as far as I recall we were never given an explanation. I know now that we were near the tropopause and were in clear-air turbulence caused by a jet-stream. At that time I doubt if the Met-men had formed any clear ideas on jet-streams and it's possible that we were among the first airmen to experience the phenomenon.

'We occasionally experienced very strong winds at lower altitudes and I remember once having a drift of 40 degrees. I stuck to my DR and found these winds, but I remember that one crew decided that their compass was u/s and went back to base. We were not really breaking new ground with these experiences because the PR Spitfires and Mosquitoes must have had it all before us, but we did not know. The Mosquito was a good-looking aeroplane of very high performance. It seldom let you down and for the 'Oboe' role it proved the ideal - there was no other aeroplane at our disposal which could have filled the bill. You could not help loving it and went to war in it with every confidence.'

Air Vice Marshal Don Bennett's Mosquitoes were to prove so successful that ultimately, eleven Mosquito-equipped squadrons operated in 8 (PFF) Group.56 In addition, 1409 (Met) Flight was established at Oakington on 1 April 1943 using Mosquitoes and crews on 521 Squadron, Coastal Command at Bircham Newton. Edwin Perry DFC AE an observer on 1409 Met Flight recalls: 'Shortly after Pathfinder Force was formed AVM Bennett appreciated that lack of up-to-date knowledge of weather conditions in the target area was inhibiting accuracy and he was permitted to form 1409 Flight. The meteorological survey usually involved one aircraft with a pilot and observer, who was both a trained navigator and wireless operator. The route to be taken was often wide-ranging and was given to the aircrew immediately before take-off; apart from their own guesses they were not told the name of the prospective target(s) being scheduled for Bomber Command's attention but on the strength of the Mosquito report the PFF marker aircraft were loaded with ground or sky-markers, which burst above the cloud, prior to bombing by the Main Force. Initially the weather reports were sent by Morse code from the aircraft but shortly after I joined the Unit the keyed frequency radio was replaced by 'Gee', which was excellent for fixing positions up to 4° east and VHF which could be used to give interim spoken reports from 200-250 miles on the return to England. On landing the observer was connected to Group and Command Headquarters to amplify and answer questions raised.

'Apart from being an excellent navigation aid, we found that it was of inestimable value in getting us down at the end of long sorties over inhospitable terrain. The 'Gee' had a screen like a television set but with two horizontal graduated traces, one set above the other. The 'fixed' blips were pre-set, one on each trace, corresponding to the airfield's ground position. The underside of each trace had the moving blip - the trick was for the observer to guide the aircraft until one of the blips was progressing slowly towards its 'fixed' mate. As the airfield was approached the blip on the other trace was also seen to approach its fixed blip. When all blips were aligned the aircraft was about 200-400 yards from the end of the runway and the pilot could go in to land the Mosquito. On many occasion we landed by this method coming down to just under 100 feet in 'nil' visibility below which altitude the flight would be aborted and the aircraft diverted. This method was developed by 1409 but Group expressed concern that, while the meteorological report was of paramount importance for the next Bomber Command operation, it was only to be used by the most experienced crews, the main anxiety being that if the attention of the ground-based blip controller, who was using a simple wheel device to maintain trace position, wandered the aircraft, its crew and the report could all be lost. However, we had no accident while I was on the unit (7.12.43-12.10.44) from 'Gee' co-ordinate drift nor from incorrectly calibrated altimeters which could also have been disastrous at the low approach levels used in very low cloud-base or fog conditions.'[57]

After having converted to the Mosquito at 1655 MTU at Marham, Flight Lieutenant Jack Richard 'Benny' Goodman DFC[58] and his navigator, Flying Officer A. J. L. 'Bill' Hickox (after 'Wild Bill Hickok' of American West fame) were posted in October 1943 to 139 Squadron at Wyton. 'Benny' Goodman had completed a tour of 37 operations and 1,300 hours on Wellingtons. 'The average time for a trip to the Ruhr was 2½ hours, while a run to Berlin took about 4½ hours. To carry out such sorties in a Wellington had taken something like 5½ hours

56 The other eight squadrons were equipped with Lancasters.
57 *The Mossie* No.28 May 2001.
58 Later Group Captain DFC* AFC AE.

and 8 hours respectively. For this reason alone, Mosquitoes were greatly to he preferred to Wellingtons - it is better to be shot at for a short time than for a long time!' Hickox had also completed a first tour on Wimpys, although he had been shot down and had to walk back through the desert.

Their first operational sortie in a Mosquito took place on 3 November 1943, the target being Cologne, as Benny Goodman recalls. 'Marking was to be done by 105 and 109 Squadrons, using 'Oboe'. Our bomb load was four 500lb HE bombs and the attack was to be an all-Mosquito affair. Out first operational take-off in DK313 was only marginally longer than out take offs from Marham in Mosquitoes without bombs. The acceleration was rapid and in next to no time we were at the unstick speed of around 100 knots and climbing smoothly away. We climbed rapidly to 28,000 feet, levelled out and settled down to an economical cruising speed of around 250 knots (true airspeed). As we neared Cologne the first of the 'Oboe'-aimed target indicators began to cascade down ahead of us. Bill took his place at the bombing panel and began the time honoured verbal directions: Left, left, Steady...' and ultimately, Bombs gone.' We then turned for home, more bacon and eggs and bed. The post-flight interrogation was much the same as on any operational squadron in Bomber Command, with one important exception. 139's full title was 139 (Jamaica) Squadron and we were all offered a tot of rum on return from every operational sortie - the rum being provided by the good people of Jamaica. When I was on 139 we had with us a Jamaican named Ulric Cross, a flight lieutenant navigator, highly efficient and well liked. Later he became Lord Chief Justice of Jamaica.

'The best 'Oboe' crews could place a bomb within a few yards of the aiming point from 28,000 feet. However, since they had to fly straight and level for several minutes in the final run to the target they were vulnerable to flak and fighters. Moreover, they could only approach a given target from two directions - in the ease of Ruhr targets, almost due north or south - the Germans quickly realized this and set up searchlight cones over the aiming point which they plastered with heavy flak. Another little trick was to position Ju 88s near the searchlight cones, at a higher level than the Mosquitoes. Thus, when coned, a Mosquito might first he blasted with heavy flak and then the barrage could suddenly cease. If the pilot wasn't in a position to react instantly, the next happening would he a highly unpleasant squirt of cannon fire from the night-fighter. The average time for a trip to the Ruhr was 2½ hours, while a run to Berlin took about 4½ hours. To carry out such sorties in a Wellington had taken something like 5½ hours and 8 hours respectively. For this reason alone, Mosquitoes were greatly to he preferred to Wellingtons - it is better to be shot at for a short time than for a long time!'

In the early months of 1943 Dick Strachan, having completed one tour on Stirlings, had pulled several strings to help him on the way towards becoming a Mosquito navigator for a second tour of operations. 'The Mosquito was already legendary, even at that early stage in its lifetime and I was very happy when my efforts were crowned with success. On 1 October I crewed up with a flying officer pilot. My new pilot was, at the age of 19, one of the youngest pilots ever to complete a tour on Hampdens, but wore the ribbon of a DFM. After about five weeks of crew training, we were posted to 105 Squadron at Marham. Came the evening of 11 November ... Düsseldorf ... 28,000 feet ... four 500lb MC (medium capacity) bombs. The tension and excitement of a first operation ... the power and thrill of take-off with a full-bomb load...a steady climb to operational height on the English coastline...the rush and panic to find two wind checks in 15 minutes ... and the even worse panic applying those winds to the two remaining legs of the flight plan in the next six or eight minutes. On the run-up to the attack leg ... switch on 'Oboe' receiver... listen for the Morse call signal ... DIT-DA ... DA ... DA-DIT DA ... switch on our transmitter...within seconds a succession of dots . . . thank goodness, we've not overshot the beam.

'On the attack run the flak started about four or five minutes before target and immediately it was apparent that it was intense and extremely accurate. 'Oboe' entailed the pilot flying dead straight and level for 10 minutes on the attack run. Suddenly a tremendous flash lit up the sky about 50 yards ahead of our nose and exactly at our altitude. Within a tenth of a second we were through the cloud of dirty yellowish-brown smoke and into the blackness beyond. I shall never forget the spontaneous reaction of both my pilot and myself. We turned our heads slowly and looked long and deep into one another's eyes - no word was spoken - no words were needed. Despite continued heavy flak we completed our attack run and dropped our bomb load on the release signal, within a quarter of a mile of the aiming point and with luck, some damage to an important German factory.

'Turning for home and mighty glad to be out of the flak, I glanced out of the window at the starboard engine and immediately noticed a shower of sparks coming from the engine cowling. A quick glance at the oil temperature gauge showed that it was going off the clock. Only one thing for it and the pilot pressed the fire extinguisher button and then feathered the engine. The sparking ceased but we now had 300 miles to go and only one engine to do it on. I remember thinking that this wasn't much of a do for our first operation, but at least we had a good deal of altitude and still had a fair amount of speed, even with just one engine. The main danger was interception by a German night fighter and I spent a lot of time craning my neck around to check the skies about our tail. The other thing I remember was a terrible consciousness of my own weight, sitting as I was on the starboard side. However, this feeling wore off and the remainder of the flight home to base was uneventful. Then came the strain of a night landing on one engine... again that awful awareness of how heavy I was... but after one anti-clockwise circuit, a superb approach and a magnificent landing. I recall the great feeling of relief as soon as the wheels touched the runway. I also remember the urgent desire to get my hands round a jug of beer to relieve the dryness in my throat and to celebrate a safe return from what was to prove my worst experience on Mosquitoes. Needless to say, the beer was not long in forthcoming...'

In Germany a new night-fighter, the He 219A-0 *Uhu* ('Owl'), might have turned the tide for the German night fighter force had it been introduced in quantity. On the night of 12/13 December 1943 when the Krupp Works at Essen was the target and I./NJG1 claimed four aircraft destroyed, one of them was a 105 Squadron Mosquito flown by Flying Officer Benjamin Frank Reynolds and Flying Officer John Douglas Phillips. They were shot down and killed by Hauptmann Manfred Meurer flying a *Uhu*.

On 24 November meanwhile, 627 Squadron was formed by the simple expedient of posting 'C' Flight on 139 Squadron from Wyton to Oakington near Cambridge that day and giving them a new squadron number-plate, as Benny Goodman recalls.'Whenever a new squadron was formed in Bomber Command it was a standing requirement that the new unit should be on the Battle Order as quickly as possible and thus 627 was briefed for operations that same night. Four crews stood by but in the event only one took off, DZ615 (a Mk.IV), piloted by myself with 'Bill' Hickox as navigator. The target was Berlin and the sortie proved to be uneventful. Only when we returned to base did we learn that DZ615 had been the only Bomber Command aircraft out that night.

'During the winter of 1943-44 'Bill' and I took part in many sorties on 627 Squadron as part of the LNSF in 8 (PFF) Group. However, the role of the squadron was changed in the spring of 1944 as a result of events which were taking place in 5 Group, which occupied the chain of airfields in Lincolnshire. All squadrons tried to attack targets accurately and some were better at this than others. 5 Group achieved striking results in precision attacks, of which the most memorable was the Dams raid in early 1943, carried out by 617 Squadron. When Wing Commander Leonard Cheshire took command of 617 Squadron he brought precision bombing to a new high level of achievement by destroying small but important targets such as factories, finding and marking them at night in Lancasters. He soon realised that the marking problem would be eased if a more manoeuvrable aircraft were used and permission was obtained to 'borrow' two Mosquitoes from 8 Group and to attempt marking with them. It was found that great accuracy could be achieved if the Mosquito dived on the target from about 2,000 feet at about 30 degrees and the pilot dropped the marker while the aircraft was pointing at the target i.e. no bombsight was employed. This proved to be a turning point, or a major jump, in the technique of marking targets and it must not be forgotten that the 'architect' was Leonard Cheshire.

'Air Vice Marshal Cochrane the Air Officer Commanding of 5 Group was quick to appreciate that if one Mosquito could mark a target for a squadron, then a squadron of these aircraft should be able to mark targets for his whole Group. After negotiations at high level it was decided that 627 Squadron should be moved from Oakington to Woodhall Spa where 617 was located. The squadron deployed to Woodhall on 13 April 1944 and was officially 'detached' from 8 Group, as were 83 and 97 Lancaster squadrons which were to become the flare-dropping force whose job would be to identify and illuminate targets by H_2S radar and to lay a carpet of flares, under which the Mosquitoes would seek and mark the targets visually. Both 83 and 97 Squadrons deployed from their 8 Group bases to Coningsby, next door to Woodhall Spa.

'After 627 had landed at Woodhall each crew was welcomed personally by the AOC. We knew then that we were in for something unusual - and probably bloody dangerous! The next thing that happened was a briefing at Coningsby, at which the method of marking targets at low level was explained. We then returned to Woodhall and for ten days practised dive-bombing at the Wainfleet range in the Wash. It was not long before we discovered, as Cheshire had said, that the Mosquito was 'just the job' for this technique and we all achieved very good results - often popping the practice bombs right alongside the target. Our 'Freshman' trip took place on 20 April, when we flew to La Chapelle railway yards, with 617 leading the way and showing us how the job was done. We then went to Brunswick, Munich (the trip that put the seal of approval on Leonard Cheshire's VC) [59] and on 26 April to Schweinfurt. Munich was very lively and a relatively very long trip - over five hours - while Schweinfurt was not one of the better trips; we had one hell of a job to find the place owing to the murk. For these trips 617 led the way and we acted as 'backers up', concentrating our markers on top of those dropped by the experts. I should, however, explain a function performed by the Flare

---

59   While no award of the Victoria Cross was ever made for a Mosquito sortie, Cheshire's contribution to the success of the Munich operation on 24/25 April, when he led four Mosquitoes of the Marking Force in 5 Group, was mentioned in his VC citation on 8 September 1944. Squadron Leader Robert A. M. Palmer DFC* a Mosquito pilot on 109 Squadron was awarded a posthumous VC for his leadership in an 'Oboe'-equipped Lancaster borrowed from 582 Squadron on 23 December 1944. Palmer, who was 24 years old and had been promoted to squadron leader at age 23, had completed 110 sorties at this time having been on bombing operations since January 1941. Squadron Leader Palmer's aircraft came under intense AA fire, smoke billowed from the aircraft and a German fighter then attacked them but he carried on and completed his bombing run. The Lancaster then went over on the port side and went down.

Force on behalf of the Mosquito markers. The point is that the Mosquitoes had only 'Gee' as a navigational aid and this was jammed by the Germans as soon as Bomber Command took off. The result was that Mosquito navigators could use Gee only as far as the Dutch coast or a short distance into France. We would therefore navigate by dead reckoning (DR) to a point about 10 miles short of the target, where the Flare Force Lancasters would lay a couple of yellow target indicators (TIs). We would fly to these indicators and set course from them to the target; a system which worked very well. However, by the beginning of May we were ready to mark targets for 5 Group, leaving 617 to carry out its 'special' tasks as laid down by higher authority.

'Our first 'solo' took place on 1 May with four Mosquitoes of 627 and the Lancaster Flare Force visiting the Usine Lictard Works at Tours. This was during the time when the Americans were doing high-level 'precision' daylight bombing in their B-17 and B-24 aircraft, using the Norden bombsight. Their contention was that they could drop a pickle into a barrel from 30,000 feet with this bombsight and they called it 'pickle-barrel bombing'. Well, the Usine Lictard Works had been attacked in this way several days before we went there and it was evident from the photos taken afterwards that the 'pickles' had jumped out of the 'barrel' - the works were virtually intact, but there were many holes in the surrounding fields.

'All that day we studied maps and photographs of the area around Tours in which the works lay. Thus, when the flares ignited above the target, we were quickly there searching for the target itself. The technique required that the first marker pilot to find the target was to call 'Tally-Ho' on his VHF radio and the other marker aircraft would then move a short distance away in order to give him elbow-room. On this occasion I was the one to see the target first and I called, 'Pen-nib 37, Tally-Ho', easing around the factory and into a position from which I could carry out a shallow dive on to the centre of the target. It worked like a charm and within a few seconds red spot fires had been dropped on the glass roof of the machine shop. Unfortunately, however, the markers disappeared inside the shop and could only be seen from directly above. This was an important lesson for us all, namely that the object of our efforts was not to drop our marker bombs on the target, but near it in a position where the red blob could be clearly seen by the main force trundling behind. On this occasion Marker Leader flew over the top and directed another Mosquito to drop his markers in the yard alongside the machine shop. This was done and the remaining aircraft backed up the blob and made a splendid, concentrated red ring of fire at which the Lancaster bombing force would aim the loads. The works was destroyed.

'It will be realised that a limitation of marking in this way is that a well-aimed stick of bombs from an early Lancaster might easily scatter the red fire blob, or at least obscure it by smoke. One method of overcoming this problem was by the use of delayed action fuses and detonators in the bombs, only one bomb in each stick being fused to burst on impact in order to give the Controller ('Master Bomber') an indication of the way in which the attack was proceeding. Many highly effective attacks were made against small targets using this refinement.

'Following the notorious Mailly-le-Camp attack, 5 Group concentrated its efforts against targets such as railway yards, the bridges over the rivers Loire and Seine and along the Channel coast and finally - in the last days before D-Day (6 June) - against the heavy anti-invasion guns along the coastline. Most of these were copybook attacks, with the marker bombs going down on time and with the heavy supporting bombers dropping their loads in exactly the right place. The experienced marker pilots on 627 Squadron were by then able to dart in beneath the flares dropped for them by 83 and 97 Squadrons, then to circle and find the aiming point within a couple of minutes and most important of all, to make accurate shallow dives and drop their spot fires within a very few yards of that point. It's doubtful if any marker pilot could say exactly how he did it; marking a target was largely a matter of practice. In other words the experienced pilot 'automatically' positioned his Mosquito in the precise spot from which to make his dive on to the target, dived at the correct angle by placing the aiming point in the right position on his windscreen, released the spot fire by means of a push-button on his control column and kept the Mosquito in the dive for another two or three seconds to ensure the bombs fell in the desired trajectory. It is on record that marking errors by Mosquitoes prior to D-Day were as low as 50 yards, while none - even on the most heavily defended targets, including Brunswick, Munich and Schweinfurt - was greater than 300 yards.'

By early 1944 suitably modified B.IV Mosquitoes were capable, just, of carrying a 4,000lb 'Blockbuster', although they did not prove entirely suitable. It was a tight squeeze in the bomb bay. To accommodate this large piece of ordnance the bomb bay had been strengthened and the bomb doors were redesigned. The B.XVI with its bulged bomb bay and more powerful two-stage 1,680hp Merlin 72/76s or two 1,710-hp Merlin 73/77s, giving a top speed of 419 mph at 28,500 feet, first flew operationally on 1/2 January 1944 when 38 Mosquitoes attacked Hamburg, Witten, Duisburg, Bristillerie and Cologne. On the night of 1/2 February 139 used H_2S for the first time, marking the target for a raid by twelve Mosquitoes on Berlin. At this time, 139 Squadron, which had pioneered the use of Canadian-built Mosquitoes, was operating a mix of B.IV, IX, XVI and XXs. A B.XVI (DZ647/B) flown by Squadron Leader Stevie Watts DFC and Flight Lieutenant Cyril Hassall on 692 Squadron was the first Mosquito to drop a 'Blockbuster' operationally, on Düsseldorf on the night of 23/24 February. There was moderate accurate flak and the searchlights were active but Hassall got the 'cookie' away at 20.45½ hours on red markers dropped by 105 Squadron.[60] Hassall went on to complete 102 ops, 67 of them on Mosquitoes. Watts was promoted CO of the Squadron but was killed on operations on 11 July 1944.

During May-June Bomber Command was, apart from three major raids against German cities towards the end of May, fully committed to destroying the Wehrmacht's infrastructure in France and bomber losses were relatively light. One exception, however, was on 3/4 May when 346 Lancaster crews, two 'Oboe' equipped Mosquitoes and four Pathfinder Mosquitoes on 617 Squadron (one flown by Wing Commander Leonard Cheshire, the 'Marker Leader') were briefed for that night's operation. 617 Squadron were the experts in marking confined and difficult targets that could not be accurately located by purely radar aids.[61] There was the usual *anticipation* of the string drawing out the route to the target. It was a short string. Everyone gave a sigh of relief as French targets were supposed to be easy. Then the Intelligence Officer introduced the reality, Mailly-le-Camp, a pre-war French Army tank depot near Epernay, about 50 miles south of Rheims. Crews were told that it was a Panzer depot and training centre

---

60 One minute later Flight Lieutenant Val S. Moore and Flying Officer P. F. Dillon in DZ534/M dropped their 4,000lb bomb while coned by searchlights and Flight Lieutenant McKeard in DZ637/C also dropped a 4,000lb bomb on the target. The next night all three aircraft went to Kiel and bombed on TIs dropped by 139 Squadron.

61 5 Group was the first wave of 163 Lancasters and was to attack the Southeast part of the camp while 153 bombers of 1 Group made up the second wave. Their target was the northwest section of the camp. Thirty aircraft were to concentrate on an area near the workshops. Five Special Duties Lancasters on 192 Squadron at Binbrook and six Mosquitoes and three ECM Halifaxes of 100 Group also took part.

reported to house up to 10,000 Wehrmacht troops. [62]

British Intelligence had received word that the Panzer Division was due to move out the next day so it had to be attacked that night. The penny dropped. It was just another raid but this one really mattered. Crews were briefed to 'get the target' because there were French people all around it.'

'Benny' Goodman and 'Bill' Hickox on 627 Squadron flew on the Mailly Le Camp operation, as Goodman recalled: 'The attack was supported by eight Mosquitoes on 627 Squadron. The idea was that while the markers on 617 looked for and marked the target, the 627 Mossies would dive-bomb anti-aircraft guns in the target area. It was thought that the presence of 'dive-bombers' would at least keep the gunners' heads down and that there might even be the bonus of a few gunners' heads blown off. The target was marked accurately but a delay in relaying information from the Master Bomber to the Main Force occurred. This resulted in the heavies being ordered to orbit north of the target for several minutes in conditions of bright moonlight; a factor which was promptly exploited by the German night fighters. Forty-two of the heavies were lost and the raid has been described as a disaster and a success. If the criterion used to determine success or failure is aircraft and crews lost then by no stretch of the imagination can a loss rate of 12½% be termed a success. If, however, an attempt is made to balance the bomber losses against the German loss of an important depot - it was 80% destroyed - together with heavy casualties among trained personnel, particularly senior NCOs and tanks and other vehicles - and all this with the invasion of Europe only weeks away - then the position becomes very different. Who can say what might have happened if the panzers of Mailly had been able to reach the landing beaches on 5/6 June? That they did not can only be described as a triumph for the Allies.

'To narrow the canvas and relate what happened to just one Mosquito during this important attack will at least give some idea of what could take place on a 5 Group operation. Leonard Cheshire led the four Mosquito markers and 'Bill' Hickox and I were in G-George (DZ484) on 627 Squadron, one of the eight supporting 'dive-bombers'. So far as we were concerned the approach to the target was uneventful. Just before midnight the Flare Force laid yellow TIs 15 miles north of Mailly and all the Mosquitoes headed for these and set course from them to the target. At 0001 hours, when all good troops should be in barracks, the Flare Force dropped the customary cloud of hooded flares over Mailly and Cheshire and his men began to search for the depot. At the same time the 'dive-bombers' found gun targets and dived on them from 1,500 feet to 500 feet releasing one 500lb bomb per dive. As the eight Mossies each carried four bombs, it will be appreciated that the gunners were at least distracted for a while.

'Meanwhile, at 5,000 feet, the heavies were fighting a deadly battle with German night fighters north of - and later, over - the target. The unfolding engagement could be seen clearly from G-George, in our worm's-eye view position, for at relatively short intervals flames would be seen above and a heavy bomber would begin its death plunge. Sometimes the burning heavy would dive straight towards us and we became exceedingly watchful in case it should crash nearby - with disastrous consequences to ourselves. Our dive-bombing of the guns was therefore interspersed with short dashes away from the trajectory of burning heavies. The raid eventually got into gear and

62   Mailly actually accommodated a Panzer regiment HQ, 3 Panzer battalions belonging to regiments on the Eastern Front and elements of two more as well as the permanent training school staff.

bombs began to crash down on the tank depot. When the 'dive-bombers' had finished their task they were ordered to return to base and by about 0020 hours G-George was on the way home. Since it was manifestly unwise to climb in the target area I stayed at low level and we set course for the French coast. We settled down at about 1,000 feet with a cruising speed of 250 mph and for a time all went well.

'The first hint of trouble came when a searchlight shone directly into our cockpit and at the same time a murderous barrage of light flak opened up from below. More lights came on and we were coned. I turned George hard to port and dived to about 300 feet above the earth, with 'Bill' Hickox exhorting me to 'watch the instruments'. We were in the unenviable position of a fly jinking close to a moving flypaper in the dark, with an irate householder swatting vigorously as it at the same time - a situation where there is no margin for error. We were literally just above the trees, with the searchlight operators shining their lights along the ground at us from all sides, while the flak gunners hosed their wares at us along the beams. Not for the first time 'Bill' and I saw streams of flak - red, blue, white and all very pretty - coming towards us; slowly at first but ever-increasing in speed until the individual missiles hurtled overhead and disappeared, to be exploded by their proximity fuses. Sometimes there was a pop or a bang, but G-George kept going.

'This game of cat and mouse continued for many minutes - it seemed like a lifetime. I would turn hard in one direction by about 30 degrees, level out on the new heading for a few seconds, then turn hard in the opposite direction by the same amount and fly level on that heading for a brief time. Lest anyone should observe that this was a more-or-less set pattern and a recipe for disaster, I would remind him that we were very close to the ground and covering it at high speed; therefore a fleeting target for any particular gunner or searchlight operator. The Germans' best chance of getting us lay in shining the maximum number of searchlights on us in the hope that a mistake would be made and control of the aircraft lost; this they did with great gusto. By the greatest good fortune we were not hit, but I do not recall ever being held in searchlights and under fire for so long and at such low level.

'The end of our ordeal came suddenly when we skipped over the summit of a low hill and there ahead of us lay the sea. I hugged the ground below the crest and 'Bill' Hickox and I were treated to a spectacle which we remember vividly to this day. The searchlights were shining through the trees and above our heads. With the coastline ahead and the lights paradoxically providing some degree of assistance, we now roared along an inlet and past a lighthouse, thence to the open sea and home. The lighthouse proved to be on the coast of Le Treport. I've since visited it, on the ground. It is quite small and as we were below the level of the light on 4 May we must have given the occupants of this some-time aid to navigation a very nasty turn indeed - tit for tat ...'

It had been while crossing the English Channel that Flight Lieutenant Tom Bennett, navigator on the 617 Squadron Mosquito flown by Flight Lieutenant Gerry Fawke that he realized how bright the moonlight was. An advantage of being in the second wave was that they could see the 'party' starting well ahead of them and the final run in could be made by visually steering towards the action. To Bennett the raid had seemed at first to be 'progressing favourably' and everything had appeared to be 'as normal as one would expect on a raid of this size'. However, he was shocked when he saw that the Yellow route markers placed north of the camp at Germinon to mark the datum point were visible from 'a long way off. If they could see them from that distance 'so could the Germans'. They were shocked again when bombs began falling as they tried to mark for the second wave. No one appreciated the chaotic conditions that were developing above.[63] For the first and only time they heard another voice across the ether. 'Well get a move on, mate,' said a calm but firm Australian voice. 'It's getting a bit hot up here.' This was the first indication they had that everything was not going according to plan. Satisfied with a job well done the Mosquito crew readily obeyed their order to 'cut and run' and Bennett set course for the return route. They had seen no aircraft shot down until they were on the first leg away from the target. Then they saw the first 'ghastly' sight of a Lancaster hitting the ground and exploding in flames. 'The fireball illuminated the pall of oily smoke that was always part of such a macabre scene. To our mounting horror and concern, that was not the only casualty. Again and yet again, the tragedy was repeated. I tried to convince myself that it was German night fighters that were being shot down but the funeral pyres were too large for that. When a fifth bomber was cremated beneath us Gerry said, 'Not a healthy area for a twin engined aircraft, Ben, let's find another way home.' It was pandemonium in the air Lancasters were jinxing in the sky trying to escape from the Messerschmitts and Junkers. Our gunners were aiming at the enemy but they could only hold the fighters in their sights for a few seconds before they had flown on. We didn't waste time. We were as likely to be shot down by one of our planes. The Mosquito could have been mistaken for a German night fighter. I gave Gerry a rough course for the nearest safe part of the coast and then busied myself in the niceties of tidying up to ensure that we crossed the coast at a reasonably safe spot. I could not exorcise from my mind the glimpse of hell we had seen or the thought of the crews that had been flying the planes that had crashed…Our worst fears were confirmed later that day - 42 Lancasters missing; fourteen from 5 Group and 28 from 1 Group. My first reaction was that 5 Group had stirred the hornet's nest and 1 Group had taken the stings.' [64]

On 11/12 May 429 bombers of the Main Force made attacks on Bourg-Leopold, Hasselt and Louvain in Belgium. The target for 190 Lancasters and eight Mosquitoes of 5 Group was a former Belgian Gendarmerie barracks at Leopoldsburg (Flemish)/Bourg-Leopold (French), which was being used to accommodate 10,000 SS Panzer troops who awaited the Allied invasion forces. The weather was bad with low cloud and poor visibility and a serious error was made with the broadcast winds. As a result, the aircraft were late over the target area and consequently flare-dropping was scattered and provided no adequate illumination. An 'Oboe' Mosquito flown by Flight Lieutenants John Burt and Ronald Curtis on 109 Squadron dropped a yellow marker. The Mosquito marking force on 627 Squadron arrived late over the target with the result that the 'Oboe' proximity marker was seen by only one of the marking aircraft and the proximity marker, unfortunately, seemed to burn out very quickly. Flare dropping was scattered and did not provide adequate illumination of the target. Haze and up to 3/10ths cloud conditions hampered the marking of the target. The 'Marking Leader' then asked the 'Master Bomber' if he could drop 'Red Spot Fires' as a guide for the flare force. The Master Bomber agreed and 'RSFs' went down at 0024 hours in the estimated vicinity of the target. Unfortunately, the 'Main Force' started to bomb this red spot fire immediately it went down and half of the main force bombed this. The result of this was the five Mosquitoes on 627 Squadron returned to Woodhall Spa with their bombs and were unable to mark the target. Immediately the 'Master Bomber' ordered 'Stop Bombing', as he realized it was impossible to identify the target but VHF was very poor, particularly on Channel 'B' and the Germans had jammed Channel 'A'. Only half the main force received

---

63   Flight Lieutenant Terry Kearns flew the fourth 617 Squadron Mosquito.
64   Squadron Leader Tom Bennett DFM writing in *Not Just Another Milk Run; The Mailly-le-Camp Bomber Raid* by Molly Burkett & Geoff Gilbert (Barny Books 2004).

the 'Cease Bombing' instruction and 94 Lancasters bombed the target. At 0034 hours a wireless message, 'Return to base' was sent out to all crews.

5 Group was now used exclusively in support of the bombing campaign against interdiction targets for Operation Overlord. 'On a purely personal note' continues 'Benny' Goodman, 'I happened to be a marker for the 5 Group attack on Brunswick on 22 May. On this occasion the AOC decided to employ the principle of offset marking; the idea being to place markers upwind of the target in such a position that they could be seen clearly by Main Force crews throughout the attack and yet could not be blown up by the bombing. The aiming point selected was a park north of the town and when we arrived - under the usual carpet of flares - we had no difficulty in identifying the park and stoking up a good bonfire in it for the heavies. Moreover, praises be, there was no flak interference. We then sculled around the park, awaiting instructions to either build up the fire of go home. We were eventually told to return to base and from our viewpoint the raid had been a gift. Not so for the heavies, however, who had difficulty in passing radio messages. The drill was that a proportion of the Flare Force would find the wind on the last leg to the target and pass results to the Flare Force leader. He in turn would calculate the mean wind, pass this to the Master Bomber, who would then work out the wind to be set on bombsights of the Main Force in order to ensure that bombs aimed at the marker flares - our park bonfire - would undershoot and hit the target. The trip was not an outstanding success due to the difficulty in getting this false wind broadcast to the Main Force; a communications problem which arose because the W/T system then in use was not sufficiently good. This problem was later overcome by the introduction of VHF radio in heavies - we in Mosquitoes had had this aid all the time and splendid it was. Thereafter 5 Group attacks improved in accuracy, with the important spin-off that morale on the heavy squadrons improved too. This offset marking technique became a standard 5 Group practice and proved to be enormously effective.

'All depended however, on accurate placing of a small number of red spot fires, which in turn depended on Mosquito pilots being able to see their target. To illustrate this point, on 28 May our target was the heavy German gun at St Martin de Varreville, just behind what was to be one of the American landing beaches - Utah - on 6 June. These heavy guns were almost invariably defended by light flak and a barrage of the latter would of course betray the gun position. However, on the night in question the German commander held his light AA in check, causing us problems with the target-marking. Although it was a clear night and the Flare Force had done their job impeccably, we found on crossing the coast that the terrain was uniform, the road running parallel to the sea, while inland there was the usual patchwork of fields with occasional tree-clumps. The gun itself was well camouflaged and we could not find it. We had begun searching at Zero-minus five minutes, but at Zero hour we still hadn't found it. The Main Force arrived but was instructed to orbit - was this to be another Mailly Le Camp? Finally, one of the marker pilots noticed a large 'empty' space with tracks leading to it and reasoned that space like that could not be as blank as it appeared. So the target was marked and the gun destroyed by 100 Lancasters, each carrying armour-piercing bombs. No aircraft was lost on this operation, though I might add that as I laid my spot fires on top of the gun a light-fingered gentleman in a Lancaster above decided to drop his load. The stick fell short but 'Bill' Hickox and I heard the crump-crump of bombs coming up behind us - we were not amused! This attack merely emphasised just how the best-laid schemes of men 'oft gang agley'...

'A regular feature of the 'new look' operations was that 'wash-ups' were held at Coningsby to assess the methods used and results achieved. These prayer-meetings were useful because they brought the markers and the Flare Force together. At times the meetings became a bit terse when something had gone wrong and at other times they were hilarious - as when my good friend Flying Officer 'Googie' Platts was accused by the Base Commander (Air Commodore 'Bobby' Sharpe) of marking the right aiming point in the wrong marshalling yard! George Platts could not be termed lucky. After this wrong marshalling yard incident, his run of bad luck continued, as when he took part in an operation against the Phillips Works at Eindhoven, Holland. Searching for the target, flying in and out of cloud, a searchlight suddenly shone directly into his face. Startled, he pulled back on the control column and the Mosquito immediately roared up and over on to its back. 'Googie' now found the searchlight apparently above his head so, in his own words, 'I half-rolled out and came home'. He was not so lucky on 29 June when taking part in a daylight marking sortie against a V-1 weapons' site at Beauvoir. Having completed the marking of the target he set course for home in stepped-down formation with another Mosquito behind and below him. After a short distance a V-1 'doodlebug' was launched from a ramp behind them and accelerated towards London, only to have its motor fail when below the Mosquitoes. It crashed and exploded right underneath them. The lower Mossie[65] was destroyed, while Platts experienced complete engines' failure. Despite all his efforts the twin Merlins remained silent and he was obliged to land with wheels up and no power. Hitting the ground hard, he broke a leg in the crash landing. However, his navigator was unhurt and after a brief council of war, they agreed that the nav' [Flying Officer G. G. Thompson RCAF] should make a run for it. This he did but in his haste to get home he fell down a well! There he stayed while a typically thorough Teutonic search failed to find him. At night he identified himself to a French farmer and they devised a scheme whereby the navigator would stay down the well by day and come up for sustenance by night. [Thompson joined the Maquis and was liberated later on arrival of the British forces]. 'Googie' Platts was not so fortunate; he was taken to Germany and spent the rest of the war in Stalag Luft III.'

An 8 Group weather report by Pilot Officer Joe Patient and Pilot Officer Norry Gilroy, a 1409 Met Flight crew, delayed the Normandy invasion by one day and D-Day finally went ahead on 6 June. 'After the D-Day landings had taken place and 627's hectic spell in the Transportation Plan was over' continues Benny Goodman 'it was time to send some of the senior crews on rest. Thus our popular CO - Wing Commander Roy Elliott - and one of the Flight commanders, 'Rocky' Nelles, both of whom had been with the squadron since its formation, were posted. In July a number of other crews found themselves on the way to other units - including 'Bill' Hickox and me. 'Bill' and I went back to 8 Group, to 1655 Mosquito TU, later 16 OTU at Warboys, near Huntingdon.[66]

'I feel I ought to add a little about 627 and the two Lancaster Path Finder squadrons 83 and 97. All had been 'attached' to 5 Group from 8 Group in April 1944 and stayed with 5 Group until the war ended. Naturally, everyone had a fierce loyalty to 8 Group at the time of the move and there was a certain amount of resentment at being shipped off to another Group. Nevertheless, it is also true that we quickly saw what a war-winner the low-marking technique was and we developed a loyalty to 5 Group. Perhaps in reality our loyalties were

65 DZ516/'O' flown by Flying Officer James A. Saint-Smith DFM RAAF and Flying Officer Geoffrey E. Heath DFM RAAF who were both killed. Both men were awarded the DFC on 15 August 1944.
66 He went to the Navigation Section, while 'Benny' Goodman was sent to the Mosquito Dual Flight. He stayed with this unit - from July 1944 until April 1947, as pilot instructor, Flight commander and eventually Chief Instructor.

The de Havilland factory at Hatfield in 1943. (MoI)

A young woman hand-paints the roundel on the side of a Mosquito at Hatfield in 1943. (MoI)

Above: Mosquito HJ728 is prepared for a test flight from Hatfield in 1943.

Right: John de Havilland checks through some details with fitters at Hatfield after a test flight in a Mosquito. During a test flight of a de Havilland Mosquito Mark VI, flying with flight test observer John H. F. Scrope, on 23 August 1943 he collided in the vicinity of St Albans with another Mosquito Mark VI flown by pilot George Gibbins, killing all four occupants. G.F. Carter was flying as an observer in Gibbins's aircraft.

De Havilland's employed a large number of women in the production of the Mosquito - here Mrs Judd prepares a strip of wood to be fitted inside the fuselage of an aircraft hull under construction (all MoI)

Two views taken on Malta showing the Commander of 23 Squadron, Royal Air Force, Wing Commander John B Selby, DSO, DFC, and his observer looking at their Mosquito II `P-Peter' while other members of the squadron watch from atop the blast wall at the Dispersal Point. The four 20mm cannon are corked to prevent dirt damaging them.

Above: B.XVI
MM364 at Mount
Farm, Oxfordshire
on being handed
over to the USAAF.

Right: PR.XVI
MM345 in the
653rd Bomb
Squadron, 25th
Bomb Group
USAAF.

B.IV DZ313 which was lost with Flight Sergeant Laurence Deeth and Warrant Officer Frank Hicks on 105 Squadron on 20 October 1942 on a raid on Hannover.

B.IV DZ476 XD-S for Scottie (note the dog) of 139 Squadron normally flown by Flying Officer G S W Rennie RCAF and Pilot Officer W Embry RCAF. This pair flew DZ476 as one of the 'shallow diver' crews on raids to the railway engine sheds at Aulnoye on 4 March 1943, to the John Cockerill Steel and Armament Works at Liège on 12 March and to the engine sheds at Paderborn four days later. In April 1943 Rennie and Embry were one of eleven crews posted from Marham to Skitten to form 'A' Flight within the newly created 618 Squadron. They finished their tour and returned to Canada on 8 August 1944. DZ476 remained with 139 Squadron until on 1 April 1944 this Mosquito swung in a crosswind and suffered undercarriage collapse at Upwood.

139 Squadron at Marham. Wing Commander Peter Shand DSO DFC in white jacket stands before XD-G DZ421. Shand and his navigator Pilot Officer Christopher Handley DFM were shot down and killed over the Ijsselmeer on the night of 20/21 April 1943 by Oberleutnant Lothar Linke, Staffelkapitan 12./NJG1.

Flying Officer Neil Munro.
Wing Commander Hughie Idwal Edwards VC, DFC (RAFM)

Opposite page: Five B.IVs of 139 Squadron in echelon rear formation. Nearest aircraft is XD-G DZ421 flown by the CO, Wing Commander Peter Shand DSO DFC. Next is DZ407/R, which joined 139 Squadron from 105 Squadron on 22 December 1942 and which failed to return from the raid on Burmeister and Wain on 27 January 1943 when Sgt Richard Clare and Flying Officer Edward Doyle hit a balloon cable and tree at East Dereham after the starboard engine failed.

B.IV DK338 was delivered to 105 Squadron in September 1942 and took part in many daylight raids over Occupied Europe. It was damaged beyond repair on 1 May 1943.

B.XVI ML963 'K-King' which served in 109, 692 and 571 Squadrons from March 1944 until it went MIA on 11 April 1945. (Charles E. Brown)

Mosquitoes of the Banff Strike Wing off on an anti shipping strike.

Ground crew attach rockets to the wing of FB.VI PZ438 on 143 Squadron of the Banff Strike Wing. (RAFM)

Banff Strike Wing Mosquito taxiing. (RAFM)

Group Captain the Hon. Max Aitken DSO DFC commanding the Banff Strike Wing. (RAFM)

PR.XVI Mosquitoes on 680 Squadron in Italy, 1944.

A B.XVI on 128 Squadron being inspected by visiting Russian general staff at Wyton on VE Day 1945. A Pathfinder demonstration was given, but only after the Soviet Embassy allowed one Russian general to fly in a Lancaster – provided that it was piloted by 'Don' Bennett. The other general and some of the six colonels flew in another Lancaster.

TR.33 TW256 of 771 Squadron, Fleet Air Arm at Lee-on-Solent in 1948. (RAFM)

BAe RR299 formates with Kermit Weeks' RS712 on September 29th 1987. Both were former 633 *Squadron* film stars and RR299 crashed on 21 July 1996 killing pilot Kevin Moorhouse and flight engineer, Steve Watson. (BAe via Darryl Cott)

evenly divided. The AOC would have noticed this and would undoubtedly have preferred crews from within 5 Group, or men who had completed an ops' tour in the Group. Anyway, the new CO and Flight commanders on 627 were all 5 Group men. The crews continued to be trained at 1655 MTU and as far as I'm aware there was never a comeback on this score.'

Although 627 Squadron was claimed by 5 Group as one of its own units, 627 stuck rigidly to its claim to remain part of 8 (PFF) group and proved the point by having a periodic visit by a Path Finder Examination Team who awarded the much coveted 'Path Finder Badge' to fully trained aircrew. 627 were mindful of the very important part 83 and 97 Lancaster Squadrons played in the visual marking operations. They illuminated the targets at night with hundreds of parachute flares to enable 627 Mosquito crews to locate the actual marking point and place their Target Indicators within yards of the intended spot. 'As for the actual techniques of low level visual marking' continues Alan Webb, who as a committed warrant officer on the ground kept the aircraft flying, 'the customary bombsight was put back into stores and a standard fighter gun button was attached to the right hand arm of the control column spectacle, connected to the bomb release selector system, transferring the actual release of TIs to the pilot, or to be precise to the right thumb of the pilot. At night the two Lancaster squadrons mentioned above had the task of illuminating the area selected and the Mosquitoes would then locate the precise aiming point, boiler house, hangar, signal box, bridge etc, dive from say 5,000 to 500 feet (sometimes to 50 feet) and at the precisely judged moment, established purely by continuous practice, release the TI. On many occasions an accuracy of 40-50 feet from the aiming point was achieved and in some instances, such accuracy could be a disadvantage with spot fires dropping through roofs of hangars, factory buildings and the like and obscuring the marker flames from the main force of heavies, necessitating the attention of a further marker Mosquito. On some of the Dortmund-Ems and Mittelland Canal operations the marking was so accurate that TIs actually dropped into the canal with obvious consequences - based on the damp squib principle.'

Flying Officer R. W. Griffiths had completed 17 operations as a Halifax navigator on 76 Squadron before he and his pilot, an experienced second tour type, were posted to training jobs but Griffiths found himself back on operations 'and on Mosquitoes at that' in October 1943 when he teamed up with Flying Officer Mike Gribbin as a crew. They arrived at 627 Squadron in December and they did their first operation on the 20th - to Frankfurt, which was, strangely, Griffiths' first destination on Halifaxes. He and Mike Gribbin flew a total of 44 operations together in the following seven months from Oakington and Woodhall Spa. One of their most eventful trips was to the marshalling yards and junction at Givors, which was the target for 178 Lancasters of 5 Group on the night of 26 July 1944. All nine of the Squadron's Mosquitoes experienced strange happenings due to the severe weather conditions of thick cloud, rain, hail, electric storm and heavy icing, which froze the air speed indicator pitot heads and affected generators, 'Gee', flying controls and worst of all, compasses which swung at intervals and generally settled on incorrect bearings.

'I don't think any of us actually found the target' continues Griffiths and 'N' DZ636 faired far worse than Mike Gribbin and I when it failed to return. Just as we crossed the south coast of England on the way out the bad weather closed in and as we crossed France at maximum altitude, in an endeavour to get above cloud, we were still in extremely turbulent conditions with frequent lightning. We circled what we thought was the target area awaiting a signal from the ground but this never came. If our instruments were out of order, as was later proved, we probably never actually arrived over the target area at all. When setting course for base we were under thick cloud and it was some considerable time before we gained clear skies where we noticed that the North Star 'was in the wrong place'. We were flying a completely incorrect course due to faulty compass bearing. Heading north using the North Star as a guide we saw flashes of light ahead, which turned out to be the Normandy fighting.'

Finally, almost out of fuel, Gribbin was forced to ditch after first jettisoning the bomb load in the sea. Griffiths did not recall much about the actual ditching as on impact with the water he was thrown forward hitting his head on the instrument panel which knocked him senseless. 'The next thing I remember was Mike shaking me and saying 'hurry up and get out onto the wing'. The dinghy had already inflated and we climbed into it. In fact there was no real urgency as the Mosquito floated for a considerable time. We had, I was told later, been the first crew to survive a night ditching by a bomber Mosquito. Having been in the dinghy only a short time we saw a small boat approaching from the German occupied coast and almost immediately a larger ship came up from the opposite direction. We visualised ourselves being in the middle of a battle over our rescue, but both boats were American, the US destroyer won hands down and landed us at Cherbourg, where we spent two or three days in the 12th Field Hospital while they patched up my nose, which had been nicely split right down the middle on the instrument panel. We hitch-hiked back to the UK in an Anson which had delivered drinks to the troops and we landed at Colerne. One of our Mossies came down and delivered us back to Woodhall where a much delayed de-briefing ensued.'

'As far as 627 were concerned' continues 'Benny' Goodman, 'the squadron continued to operate skilfully against all kinds of targets - marking on behalf of 5 Group and at times for 617 Squadron. The off-set marking technique reached a very high level of efficiency on 11 September 1944 when 218 Lancasters, led by four Mosquito markers, destroyed Darmstadt. The aiming point was a parade ground one mile west of the town centre and here a bonfire of red spot fires was lit. The clump of red markers was backed up with greens and the Master Bomber then called in the Main Force who attacked on no less than seven different headings and at varying times of release to give the maximum bombing spread. To summarise what I thought of 627 Squadron, two words will suffice - 'Just great'.'

The designated Master Bomber on the night of 19/20 September when the twin towns of Mönchengladbach/Rheydt were the targets for 227 Lancasters and ten Mosquitoes of 1 and 5 Groups was unavailable and Wing Commander Guy Gibson VC DSO* DFC* the famous Dam Busters leader and navigator Squadron Leader James Brown Warwick DFC took off from Woodhall Spa in a 627 Squadron Mosquito to act as Controller for the raid on Rheydt. They did not return. Barnes Wallis said of Gibson: 'For some men of great courage and adventure, inactivity was a slow death. Would a man like Gibson ever have adjusted back to peacetime life? One can imagine it would have been a somewhat empty existence after all he had been through. Facing death had become his drug. He had seen countless friends and comrades perish in the great crusade. Perhaps something in him even welcomed the inevitability he had always felt that before the war ended he would join them in their Bomber Command Valhalla. He had pushed his luck beyond all limits and he knew it. But that was the kind of man he was... a man of great courage, inspiration and leadership. A man born for war...but born to fall in war.'

Chapter 5

Light Night Striking Force

'The 8 Group crews had been encouraged to regard themselves as a corps d'elite' recalls Jack Currie, who before joining 1409 Met Flight had flown a first tour on Lancasters and had been to Berlin nine times. 'Most of them made an attempt to look the part. The wealth of smoothly-barbered hair, of neat moustaches, cool, clear eyes and well-pressed battle-dresses made a striking contrast with the more outré appearance of the main force men at Wickenby. There were no Stetson hats or cowboy boots at Wyton; nobody wore Irving coats or sweaters in the splendid Mess. For once, it was the officers of other trades - administrators, engineers and flying controllers - who seemed, comparatively, less sartorially aware. Of a chaplain and one of the doctors, down-at-heel and out-at-elbow, this was particularly true. Even among such image-conscious fliers, the Met Flight crews were noticeably elegant and couth.'[68]

'Nuisance' raiding had begun in April 1943 and was so successful that by the summer a Light Night Striking Force (LNSF) of Mosquitoes was established. Mosquitoes went in up to an hour before the main attack, descended slowly and released their Spoof cargoes of two 500lb bombs, two target indicators (TIs) or 'sky markers' (parachute flares to mark a spot in the sky if it was cloudy) and bundles of 'Window'. German fighter controllers immediately sent up their night fighters, so that when the 'heavies' did arrive, the Nachtjagdgeschwaders were back on the ground having to refuel. 139 Squadron first tried Spoof raiding on the night of 18 November 1943 when flares and bombs were dropped on Frankfurt. Various plain colours with starbursts of the same or a different colour prevented the enemy from copying them.

On 26 November three Mosquitoes on 139 Squadron, flying ahead of the Main Force, scattered 'Window' on the approaches to Berlin and returned to drop bombs.[69] On 26 November three Mosquitoes on 139 Squadron, flying ahead of the Main Force, scattered 'Window' on the approaches to Berlin and returned to drop bombs.

692 Squadron was formed at Graveley on 1 January 1944. In the 12 months

---

68 *Mosquito Victory* by Jack Currie (Goodall Publications 1983)

69 On 18/19 November 1943 'Bomber' Harris began his nightly offensive against Berlin. The raids, which were to last until the end of January 1944, brought added demands for bomb damage assessment (BDA). Flights over Germany were being made more difficult by enemy action, bad weather and factors such as smoke from still burning factories and houses - it took no less than 31 PR Spitfire and six PR Mosquito sorties before the results of the bombing of Berlin on 18/19 November were obtained. BDA became such an issue with both the RAF and USAAF bomber commands that PR aircraft were required to cover targets within hours of a raid being carried out - sometimes even before the returning bombers had landed.

January-December 1944 five more Mosquito squadrons joined 8 Group.[70] Bennett wanted only experienced pilots with 1,000 hours total time for his squadrons. Group Captain 'Hamish' Mahaddie DSO DFC AFC, SASO at Group HQ in Huntingdon, was tasked with recruiting volunteer aircrew from the Main Force bomber groups. Thomas Gilbert 'Hamish' Mahaddie, an incorrigible Scot from Leith, had started his RAF life as a non-commissioned metal rigger at the age of 17. In 1933 he was posted to RAF Hinaidi near Baghdad in Iraq. A year later he was accepted for aircrew training and earned his wings in Egypt, flying Avro 504Ns. Posted to 55 Squadron for two years, he bought a horse called 'Hamish' but his fellow aircrew claimed that there was no real difference in appearance between the horse and its owner and Mahaddie acquired the nickname 'Hamish' for the rest of his life. Potential Mosquito crews were posted to 1655 Mosquito Training Unit at Warboys for conversion.

Mosquito bombers flew a series of operations to German cities in March. On some nights, including 18/19 and 22/23 March, when Frankfurt was raided by the heavies and Berlin on 24/25 March they acted as diversions for the Main Force effort with raids on German night-fighter airfields. The night of the 30/31st fell during the moon stand-down period for the Main Force but the raid on Nürnburg, destination of 795 RAF heavy bombers and 38 Mosquitoes, went ahead as planned. The Met forecast indicated that there would be protective high cloud on the outward route when the moon would be up. A 1409 Met Flight Mosquito carried out a reconnaissance and reported that the protective cloud was unlikely to be present and that there could be cloud over the target, which would prevent accurate ground marked bombing, but the raid went ahead. It was a disaster. Mosquito spoof attacks on Cologne, Frankfurt and Kassel were identified for what they were because to the German defences they were apparently flying without H_2S. As the bomber stream was clearly recognized from the start, 246 twin- and single- engined night fighters were sent up to engage the heavies. British jamming of the first interception of the bomber stream in the area south of Bonn was successful but from there on in the bomber stream was hit repeatedly and the majority of the losses occurred in the Giessen-Fulda-Bamberg area. A staggering 82 bombers were lost en route to and near the target. In all, 64 Lancasters and 31 Halifaxes (11.9 per cent of the force dispatched) were lost (and ten bombers crash-landed in England); the worst Bomber Command loss of the war.

It was evident that the German night fighter force was far from defeated. On the night of 10/11 June 1944 two Mosquitoes failed to return from a raid by 32 of the aircraft on Berlin. One of the German night-fighter crews on patrol this night was Oberleutnant Josef Nabrich and his Bordfunker, Unteroffizier Fritz 'Pitt' Habicht of 3./NJG1 who after many requests were flying a cleaned up He 219 Uhu with the armour plating and four of the cannons removed especially for hunting Mosquitoes.

70 On 7 April 1944 571 Squadron was formed at Downham Market. A shortage of Mosquitoes meant that 571 had to operate at half-strength for a time. On the night of 13/14 April two crews from 571 and six Mosquitoes from 692 attacked Berlin for the first time carrying two 50-gallon drop tanks and a 4,000lb bomb. On 1 August 1944 608 Squadron at Downham Market joined LNSF. On 25 October 142 Squadron re-formed at Gransden Lodge and that same night they flew their first operation when their only two B.XXVs were dispatched to Cologne. On 18 December 162 Squadron re-formed at Bourn with B.XXVs and soon accompanied the veteran 139 Squadron on target-marking duties. 163 Squadron, the 11th and final Mosquito unit in 8 Group, reformed at Wyton on 25 January 1945 on B.XXVs. Commanded by Wing Commander (later Air Marshal) Ivor Broom DFC the squadron flew its first LNSF operation just four days later when four Mosquitoes dropped 'Window' at Mainz ahead of the PFF force.

Nabrich, Kapitän of the Third Staffel was looking to add to his claims for four bombers destroyed during May, including two in one night (on 24 May). Habicht recalled: 'We must already have flown about twenty trips from Venlo in spring 1944 in addition to our normal interception operations and all we had got for our trouble was 'friendly' flak, altitude sickness and one long but inconclusive chase of a Mosquito 'Intruder'. But things were about to change. We were circling on wait over the Zuider Zee at 9800 metres at about 10 o'clock when our ground station suddenly announced that a group of light bombers was approaching. We were quickly controlled by radio into the gaggle of Mosquitoes, which was flying rather lower than we were and we felt the first turbulence from slipstreams. In a few minutes I had a clear response at a range of six kilometres on my SN-2. The enemy machine was flying so fast that despite using our height advantage to gain speed it wasn't until we were in the Osnabrück area that we obtained visual contact. We positioned ourselves about thirty metres beneath him and identified him positively as a Mosquito [B.IV DZ608 on 692 Squadron at Gransden Lodge flown by Flying Officer I. S. H. MacDonald RAAF and Flying Officer E. B. Chatfield DFC]. Now it was a matter of stalking this rare bird carefully and scoring a direct hit. As I was checking our position my pilot attacked, aiming at the left engine and wing in order to give the two Englishmen in the aircraft a chance to escape. At first the engine burned strongly, then more weakly. Burning gently, the Mosquito began to fly in circles, losing height gradually. After a few minutes, when we were just about to make a second attack from above, the enemy machine, together with its bomb load, exploded. We were thrown to one side by the pressure wave, but our pilot regained control of the He 219 at 4000 metres, just above the cloud. We made an orbit over the spot where the Mosquito hit the ground and then we made our way back to our base at Venlo without any trouble, where our combat report was received by our friends in the Operations Room with surprise and with congratulations.

'The following morning only widely scattered fragments of the Mosquito could be found where they had been flung by the explosion. And the two British flyers? They were taken prisoner almost unharmed and a few days later told us personally how lucky they had been. Immediately after our attack they had switched on the automatic pilot and bailed out, both landing uninjured. They had thought at first that they had been the victim of a new anti-aircraft weapon, because they didn't expect to meet a night-fighter at that height.'

This same night a B.XVI on 571 Squadron flown by Flight Lieutenant Joe Downey DFM was shot down returning from Berlin by Hauptmann Ernst-Wilhelm Modrow of I./NJG1 flying a He 219 Uhu 'Owl' for his 19th victory. Downey's navigator, Pilot Officer Ronald Arthur Wellington, recalls. 'The attack on our aircraft consisted of a short burst of cannon fire, no more than five rounds. The starboard engine was hit and burst into flames. The aircraft immediately went into an uncontrolled dive and on receiving the order 'Bail Out' I made my exit from the normal escape hatch. At the time Joe was preparing to follow me. Very shortly after pulling the ripcord I saw the aircraft explode beneath me. It is therefore; very unlikely that Joe was alive when the remains of the aircraft crashed onto the dunes near Bergen, a small seaside town three miles northwest of Alkmaar.'

Scarcely twenty-four hours later when the LNSF sent 33 Mosquitoes to Berlin again as the heavies bombed rail targets in northern France, Oberleutnant Josef

Nabrich and Fritz Habicht were chasing another Mosquito in the direction of Berlin. It was B.IV DZ609 on 139 Squadron at Upwood flown by Flight Lieutenant Charles Anthony Armstrong DFM MiD RNZAF and Flying Officer George Leonard Woolven. 'This time' recalled Habicht 'it took us even longer to reach the fast bomber, flying as it was at 9700 metres, because we didn't have a height advantage. At last, to the west of Salzwedel, I was able to hand over the Mosquito to my pilot for him to approach visually. We tracked him in the normal manner, but we had difficulty in getting into a firing position because the enemy aircraft was making energetic evasive manoeuvres. Finally two bursts of 20mm cannon, which we saw strike home, caused the Tommy to dive vertically downwards. After a few tense seconds of waiting I saw the flash of a gigantic explosion as the aircraft hit the ground below the clouds. Even as I was reporting our kill to ground control our starboard engine began to falter. It had apparently been overstrained by the long period of running at full revolutions. It was imperative for us to get down at any available airfield in the vicinity. My Mayday call was acknowledged immediately by Perleberg and we landed there a few minutes later. To our astonishment we were greeted on the airfield by the duty officer and a number of girls with bunches of flowers - they had heard by radio of our rare success.'[71]

On 28/29 June 230 bombers hit the railway yards at Blainville and Metz for the loss of 18 Halifaxes and two Lancasters[72] while 33 Mosquitoes of the LNSF went to Saarbrücken and another ten were despatched to drop 4,000lb 'Cookies' from 32,000 feet on the Scholven/Buer oil plant in the Ruhr. All the Mosquitoes returned without loss. In one month, 15 July-15 August 1944, Mosquitoes dropped 336 4,000lb bombs on the 'Big City'. On the night of 20/21 July the LNSF sent 26 Mosquitoes to raid Hamburg. It was at this time that Jim Foley, a navigator who had flown a first tour on Lancasters, was posted to 1655 MTU at Warboys where he crewed up with Flight Lieutenant 'Hank' Henderson, a Canadian. Jim Foley recalled: 'At the beginning, the number of operations to complete a tour on Mosquitoes was fifty - it seemed a lot at that time. A navigator in a Mosquito was a more interesting function than in a heavy bomber. He sat by the side of the pilot, his chart on his knee, 'Gee' box to the left and the nose of the aircraft directly ahead in which was the bomb sight. Instead of being enclosed, as in the Lancaster, the navigator saw everything that was happening, but was not quite so comfortable. A consolation was that the flying time to a like target was very much shorter. For instance my Berlin trip in a Lancaster took seven hours plus, whereas the average Mosquito op on the same city was about four and a quarter hours. We were posted to 139 Squadron at Upwood. In the event we were there for just over a week, doing just three operations. Flying fast and high the ops were less than four hours and the initial experience quite exciting. After the three operations at Upwood we were posted to Downham Market, to 608 (North Riding) Squadron which had just been formed. One of the first people I met was Harry Erben, which

---

71 Armstrong and Woolven were killed. Generalleutnant Josef 'Beppo' Schmid sent Nabrich and Habicht a congratulatory telegram and a gift of several bottles. Nabrich was killed during a strafing attack on Münster-Handorf on 27 November 1944. Habicht crewed up with Hauptmann Alexander Graf Rességuier de Miremont, Habicht was severely injured during his last sortie on the night of 3/4 February 1945 when his He 219 was shot down by return fire from a Lancaster over Roermond. See *Nachtjagd: The Night Fighter versus Bomber War over the Third Reich 1939-45* by Theo Boiten (Crowood Press 1997).
72 13 Tame Boar crews were credited with 21 Viermot kills.

was good news. Harry had been on my course. He was an Austrian born in Vienna who wore Czech flashes on his upper arm to avoid precise identity if he had to bail out and land in Germany. If it was discovered that he was from Austria he would be treated rather roughly, Austria being part of Germany at that time.

'I started operating with my new squadron on 2 September, the first target being Karlsruhe. After a bombing trip to Hamburg I went on leave and took my fiancé to Yorkshire for the first time to meet my family. Back to Downham Market to re-commence operations. At this time the targets were varied: Wilhelmshaven, Cologne, Hamburg, Berlin, Hanover and Gelsenkirchen. On each we carried four 500lb bombs. Although the losses on Mosquitoes were minimal as compared to my Lancaster tour, the odd one in my squadron failed to return and the same anxieties existed. The Mosquito was very well heated; I never wore flying boots, just a battledress and shoes. Crews wore 'Mae Wests' at all times in the air and my parachute fitted under my seat to be near at hand ready to be clipped on in case of emergencies. Being a small aircraft the Mosquito did not have any proper toilet facility. If you wanted to pee, there was a funnel connected to a flexible pipe which led to the outside of the plane. It wasn't easy to do it at 28-30,000 feet as the air pressure at that height wasn't very conducive. I suppose when it left the aircraft it vaporised, otherwise perhaps some German town or field got the odd slight drenching. The Lancaster had a proper Elsan (portable toilet) situated towards the rear of the aircraft with oxygen and intercom points adjacent. Some unfortunate ground crew member had the job of emptying same.

'The routine was invariably the same, air test in the morning, briefing, navigation preparation, supper, draw parachute, get all equipment together, transport to dispersal point, start engines at the appointed time, taxi, take off when given the green signal, climb to altitude, navigate to target, view with some apprehension if lots of flak over target, fuse bombs, crawl into nose of aircraft, set calculated wind on the bomb sight, bomb doors open, instruct pilot left-right etc. until target lined up in sights, press bomb tit to release and call 'bombs gone', close bomb doors, resume navigation position having previously given pilot course to steer for home. At all times ensure that the oxygen mask was on and intercom plugged in. navigate home, avoiding dangerous flak areas and hoping that no German fighters were being vectored onto you.

'Halfway through the tour Boozer was fitted to the instrument panel, which would light up if there was a German fighter on our tail. Several times the light came on which meant immediate corkscrewing or diving at speed to shake off. It was always a good feeling to cross the enemy coast and then over the North Sea; always remembering to switch on our IFF (Identification Friend or Foe) to tell the home defences that you were a friendly aircraft. Halfway across the sea we would gradually lose height crossing the English coast, invariably Norfolk or Suffolk, at the required operational height. From the coast gradually lose more height until about 10 miles from home, then call up for a QFE (Ground Pressure) and set the altimeter accordingly. Request to join circuit and at what height, hoping to be one of the first back to avoid circling to take turn to land. There was usually a race to get back, land and be first to de-briefing. Latecomers had to hang around as there were usually only two or three intelligence officers to interrogate the returning crews. I must admit that whenever possible we cut corners to try to return in the first batch. After de-briefing, egg and bacon and then bed.'

Derek Smith DFC was another ex-Lancaster navigator who crewed up for his second tour at 1655 MTU when he teamed up with Philip Back. 'I had done a tour on Lancs on 61 Squadron in 5 Group while Philip was very much a new boy. Philip said of our crewing up, 'Not only did I feel extremely honoured, I felt extremely lucky that you had chosen me'. This was because he had seen my DFC ribbon. In turn, I was to find I had been extremely fortunate in my choice as I soon found him to be a very skilful and courageous pilot equal to, or in most cases better than, those I knew with a great deal more experience. In all of our 246 airborne hours together there was never a sign of 'twitch', panic or indecision in the cockpit we shared. On reflection, doing our first op together from Graveley on 5 September I was probably very blasé about operating in a Mossie at 27,000 feet while Phil must have been a little on edge to say the least. For me, it was very much routine and we arrived on the target exactly on time only to find it obscured by 10/10 cloud. A Wanganui marker went down exactly ahead so that we were on it in seconds. I said, 'Bombs gone - OK Phil, let's go home, steer 270°.' He looked round and said, 'Is that it then?' I replied on the lines of 'Yes, that's all for tonight', but I wonder if he really believed me as there was a complete absence of flak at our height.'

'The look came again on another occasion when we landed at Woodbridge with no engines. We were about 12 miles out when the second engine stopped and after looking at the options he said, 'I think I can get it down at Woodbridge, are you with me?' To which I must have replied on the lines of, 'Well I'm not staying out here on my own!' Having made a perfect landing, after losing about 12,000 feet in the circuit, he would have looked round and said, 'How about that then?' only to find me more interested in a Lanc bearing down on us at a very high speed. Fortunately, it just missed us on the starboard side having landed without any brake pressure.

'Again, it could have been when we were passed by a German jet, fortunately going in the opposite direction, or when a V-2 rocket went up extremely close to our starboard wingtip. Another occasion was when a piece of flak passed right through the canopy in front of me and just behind Philip, or possibly it was when we were bracketed by two AA shells much too close for comfort. All our Mossies were fitted with 'Boozer' which glowed pink if radar controlled AA was operating in the area and red if we were the object of their attention. Both were very common occurrences so it was a matter of familiarity breeding contempt when we ignored it. However, we suffered a rude awakening when, at 27,000 feet', the red was followed immediately by the shell bursts - one on either side. It was a valuable lesson, well learned and we never ignored it again.'

On 12 September on Berlin the raid did not go well for Flight Lieutenant Norman Griffiths and Flying Officer Bill Ball on 571 Squadron in B.XVI MM127 K-King. Bill Ball wrote. 'There were wavering clusters of them all around the city, in the city and on the approaches to the city. A complete forest of blazing lights. Some were almost stationary, holding one or more of the early arrivals. Others were waving about like tall trees in a high wind, seeking the Squadron's Mosquitoes. Bombs were going down all the time as we approached. Great flashes and fires on the ground showed where the blockbusters were bursting. Flares and target indicators added to the illuminations. The whole sky on the bombing run and over the target was filled with vivid, vicious flashes and ugly grey and white puffs of smoke. The flak was crabbing nearer, bursting all around; a deadly barrage just above the cockpit, outside the port window and all along the starboard fuselage... it was so near I could feel K for King shuddering with the impact. So close I could see every detail of the cotton-wool puffs slowly unfolding!' (K-King limped back towards the Norfolk coast on a rapidly depleting fuel supply and was abandoned over the sea. K-King came down in a beet field near the village of Bacton, having missed houses in the village by a fair margin).

Warrant Officer Tommy Tomlinson and Flying Officer Dick Richards in B.XVI PF394 were also given 'the full treatment' as Richards recalls: 'We dropped, but while still held in the glare the guns stopped. Twice fighters attacked us and the second attack smashed all our hydraulic systems. Eventually we got away and Tommy (I was lucky enough to do most of my trips with the tearaway Warrant Officer Tommy Tomlinson); remembering Magdeburg wanted to do another low level night X-country across Germany. (On 25 August to Berlin we had an engine shot out near Magdeburg. We returned the compliment with our 4,000b 'Cookie' and turned for home. The aircraft would not hold height and we were contemplating jumping but with the throttle through the gate we staggered home at lowering altitude with Tommy loving every minute of it). I persuaded him that, with two engines operational it was silly to lose the advantage of height. He reluctantly agreed and eventually he made his usual immaculate landing at Woodbridge, but this time with no undercarriage or flaps and at a speed close to 200 mph.'

Berlin at this time was the 'favourite' destination for the Mosquitoes. 'A' and 'B' Flights at 8 (PFF) Group stations were routed to the 'Big City' over towns and cities whose air raid sirens would announce their arrival overhead, although they were not the targets for the Mosquitoes' bombs. Depriving the Germans of much needed sleep and comfort was a very effective 'nuisance' weapon, while a 4,000-pounder nestling in the bomb bay was a more tangible 'calling card'. The 'night postmen had two rounds: After take-off from Wyton crews immediately climbed to height, departed Cromer and flew the dogleg route Heligoland-Bremen-Hamburg. The second route saw departure over Woodbridge and went to The Ruhr-Hannover-Munich. Two Mosquito bombers, which failed to return from the attack on Berlin on 13/14 September were claimed shot down SE of the capital by Oberfeldwebel Egbert Jaacks of I./NJG10 and at Brunswick by Leutnant Karl Mitterdorfer of 10./JG 300. Two nights later, on 15/16 September, 490 aircraft bombed Kiel for the loss of four Halifaxes and two Lancasters. Three Mosquitoes and a Stirling on 199 Squadron in 100 Group were lost on Bomber Support and a Mosquito XX on 608 Squadron failed to return from a raid on Berlin. Leutnant Kurt Welter claimed two of the Mosquitoes, one south of Berlin and the other north of Aachmer and Feldwebel Reichenbach of 10./JG 300 one other northwest of Wittenburg.

At Wyton on the night of 10/11 October Australian pilot Doug Swain and his navigator Michael H. A. T. Bayon on 128 Squadron were briefed and ready to take off for their first bombing trip. Bayon, a classicist who later taught Greek and Latin, was also a frustrated fighter pilot, as he recalls. 'Of course, I would be a fighter pilot. Nothing else occurred to me as even a possibility. And so I went to flying school; and took longer than the average to fly solo and on my first solo landing bounced so high my instructor suggested that I should have switched on my oxygen again. At the end of the course I failed ignominiously. I was summoned to the selection committee 'you will be a navigator,' said the voice of authority. So more, tests. I couldn't really see the letters with one eye; luckily they tested my good eye first and I memorised the letters. We stayed in huge blocks of flats in Saint John's Wood and heard the lions roaring at night in the Zoo. We went first to the Grand Hotel, then to the Hotel Metropole at Brighton. There a Messerschmitt came in low from the sea, machine guns blazing. We all dived for the floor. There was one casualty - a bloke was scalded as the tea urn was riddled with bullets. We were sent up to Manchester. I was put to swilling out the cookhouse with John Sidgwick, a slightly effete musical scholar from King's College, Cambridge. From there we went to Canada and I began to learn to navigate. If your pilot asked where you were, you put your thumb firmly down on the map, covering perhaps 100 square miles and said confidently 'just there'. Then he felt secure and you could sweat it out in peace. I flew across Montreal and was told to photograph a bridge over the St. Lawrence but I pressed the wrong bit and dropped a bomb on it instead. I must have missed as I heard no more of it. I went to bombing school in Ontario and discovered that I was rather good at it. Quite a surprise. The rest of the course was sent to heavy bombers, to Coastal Command, to reconnaissance planes. I alone was sent to Mosquitoes, Pathfinders - the elite of Bomber Command. We were to be a brand new squadron [128], three British, one Canuck, the rest Aussies. For some reason, I was the only member of flying crew on the whole unit who was not an officer.

'So, on the first evening, over drinks in the Mess, all the blokes teamed up. Next day we turned up for briefing. I was the only one without a pilot. I looked at the various pilots and I thought, 'there's the one I'd like as my pilot.' A tall raw-boned blond Aussie called Doug Swain. We all went along to the decompression chamber to test our ability to withstand low-pressure. One navigator dipped out - Doug Swain's. He got agonising bends, so in actual fact did I - but I decided not to say so.'

All 8 (PFF) Group airmen had to undergo decompression tests to make sure that none was subject to aeroembolism or 'bends'. But although the XVI was pressurized up to 2 psi, sufficient to reduce the effect of altitude by 5-6,000 feet, crews never used it on operations because they could not drop 'Window' and because if their aircraft was holed it would reduce pressure suddenly and injure the crew. They could still fly at 30,000 feet and above on oxygen.

Flying Officer F. A. 'Sandy' Saunders on 627 Squadron experienced the bends while undergoing high altitude testing in the pressurization chamber, as he explains. 'Towards the end of my flying instructing tour I was anxious to get posted to a Mosquito Squadron and if it could be with the Pathfinder Force, so much the better. This high altitude test was an early obstacle in that path. Picture if you can the interior of a decompression chamber. It is a tube like structure, which can accommodate about eight people on opposite facing benches. A medical orderly can view the interior and the occupants through portholes. There is a telephonic communication between the occupants and the person in charge of the tests. The first run is a demonstration to show the effects of oxygen-lack. You are given pencil and writing pads and under instruction from the orderly you write simple things like your name and address and do simple problems that require a little exercise of that muscle between your ears. Oxygen is gradually withdrawn from the air and you find that you require more and more explanation of the current problem. It takes longer to say anything because the right words don't spring to mind. Your writing becomes increasingly sprawled and scribbly and the sight of it appears to you as increasingly funny. There is no pain or distress whatsoever. Our little jokes become increasingly hilarious and at the end of the test a happier band of warriors you never did see.

'You are slowly brought 'back to earth' and when you review your test writings, it brings home with a severe jolt what oxygen-lack is about. I was later to benefit from this experience. So much for that demonstration - but now the real test begins. The test is for the decompression chamber to 'climb' to a height equivalent to 37,000 feet and the occupants would be breathing through oxygen masks. A full two-hour dwell at that height repeated for two separate occasions is the standard. Should any occupant get the 'bends' as this affliction is know during this time, the height is brought down again in a controlled sequence, which itself takes time. During this the victim is in varying stages of pain, nausea and discomfort and of course the test is void not only for the victim but is also void for the others taking the test. So the victim - in addition, has the embarrassment of facing his colleagues who will all have to retake the tests. I failed my first decompression flight. A minor irritation started in one knee and however much I tried to rub it away, it steadily got worse until I was left with an excruciating pain and I eventually collapsed in my seat. A bubble form's in the blood and the blood begins in effect to boil. It could be a dangerous situation. The safest place to be is inside a pressure chamber. Anyway, we were all brought back to earth and I had to apologize to all my fellows, who of course all took it in good spirit. My visions of Mosquitoes were fading but you were allowed one failure in the chamber. Later I took the tests and I sailed through those with no trouble at all.[73]

'So Doug and I were now a partnership. Doug said, 'right now - my ambition is quite simple. I want us to be the best bloody aircrew in the RAF and that means in the world. As for you, you can make any bloody mistake you like ('that's good of him,' I thought contentedly) - 'ONCE' he added menacingly. We went up for our first flight together and Doug decided to feather one engine. What he did not know was that you could not restart an engine in midair, so our first ever landing together was a single engine landing.

'Cologne was quite a short trip. As we got over the target I was amazed how vivid the scene was. Lots of searchlights raking the sky and occasionally a plane would be caught in a cone of searchlights glow luminously like a moth. Vivid cascades of target indicators in fluorescent red, yellow or green. Decoy German indicators, subtly different in colour, bomb bursts, flaming buildings, tracer bullets and flak bursts. It was all very stimulating. I crawled down into the nose of the plane, to lie on my belly and guide Doug in on the target. But I got a kink in the oxygen pipe, so I was a bit drunk from Anoxia. 'Port, port, port' I said. I felt the plane slew slightly. 'Port, port, port. Now starboard'. I gave a little giggle. 'Now back a bit'. Doug didn't panic. He realised the problem and began to drag me out by the legs. I protested. 'It's pretty out there', I said. He hauled me back, took off my oxygen mask and put his mask over my face. I recovered. Doug was slumped over the steering column and we were plummeting down. I took off his mask and put it back on his face - well, if you survive the idiocies of your first ten or twelve operations, you may well survive. Obviously all the worst mistakes occur early in your tour of operations. Like young birds, if you can survive the first few hazardous weeks, the odds lengthen.

'I decided that if radar was the key to success, I would master it; we used to have two nights of operations and then one night off. On my nights off, I would go along to the radar unit, where a thin, dark radar aircraftsman and his plump jolly girlfriend would teach me all they knew. I became an expert, accurate at finding my position anywhere on the airfield to within six feet, sight unseen. This was to save our lives, later on. Here an odd story follows. The boffins came up with 'Oboe', a highly sophisticated form of radar. Yes, but how accurate was it? A subtle plan was concocted which would require no time lapse, no risk to spies or undercover agents. A lull in the bombing was planned and only three planes were sent out, bombing on 'Oboe'. The target was a small German cemetery. The next day the German news was jubilant. Ze British have Germany last night bombed. But - ha ha ha - zere were no casualties; bodies were attacked - ha ha ha - but zey vere all dead bodies. Ze stupid British a cemetery have bombed. The British scientists hugged each other and the production go ahead was authorised. Radar was our seeing dog, our white stick. And so one day soon after we took off, the radar blew a fuse. I put in another and that one blew. Then, as I'd learnt in the radar shed, I put in a penny. I got my three fixes; and then the radar caught fire. I beat out the flames with my cap and my bare hands, we got to target and returned; Doug was furious. Then I was mentioned in dispatches for outstanding intelligence, initiative and refusal to admit defeat. Even in those days the radar set cost £600 which would buy a three-bedroom house in Cambridge.

'About now, a pretty little blonde WAAF called Rose (I never took her out and I don't think I ever learnt her surname), began to feel that she was my good luck mascot. If she kissed me goodbye on every trip, I'd never be killed. So, even if take off were at 3 am, she'd be there to kiss me. She'd come back from leave to see me off. She never once missed out. I wonder what happened to her.

'I suppose I might just describe a typical day if you are flying that night. In the morning you would contact your ground crew and when they gave the whole plane the OK, it was ready for a test flight. We had a magnificent ground crew, they really were our friends; and they would work any hours to get things right for us. So we'd fly for perhaps merely half an hour, testing, testing. Or perhaps we'd fly for almost two hours, including a trip to the practice bombing range on The Wash. You would sort out your hours to fit in your meals. It might be a 5 pm take off or any time up to 3am. Whatever the time, the kitchen staff would be on duty and if you didn't feel like a proper meal there was a huge cauldron of soup always simmering on the stove, a kind of huntsman's stew. Air crew were allowed fresh oranges with any meal, while the Weathermen, Air Controllers and so on looked on, slavering. I knew I simply must not give the precious things away, so I hardly ever ate mine; some of the aircrew delighted to gloat!

'Perhaps an hour or two before take-off you'd go along to the Briefing Room, sitting in pairs, each with his crew member. You'd learn the target, the route there and back (Doug and I always came back in a straight line - never mind the subtle route worked out by control), the weather and above all, the winds expected, what load you'd carry, what trouble spots you might expect. A great deal to work out. The pilot was captain of the plane, but in fact his job was often surprisingly boring not quite that, I suppose; perhaps the word is 'undemanding'. He would have three moments of high drama. Take-off with full bomb and petrol load; over the target and landing when you were tired. Although you might have heard and felt the shrapnel hitting your plane, you had no real idea of what damage had been done, what state the hydraulics might be in, whether the flaps would respond and so on. Of course, the target area was the high spot of the performance for both of you. But for the navigator, take-off and landing were comparatively relaxed. There wasn't a thing you could do. All you had to do was to be supportive by showing your complete faith in your pilot and in Doug I had an outstanding flier. He had all the qualities.

'Obviously, there were a few mini crises crossing the coast of Europe, or if you went too close to the islands of Heligoland, or if a night fighter picked you up. In fact you had a form of radar (called rather endearingly, Boozer), which told you by a dull red light when you were being tracked by German radar. Within a couple of minutes of take off this always came on. (The first flight you think 'My God - they know we're coming'. It reminds me of the new air gunner who said excitedly to his battle-worn pilot, 'Skip, Skip - they're firing at us'. 'I know' came the weary reply, 'they're allowed to'). Right, so Boozer glowed dull red. Then it would shine bright red. This meant they were training their guns on you, not on the next plane. Here the navigator, however busy he was (and often you would work at an intensity to make you sweat) had to take over. If you merely swerved about like a headless hen, the Germans marked down your track as perhaps half a mile wide and automatically cut down on your airspeed. Then up would come the box barrage; and I suppose, down you'd go. Though I did not mind the thought of death, I did hope I wouldn't be burnt to death. No. What you had to do was to turn a full 69 degrees to port (the light would fade as they lost you). Then, as it glowed bright red again, give it 20 seconds for them to lay the guns and the flak to travel up - after all, we were five miles up in the air - and then turn 600 starboard. It used to make Doug and me laugh delightedly to see the box barrage wasted where they hoped we'd be. Of course, over target, the Boozer would be bright red pretty continuously. However, there was another little light on Boozer, which did not come on often. This was a little white light and meant an enemy night fighter was on your tail, tracking you with radar. (If you had a cat's eye night fighter, the first warning you'd get would be the tracers going past; but both of you had a seat back of heavy armour plate). If the white light came on, it was like being on a 'Bucking bronco', or in a dinghy on a rough sea. Your pilot would go mad and chuck the plane all over the sky. It was rather exhilarating.

'I digress; the operational flight. I always wore my pyjamas under my uniform. When you got back at 5 o'clock in the morning, you were tired and cold; and the last thing you wanted was to clamber into cold pyjamas. At Briefing, the pilots are almost spectators (bus drivers, we'd call them). Doug was rather an exception. He wanted to know and understand everything that went on. The navigators, each with his individual style, would have to work fast, working out their flight plan, sorting out charts, preparing the logs, like preparing for a party; really rather fun. Then into the crew bus and out to the various dispersal points. Each crew was dropped at their own plane, greeted by their ground crew (statutory kiss from Rose). Called out in order, taxi to end of runway, take off and set course. Then two or more solid hours of intense work by the navigator (with the pilot telling you your pinpoint of light to work by is a blazing beacon for night fighters and do you think you're Piccadilly Circus on Christmas Eve? (You dim it down and furtively turn it up again). You take a radar fix, then another exactly three minutes later and then another three minutes on. This gives you how far you have travelled over the ground in six minutes. Multiply by ten, compare air and ground position and you know what the wind is. Apply this to the predicted wind and you have a vague idea of how things will be. The normal wind at that height would be about 60 mph, so if you ignored it, you'd be bombing somewhere about 120 miles from where you wanted to be.

'When you were inexperienced, you did carry target indicators - but they might be yellow and the main force was told to bomb as primary targets perhaps the red; as secondary targets the green and if all else failed, the yellows. What made your pilot smile was if you said, 'The first indicators should go down in about another fifty seconds' and then dead ahead, suddenly the indicators were there. What did not make him smile was if they appeared behind us. We would then have to do a U-turn and fly back through perhaps 600 planes. This sort of thing made pilots inexplicably tetchy and for years cured me of being early for an appointment!

'On one flight, as we left target, my nose started to bleed. Nothing I could do, with my oxygen mask on, so it contentedly bled on till I'd lost between half a pint and a pint of blood; and then it stopped of its own accord. When I got out of the plane, the front of my uniform was sodden and red with blood. 'Mike's wounded - get the blood wagon,' said one of the ground crew. I took off my oxygen mask to say that it was only a nosebleed. The blood had clotted and congealed. 'Christ, they've shot his face off' said the young fitter and he fainted. Not a nice cushiony sort of stage faint, with the legs buckling. No, he fell straight back like a board and I heard the crack of his skull on the concrete. The blood wagon tore up; he was put on a stretcher and away he went. This was the sort of thing that tended to upset Rose.

'Churchill had decided that as a propaganda ploy, Germany should be bombed for 100 nights in a row. If the forecast was appalling four engine bombers with their crews of eight men were not to be involved. Icing at height would distort the wing shape so that you just fell from the sky. Heavy fog on return; or towering cumulus clouds containing 100 mph up and down draughts within a few feet of each other, were strong enough to toss a Lancaster around like a leaf. Send in the Mosquito boys. A plywood body and a crew of only two were expendable. We had no defences, except our speed and manoeuvrability with which to elude an enemy fighter. It did make one feel somewhat wimpish! A tour of operations was 30 for the heavies who bombed at 15,000-18,000 feet; 50 for Mosquitoes, who bombed at 25,000 feet, so we were much less vulnerable.

'One night of appalling weather only two Mosquitoes from another squadron and Doug and I from Wyton took off. The idea was for us to do a Cook's tour - come very close to Hamburg, then veer off; the same for Bremen, Kiel, Hanover, Essen etc, so as to alert the air raid wardens, fire-fighters, flak crews, searchlights, night fighters - the lot; and rob them of their sleep. I plotted a bad wind and then lost the radar picture under intense jamming from the Germans and a host of false signals. Later I came to recognize the true from the false. We came up to Hamburg and passed straight over the centre of the city. Every gun opened up. Over 200 searchlights coned on us. The light was incredibly strong and sharp I have seldom been so embarrassed in my life. It was like walking down Bond Street naked. Doug's mouth was a grim line as we did our standard evasion tactics. Whatever, we did, we must not lose our nerve and lose height - that was how many were killed. Sure, you gained speed - but you became an easier target, by widening the angle of effective fire. We moved on to Bremen and all alone we sailed over the centre of the city. We reached Kiel - naval guns here, first class gunners. I could hear the flak hitting us. One large piece went straight through our two-ton bomb and out the other side. Another cut the steel struts for the bomb doors like scissors cutting a stick of macaroni - sheared through, shiny, clean, not snapped. This bar was thicker than my thumb. Our petrol tanks were pierced again and again, but they were self-sealing so that was all right. Our auxiliary tanks had no self-sealing but Doug always used them first, for this reason. We jettisoned them, to add an extra 5 knots to our speed.

'As we were in the middle of Kiel I found myself thinking, 'I wonder if I'm frightened?

How do I test it?' I held my hand out - it was brilliantly light and I could see that it was rock steady. I put my hand on my heart. It seemed to be beating slowly and strongly. My mouth was not dry and nor were my hands clammy. Then I noticed that I had a thin line of sweat on my upper lip. 'Perhaps this is what fear feels like' I thought. But I was certainly scared of Doug's reaction and with reason. We landed in stony silence and after the debriefing he said 'Go to bed now but I want you to get up early and I want a complete reconstruction of the whole flight, finding out where you went wrong before we flight test tomorrow'. That's right. 'You can make any bloody silly mistake you like - once'.'

On 23 October the weather was fine and the forecast for later in the night, when 38 Mosquitoes were detailed to bomb Berlin and ten were given a 'spoof' raid on Wiesbaden, would change very little. Another two Mosquitoes went to Aschaffenburg. Like all German cities these targets were heavily defended by anti-aircraft guns and searchlights but no aircraft were lost on these three operations. The following night the largest Mosquito raid was on Hannover which was visited by 57 Mosquitoes. Again no aircraft were lost. It was the same story on the night of 27/28 October when 60 Mosquitoes attacked Berlin and 21 others visited six other targets and the next night also, when 30 Mosquitoes went to Cologne. During October just nine Mosquitoes of the LNSF were lost on operations. Despite the intensity of raids, LNSF Mosquito squadrons would register the lowest losses in Bomber Command (one per 2,000 sorties) which is even more amazing when one considers how many ops crews were increasingly expected to fly, as Jim Foley on 608 Squadron recalls:

'By September/October I had 21 ops under my belt and I thought I was near halfway on his second tour - but it was announced that to complete a tour on Mosquitoes the number had been increased to 55. This meant that if I was to successfully complete the tour I would have done well over 80 bombing operations. In November I did nine operations of which three were to Berlin. We had to turn back from a raid on Gelsenkirchen as the generator and ASI packed in (this didn't count towards my total ops). Also in this month, I did my first daylight raid, the target being Duisburg. The bombing tactics were different, as approaching the target the squadron flew in gaggle formation and the leader bombed visually, i.e. ground target identified by eye. The rest of the gaggle dropped their bombs on seeing the leader's bombs leave his aircraft. To actually see the bombs falling was quite a sight. The pattern made on the ground in relation to the target could clearly be seen.'

On 6/7 November RAF Bomber Command sent out two major forces of bombers. Some 235 Lancasters of 5 Group, together with seven Mosquitoes again attempted to cut the Mittelland Canal at Gravenhorst but crews were confronted with a cold front of exceptional violence and ice quickly froze on windscreens. Only 31 Lancasters bombed before the Master Bomber abandoned the raid due to low cloud. Ten Lancasters failed to return from the Mittelland debacle. Meanwhile, 128 Lancasters of 3 Group carried out a night Gee-H raid on Koblenz. Eighteen Mosquitoes raided Hannover and eight more went to Herford, while 48 Mosquitoes of the LNSF carried out a Spoof raid on Gelsenkirchen, to draw German night fighters away from the two Main Force raids. The Gelsenkirchen raid began as planned, five minutes ahead of the two other attacks, at 19.25 hours. The city was still burning as a result of an afternoon raid that day by 738 RAF bombers. From their altitude of 25,000 feet the Mosquitoes added their red and green TIs and high explosives to the fires. A few searchlights and only very light flak greeted the crews over the devastated city. On the return a Mosquito B.XX on 608 (North Riding) Squadron iced up in cloud and both crew died when they struck overhead electric power cables before crashing into a village church.

On 15/16 November 36 Mosquitoes visited the 'Big City' and just one aircraft was lost. A further 21 Mosquitoes attacked four other targets and all returned safely. Three nights' later 31 Mosquitoes carried out a 'spoof' raid on Wiesbaden, 21 went to Hannover and six visited Erfurt, all returning without loss. On the 21st the night was of mainly good visibility and 78 Mosquitoes attacked four targets without loss. Two nights' later 82 Mosquitoes hit four targets again without loss and the same was true on the 24/25th when 58 Mosquitoes raided Berlin again and six visited Göttingen. One Mosquito was abandoned over Calais on return from the raid on Nuremberg on the 25/26th when a force of 68 Mosquitoes was dispatched to the city and ten visited Hagen and nine each went to Erfurt and Stuttgart. Seven Mosquitoes were dispatched on the 267/27th to Erfurt and six to Karlsruhe on a 'spoof' raid when the target for the main Force was Munich. On the night of 27/28 November 67 Mosquitoes raided Berlin and 19 more went to three other cities; all returning safely. The night following 75 Mosquitoes visited Nuremburg and nine more went to Hallendorf. A 128 Squadron Mosquito XVI and its crew were lost on the operation on Nuremburg. The following night 67 Mosquitoes went to Hannover and four to Bielefeld. Six Mosquitoes of 5 Group that set out to lay mines in the River Weser were unable to complete the operation because of 10/10th cloud over the target area. On the 30th the LNSF mounted the second major daylight raid of the month when Mosquitoes on 128, 571, 608 and 692 Squadrons were dispatched to the Gessellschaft Teerverwertung tar and benzol plant in Meiderich, a suburb of Duisburg. 'Sky markers' dropped by three formations of Mosquitoes on 105 Squadron each led by an 'Oboe' Mosquito defeated the solid cloud cover and smoke seen rising to 10,000 feet was testimony to their bombing accuracy.

On the cold winter night of 2/3rd December 1944 23 Mosquitoes of 8 Group took part in the Main Force raid on Hagen just south of Dortmund in the Ruhr. The Mosquitoes took off early, around 17.56 hours and after about three and-a-quarter hours in the air all of them returned safely a few minutes after 9 o'clock that night. In a separate raid, 66 Mosquitoes were detailed to bomb Giessen. Flight Lieutenant D. F. Gosling DFC arrived on 142 Squadron at 11am on 2nd December and was told to test fly an aircraft, a Mosquito Mk.XXV coded 'K' immediately! 'All was well with the aircraft' recalled Gosling. 'I then found myself down on the Battle Order for that night! The route was 890 miles and the target was the railway marshalling yards in Giessen. The bombing height was set at 12-15,000 feet, somewhat below the usual bombing height for night operations. Before take-off whilst taxiing along the perimeter - the brakes failed. I fired off the Very light and when all the other aircraft had taken off the CO arrived and collected us and the spare aircraft. We took-off late (about 30 minutes) and cutting off part of the outward bound leg arriving 30 minutes' late. We encountered little flak and bombed on the largest fire visible, running in off a west to east course. I recall it being a rather peaceful scene with odd fires burning. The river and built area of the town were clearly visible as crews made their respective bombing runs. The first red markers fell four miles north-west of the aiming point on the west bank of the river but subsequent yellow markers formed a triangular shape across the marshalling yards. The bombing was well concentrated around the yellow markers and the marshalling yards were badly damaged in the attack. We returned to base with no interference. Total flying time 3 hours 40 minutes.'

Jim Foley on 608 Squadron was to do ten operations in December starting with a special duties one on Hagen, followed by Nuremberg.

'On 8 December we were briefed for a daylight raid on Duisburg which at one time looked like being my last. We took off at 12.45 and the orders were, as in the previous daylight raids, to bomb in gaggle formation. On crossing the North Sea we saw cumulus cloud up to a height of 15,000 feet - this type of cloud is particularly unpleasant to fly through. The run to the target was fairly uneventful until, on the run in, we were hit by flak and immediately lost an engine. With this loss of power we could not maintain height and speed. We set course in a generally westward direction and realised we had no chance of getting back to England, bearing in mind the cumulus cloud. We were soon on our own as the rest of the formation was well on their way home. Once clear of the German defences and near the Dutch-Belgian border we put out a continuous Mayday call. As we crossed what was presumably the front line we were attacked by anti-aircraft fire, whether this was 'enemy' or 'friendly' we would never know. Fortunately, whoever it was did not fire very accurately and we were safely in Belgium. After crossing into Belgium we had an answer to our distress call. It was the airfield at Brussels. We were having difficulty in maintaining height and after they gave us a course to steer to reach Brussels it was a question of whether we would run out of sky before we got there. Fortunately we were still at about 2,000 feet when we sighted the airfield - it seemed just a question then of making a single engine landing - but as we were on our approach a Spitfire was just ahead and control told us that he had no engine at all - could we overshoot and go round again. We were so committed to land that it took quite a feat of airmanship by Hank Henderson my pilot to get round and come in again. I thought we wouldn't make it and would end up, we hoped, in a ploughed field all in one piece. He made it. He was awarded an immediate DFC for this exploit.

'The adjutant informed us that we would stay the night in a hotel in Brussels and fly back to England at the first opportunity. He arranged for us to be given some Belgian francs and we took a tram into the city armed with directions. An old lady, sitting opposite me patted my knee and said in broken English, 'Thank you and your comrades for all that you've done for us'. It made me realise that our efforts had not been in vain and were appreciated. We eventually boarded a Dakota and took off for England at 13.45. The interior had been stripped and we and about half a dozen more servicemen had to sit on the hard metal floor. I was fairly well laden having a Mae West, parachute and navigation bag containing my navigation equipment. The trip was uneventful and we landed at Down Ampney in Wiltshire after a flight of two hours duration. When we got back to camp, much to our astonishment, we were down to fly on ops that night. It was already about 3pm. We saw the CO and under the circumstances he stood us down. However, the next night we were on - Essen the target, a tough one. The blessing was that it was only a trip of just more than three hours - short, sharp but tough.'

On the night of 9/10 December twelve Mosquitoes on 142 Squadron were detailed to attack Berlin as part of a 60 strong attacking Mosquito force; with take-off scheduled for 19:42 hours. The weather at Gransden Lodge started off hazy and fine but as the day progressed, conditions got worse with wintry showers sweeping in over the airfield during the evening. It was to be a rather disastrous night as far as operations were concerned, with numerous mishaps occurring. At dispersal 'A-Apple' could not take off, as the electrical system was found to have failed. Then 'U-Uncle' was found to have low brake pressure, so only ten aircraft proceeded to taxi out for take-off. Flight Sergeant D. S. Courage in 'D-Dog' did not have a good take-off and the aircraft ploughed through the top of the trees at the end of the runway, smashing the aircraft's Perspex nose cone. Courage continued to climb to 10,000 feet and then flew away from base until all the other aircraft had taken off. At 20.17 the crew landed back at Gransden complete with the bomb load.

'J-Johnny' flown by Flying Officer John Whitworth and Flying Officer W. A. 'Bill' Tulloch got away on time and climbed to operational height and crossed the Channel but then the constant speed unit on one of the engines packed up and the engine had to be shut down. Whitworth aborted the sortie and headed back to the bomb jettison area before making a single engine landing at Gransden at 21.07. He recalled. 'I have only a foggy memory of KB408 with which came in to a fast 'on one' and went through the end of the runway. It was the only kite I ever even scratched in 450 operational hours of flying.' The Mosquito ran through a hedge on its belly and was badly damaged, never to fly again.

Flying Officer K. Pudsey and Flying Officer J. R. D. Morgan in 'K-King' got only a little way further than KB408. The 'Gee' set packed up on the way out and shortly afterwards a supercharger failed to engage properly. The aircraft could not maintain operational height and so Pudsey had no option but to turn back for home. He landed at base with a full bomb load at 21.30. At this point the Squadron was down almost to half strength, with just seven out of the 12 aircraft still en route for Berlin. S-Sugar crewed by Flying Officer J. M. Ellison and Flying Officer H. J. Farquahar were the first crew to arrive over the Big City which had only 3/10ths cloud cover and a ground haze. They saw the first Green TIs go down at 21.52 and at regular intervals following this, Yellow TIs. The crew bombed a group of these from 23,000 feet. In 'N-Nan' Flying Officer W. E. Martin and Sergeant F. L. Lilley missed the first three Yellow TIs which cascaded on the north bank of the river. They went into an orbit over the city to await developments. Moments later they saw some Yellow TIs going down and so they began a bombing run on these. A number of Red TIs were burning on the ground two thirds of a mile to the south east of the Yellow TIs. Many searchlights lit up the sky but none operated in cones. The flak opened up briefly, bursting between 24-25,000 feet amongst the attacking Mosquitoes. In E-Edward Sergeant W. K. Brown observed 'bags of searchlights. No flak or fighters.' N-Nan was the last Squadron aircraft to bomb the target at 22.11. Flying Officer W. E. Martin's navigator, Sergeant F. L. Lilley, could see bombs bursting near to the Red TIs, with the main effort concentrated on the Yellow TIs: cookie blasts which appeared near to the Aiming Point started several small fires. The return trip home was without incident and everyone was back on the ground by 00.29.[74]

Daylight raids were dispatched on 11 December when two waves drawn from 128 Squadron raided Hamborn and two 'Oboe'-led raids were made on targets in Duisburg. Hamborn was a 'shortish' trip of three and a-half-hours and clear all the

---

74 Adapted from an article by Barry Blunt in *The Mossie*. Feldwebel Reichenbach of 4./NJG11 claimed a Mosquito near Berlin but the Mosquitoes that attacked the 'Big City' returned without loss.

way. At 24,000 feet crews could see the troop concentrations and supply columns winding their way inland towards the front line. Another 48 Mosquitoes of 8 Group attacked the benzol plant at Meiderich again and 32 more Mosquitoes bombed a cocking plant. Most of the bombing on the benzol plant and about half of the cocking plant appeared to be accurate. No aircraft were lost. That night 38 Mosquitoes went to Hannover, 28 to Hamburg and 23 other aircraft visited Schwerte, Bielefeld and Duisburg. A 128 Squadron Mosquito XVI (MM190) piloted by Flight Lieutenant Ronald Charles Onley lost on Hamburg was claimed by Oberleutnant Kurt Welter of II./NJG11. Onley and his navigator, Flying Officer George Barrowby Collins RAAF were killed. A 105 Squadron Mosquito crashed near Newmarket on return from Bielefeld and this crew also died. On the night of the 12/13th 49 Mosquitoes of 8 Group set out for Osnabrück but by the time crews had reached their en route cruise height the operation was scrubbed. They were ordered to keep their drop tanks and not jettison fuel but to drop their 4,000lb bombs in the North Sea. Unteroffizier Scherl of 8./NJG1 claimed a Mosquito east of Hagen when 540 aircraft of the Main Force attacked Essen but though six Lancasters were lost, all 28 Mosquitoes that attacked Essen and 49 others that raided Osnabrück returned safely.[75]

When the 13th day of December broke it was under a very heavy frost and towards mid-morning thick fog enveloped stations in Norfolk and operations were scrubbed very early. That night 52 Lancasters and seven Mosquitoes of 5 Group flew to Norway to attack the German cruiser *Köln* but by the time they reached Oslo Fiord, the ship had sailed so instead other ships were bombed.

'Winter was setting in' recalls Jim Foley on 608 Squadron. 'Downham Market, being a wartime airfield, did not have the comforts of the peacetime ones. Sleeping in Nissen huts whose sole heating was a stove and having to walk 100 yards to the ablutions - life on site was a little rigorous. Also it was the best part of a mile to walk to the flights if not on operational duty; transport was supplied if you were. After the trip on Essen I did three more before Christmas - Hanover [on 15/16 December when 62 Mosquitoes were dispatched] and then an unusual one, as we took off at 03.45 on 17 December, the latest completed night op I had ever done from the take-off point of view, arriving back at 07.30. The target was Münster. [The Main Force attacked Duisburg and the 24 Mosquitoes of 8 Group that took part flew a trip lasting almost four hours, one and a half hours of which were on instruments]. 'On our way home one night from a raid we were flying at our usual height of 28,000 feet feeling a little relaxed, as in theory, we were flying over what we thought was a comparatively safe area of Germany, if one existed, when suddenly ominous puffs of smoke appeared off our starboard wing. Flak - they had our height but fortunately not quite our direction. That woke us up. Hank put the nose down to gain more speed to 'get the hell out of there' smartly. We never relaxed again. In complete contrast I took off to bomb the railway yards at Limburg two days before Christmas at four in the afternoon. Off in daylight but being December it was dark by 5pm and back in good time to have a drink in the mess before closing time.'

Altogether, 52 Mosquitoes were detailed to bomb the Limburg railway yards and 40 more visited Siegburg. Flying Officer John Whitworth and Flying Officer Bill

75   The only Mosquito lost was a 306 Squadron NF.XXX that was hit by a V-2 in mid air during an Intruder patrol!

Tulloch were one of six Mosquito crews on 162 Squadron that went to Limburg. Whitworth had completed a first tour on Wellingtons in 1942 in the Middle East but in all his 87 ops this was the one which stood out.

'Our job in the LNSF was to wake up Germany, especially Berlin, every night if possible, in almost any weather circumstance. Bomb loads were small. Routes to Berlin were always skirting Bremen, Hamburg, Hanover, Magdeburg etc. It wasn't good on take-off, but on return cloud was down to about 350 feet. The first aircraft got down on SBA (Standard Beam Approach) OK, but just in front of me Bill Lucas came in too fast (who didn't in nasty conditions!) and went through the end of the runway. Immediately the rest of us, struggling with the dots and dashes of SBA, were diverted to Graveley. What a wonderful sight Graveley was. There in the middle of all the low cloud and fog was this great hole of flames and clear air, with the runway lights down the middle! The tension went and despite the much talked about 'uplift' on approach (which was nothing); we were all four rapidly down safely. FIDO (Fog Intensive Dispersal Operation) was a great invention, which not only saved many lives and aircraft, but also relieved so much tension among crews at a time when we were all at our most fearful - bad conditions at the end of an op.'

Christmas came and as Jim Foley on 608 Squadron recalled, 'it was pretty quiet'. 'I had hoped to get to Ickenham but was told that it wouldn't be advisable to go too far away as operations, weather permitting, would continue. This proved to be true for we were on the battle order for Boxing Day night - what a night it turned out to be. We were briefed for a midnight take off although the weather forecast was pretty dodgy. Take off was postponed several times owing to fog and frost and particularly bad icing conditions. Eventually we took off at 4.35am but within ten minutes we were recalled and the raid aborted. We were airborne for 25 minutes. Landing with bombs on board was always a little scary. We were still carrying four 500lb bombs. Three more before New Year, all taking off early evening and back by 9pm. I liked this timing if one could say that flying operationally could be enjoyed. I had completed twelve in December to add to my total that added up to sixty. The winter was proving to be very severe and I only did five trips in January including two to Berlin, on the second of which we couldn't land at base and were diverted to Wyton. We spent the night there and returned to Downham Market the next day.'

Throughout his operational tour Flying Officer Douglas Tucker DFC a pilot on 571 Squadron suffered from an awful feeling from the time he saw his name on the Battle Order until the wheels touched down on return. 'It is impossible to describe. A combination of terror, fright, fear, worry, possible a feeling most people get when visiting a dentist, the fear of the unknown. I don't think that I was alone in my feelings. There were a few that seemed to revel in the feeling. It did not affect our performance in flying or navigation; it possibly made us more aware and therefore more careful in carrying out all our flying procedures. There was no 'seat of the pants' flying in night bombers, it involved precision instrument flying from take-off to landing with no auto-pilot to relieve the monotony it was sheer hard work.

'The difficult times occurred when after staring at the Blind Flying panel for some time the pilot became almost mesmerised until the instruments seemed meaningless. It was not a question of being sleepy. When this occurred it was advisable to turn up the oxygen, take deep breaths and try to re-orientate yourself. All the aircraft had VHF transmitters/receivers. Transmitting was forbidden unless in an emergency.

Occasionally a pilot could press the transmit button by mistake and continue talking to his navigator about anything from his love life to the film at the local cinema. When this happened it stopped anyone else transmitting and there was no way to let the crew know they were on transmit. Usually they would suddenly realise what was happening because of no other transmitting noise in their headphones and would hurriedly switch back to receive. Although it was something easily done, it could also be dangerous, giving away information which could help the enemy for it was certain they were listening.

'The operational flights were neither boring, or exhilarating. It became a job to us, a job which required all one's concentration from the commencement of briefing to the landing on return. One of the more pleasant happenings was de-briefing. On entering the room the crews were given a cup of hot, real strong coffee topped up with rum from a store jar. This helped considerably in relaxing after a trip. The interrogation was very full, asking pilot and navigator questions on the weather en route and at target and any sightings of enemy aircraft, flak (if any) and at what height it exploded, searchlights etc. Did the TI's go off at the right time and heights, did we see any TI's that could have been dropped (or set off on the ground) by the enemy; what time did we release our bomb, did we manage to get any photos or did we have to take evasive action after dropping the bomb? De-briefing over, we were taken to the Mess for another breakfast and then to bed. It was unlikely we would be flying that night, but usually reported to the Flight Office after lunch.

'When we had the occasional 24 or 48 hours off I found it best to set off after return from ops, better still if in the middle of the night, because there was very little traffic at that time. After eating the 'breakfast' the Mess staff would fill a vacuum flask with coffee to drink on the way home. Invariably, I arrived home just as everyone was getting up. I never told anyone where I had been a matter of a few hours earlier. If asked, I would say that I had made an early start to make the most of my time off. We would try and switch off completely while at home and not think about flying until the time came to set out for base. This was sometimes made difficult when the BBC news kept reporting that the RAF had bombed a certain German town and you knew that you were one of those involved. The local newspapers although very restricted in size invariably carried such news on the front page. On reflection, I feel certain that had I told people where I had been a few hours earlier they would not have believed me. The hours at home simply flew until the time came to go back to camp. As aircrew we were allowed petrol for recreational purposes, so I was able to drive home. This saved considerable time. The only time I stopped in either direction was to give a lift to service personnel trying to get home or back from leave. During the war there never seemed to be any reason to worry about stopping in the hours of darkness and giving someone a lift. The journeys took about four hours each way. The return journeys were always something of an anti-climax. As we got nearer and nearer to camp that indescribable gut feeling returned. Most people talk about feeling in their heart or head when invariably the various emotions are felt in the stomach.

'Immediately upon return we would report to the Flight Office to see whether we were on the Battle Order for that night. If we were it was a matter of arranging an NFT on the aircraft allocated to us and discovering times of briefing. If not on the list it was a case of hanging around to see if there were any odd jobs to be done before going back to the Mess. Usually one crew was asked to stay on call in case of sickness.

'I continued flying with my navigator Bert Cook. We shared some odd moments, some terrifying ones and some humorous ones. A few of the terrifying moments were not necessarily dangerous, but in the dark with our nerves taut it did not take much to make us jump. The top section of the cockpit was a metal frame with Perspex panels and this had a release lever to detach it. If it was necessary to bail out, the panel was detached and exit was made from above. The entrance in the bottom of the aircraft was not suitable for a quick getaway. On one night we had dropped our bomb and were flying towards home at about 26,000 feet. Then suddenly 'it' happened. It was as if a giant hand had slapped the bottom of the aircraft. It was very loud, although not a bang. At this moment a hurricane blew through the cockpit, blowing loose papers and articles around like feathers. We were well strapped in, but anything that wasn't clipped down was disappearing. For an interminable few seconds we could not contemplate what had happened. The dim cockpit lights were concentrated on the instruments and did not shed any light on the problem.

'For a split second both of us imagined the worst, that the aircraft had started breaking up and that 'this was the end'. As the seconds ticked by and the engines were still running the aircraft was responding reasonably well to the controls it became apparent that we were still flying, even if it had suddenly become very, very cold (as well as a hurricane blowing). My navigator was now hanging onto his chart board and chart like death. It was by then apparent that we had no roof to our aircraft. The whole episode from the 'big slap' to this realisation only took a few seconds. We had been taught emergency drill for most of the mishaps that might befall us, but we had not been taught the procedure for flying without a cockpit roof.

'We had exercises in abandoning the aircraft by detaching the roof and getting out that way, but not for continuing with it missing. We were now in no actual danger but it was important to take action of some sort. Firstly, it was essential to reduce speed, in case the air pressure built up inside the aircraft and caused structural damage, secondly it was important to lose height before we started freezing. As we wore oxygen masks there was no problem from this source. We were still over enemy territory and we were not keen on flying lower and slower, but we had no alternative. The remainder of the flight was fairly uneventful and we returned to our own base a little later than the others. We reported the occurrence at de-briefing. As usual no-one showed much interest, it was almost as if they thought we had done it on purpose. I never discovered what really caused it. The only feasible reason can be that a rather large shell exploded under us and a shock wave hit us with sufficient force to wrench the roof off.

'Bert and I continued together, not enjoying it, but between us thought there was a remote chance we might survive if we did our job properly and tried not to do silly things. [Bert was killed in a crash landing on returning from ops on the night of the 1 January 1945

Doug had to re-crew with a new navigator]. The loss of Bert was bad enough but now I had sufficient experience to notice the short comings of a new navigator.

'The most disastrous of my experiences was on a trip with a Canadian navigator. He was an extremely nice person, but his navigation left a lot to be desired. Maybe he thought I wasn't a very good pilot, but when I got back I refused to fly with him again. The trip in itself was not memorable in any particular way, but for some reason or other he must have given me the wrong course because on the way back we were running very late. On our VHF radio we could hear other planes asking for permission to land and we were still some way from the station. To make matters worse, the weather was closing in. It was raining hard and the cloud base was getting lower. My own navigator would get us straight back to the airfield, this time I don't think this one had the slightest idea. We were gradually losing height and still in cloud. In rain the windscreen of the Mosquito became almost opaque, which did not help matters. The navigator was frantically trying to get a position from the 'Gee' set without much success. We were fitted with a beam approach receiver. Unfortunately it was a multi-channel Beam Approach with a handle to tune in to station. This was fine if you had time, as it was necessary to tune into a beam and listen for the call sign; from this it was possible to check which signal you were receiving. We did not have time with the cloud base getting lower.

'I tried tuning in but the handle fell off. There was no time to try to repair it. I was now flying at about 1,000 feet and completely in cloud. Should I fly lower and try to break cloud in the hope of seeing a landmark? I knew that I dare not risk this as I was not certain where we were. I called the station and asked for a fix and a course to head homewards. I gave a short transmission and quite quickly they gave me a heading to fly. It was fairly certain that I was within 20miles of the station. I decided that I would have to fly lower otherwise I would miss the airfield even if we passed over it. I reduced height continuously to about 600 feet. As I did, I momentarily broke cloud and at the same time lights glimmered through the rain.

'When full lights were on at operational stations it consisted not only of runway lights but a ring of lights on poles forming a circle around the airfield for aircraft to follow in poor visibility. Also, two large letters were illuminated designating which airfield it was. By a stroke of luck the lights we came across were the station's code letters. It was an airfield (Waterbeach) about seven miles East of Oakington. From this position we could not see the runway lights, although they were only half a mile away. In a second the lights were gone and we were in darkness. I shouted to my navigator to give me a course to get back to Oakington. In these conditions I preferred to try for an airfield that I knew well. At the same time I turned to an approximate course that which I knew was in the right direction. As I straightened out my navigator gave me an accurate course. If all was well we should see the airfield in a couple of minutes.

'It suddenly dawned on me that the course we had been flying was taking us away from the airfield. It transpired it was possible to show a reciprocal bearing from the equipment used to give a fix, if the aircraft was low and close to the transmitter. I knew that it was fairly safe to continue at about 600 feet between the two airfields. I couldn't go back into cloud again and I certainly couldn't fly any lower. Luck was with us again, we flew over the airfield directly above the runway, it now required a circuit to come in and land. If I could locate the outer circuit lights and follow them in we might be successful in finding the runway again and in landing. I turned to the left in the hope of picking up an outer light. From out of the gloom through an almost opaque windscreen, the glimmer of a light was seen. As soon as we passed this light darkness closed in and we peered to see the next one. This continued until the funnel of lights became visible, although still only one at a time. During this circuit it was also necessary to lower the under carriage and prepare for a landing. It was no good arriving at the runway at 600 feet again. We were running short of fuel, so I began to lose some more height. At long last the lights at the end of the runway came into sight. I cut the throttles and pushed the nose down, levelling off at the last moment then gently forcing the wheels onto the concrete to slow the plane down. The tail wheel dropped and we were down. I radioed to the Control Tower that I had landed as they hadn't seen the plane come in.'

'You'd think that bombing Germany was challenge enough and at first it was' recalls Mike Bayon on 128 Squadron at Wyton. 'But then, we wanted to swagger a bit, to take an early bath, to field close to the bat. We knew that if we switched on our radios (which should only be used as you bailed out to let the rest of the squadron know you were alive or unwounded as you left the plane) the Germans could home in on us. Yet our squadron had a tuneless little ditty and as we swung away after the photographic run one harsh Aussie voice would come over the air and then another and another and another would join in the refrain. And we'd be laughing with the sheer risk of it.'

I saw a ****** boy sitting by the fire.
I saw a ****** boy pulling his wire.
Hold him down while I get at him.
Hold him down as I snatch his ring.

'Odd, unusual and not very wholesome! One of the heavy boys used to get the whole squadron to use his Elsan and then he'd make one bombing run - then do a U-turn against all the stream of bombers, make another bombing run to drop his Elsan, shouting obscenities in broken German as he did so.

'The backroom boys put much thought into bombing. How about high explosive first, to shatter the roofs and the gas mains? This would make the incendiaries infinitely more lethal instead of their bouncing off roofs on to the pavement. How about incendiaries first? Then the ARP and fire fighters would swarm out to deal with them and be killed by the HE. How about a mixed grill? In fact, this was the usual pattern.

'I tried not to think of cities and people and treasured possessions and pets and children. London had been in the grip of the Blitz. If you went up you would sleep in the tube shelters, all along the platforms. Not a restful night - babies might cry and trains started at 4.30 am. But there was a great feeling of camaraderie - no theft, no mugging. From Cambridge nightly we saw the glow in the sky, fifty miles away. I tried to concentrate on the essential. If Germany won; the whole world would be enslaved. Then one night Ivor Broom the CO said, 'Berlin tonight - again. A night on the Spree (Berlin is on the River Spree); and it will create chaos. The city is jam-packed with refugees fleeing from the Russians on the Eastern Front'. That night I had a nightmare. I dreamt that I saw, in the cold light of dawn, a great heap of bricks and rubble. Drifts of thin smoke wafted around. A woman, swathed in black, was clawing desperately at the rubble. I could see that her breath was rasping in her chest but everything was completely silent. I could see her nails tearing, her hands bleeding and the desperation in her. Suddenly she saw a child's thin bony hand poking out of the rubble. She called out and clawed and scrabbled even more desperately; and as she cleared almost to the elbow the hand just went limp and I woke, sweating. I did not sleep for the rest of that cold, frosty night. I just walked round the deserted airfield with Sheba my nuzzled spaniel. There was a full moon, the stars were very vivid and it was very cold. I found a £5 note, sodden, in a ditch. From then on, almost every night and long after the war was over; I had that same dream. Yet I was happy. I was doing something important, something which had to be done; and I was doing it well.

'Another odd thing; we were strongly individualistic. Unthinking obedience was anathema to us, yet we were disciplined, deeply disciplined. We had very little time for indiscipline. I remember flying over Alconbury, an American base. If the Yanks got back to base damaged or with wounded aboard, they'd contact control and take their place in the circuit, in order of priority. The Yanks were back from a daylight raid. The airwaves were throbbing with their cries of 'May Day'. Then they abandoned control altogether and came in huggermugger - down wind, cross wind, any old how. No less than five collided about at the junction of the runways and a great pall of smoke rose. It made me very angry.

'In spite of our casual dress, behaviour, cars and moustaches, we were surprisingly caring of our 'best blue', or new forage caps; or gloves; like the Guards Officers at Waterloo, oddly dandified.

'The Mosquito boys had another chore, which we did not much enjoy. We would set off, on the same route and almost at the same height as the Lancasters and Halifaxes - the heavy boys; then they would swing off one way and we would swing off on our own route. BUT - we had to drop thousands and thousands of strips of tinfoil to simulate a heavy stream of aircraft to the German radar. It was fiddly work splitting the packages and pushing them down the chute, cold too; and the slight pressurization we had in the plane would dissipate. But worst of all, to entice the enemy fighters away from the soft target of the heavies, we had to fire off vivid flares and Very lights every few hundred yards. It's not very nice to be told that you don't count and that you're expendable!

'But now we had done twenty or thirty trips; we were good and we knew we were good. By hours and hours of work in the radar shed I had become an expert on radar. And I, who can't even mend a fuse and who usually, put in the petrol and leave my companion to see if we need any oil! Donald Bennett had me to dinner a couple of times with his Swiss wife Ly, to see if I could explain exactly how I knew which were our radar signals on the screen and which were the German ones. I couldn't. I just knew. I would sometimes be getting accurate radar fixes fifty miles further east than anyone else on the raid. It gave us a great edge and Doug was pleased. If we were dropping a 4,000lb bomb - which we often were; its terminal velocity in falling was something like 460 feet per second. In other words, if we had gone into a dive we could easily have passed it. It was a great big clumsy thing, like a cylindrical hot water tank. So, you would release it and all of us had enough pride of performance to do a very steady run up to the bombing, however the flak might rattle and the plane would give a great surge as the bomb left it. An anti-aircraft shell bursting nearby could feel much like this, actually. Then you had nearly a minute before the bomb burst. Obviously, standard practice was to take evasive action directly the bomb left, with the navigator timing it to photograph the bomb burst. Once, Mick Solomon took off with a 4,000lb bomb aboard. One engine cut out at 10,000 feet so he jettisoned his bomb, safe - not fused. The bomb did not care; it went off anyway and almost blew him out of the sky. That's at a range of two miles. Next day was very hot. Mick was wearing an overcoat, gloves and a scarf and he was still cold. Shock, of course; but we thought it hilarious. He had to go, of course. They should have known earlier when he refused to join 571 Squadron - because it added up to 13.

'Doug decided that he wanted 'The Best Photographs' in Bomber Command. To his way of thinking, this involved straight and level not only for the minute of run up, but also for the minute of bomb fall. It was rather exciting to work at this level of perfectionism.'

A successful daylight raid was carried out on 31 December against the Oslo Gestapo Headquarters, in Victoria Terrasse (last bombed by 105 Squadron Mosquitoes on 25 September 1942) by the low level Mosquito diver specialists on 627 Squadron. Back to night operations again and on the night of 31 December 77 Mosquitoes were dispatched to Berlin and twelve to Ludwigshafen.

At Wyton Doug Swain and Mike Bayon had now worked out a way of always being first back. 'Sure, we did come back in a straight line but so did lots of others' recalls Mike Bayon. 'Our secret was to climb to 32,000 or higher for the return journey, when bombs or petrol didn't weigh us down. On the indicator, the reading was very low for our airspeed, owing to the thinness of the air; and the climb did take time. But at that height we went like a bullet. In fact, every time I suffered from bends; but it seemed ungenerous to mention it. Doug would stay at height till the last possible moment and then scream down to take first place in the circuit. Obviously, our ears could not cope with this change of pressure. Later, when I shared a room with Doug, whoever woke first would hold his nose and blow and the high pitched squeal as the pressure equalised would wake the other.

'I was now an officer. The CO called me in and said I should be commissioned. I said I saw no necessity for it. I was perfectly satisfied with the pay, in any case the ground crew treated me as an officer and I saw no point in going on a course to learn to behave like an officer. The CO said that I must be an officer. I said I hadn't time. I was busy. 'All right' he said. 'You can skip everything. We'll bypass it by saying you were commissioned on the battlefield.'

Eighteen crews on 692, 571 and 128 Squadrons were now briefed for a daylight raid on 24 strategic tunnels in the Eifel and Ardennes area. Each Mosquito would carry a 4,000lb bomb with orthodox casing and fitted with a 30-second delay fuse which was to be dropped as low as it was possible, aiming for 50 to 100 feet above ground level to avert any possibility of the crew being blown apart by the blast. 'For days we practiced - thrilling;' recalls Mike Bayon. 'I remember swooping over the brow of a Welsh hill and seeing the sheep scatter. Then the raid was postponed and when it did take place [on New Year's Day] we were on leave. We were deeply disappointed. One pilot came back with blades of barley in his tail wheel. One saw a train accelerating into a tunnel. Just as it shot in, like a rabbit into its hole, he dropped his bomb to collapse the entrance to the tunnel. What neither he nor the train driver knew was that the other end had been collapsed ten minutes earlier.'[76]

During January-May 1945 LNSF Mosquitoes made almost 4,000 sorties over the dwindling Reich for the loss of 57 Mosquitoes shot down or written off. No opportunity, it seemed, was missed to wake up the harassed inhabitants of Berlin and the LNSF bombed the 'Big City' on 61 nights running but the main purpose was for the BBC to be able to announce to the world that 'aircraft of the RAF have bombed Berlin for another consecutive night'. Tom Empson completed initial pilot training in New Zealand in 1941 followed by Canada and then two years as an instructor on twins before his much desired posting to 128 Squadron with his navigator Bert Dwerryhouse. Empson recalls:

---

76 A 128 Squadron Mosquito crashed on take-off, killing the crew. Six out of seven Mosquitoes on 692 Squadron bombed tunnels near Mayen, losing Flight Lieutenant George Nairn and his navigator Sergeant Danny Lunn to light flak. One bomb, dropped by B.XVI ML963 K-King, crewed by Flight Lieutenant Norman J. Griffiths and Flying Officer W. R. Ball, totally destroyed a tunnel at Bitburg. Twelve tunnels were blocked in the Eifel and Ardennes area, holding up German lines of communication.

'Calculated risks in time of war were considered acceptable. Sometimes they were taken for unwarranted reasons. Take the occasion on 14/15 January when eight of us were went to Berlin in dangerous conditions rather than break the sequence of continuous nightly raids on that city. The forecast was for pending snow storms with zero visibility. As it was not due for a few hours the planners decided a small force of [83] Mosquitoes had time to visit Berlin and return before it clamped. So the eight were selected from 128 Squadron and Bert Dwerryhouse and I were one of the 'privileged' crews.' So too were Doug Swain and Mike Bayon, who recalls: 'A disastrous night, Doug and I had quarrelled, so we were split up as a crew for that night. I was to fly with Alan Heitman an Australian pilot and Doug had Nat [Pilot Officer A. N. Gold], Alan's navigator; a ratty little POM. Briefing was over and we were all in the crew bus. Doug came over 'I don't know whose fault the argument was and I don't care. You're the best navigator in the world and I don't trust anyone else. Will you fly with me tonight? I've fixed it up with Alan and Nat'. So, I got out at our usual dispersal point.'

'We took off at perhaps 10 pm. An early dawn landing. The predicted winds were high that night - 130 mph from the West. I plotted my first wind; 130 mph - from the East. I told Doug. He said, 'You must have made a mistake'. I took my next wind. Same result. He said. 'Look, this is absurd. Try again. I'll concentrate like buggery on my height and airspeed'. Third wind, same result. 'We've got to believe it,' I said. What had happened was that the anti-cyclone had gone through faster than predicted, so that we were on the other side of the trough. We were meant to reach Berlin in perhaps two hours - it took us 3½ hours, all right, so we'd come back fast, but we'd have been bucking a head wind for 3½ hours with full petrol and bomb load. We knew we'd be pinched tight for fuel on return.'

Tom Empson adds: 'When we left we entered a very thick cloud at about 500 feet and we didn't break it until we were at over 23,000 feet where it was a beautiful moonlit night. The only uncomfortable factor was that we were leaving clearly defined condensation trails behind us. We consoled ourselves with the thought that the stormy conditions were forecast for all of Europe and the Luftwaffe would have more concern for their crews than those of the 'mad dogs of Englishmen' and the one from New Zealand. We completed our op to the best of our ability, but we still had to get down. We started our let down over the enemy coast as per usual, entering and breaking cloud again at the same height as on the journey out. Navigation lights on, we were just able to see a faint glow on each wing tip, although it would be almost invisible to the seven other planes heading for the same area as we were. We continued regardless with Bert glued to his green screen. We were down to 500 feet again, still in cloud when Bert said we were overhead. About then another aircraft called for permission to land saying that visibility was very bad with the cloud base at 220 feet and it was snowing. I recognised the call sign as that of our Flight Commander Ivor Broom. This was very disturbing and I told Bert to lower the undercarriage and 20° of flap just to be ready for an emergency landing.

'I called up control to say we were orbiting overhead at 164 feet and needed urgent clearance and confirmation that they had sighted us. Confirmation came just as Bert indicated the blurred lights below. Fortunately, we were in a position from which we could do a steep turn and without power, with full flap and make a good approach. We got off the runway as soon as we could because another aircraft said it had a visual and was coming in. It was too high but the pilot wisely decided to put down rather than risk losing the 'drome in another attempt. He couldn't pull up in time and ran off the end of the runway and through the hedge beyond. We then heard control calling Sparhawk aircraft ordering them to climb to a safe height and bail out. They were getting near the end of their endurance and needed fuel to climb to at least 5,900 feet. The outcome of this disastrous sortie was that one crew spotted runway lights through a small gap and managed to get down just before their motors stopped. Of the others, one couldn't reach height and the crew perished. Two others did escape successfully, leaving one unaccounted for. It was not until next morning that a report came in that the eighth plane had been found a distance from the end of the take off runway. It had crashed and miraculously not exploded or caught fire. All in all the cost of that bit or propaganda was two crews lost, with one aircraft badly damaged and four written off. Hardly worth it they had to admit and all because the Met had miscalculated the arrival time of the weather front.'

Doug Swain and Mike Bayon got back to base and their fuel tanks registered empty. 'Moreover', says Bayon 'a great blanket of warm air had slid over the cold air, trapping fog, which was forming on a nucleus of the ashes of burning London. Doug contacted base. 'Why aren't the runway lights on?'

'They are'.

'But we're right over base at only 10,000 feet'.

'There's a bit of fog down here.'

'The rest of that night is easily told. Half a dozen Mosquitoes gained height and crews bailed out, leaving crewless planes to crash. [77]

One plane aborted and came back early with radar trouble - once when we had radar trouble we just carried on. They were pretty 'wet' we thought. The planes limped in, exhausted, frustrated, short of fuel and no airfield visible. One diverted to Bassingbourn and landed safely. 'Taxi in to the perimeter' radioed control. He couldn't - he had no fuel. One crew who tried to land was not quite accurate enough and they landed on a petrol bowser. Even this great sheet of flame was not visible through the clinging fog. Next day the Medical Officer went to search for their bodies. All he found was one thumb and he callously trod it into the ground with his heel. John Smith, a good bloke and a bloody fine fly half at rugby, found base but could not land. 'Gain height and bail out' ordered control. He tried and ran out of fuel. His navigator bailed out safely. Parachutes were designed to open within 400-600 feet. John got out at 180 feet and his parachute was still only half open when he hit the ground. He must have hit at well over 80 mph, but he was fit and relaxed. He rolled with the fall and wasn't even bruised. When he got back he said, 'I'm going to look there tomorrow. Just before I jumped I chucked out my forage cap - it was brand new'. The plane hit the ground less than 200 yards from where his cap was found.

'Alan Heitman was less lucky. He got back over base, saw no runway, was told to gain height and bail out. Nat opened the escape hatch and froze with fear. A red haired WAAF was talking the planes in. In fact, she was engaged to Alan and they were due to marry on their next leave. She could hear Alan telling Nat to jump and then his urgency as he said, 'The engine's overheating. Christ - it's on fire. Jump! Jump!' Still

---

77 Five Mosquitoes from the Berlin raid crashed in England and three crashed in Belgium. Flying Officer T .J. S. Adam and Flight Sergeant A. J. Casey RAAF on 128 Squadron died trying to force-land at Woodhurst, 5 miles NE of Huntingdon.

Nat clung to the plane. Now Alan was losing control of the plane and the flames were beginning to lick at the cockpit. He even struggled with Nat and still Nat clung neurotically to the plane. Suddenly he jumped and landed safely. But by now it was too late for Alan. The plane was in a spin, burning fiercely. The red haired WAAF could hear Alan screaming all the way down and she even heard the plane hit the ground, though by now she was on hands and knees under the desk, trying to blot out the sounds. She was sent on a week's immediate compassionate leave.[78]

'And Doug and I? Well, this was my chance to test the theory of blind landing I had worked out. Run down one radar line till you hit a cross-line, do a steady 30° turn port and you'd be lined up with the centre of the runway. Accurate to six feet. We tried it at 300 feet. No joy. We simply could not see the massive sodium lights. We went round again. Two hundred feet. Not a sausage. 'We'll just have to go lower,' I said. 'Well I'll go in at 30 feet,' said Doug. 'But you'd better be bloody accurate. The hangars are higher than that.'

'Oh that's OK' I replied. 'It will work'. We came in at 30 feet. 'Crossing perimeter' I said. Then, 'Start of runway'. Then 'You'd better be quick - we're halfway down the runway'. Doug gritted his teeth. 'I hope you know what you're doing he said. 'I'll chuck her down'. We hit the runway and seconds later we were off the runway and on the grass verge. Then we tore through the concertina wire and barbed wire entanglements and perimeter fence as though they were cobwebs. We were still travelling at over 100 mph. Then we hit the hedge and the ditch and the main road from Cambridge to Huntingdon and still Doug was fighting to keep her straight. We hit the hedge and the ditch the other side of the road and now we were in a field of sugar beet, sodden soil. Suddenly the undercart collapsed and we skidded along on the belly of the plane. Then we were still and after all of the intense drama of the last half-minute it was amazingly silent - so silent that you felt you could have gathered great handfuls of it. I've never known a feeling like it. I broke it. 'Thank you, Doug' I said. 'That was good'. Still we sat; we knew we ought to get out in case the plane caught fire; but we felt curiously drained, as though we were waiting for all out innards to catch up with us again.

'Again, I was the one to break the silence. I said, 'I've got some chocolate in my navigation bag. Would you like some?' It was another of our perks, like oranges, that the aircrew got extra rations of, coarse rather bitter heavy chocolate. 'Christ, yes,' said Doug and suddenly we both realized that we were ravenously hungry. I broke the huge slab equally in two and both of us just stuffed the whole lot into our mouths barbarously. At that moment, the CO climbed onto the wing of the plane and battered on the Perspex of the cockpit. 'Is anyone alive? He shouted. He had come by van as far as the perimeter fence and then run through the gap left in the defences by our plane.

'Our mouths were stuffed with half chewed chocolate. We were incapable of coherent speech. I tried to say 'Don't worry, we're OK'; but it was unintelligible. 'Bring the stretchers - they're alive. I can hear them groaning', shouted the CO. Doug and I collapsed. We were laughing till the tears came and choking and doing the nose trick. It was all very silly really. But of course, next day when it came round to seeing what had happened to the squadron that night, things were different. Doug said to me pretty solemnly, 'Look, Mike, if you'd flown with Alan Heitman last night, he'd be alive now and I'd he dead'.

---

78 Flying Officer Alan Walter Heitman RAAF an Australian from Tasmania was 23-years old. The Mosquito crashed near Chatteris, Cambridgeshire.

'If a friend was killed we were actively encourages to get very drunk that night. Next day the day before felt quite distant. On mess nights at the end of the evening we would sing a song from *The Dawn Patrol*, a film of the Great War starring Errol Flynn and David Niven.[79]

> '*So stand by your glasses, steady*
> *Each man who takes off and flies.*
> *So here's to the dead already;*
> *Three cheers for the next man who dies.*'

'And then we drained glasses. Unfeeling? Disrespectful? Insensitive? I don't know. Perhaps it was a kind of denial or defiance.'

On 25 January 1945 163 Squadron reformed at Wyton on B.XXVs under the command of Wing Commander Broom. Wing Commander Broom had instructions from AVM Don Bennett for 163 Squadron to become operational immediately and 163 Squadron flew its first operation on the night of 28/29 January when four B.XXVs dropped 'Window' at Mainz (a 'spoof' raid for the attacks by 602 aircraft on Stuttgart). On the night of 29/30 January when 59 Mosquitoes were despatched to Berlin and 50 reached and bombed the city without loss. In February the LNSF flew 1,662 sorties. The 1/2 February attack on Berlin was the largest Mosquito bombing attack on the Reich capital since the formation of the LNSF with 122 aircraft dispatched in two waves. No aircraft were lost. On the night of 2/3 February raids were carried out by the Main Force on Wiesbaden and a huge synthetic oil plant at Wanne-Eickel just ten minutes beyond the Dutch border near Venlo. Another raid by 250 Lancasters and 11 Mosquitoes of 5 Group would attempt to bomb Karlsruhe. Cloud cover over Karlsruhe caused the raid to be a complete failure and the Mosquito marker aircraft that dived over the city failed to establish the position of the target. Fourteen Lancasters were lost on the raid. German cities were continually bombed early in the month and all were marked by Mosquitoes of 8 and 5 Groups.

On 5/6 February 63 Mosquitoes attacked Berlin seven went to Magdeburg and six to Würzburg. One Mosquito, on 571 Squadron at Oakington, was lost without trace on the raid on Berlin. By way of a change, on 7/8 February 177 Lancasters and 11 Mosquitoes of 5 Group attacked a section of the Dortmund-Ems canal near Ladbergen with delayed action bombs but all missed their target. Another 38 Mosquitoes attacked Magdeburg, 16 bombed Mainz and 41 others attacked five different targets. One Mosquito, on 692 Squadron at Graveley, failed to return from the raid on Mainz. On 8/9 February seven Mosquitoes of 5 and 8 Groups marked the Pölitz oil refineries for 472 Lancasters, 12 of which were lost. The first wave's objective was marked by the 5 Group method and the Pathfinder Mosquitoes of 8 Group marked the second. The weather was clear and the bombing was extremely accurate and severe damage was caused. Nine Mosquitoes flew a 'spoof' on Neubrandenburg for the raid on Pölitz and four more bombed Nuremberg. Another twenty Mosquitoes took part on another raid on the oil refinery at Wanne-Eickel. On 10/11 February 82 Mosquitoes bombed Hannover and another eleven raided Essen. The weather clamped down on the 11th

---

79 Edmund Goulding's 1938 remake of Howard Hawkes' early talkie semi-classic. The 1930 version starred Richard Barthelmess and Douglas Fairbanks Jnr of the RFC over Flanders in WWI, which provided much of the footage for the aerial action for the 1938 film. See *Brassey's Guide to War Films*. Alun Evans (Brassey's 2000)

80 Later Air Marshal Sir Ivor, KSB CBE DSO DFC AFC.

with a mixture of rain and sleet blowing in the air. The weather was still less than hopeful on the morning of the 12th but it eased off slightly after lunch and by take-off time in the late afternoon it was at least flyable and 72 Mosquitoes raided Stuttgart and 15 others bombed Misburg and Würzburg. The latter, a small town set among mountains, had a special significance for Mike Bayon on 128 Squadron, as his father had been at Würzburg University before the war.

'We had a 4,000lb bomb and were told by Met that it would be a clear night so the markers would be on the ground. We arrived over target and could just see the glow through heavy cloud. 'Let's go lower' said Doug. Well, once we were on that course there was no stopping us. We suddenly came into clear air at just under 4,000'. By now it was really exciting. We were bucketing about and tossed around by the bomb bursts (we'd been told that at anything less than 5,000 feet the explosion would rip our wings off) and we were right into the light flak. We'd never experienced that before. We were both laughing with sheer exhilaration and excitement. This was a brand new experience. With the fires and the bomb bursts and the target indicators, it was vividly, luridly lit up. I'd never bombed visually before. I could see squares and streets and the University. I picked on the railway as my target, two tall towers like King's Cross. Then we were climbing and wheeling steeply to avoid the pine clad mountains.

'We got back last. Rose had given us up as missing. We were last in the queue for debriefing. We were last in the queue for rum, hot water and sugar - better than any sleeping draught if you are cold and keyed up. One after another came to the table.

'What did you bomb?'

'Glow in the sky'.

'Again and again and again. The Intelligence Officer was in the rhythm. Donald Bennett was leaning negligently against the wall. A lot of the crews had gone to bed. Doug and I were smiling secret smiles and even nudging each other, like kids. We reached the table.

'What did you bomb?' asked the bloke.

'I looked at Doug. He said, 'You saw it best. You say.' I said, 'We bombed the railway station'. The Intelligence Officer had already written, 'Glow in the sky' and switched off. Suddenly he shouted 'WHAT?' Donald Bennett hurried over; as the news spread, all the other crews on the raid came back - some in 'jamas, some half-undressed. Then the various cooks, electricians and firemen on night duty all flooded in. Ours was the only eyewitness account of how the raid had gone - where the bombs had dropped, how accurately the target indicators were. Doug received an immediate award of the DFC. Mine followed two or three weeks later.'

'February came,' recalled Jim Foley on 608 Squadron 'and from now on to the end of my tour Berlin, weather permitting, was going to be the target. The war had progressed with the Allied armies pressing towards the Rhine and the Russians advancing rapidly through Poland towards Germany. It obviously became Bomber Command policy that the Light Night Striking Force should keep the German capital awake as often as possible. These were more than pinpricks, as on each raid up to one hundred tons of bombs were dropped. While it was still a long way to fly to Berlin, we were never sure of the reception we would get, as more often than not they put up a heavy anti-aircraft barrage. On one occasion no defence at all was evident - as though they were saying 'we can't do anything about these buggers, we'll just have to take it'. In February I did six trips, five to the 'Big City', one of which I flew with Squadron

Leader McArdle as Hank was not able to fly on this particular trip. When we reached the target area we were completely in cloud and could not see anything. The bombs were dropped blindly on target ETA (dead reckoning time over target). I had a week's leave in this month and spent it with Peg and visited brother Syd in Staffs. I think on this leave I mentioned to 'Pop' Sheffield about marriage and he nicely told me that he didn't think it a good idea to get married until I had finished flying operationally, for obvious reasons.

'One snowy afternoon I was sawing logs with another airman using a two handed saw when the CO Wing Commander R. C. Alabaster DSO* DFC* sent for me. He said, 'Jim, you had better go to the stores and get some purple and white ribbon - you've been awarded the DFC.' He said I had done a magnificent job pressing home attacks against the most heavily defended targets, calmness under fire and on more than one occasion navigated the crew back to safety after problems. He went on to say that it was well overdue, considering the number of ops. I had done in both Lancasters and Mosquitoes, as a member of Pathfinder Force and the Light Night Striking Force. Naturally I was elated and fortuitously not operating that night so was able to have a few drinks at the 'Crown and Sceptre' in Downham Market to celebrate.'

On 13/14 February Dresden was bombed in two RAF assaults three hours apart, the first by 244 Lancasters of 5 Group and the second by 529 Lancasters of 1, 3, 6 and 8 Groups. 5 Group attacked at 22.15 hours, using its own pathfinder technique to mark the target. This was a combination of two Lancaster Squadrons; 83 and 97, to illuminate the target with Primary Blind Markers and parachute flares to light up the target and 627 Mosquito Squadron to visually mark the aiming point with TIs from low level. The aiming-point was a sports stadium in the centre of the city near railway lines and a river, which served as a pointer to the Stadium for the Marker Force. There were six such stadiums in the area so particular care had to be exercised. At 22.13 hours 244 Lancasters, controlled throughout by the Master Bomber, began their attack. A second raid started at 01.30 hours on the 14th by another 529 aircraft of Bomber Command. Calculations were that a delay of three hours would allow the fires to get a grip on the sector (provided the first attack was successful) and fire brigades from other cities would concentrate fighting the fires. In this second attack target marking was carried out by 8 Pathfinder Group. The Mosquitoes were aided by the newly installed Loran sets, which enabled reliance on radar to be greatly extended as they went further east and out of Gee range. The backing-up by all markers was described as 'first rate'. The US 8th Air Force dispatched 450 B-17s of which 316 attacked Dresden shortly after 12 noon on 14 February to add to the destruction.

PRU photographs, taken later that day, showed that the marking went smoothly, the bombing was accurate and there were very few casualties in the bomber force. This was due in no small part to the Mosquitoes, of which 59 night-fighters were on patrol and in 8 Group, 71 went to Magdeburg, 16 to Bonn and eight each to Misburg and Nuremburg and six to Dortmund. On the raid on Magdeburg a Me 262 jet fighter was seen by Wing Commander Ivor Broom and also by Flying Officer Price on 163 Squadron. There was no certainty that it was even the same one. So great were the conflagrations caused by the firestorms created in the great heat generated in the first attack on Dresden that crews in the second attack reported the glow was visible 200 miles from the target. In a firestorm similar to that created in Hamburg in July 1943, an estimated 50,000 Germans died in Dresden. The night following, Operation Thunderclap continued with an all-out assault on Chemnitz. Small numbers of Mosquitoes were dispatched to targets at Rositz, Mainz, Dessau, Duisburg, Nuremburg and Frankfurt and 46 Mosquitoes visited Berlin.

On the night of 19/20 February Böhlen was the target for 254 Lancasters and six Mosquitoes of 5 Group. This raid was not successful, probably because the 627 Squadron Mosquito on loan to Wing Commander Eric Arthur Benjamin DFC* of 54 Base, the 25 year old Master Bomber, was shot down by flak over the target. Benjamin and his navigator, Flying Officer J. E. Heath DFM were killed. The following night Mosquitoes carried out the first of 36 consecutive nightly raids on the 'Big City', 1,896 sorties being flown for the loss of eleven Mosquitoes, a loss rate of just .58 per cent.

In February 1945 24-year old Squadron Leader Peter Whitaker and Flight Lieutenant Hoare as his navigator on 105 Squadron at Bourn in Cambridgeshire flew 36 hours by night to ten different targets - including Würzburg, Kassel, Nuremberg, Mainz and Mannheim. Whitaker, who had flown two tours on Wellingtons, had experienced worrying cardiac irregularities during decompression tests simulating flight at 37,000 feet in October. Asked why he did not report this at the time, he stated he had no intention of being discharged as LMF (Lacking Moral Fibre) and in November he commenced conversion on the Mosquito. On 21 February, when 77 Mosquitoes went to Berlin, Peter Whitaker and Flight Lieutenant Hoare flew the first of their three raids on Bremen - then considered the most heavily defended target in Germany. No aircraft were lost. On the following night, 73 Mosquitoes returned to the 'Big City'; again without loss, although one of four Mosquitoes was lost on a raid on Erfurt when it was abandoned SE of Bruges in Belgium. The following night, on a sortie to Essen, which was attacked by 324 heavies and 18 Mosquitoes of 4, 6 and 8 Groups, Peter Whitaker shut down one of their two engines immediately after take-off, but still completed the operation. Asked why he had not aborted the task, Peter stated it was safer to continue to the target than to explain a turn back to AVM Bennett! The target area was cloud covered and all the bombs were dropped on sky markers. Such was the accuracy of the marking that 300 HE and 11,000 incendiary bombs fell on the Krupps works. On the night of 25 February, when 63 Mosquitoes went to Erfurt and ten each to Berlin and Mainz, Peter Whitaker and Flight Lieutenant Hoare were one of six Mosquito crews that went to Bremen again. This time, carrying a 4,000lb bomb, Peter Whitaker and Flight Lieutenant Hoare were hit by anti-aircraft flak during the attack. They were again one of six crews that returned to attack the same target on the night of 27 February when 96 Mosquitoes also attacked Berlin and were again hit by flak when pressing home a 4,000lb bomb attack. The following month, although the weather was much worse, they marked a further seven separate targets during a total of 25 hours night flying.

In March the LNSF raided Berlin on no less than 27 nights, flying 1,222 sorties and losing seven Mosquitoes on operations. On 6 March, the last day raid by Mosquitoes, 48 Mosquitoes led by 'Oboe'-equipped Mosquitoes on 109 Squadron to provide marking, took off at around 15.00 hours for Wesel, which was believed to contain many German troops and vehicles. Shortly before the attack a fighter escort rendezvoused with the Mosquitoes. Over the target there was 10/10th cloud cover reaching to 15,000 feet. On 128 Squadron Doug Swain's and Mike Bayon's experience of their only daylight raid was 'rather dull; but different', so it stuck in Bayon's mind. 'Our troops had reached the Rhine and were held by stubborn resistance at Wesel. By now we had virtual command of the air. I don't know how many planes - certainly around 2,000 bombers -

were in the air. We took off, made our rendezvous and flew over the North Sea in tight formation while above us and below us the fighters weaved and patrolled. We came North of Wesel and swung onto the target run - no flak, no fighters. A feeling of unreality, like performing in an empty hall. No audience! Contrails were forming and we ran down them, as though they were rails. The leader of our formation opened his bomb doors - we did the same. His bomb dropped and we also pressed the tit as his plane surged up under the release of its load. That was it. A non-event but I met an Army officer who was on our bank of the Rhine that day. He said they themselves were almost in a state of shock, shattered, deafened, addled. Then they crossed the river and the Germans were paralysed - incapable of speech, thought or movement.'

That evening 87 Lancasters of 3 Group and 51 Mosquitoes of 8 Group continued the attack on Wesel with two separate raids. Two Mosquitoes on 109 Squadron were seen to collide. One of them returned safely to Little Staughton but the other crashed killing the crew. A 105 Squadron Mosquito was attacked on return by a British night-fighter and was abandoned south of Frayling Abbey in Norfolk. Both crew who were injured, bailed out safely. A second Mosquito crash landed at Bourn.

The following night 80 Mosquitoes visited Berlin, ten went to Frankfurt, nine to Münster and five to Hannover. One Mosquito was lost on the Berlin operation. On 8/9 March thirty Mosquitoes were dispatched to the 'Big City', 33 to Hannover, seven to Hagen and five each to Bremen and Osnabrück. The night following no less than 92 Mosquitoes went to Berlin and 16 more went on 'siren tours' of Bremen, Hannover, Osnabrück and Wilhelmshaven. On 10/11 March when no heavies were operating, sixty Mosquitoes were detailed to bomb Berlin, with four each going to Gotha, Jena and Weimar. Nine aircraft including two H$_2$S-equipped Marker aircraft were dispatched by 162 Squadron.

Flying Officer Burgess and Flight Lieutenant Wallis suffered engine problems over the North Sea. The port engine began to give trouble and Burgess decided to shut it down. However, before he could complete the task the starboard engine suddenly began to fail. The crew decided to abort the sortie to Berlin and drop the bomb load on Hamburg. An alteration in course was made and at 21.05 the bomb load was released from 24,000 feet over the city. Once clear of Hamburg a direct course was set for base and on nearing the English Channel was notified of the problem. The aircraft was diverted to Carnaby and the crew made a landing there at 22.04.

Flight Lieutenant Abraham and Flight Lieutenant Gannon in one of the Marker Mosquitoes arrived over Berlin to find the target covered with a layer of alto-stratus topping out at around 20,000 feet. They approached the glow of two sets of TIs which were visible on the cloud and then they made their bombing run from 27,000 feet, releasing three TIs and a 500lb MC bomb on an H$_2$S aiming point over the cloud. Flying Officer Rhys and Flying Officer Kennelly saw the first Red and Yellow Floaters go down as they approached at 26,000 feet. TIs were seen going down at one minute intervals until. The defences were active and some flak was put up against the attacking Mosquitoes. Flying Officer Ben Knights and Flight Sergeant 'Robbie' Robjohns bombed and were hit by a flak burst about 30 seconds later as they completed their camera run. A fragment of flak partly severed a fuel pipe from one of the main inner tanks to the fuel distribution box, causing a fuel leak on the return trip. Knights recalled: 'It was a straightforward trip to the Big City except that we caught a packet in the target area. As was my wont I checked the petrol gauges when I had cleared a difficult passage through heavy flak. Berlin had special flak towers equipped with 120mm AA guns, far out gunning any other German defences. I never knew at this time but was frequently surprised by the number of small holes picked up on the Berlin raids. On this occasion my caution proved worthwhile as it soon became clear that we were losing fuel quite rapidly. We identified the holed tank and switched over to it to make use of the remainder. It then became a question of whether we could venture across the North Sea. If not, was a friendly aerodrome within reach or would we have to bail out in a suitable area? Robbie had to do the calculations on the elementary computer supplied by the engine maker and I had to set the engines to the most economical running. We used our VHF to request permission to land at Woodbridge but we were diverted to Coltishall. As it turned out the main DREM lighting system at Coltishall was out of order and we had to land on the bumpy grass aerodrome by old fashioned glim lamps. It transpired that Coltishall was used by gun firing Mosquitoes to intercept low flying V-1s.'

The second Marker crew of Wing Commander Bolton and Squadron Leader Waterkeyn suffered a series of major equipment failures as they flew over the English Coast. Both the 'Gee' and H_2S sets failed. However, the crew decided to press on, Waterkeyn navigating using the compass and DR fixes assisted by the Route-markers to reach the target area. They dropped a single 500lb bomb on a cluster of TIs visible beneath the cloud. Leaving the target area what appeared to be 'dummy' TIs were seen beneath the cloud 10 miles north of the target. As a consequence of the H_2S failure the TIs were not released; they were brought home. Flight Lieutenant Haden and Flight Sergeant Nichols, who bombed from 25,000 feet at the same time, saw bomb bursts around one set of TIs. Amongst them were one or two scattered cookie blasts. 30 seconds later Flight Lieutenant Goodman and Flying Officer Jarrett dropped their bomb load on to TIs from 26,000 feet. Because of the cloud cover it was impossible to assess the effectiveness or accuracy of the bombing. [81]

The 21st March was an almost perfect spring day and that evening some crews flew two sorties when no less than 142 Mosquitoes were detailed for two attacks on Berlin. The first wave of 106 Mosquitoes headed off at about 19.00 hours and the second wave of a further 36 Mosquitoes following just before 02.00 hours. All told, 118 crews got their bomb loads away on the 'Big City'. Seven Mosquitoes of 5 Group dropped mines in Jade Bay and the River Weser and three Mosquitoes visited Bremen. One Mosquito failed to return from the raid on Berlin and another returned early with engine trouble and crash landed at Upwood. Both crew members survived the crash but the navigator died of his injuries later in Ely Hospital.

Two nights' later 80 Lancasters and 23 Mosquitoes of 5 and 8 Groups carried out the last raid on Wesel at 3.30pm. Wesel was an important troop centre behind the Rhine front in the area about to be attacked by the 21st Army Group massing for the Rhine crossings at dawn. It was an important point in the defensive system on the east bank of the Rhine and the Germans had not only turned it into a massively fortified position, with strong points, machine gun nests and tank obstacles, but had concentrated troops and armour there for the expected British crossing. Once a town of 25,000 people, Wesel was, because of its tactical importance one of the most devastated places in Germany.

81   *162 Squadron - Just another trip to the Big City?* Written and researched by Barry Blunt. *The Mossie,* No.34 September 2003.

It was an important point in the defensive system on the east bank of the Rhine and the Germans had not only turned it into a massively fortified position, with strong points, machine gun nests and tank obstacles, but had concentrated troops and armour there for the expected British crossing. In ten minutes, the roads, which had been cleared from the previous attacks were blocked and pitted with fresh craters. More than 400 tons of bombs were dropped on the troops and many strong points were destroyed. Five hours later, at 2230 hours, only a short time before Field Marshal Sir Bernard Montgomery's zero hour, as the 1st Commando Brigade followed by the 51st Highland Division closed in, over 190 Lancasters followed it up with another attack to complete the work of the afternoon. In exactly nine minutes, well over 1,000 tons of bombs went down on those troops who had crept back into the ruins to await the British commandos' attack. In all, more than 1,500 tons of bombs were dropped in the two attacks - a weight of bombs which had already almost completely wiped out cities eight times the size of Wesel.

One of the most dramatic marking operations of the war had occurred on 14 March when a Mosquito of 5 Group and eight 'Oboe' Mosquitoes on 105 and 109 Squadrons set out to mark for 5 Group Lancasters in attacks on the Bielefed and Arnsberg viaducts. Four Mosquitoes attempting to mark the Arnsberg viaduct for 9 Squadron failed in the attempt, with no damage to the viaduct. Three of the 'Oboe' Mosquitoes were unable to mark the Bielefed viaduct for 617 Squadron but Flying Officer G. W. Edwards on 105 Squadron, succeeded in getting his markers on target and more than 100 yards of the Bielefed viaduct collapsed under the explosions.[82]

On 14/15 March Lancasters attacked Lützkendorf and Zweibrücken and Hagen and Misburg the night following - all of which were marked by Mosquitoes. The LNSF was out in force on both nights, with a total of 129 Mosquito sorties on Berlin and no Mosquito losses and again on 16/17 March when 56 Mosquitoes visited the 'Big City'. Again there were no Mosquito losses though 24 Lancasters were shot down attacking Nuremburg and six were lost on the raid on Würzburg. One of these was attributed to Hauptmann Wilhelm 'Wim' Johnen, Kommandeur of III./NJG6 for his 32nd and final victory of the war. He could have destroyed more but as soon as his Bf 110 was in position his Bordschütze shouted; Auchtung! Moskito! Forty Mosquito night fighters were on patrol to cover the two raids. Johnen had instructed Mahle only to warn him in case of great danger. They could hardly watch the Lancaster crash on the ground before the Mosquitoes set upon the Bf 110. Johnen wrote: 'The Naxos apparatus [FuG 350 homing and warning radar] lit up constantly. Mahle no longer shouted Achtung! but sat and fired his tracers at the Mosquitoes. No avoiding action - no banking - no hide and seek in the clouds was of any avail. The British pilot remained on my tail. Fortunately he always began from long range and his aim was inaccurate. And then suddenly Mahle shouted in terror, 'Mosquito close behind us.' His voice made me shudder. Even as I banked the burst hit my machine. There was a reek of smoke and fire. Terrifying seconds ahead, but I let my machine dive to be rid of my pursuer. The altimeter fell rapidly - 2500... 2000...1500...1000. Now I had to pull out unless I wanted to go straight into the ground. I pulled with all my might on the joystick and got the diving machine under control. Luckily the controls answered. There was still an acrid smell of smoke in the cabin. Perhaps a cable was smouldering, but the engines were

82 Twenty-eight of the 32 Lancasters dispatched carried 'Tallboy' bombs and one from 617 Squadron dropped the first 22,000lb 'Grand Slam' bomb.

running smoothly. We hedge-hopped over Swabia towards our airfield at Leipheim.

Almost out of fuel Johnen reached Leipheim, pursued by a Mosquito all the way. Johnen lowered the wing flaps to 20° and circled at low speed over the airfield. The British were searching. The ticking in his headphones from the Naxos tail warning device was continuous and perspiration was pouring from his forehead. Mahle suddenly shouted: 'There's one ahead to starboard. A bit higher.' Johnen only caught a glimpse of exhaust pipes disappearing in the darkness.

'For God's sake don't shout so loud, Mahle,' he replied.

The seconds passed. Throttle back. Float... The wheels touched down. Johnen applied the brakes and the 110 gradually came to a standstill. Grasshof his Bordfunker opened the cockpit roof.

'Herr Hauptmann, the Tommies are droning right overhead. Something's up.'

Johnen cautiously gave a little throttle to prevent the flames darting from the engine. Any reflection would betray them. In the darkness he taxied to the dispersal pen. Then an over-eager mechaniker, trying to be helpful, flashed his green torch. The Mosquitoes were on the watch. Johnen turned the 110 into wind and cut off the engine. Mahle shouted: 'Put that torch out, you bloody fool.' At that moment the crew heard an increasingly loud whistle in the air. The Mosquito was diving on the airfield. The 'Intruder' fired and the tracers made directly for the German crew. Johnen sprang out of his seat on to the left wing and fell over Grasshof and Mahle as he slipped to the ground. A Feldwebel was writhing on the ground. Then the second Mosquito made its attack. 'The burning machine made an easy target' wrote Johnen. 'With a few leaps we got clear of the machine and lay flat on the ground. Grasshof and Mahle were close behind me. The second burst was a winner. Our good Me 110 exploded and went up in flames. Now the British were in their element. Powerless, we had to watch two more night fighters go up in flames.' [83]

On the night of 18/19 March just over 300 Lancasters and twenty Mosquitoes of 4, 6 and 8 Groups carried out an area raid on Witten and another large force of Lancasters of 1 Group raided Hanau. Included in this force were nine Mosquitoes and 47 Lancasters of 8 Group. Two of the Mosquitoes were abortive. The attack opened at 0425 hours when the first red TIs were seen cascading. Other Red and mixed Red/Green TIs quickly followed and formed a good group on and around the aiming point, which could be clearly seen in the light of the illuminating flares. The Master Bomber broadcast instructions directing the bombing on to the markers, but many crews do not appear to have heard him. However, the bombing was all well concentrated on the markers and the town was described as being a mass of flames as aircraft left. One large explosion was observed as 0432 hours and fires were visible for up to 80 miles distance on the return journey. The defences were negligible and just one Lancaster failed to return. Seven heavies and a Mosquito were lost on the raid on Witten. Sixty-two per cent of the built-up area in Witten was destroyed and Hanau too, was devastated.

The largest operation ever on Berlin occurred on the night of 21/22 March when 138 Mosquitoes set out to attack in two waves. It was the 30th successive raid on the 'Big City' and PFF HQ had invited the media to visit Wyton. 'All the newspapers and the BBC were there covering the preparations during the day, briefing, take-off and return' recalls Tom Empson DFC pilot of A-Apple on 128 Squadron. 'Bert Dwerryhouse and I

---

83 *Duel Under The Stars* by Wilhelm Johnen (Crecy Books 1994)

were on our 14th trip to the 'Big City'. Not much significance in that except that over Berlin we caught a piece of flak in the port motor radiator. We weren't aware of this until it was noticed that the temperature was climbing rapidly. So we had to shut the motor down and feather. Again no big deal except that the motor drove all the nav' radar. Then it was back home on one motor and Bert's dead reckoning. Down at about 17,000 feet and some 150 knots and all lonesome we attracted more than the usual attention. This we particularly noticed when we wandered over defended towns, we copped the lot. Boozer was working overtime bless it, especially when a fighter beamed on to us. We all but toppled our gyros shaking him off. Called for a QDM when we reckoned we were in range. In spite of Bert's good navigational ability we were surprised to get one from Manston so far south of track so decided not to be heroic and go in there. Next day Archie Robinson came down in an Oxford and took us back to Wyton. Reported to the Winco and he said, 'Good Show, but it would have been much better if you had come home and given the media a bit of drama'!

'We were not heroic and had forgotten all about the media any way. A-Apple's adventure did not end there. When a new motor had been fitted Archie flew me down in a Proctor to collect it. Just as I was getting airborne with attention focused outside a sixth sense made me aware that the oil pressure of the new motor was falling off the clock. Another shut down and SEL at Manston. The problem was soon solved. The drain plug had not been wire locked allowing all the oil to escape. This was my only experience of a mistake by those wonderfully efficient ground crew, how we depended on them. Had this happened with a full load we no doubt wouldn't have made it. Luckily no damage to the new motor was sustained and I was soon on my way. We were to do another ten trips to Berlin before the Russian army took over. Towards the end we wore Union Jacks over our Mae Wests and were drilled to shout Ya Anglicanen if we bailed out in their vicinity.'

Only one aircraft was lost on the 21/22 March raid but on 27/28 March three Mosquitoes of the Light Night Striking Force were missing from a raid on Berlin and a 627 Squadron Mosquito was lost during a 5 Group minelaying operation in the River Elbe. One of the Berlin losses was a Mosquito on 692 Squadron which was lost without trace and the other two were involved in a collision. Throughout the attack on Berlin the searchlights were active across the city and a jet fighter was spotted in the area on the 128 Squadron bombing run. Flight Lieutenant Jim Dearlove and Sergeant Norman Jackson's Mosquito was coned on the bomb run and it was attacked by a Me 262 of 10./NJG11 just after they had dropped their 'Cookie'. He fired two short bursts of cannon fire, which missed the Mosquito and Dearlove was able to take evasive action and escape. Two other Mosquitoes, which failed to return, were claimed shot down by Me 262 jet fighters. Oberfeldwebel Karl-Heinz Becker flew one of 10./NJG11's three Me 262A-1a's this night and claimed his sixth victory. At 2138 hours and flying at 27,600 feet Becker clearly saw the RAF aircraft and opened fire at 150 meters whilst pulling up the nose of his aircraft. He hit the Mosquito squarely. Pulling away to the left Becker observed large burning parts of the Mosquito falling and scattering the ground near Nauen.[84]

---

84 Becker's victim was FB.VI MM131 XD-J on 139 Squadron, which had taken off from Upwood at 1912 hours for Berlin. Squadron Leader H. A. Forbes DFC, the navigator/bomb aimer escaped and was taken prisoner but no trace has ever been found of his pilot, Flight Lieutenant André A. J. van Amsterdam, a Dutch escapee decorated with the DFC and the Dutch AFC.

'The weather in March was much improved' recalled Jim Foley 'and I did eleven sorties of which eight were to Berlin. The others were to Kassel, Zweibrücken and Bremen. At one period in the month I did three in four nights.

Again Hank Henderson was unable to fly and the first one in the month I did with Flight Lieutenant Bartholomew. The second, the CO Wing Commander Alabaster, asked me to navigate him to Berlin and back, quite an honour and an indication I took of my standing as a navigator. We successfully completed the operation, but on return again were unable to land at Downham Market and were diverted to Little Staughton twenty miles away, returning the next day. Toward the end of March our aircraft were modified to carry a 4,000lb bomb, twice the bomb load we had previously carried. In order to carry this 'cookie' it was not possible to close the bomb doors. This meant that once we were airborne it was inadvisable to land still carrying it and orders were to jettison at sea. The take off technique had to be amended, needing a lot more runway to get off the ground. Excitement at carrying this huge bomb was mixed with slight apprehension, especially when we did it for the first time. Just think, this wooden two engined aircraft with a crew of two was carrying the same bomb load as a Flying Fortress, which had a large crew and half the load carried by a Lancaster with a crew of seven. What an aircraft. Pound for pound, as they say in the fight game, we were the greatest! Inevitably the target was Berlin for our first 4,000 pounder and I must admit that I was very relieved when we got off the ground safely, as it seemed an eternity reaching take off speed. When I released the bomb over the target the aircraft gave a noticeable lurch upwards.

'The end of my second tour was in sight and at the end of March I had one op left to do. An historic day for me, 3 April, [when 95 Mosquitoes went to Berlin, eight to Plauen and five to Magdeburg] target Berlin again and if I successfully completed this one I could look forward to three weeks leave, getting married and the end of the war in sight. I tried to be blasé but such a lot seemed at stake; recently we had lost a couple of crews including my Flight Commander. We took off at 22.55 carrying the, by now, usual 'cookie'. Everything went well and we returned safely at 3am. I had completed 82 operations.' [85]

On the night of 16/17 April Jack Currie and his navigator, Flying Officer Norman Pittam DFM on 1409 Met Flight at Graveley heard the Lancaster squadrons from the nearby airfields go while they were dressing - 7 from Oakington, 35 from Graveley and 156 from Upwood - but the Mosquito crew had lots of time ahead to take a look at Europe's weather and still make rendezvous with them before they reached their target. Over 160 Lancasters and eight Mosquitoes of 6 and 8 Groups were to attack the railway yards at Schwandorf in south-east Germany on the edge of the Bavarian Forest. It was a communications link with Hitler's 'Redoubt' at Berchtesgaden.

'Like all good aeroplanes' recalls Jack Currie, 'the Mosquito looked as though it ought to fly well - the first glance told you that. There were those two, great, sharply-pointed engines slung below the tapered wings; the typically towering tail that said de Havilland's had made it; and the narrow fuselage, the famous mix of ply and balsa wood, which gave so high a ratio of power to weight. Sitting in the cockpit was like

---

85 A Mosquito on 139 Squadron flown by Canadian Squadron Leader Roy Dow DFC and Flight Lieutenant J. S. Endersby was shot down on the raid on Magdeburg by a Me 262 of 10/NJG 11 for the only loss of the night. Roy Dow was on his 90th op.

eating at a crowded table - not a lot of room for knees and elbows. It would have been extremely cramped if you had needed lots of clothes, as in the freezing heavy bombers. Luckily, the cabin was as warm as toast and I found that one issue polo-necked jersey underneath the battle-dress was quite enough for comfort.

'East Anglia lay dark beneath us as we climbed towards the coast - so dark that it might have been anywhere, or nowhere. Only Pittam's radar recognised that shapeless nothingness for what it was. Those radar blips lit Pittam's world for him, as the cool, blue panel dials lit mine. Outside my cabin window, the exhaust-pipes on the engine's inboard side gave six dancing, yellow flames; beyond the flames was total darkness. If you liked flying in total darkness, this was the time to do it.

'We crossed the Essex coast at Clacton and flew south-east for 40 minutes, until Liege was under the port wing; there I turned A-Able easterly, over the Ardennes and on across Koblenz, then swung north-east towards Berlin. It was now almost two hours since I had pulled the wheels up over Wyton and the darkness, as it always did, had made itself my friend. It gave me little hints to know it better as time passed; nuances to see its character in all the variations from black to not so black. There was as yet no moon and high, thin veils of cirrus hid a million stars, but I could sense, if not actually see, where the long curve of the horizon met the sky. Then a flickering of gunfire 30,000 feet below came as a reminder that, down there, the war was going on.

'We flew south across the Elbe, past Dresden on the left and Chemnitz on the right and on across the Czechoslovak border until we came to Karlsbad on the starboard beam. There we turned south-west towards Bavaria and the bombers' target. They were to arrive just after 5 am and I meant to complete the recce thirty minutes earlier, which would give me time to tell the Master Bomber what the weather was while he still had a hundred miles or so to go, although - unless there was a sudden change - I was not going to have a lot to tell.

By now, the night had got to know me well enough to let me see more of its secrets - the total blackness that meant forest and the dull gleam of the Danube as it flowed through Regensburg. If I could see that much from 30,000 feet, the marker crews should have no problem over Schwandorf. There was no need, in that clear sky, to find the cloud-base for the Master Bomber, but a descent would make a change from being six unearthly miles high and give a chance to take the mask off for a while.

'With the Merlins throttled back and half-flap down to cut the speed, the Mosquito lost height like a falling star... Bavaria went by at 300 mph - woodlands, open fields, a flash of metalled roadway. Perhaps a villager, behind his blackout boards, was awakened by the Merlins' passing roar and murmured, nestling closer to his wife, 'Don't worry, dear, it's probably one of ours.' In half-an-hour he would be reawakened and the Lancasters would leave him in no doubt as to whose aircraft they were. I climbed to meet them, leaving Schwandorf to its fate and kept on climbing, well above their bombing height.

'Some 20,000 feet below the bomber force, the US 7th Army were coming south-east too, on their push for Nuremberg. We must have passed above their vanguard somewhere south of Wurzburg, but there was no more sign of them than of the Master Bomber when I called him on the radio at the appointed hour. 'No.1, are you receiving me?' went unanswered - I might as well have called out to the soldiers, or the night.

'Maybe he's got RT trouble,' I conjectured.

'Maybe he's got the chop,' said Pittam. 'Better try the Deputy.'

After two attempts, the Deputy Master Bomber's voice came through against a heavy static background. He said that he was receiving me strength three. In the RT jargon, five was perfect - three was not too bad.

'Here is your weather, No 2,' I said, sharpening my voice and spacing out the words. 'No cloud over target, visibility good, over.'

'Roger, out,' said the Deputy, obviously no gossip, either and more concerned, perhaps, about where No.1 had gone than he was about the weather.

'10,000 feet below A-Able's height, the bombers moved on steadily to Schwandorf, lugging their loads of phosphorescent flares, incendiary and high-explosive bombs, as soundless and unseen to me as Eisenhower's tanks.

'An hour or so later, high above the Channel, the first pale light of dawn was in the sky behind us, but we plunged into the night again on the long descent to base. When the wheels touched Wyton's runway, we had been airborne for four hours and a half and covered nearly 1,500 miles. I checked the fuel-gauges: the tanks still held about 150 gallons. It was comforting to know that Able could have stayed up for another 90 minutes if I had needed her, to do so. It was even more comforting to know that I did not.

'In the next few days... the Met Flight aircraft made their sorties - four or five a day - to hunt down all the weather in the European skies: Not the smallest cloud, from the Russian front to the Atlantic, from Norway to the Alps, from MSL to 40,000 feet, was left to live its life in privacy. A blue Mosquito would be sniffing round it, seeking out its secrets and running home to tell - to Bomber, Fighter, Transport, 2nd T AF and USAF, to anyone who was prepared to listen.'

The last attack on the 'Big City' by Mosquitoes took place on the night of 20/21 April when 76 Mosquitoes made six separate attacks on the German capital. Flying Officers A. C. Austin and P. Moorhead flying Mosquito XVI ML929 claimed the last bombs dropped on the Big City when they released four 500 pounders at 2.14 am British Time. All the aircraft returned safely. Two Mosquitoes were lost on 21/22 April when 107 Mosquitoes bombed Kiel. Another attack was flown against Kiel on 23/24 April by 60 Mosquitoes who returned without loss.

In April Squadron Leader Peter Whitaker and Flight Lieutenant Hoare on 105 Squadron flew 40 operational hours and marked targets as far apart as Magdeburg, Ludendorf, Munich, Potsdam, Heligoland, Eggebek and Travemünde. On 25 April the target was Adolf Hitler's Austrian border retreat and fortified command post - the Adlerschanze (or Eagle's lair) at Berchtesgaden. Bomber Command's was detailed to prevent its use as a Nazi High Command second HQ. The Mosquito Pathfinders marked the target for a daylight raid by 395 Lancasters. The Adlerschanze was totally destroyed. Hitler committed suicide in Berlin five days later. The trip from Bourn to Berchtesgaden and back took just 4 hours 35 minutes - at over 30,000 feet, unpressurised and with an outside air temperature of minus 40°. The war had now lasted over five years. By VE Day, Peter Whitaker had flown a total of 89 operational sorties, 17 of these as a Pathfinder pilot. This was one operation short of three full Bomber Command tours. He was awarded the DFC for Mosquito Pathfinder operations.

In the period January-May 1945 LNSF Mosquitoes had flown almost 4,000 sorties. Altogether, 8 Group's Mosquito squadrons flew 28,215 sorties, yet they had the lowest losses in Bomber Command; just 108 (about one per 2,800 sorties) while 88 more were written off on their return because of battle damage. From 5,421 sorties 109 Squadron lost only eighteen Mosquitoes. As a comparison, another Pathfinder squadron, 156, flew 4,238 sorties from the inauguration of PFF until the end of the war and lost 121 aircraft. In percentage terms this was between nine and ten times as high. [86]

8 Group's record is an incredible achievement, even more remarkable when one considers that well over two-thirds of operations were flown on nights when the heavies were not operating.

When Doug Swain and Mike Bayon had done 48 raids they had transferred to another squadron 'hoping to do 98 raids on the trot'. 'In fact' recalls Bayon 'when we had done 52 raids the war in Europe ended. We volunteered for Japan as a crew and while we were on embarkation leave, the atom bombs were dropped. Doug went back to Melbourne. Six months later he was killed in a civil flying accident. [87]

'After the war I taught boys Latin at St. Faith's School, Cambridge and later St. Pauls. The intellectuals loved it - the Rugger buggers found it a sore trial. They'd ask me 'Why do we do it?'

'Because it's difficult', I'd say.

'That's no reason' they'd reply scornfully.

'All right, what's the point of rugby?'

'To score tries'.

'How?'

'You put the ball down beyond the line. Under the posts, if possible'.

'OK' I said. 'But why don't you wait till everyone has gone and then you can put it down as often as you like?'

'Oh Sir - that's stupid'. And then they'd think and they'd say, 'Wait a minute, no it's not. I see; it's the challenge that makes it exciting'.

'It seemed to me that the whole world had gone mad. And sometimes perhaps it had. Yet we had our own rules of sanity, which are hard to explain now. Our Art Mistress used to say to the 1st XV 'How can you look forward to a match? You know it will be cold, wet and muddy; that you'll be hacked and trodden on and knocked about'.

'True' they said, 'That's the point of it'. They did not know, so could not say, that pride was the motivation; and a kind of self-confidence the target.

'I'd always longed to bail out. But why did we risk death to save our planes? Why did we join the most perilous and casualty ridden branch of the Forces? Why did we refuse to turn back when instruments failed? Were we just conditioned lemmings? I don't think so. Some of it was competitiveness, a bit was bravado; but most of all, it genuinely was pride of performance; the Olympic ideal, pursuit of excellence. I can't believe that was bad. Personally, I am happy to have been part of it.'

---

86   *The Other Battle: Luftwaffe Night Aces versus Bomber Command* by Peter Hinchliffe (Airlife 1996)
87   On the afternoon of 14 September 1954 Captain Doug Swain, his co-pilot and a passenger aboard a Lockheed Hudson owned by *The Sydney Morning Herald* went missing while delivering newspapers on the regular 'milk run' from Mascot to Taree, Kempsey, Armidale, Glenn Innes, Inverell and Bingarra. Seven months later his son was born and his widow remarried.

Chapter 6

The Banff Strike Wing

Mosquitoes featured significantly in the dangerous low level daylight campaign of attacks on the German Kriegsmarine in WWII. Mainly, the Strike Wings in Coastal Command targeted German ships in the Baltic, which sailed between Germany and Norway, often laden with iron-ore and the U-boat wolf packs in the Bay of Biscay and the Western Approaches. U-boats were quite often protected by numbers of Ju 88s and Ju 188s and they could also put up a fearsome defence of their own. Not surprisingly, the German Unterseeboote were highly respected adversaries. A U-boat for example, could be armed with an 88mm gun and two 20mm guns forward, or four 20mm cannon, or a 37mm gun. Either way, when they cornered one, the Mosquito crews knew they were in for a fight, especially when Karl Doenitz, the U-boat Commander-in-Chief, ordered that U-boats, when attacked, were to remain on the surface and 'slug' it out with their low level attackers.

In 1943, to help Coastal Command in their onerous task, Mosquito fighters were detached to Scotland and to Predannack at the southern tip of Cornwall, for sorties far out to sea. It will be remembered that from 1943 to early 1944, a few NF.II squadrons in Fighter Command assisted Coastal Command with Instep anti-air and anti-shipping patrols in the Bay of Biscay and the Western Approaches. One of them, 307 (City of Lwow) Squadron, flew its first such patrol on detachment from Predannack on 13 June. Bad weather, however, caused the Poles to abort the operation. Next day four more Polish-crewed NF.IIs led by Squadron Leader Szablowski took off and headed for the Bay, accompanied by a 410 Squadron RCAF NF.II. Szablowski and his navigator, Sergeant Gajewski, spotted five U-boats on the surface and went in to attack from line astern. Szablowski fired and hit the second U-boat before hitting the third submarine. The U-boats returned heavy fire and Szablowski's port engine was hit and put out of action. Flying Officer Pelka, the No.2, attacked but found that his cannon would not fire, while the third and fourth Mosquitoes did not attack because by now the flak was intense. Szablowski nursed his ailing Mosquito back 500 miles to Predannack, while the others completed their patrol and he belly-landed successfully. Five days later, on 19 June, Szablowski's three Mosquitoes and a 410 Squadron NF.II destroyed a Blohm und Voss Bv 138 three-engined reconnaissance flying boat in the Bay.

Another of Coastal Command's tasks was to attack German capital ships which lurked in the Norwegian fjords ready to break out for raids on the rich shipping lanes of the North Atlantic. One of the capital ships that posed the greatest threat to Allied shipping in 1943 was the *Tirpitz*, but sinking it with conventional weapons was out of the question. 618 Squadron therefore, was formed at Skitten, a satellite airfield for Wick in Coastal Command, under strict secrecy, on 1 April 1943 and just one month before 617 Squadron's attack on the German dams on 16/17 May, for the sole purpose of using Dr Barnes Wallis' 'Highball' weapons against the Tirpitz and other capital ships at sea.

Highball weighed 950lbs with a charge weight of about 600lbs and a diameter of 35 inches. Based on the Upkeep 'bouncing bomb' which 617's Lancasters had dropped on the German dams, Highball was significantly smaller and lighter (about 10 per cent of the weight of the larger weapon). Each modified Mosquito B.IV could carry two Highballs, launching them at low level with a back spin of approximately 500rpm from about ¾ mile. On 28 February 1943 an Air Staff paper called for two squadrons of Mosquitoes and 250 'Highball' bombs and two squadrons of Lancasters and 100 Upkeep bombs.

Using a nucleus of nineteen crews, including, from Marham, eleven crews late of 105 and 139 Squadrons and their aircraft (the other eight crews, including the CO, Wing Commander G.H.B. Hutchinson DFC and his navigator, came from Coastal Command Beaufighter squadrons), 618 spent much of 1943 perfecting the weapon and flying assimilation sorties. However, by 14 May, the day before Operation 'Servant', the intended strike on the Tirpitz, only six suitably modified B.IVs were available at Skitten and the strike was called off. (Twelve other Mk.IV s were at Hatfield for long-range tanks to be installed.) 'Highball' trials continued but by September the Squadron had been reduced to a cadre at Benson.

618 Squadron was re-tasked for re-assignment to the Pacific so, in July 1944, it was brought up to full strength. Its mission now was to attack, with 'Highball', the Japanese fleet at Truk, which, because of the distance involved, meant that the Mosquitoes would have to operate from a carrier! Ten crews arrived from 143, 144, 235, 236, 248 and 254 Squadrons, while from 540 and 544 PR Squadrons there arrived ten pilots and navigators whose task it would be to find the Japanese ships.

Pilot Officer John R. Myles, who with Flying Officer H. R. Cawker formed one of the five PR crews, recalls.'We were attached to the Naval Air Torpedo School for carrier training using Barracuda II aircraft. After 72 aerodrome dummy deck landings (ADDLs), we five PR crews made more ADDLs during August, September and October, in Mosquito VIs, VIIIs and XVIs. Then we had to make a real deck landing and take-off from a carrier using Mosquito IVs modified with arrester hooks and four paddle-bladed props. On 10 October I made my first ever deck landing and take-off, from HMS *Implacable*. Quite an experience! On 31 October we [and twenty-four Mk IVs and three PR.XIs] were ferried out to the Pacific on two escort carriers, HMS *Fencer* and HMS *Striker*. We berthed at Gibraltar on 4 November and went through the Mediterranean and the Suez Canal. Unfortunately, I was quarantined with measles so I didn't see much. We spent two weeks at the Naval Base at Trincomalee in Ceylon and then proceeded to Melbourne, where we arrived on 23 December. (Fortunately, the Yanks sunk the ships before we reached Australia, otherwise it would have been a fiasco.) In January the aircraft were unloaded and on 7 February we proceeded to Narromine in NSW. I organized a trip to Alice Springs where we were conveniently grounded with engine trouble and I was able to do some sight-seeing out in the desert. We then proceeded to Darwin where a PR unit was stationed. We were scheduled to do a trip to New Guinea, but it had to be abandoned due to bad weather. On ANZAC Day, 25 April, nine of us flew a formation flypast of Mosquito IVs over Narromine and surrounding towns. We finally left Australia on VE Day on board the Nieuw Amsterdam and returned to England via Durban and Cape Town.'

Not all of 618 Squadron's crews went to the Pacific. By December 1943 248 Squadron based at Predannack flying Beaufighter Xs had received a detachment of five crews on

618 Squadron. They flew Mk.XVIII 'Tsetse' Mosquitoes, so named because of their fearsome 57mm Molins automatic weapon for use against U-boats on the surface, which was installed in the nose in place of the four 20mm cannon. An arc-shaped magazine, holding twenty-four rounds of 57mm armour-piercing HE shells capped with tracer, was positioned vertically about midships, feeding into the breech-block behind the crew. The barrel extended below the floor of the cockpit, the muzzle protruding below the fairing of the nose. Two, sometimes four .303 inch machine guns were retained, however, for strafing and air combat. All these guns were sighted through one reflector sight, the firing buttons being on the control column. The Molins gun had a muzzle velocity of 2,950 feet/second and the ideal range to open fire was 1,800-1,500 yards. The gun and its feed system were sensitive to side-ways movement and attacking in a XVIII required a dive from about 5,000 feet at a 30° angle with the turn-and-bank indicator dead central. The slightest drift would cause the gun to jam.

On 22 October 1943 the first two 'Tsetses' arrived at Predannack for anti-shipping operations in the Atlantic. 248 Squadron was equipped mainly with Beaufighters but earlier that month, five Mosquito crews and thirty-four ground crew from Skitten were transferred in as the 618 Squadron Special Detachment, to fly and service the new Tsetses. Amid great secrecy three 'Tsetses' were prepared for action. Operations commenced on 24 October with two 'Tsetses' flown by Squadron Leader Charlie Rose DFC DFM and Sergeant Cowley and Flying Officer Al Bonnett RCAF and Pilot Officer McD 'Pickles' McNicol but they returned empty-handed. After some modifications to the aircraft, on 4 November Charlie Rose and Flight Sergeant Cowley and Flying Officers Doug Turner and Des Curtis headed south to the Bay of Biscay. Rose and Cowley failed to return when they crashed into the sea during a diving attack on an enemy trawler. Rose got off two shells and was either hit by return fire or knocked out of the sky by a ricochet from one of his shells. Three days later, on 7 November, Al Bonnett scored hits on U-123, a Type IXB of 1,051 tons, which was returning on the surface to Brest at the end of her thirteenth war cruise. (The mine-swept channels off the French Atlantic coast leading to the U-boat bases at Brest, Lorient, St-Nazaire, La Rochelle and Bordeaux, were ideal killing grounds because the water depth was too shallow to permit the U-boats to crash-dive if attacked). After the first dive Bonnett's cannon jammed and he was forced to strafe the U-boat with machine gun fire. As a result of this attack the Kriegsmarine was forced to provide escort vessels for its U-boats from now on.

By 1 January 1944 248 Squadron Mosquito Conversion Flight had mustered sixteen Tsetses and four FB.VIs available for anti-shipping operations. On 16 February 248 and 618 Squadrons were moved to Portreath and the former would now provide fighter cover for the Tsetses for 618. On 20 February 248 Squadron flew its first interceptor and anti-shipping patrols in the Bay of Biscay. On 10 March four Mk.VIs which escorted two XVIIIs to an area about 30 miles north of Gijon on the Spanish coast, got into a vicious dog-fight with eight to ten Ju 88s flying top cover for a German convoy of four destroyers and a U-boat. One of the Ju 88s immediately fell to a head-on attack by the four VIs and a second was shot down into the sea in flames shortly afterwards. The XVIIIs, meanwhile, went after the convoy. Squadron Leader Tony Phillips carried out four attacks on the U-boat and Flying Officer Doug Turner, two. They damaged a destroyer and Phillips blasted a Ju 88 out of the sky with four shots from his Molins gun. One of the shells literally tore an engine from the Ju 88 and it spiralled down into the sea. On 25 March two 'Tsetses' crewed by Flying Officers Doug Turner and Des Curtis and Flying Officer A. H. 'Hilly' Hilliard and Warrant Officer Jimmy Hoyle, escorted by four Mk.VIs on 248 Squadron came upon a formation of two armed minesweepers and a destroyer. In the middle of these escorts was U-976, a Type VIIe of 769 tons, commanded by Oberleutnant zur see Raimund Tiesler, which was returning to St-Nazaire after being recalled from her second war cruise. The two pairs of escorting Mk.VIs dived on the escorting ships down sun and opened fire with cannon and machine guns. A heavy fusillade of fire from the ships came up to meet them. Doug Turner opened the attack on U-976 and got off five rounds with the Molins. Every burst was accompanied by recoil which whipped the needle of the airspeed indicator back to zero. Turner made four attacks in all and fired off all his twenty-four rounds. One of the shells in the first diving attack destroyed one of the guns on the U-boat. Hilliard attacked U-976 on the waterline below the conning tower before breaking off. About ten hits were seen on the conning tower and on the forward deck near and below the waterline. After the attacks U-976 sank and Jimmy Hoyle saw an oil patch which he estimated to be 100 yards long and 30 yards wide. Survivors from the U-boat were picked up by the minesweepers.

On 27 March the same 'Tsetse' crews, but with six FB.VI escorts on 248 Squadron (which had begun conversion from Beaufighters in December), set out for the same area again. Intelligence had monitored the course taken by two Type VIIe U-boats, U-769 and U-960, which were due to arrive at La Pallice escorted by four 'M' Class minesweepers and two Sperrbrechers (merchantmen converted to flak ships). RAF anti-shipping aircrews regarded these vessels, which were bristling with AA guns, as their most dangerous enemy. U-960 was commanded by Oberleutnant Oberleutnant zur see. Günther 'Heini' Heinrich, who had enlisted in the Kriegsmarine in October 1938 and had taken charge of U-960 on 26 January 1943.

Hilliard's intercom and VHF set in HX903 went u/s, but he decided to continue. Rounding the northwest peninsular of France the formation was spotted just over two hours after take-off. When they reached 2,000 feet heavy flak began bursting all around them. Hilliard banked to port and his Mosquito escort did the same, so the pair broke from the formation for an attack, while the rest climbed. The escort went for a Sperrbrecher while Turner and Hilliard dived on U-960, firing off seven shells during their run-in, 'five of which I claimed as hits,' recalls Hilliard, (One of the shells hit the armoured conning tower.) He goes on.

'We screamed over the U-boat at zero feet and I noticed the gunners stripped to the waist pulling their 37mm gun into a vertical position. Then I heard and felt a thud, seconds later followed by the machine gun inspection panels in front of my windscreen splitting open. I thought that the nose section had split from the shell I had collected, but looking around there was no apparent damage. [The 37mm shell had hit the Mosquito right on the nose cone but fortunately, the armour plating under the instrument panel cushioned the impact of the flying shrapnel]. Flak by this time had opened up from coastal batteries.'

Altogether, the four mine-sweepers fired forty-five 88mm shells and 1,550 20 mm shells and claimed one Mosquito 'definitely' shot down. Hilliard and Hoyle however reached Portreath safely despite the ruptured nose cone protruding into the slipstream and they landed almost out of fuel. Turner had started his dive as Hilliard cleared the target and in all, four shells were seen to hit the metalwork. Five other Mosquitoes were hit in the attack. Flight Sergeant C. R. Tomalin managed to put his FB.VI down at Portreath despite a large hole in the starboard main plane. Flight Sergeant L. A. Campton and Sergeant Peters crash-landed also, with the hydraulics shot out. Aboard *U-960* the conning tower, periscope and control room were badly damaged by Hilliard's 57mm shells. Ten men, including Heinrich, who was hit above the left knee, were wounded, some of them badly. *U-960* managed to put into La Pallice for repairs. A year later she put to sea again and was sunk in the Mediterranean on 19 May by the combined efforts of four US destroyers and two squadrons of Venturas.

While at Portreath a problem arose with the Molins on some of the Mosquitoes, which when fired split the nose cone fairing above the gun muzzle. When the six pounder shell left the gun barrel at roughly half a mile per second the recoil felt in the Mosquito was quite considerable and the aircraft's instruments momentarily returned to zero. It appeared that on some of the Mosquitoes the effect of the gun recoil together with the closeness of the muzzle to the nose, jarring with related air disturbance, all contributed to the nose cone fairing splitting. Hilly Hilliard, together with his navigator Jim Hoyle, had flown their aircraft for repair to de Havillands at Hatfield on 2 March but the problem was not resolved. However, 618 Squadron's NCO flight sergeant in charge of the maintenance team came up with the idea of removing the two outer Browning machine guns allowing him to use the space made available to install Tie-Rods thus strengthening that part of the nose which was splitting.

The first ten days of April produced no results and then on the 11th, two Mk XVIIIs on 618 Detachment escorted by five FB.VIs on 248 Squadron and six on 151 Squadron at Predannack, took off on another coastal patrol from Portreath. One Mosquito crashed into a hill on take-off and one of the Tsetses returned early with mechanical problems. The others pressed on to St-Nazaire where they came upon a U-boat with a four ship escort and an air umbrella of about a dozen Ju 88s. The FB.VIs attacked the escort ships and then turned their attention to the Ju 88s while Flight Lieutenant B. C. Roberts went after the U-boat. He saw spouts of water near the hull of the U-boat as he fired his Molins but could claim no definite hits. Flak was extremely heavy and Wing Commander O. J. M. Barron DFC, CO of 248 Squadron and another Mosquito, were shot down. Two of the Ju 88s were claimed destroyed. A third Mosquito was lost in a crash landing at Portreath.

At the end of April 248 Squadron began attacks on land targets and in May the 618 Squadron Special Detachment joined 248, the Tsetses now making attacks on surface vessels as well as U-boats. Their technique was to fire the armour-piercing shells through the wooden deck planking of the ships while rocket-firing Beaufighters went in at 500 feet in a shallow dive. On D-Day, 6 June, 248 Squadron flew anti-shipping, escort and blockading sorties off the Normandy, Brittany and Biscay coasts, including one operation as escort for seventeen anti-flak Beaufighters on 144 Squadron and fourteen rocket-armed Beaufighters on 404 Squadron. During one of these sorties, a 248 Squadron Mosquito shot down a Ju 188. On 7 June two 'Tsetses', flown by Doug Turner and Des Curtis and Al Bonnett and 'Pickles' McNicol, each made a run on a surfacing U-boat. A dozen 57mm shells were fired at *U-212* but on his second run, Bonnett's cannon jammed and he only made a series of dummy runs on the U-boat which crash-dived, leaving a pool of oil and a crewman on the surface. (*U-212* limped into St-Nazaire for repairs and when she put to sea again, was sunk by frigates in July). Turner's Tsetse was hit by flak in the port wing and engine nacelle but he and Bonnett made it back to

Cornwall safely. Bonnett and McNicol were killed two days later, following a search for survivors of a German destroyer in the Channel, when Wing Commander Tony Phillips DSO DFC, now CO of 248 Squadron, collided with his Mosquito while approaching the airfield. Phillips lost 6 feet of his outer wing but landed safely.

On 10 June four 248 Squadron Mosquitoes attacked U-821 near Ushant with such ferocity that the crew abandoned ship, which was then sunk by a Liberator on 206 Squadron. That afternoon Flight Lieutenant E. H. Jeffreys DFC and Flying Officer D. A. Burden on 248 Squadron were shot down by a motor launch carrying the survivors of U-821. The launch was promptly sunk by the other Mosquitoes. On 22 June, wing-mounted 25lb Mk.XI depth charges and A.VIII mines were used operationally by Mosquitoes for the first time and 235 Squadron at Portreath, which had been equipped with Beaufighters, flew their first Mk.VI sortie (the last Beaufighter sortie was flown on 27 June). The Mosquitoes now flew escort for the Beaufighters and they were also used to intercept Dornier 217s which carried Henschel 293 glider bombs for attacks on Allied shipping. On 30 June Pilot Officer Wally Tonge and Flight Sergeant Ron Rigby were shot down by flak whilst on an anti-shipping strike off Concarneau in Brittany. Tonge successfully ditched a mile or two from the shore and the two men were seen in their dinghy shortly afterwards but they did not survive and were buried in the grounds of a small church in the village of Combrit.

On 4 July Wing Commander Tony Phillips with Flying Officer R. W. 'Tommy' Thomson DFC and Squadron Leader 'Jean Maurice', the Free French pilot, with Squadron Leader Randall, flew a costly 248 Squadron operation to the Brest Peninsula. 'Jean Maurice' was the nom de guerre adopted by Max Geudj, a Frenchman of the Jewish faith, to safeguard his family in France. He had flown 75 operational sorties on Coastal Command Beaufighters. The two Mosquitoes found a group of mine-sweepers anchored in Penfoul Cove and the Kercreven docks. For greater accuracy they closed right in on their targets, skimmed over the masts of the enemy ships and dropped their bombs. AA guns were firing from Creach-Conarch heights and the ships. It is unclear if the Mosquito crewed by Phillips and Thomson was hit by flak. A witness claims that they hit the top of the mast of one of the ships. The Mosquito crashed near the Keranguyon Farm and the crew were ejected in the explosion. Phillips was found near the aircraft, Thompson falling a hundred yards away, in front of the doorstep of Madame Berrou's farm, which caught fire after being hit by flying debris. Two farm workers, Yves Glernarec and Yvonne Laurent, a young girl, had their clothes set alight. Glernarec badly burned, survived, but Yvonne died twelve hours' later. For two days the airmen were left where they lay before a German officer gave the order to bury them. Flight Lieutenant Charles Corder was the long-serving navigator of the Mosquito flown by 'Jean Maurice', which managed to return against all the odds after it had been severely damaged by a Luftwaffe fighter. It was their 71st operation together. When they encountered a Junkers 88 long-range fighter, Guedj attacked and sent it crashing into the sea. Return fire from the German fighter's gunner severely damaged the aircraft. Guedj was wounded during the attack and the intercommunication in the aircraft was put out of action. With the situation appearing hopeless, Corder crawled forward to assist the pilot before returning to his seat, where he obtained radio bearings and gave Guedj a course to steer for their base in Cornwall, 180 miles away. One of the two engines failed and Guedj had difficulty keeping control, forcing him to fly a few feet above the sea. Corder once more crawled forward to assist him, having managed to repair the intercommunication system. Just before they reached the English coast the second engine caught fire, which spread to the cockpit. Corder transmitted an SOS and fired distress cartridges to attract the attention of those ashore. As they approached Cornwall, it was clear that the aircraft had either to ditch in the heavy seas or clear the cliffs. As Corder guided Guedj to the cliffs' lowest point, observers on the ground were convinced that the aircraft would crash; but Guedj managed to clear the cliffs by a few feet before making an emergency landing as the second engine finally failed. Corder's navigation had been so accurate that they managed to crash-land on their own airfield at Predannack.

On 11 July two Tsetses flown by Doug Turner and Des Curtis and Flying Officer's Bill Cosman and Freedman and escorted by sixteen FB.VIs, made an evening raid on the approach to Brest harbour where a surfaced U-boat was proceeding slowly with no wake along the Goulet de Brest, escorted by three minesweepers and a Sperrbrecher. The shore batteries combined with the ships to put up an intense flak barrage yet Cosman made a diving attack on the U-boat, breaking off at 50 yards and claiming two possible hits out of four shots fired. Doug Turner scored five hits on the Sperrbrecher and Cosman's parting shot was a salvo of two 57mm shells at the leading minesweeper, as the Mosquitoes weaved their way through the flak to the mouth of the harbour.

Flak was intense on 14 August when 26 Mosquitoes on 235 and 248 Squadrons at Portreath led by Wing Commander Bill Sise DSO* DFC, CO of 248 Squadron, carried out a shipping strike in the Gironde Estuary with rockets, cannon and the six pounder Tsetse gun. Warrant Officer Harold Arthur Corbin and his navigator Flight Sergeant Maurice Webb in Mosquito HP866 drew heavy AA fire from both ships and land batteries. Corbin was born in 1923 and joined the RAF in November 1940, four days after his 17th birthday. He joined 235 Squadron flying Beaufighters on anti-shipping sorties from Portreath, but after a few operations he was posted to 248 Squadron at Predannack. Corbin attacked and damaged a Seetier Class destroyer but his Mosquito was hit in both outer fuel tanks by heavy flak. The port inner tank was also pierced and all the fuel lost. One shell smashed into the Mosquito through the floor of the fuselage and wrecked the IFF and 'Gee' apparatus. Corbin set course for Vannes airfield in Brittany, now occupied by the Allies, with fuel streaming from his punctured tanks, the port engine U/S and the starboard engine damaged. When he arrived over Vannes, Corbin climbed to 4,000 feet and ordered Webb to bail out and then he went out himself. Both made successful landings and spent the night under a hedge before making contact with American troops the next day. [88]

Germany's seaborne traffic travelling daily along the Norwegian coast with large quantities of supplies now assumed a much higher priority and early in September

88 (Squadron Leader Cook on 235 Squadron and 'Taffy' Stoddart on 248 were both killed as were their navigators. Warrant Officer Bob Gennoe and his navigator 'Benny' Goodman were shot down and after standing on the wing of their ditched Mosquito, they were also taken prisoner by the Germans). Initially Corbin was recommended for the DFC and operations mentioned were an attack on an M-Class minesweeper on 30 June and an attack on a convoy off the French coast on 27 July, when he was hit and had to return on one engine and a punctured tyre. The recommendation, however, was changed to the CGM by AVM Brian Baker, AOC 19 Group. Flight Sergeant Webb received the DFM. In Action With the Enemy: The Holders of the Conspicious Gallantry Medal (Flying) by Alan W. Cooper (William Kimber 1986). On 18 September Corbin attacked U-867 on the surface near Bergen with cannon and machine gun fire and then dropped depth charges astern of the submarine. The U-boat was sunk the next day by a Liberator of 224 Squadron.

Coastal Command ordered 235 and 248 Squadrons to Scotland. The last operation from Portreath was flown on 7 September by four Mosquitoes on 248 Squadron, in poor visibility near Gironde, while searching for U-boats. Now, 235 and 248 joined 333 Norwegian Squadron and 144 and 404 RCAF Beaufighter Squadrons to form the Banff Strike Wing under Group Captain Max Aitken DSO DFC. 333 Squadron had formed at Leuchars on 10 May 1943 from 1477 (Norwegian) Flight and commenced its first Mk.VI operations on 27 May. The Banff Wing carried out their first strike on 14 September, when 22 FB.VIs and four Tsetses from 235 and 248 Squadrons and nineteen Beaufighters, attacked shipping between Egero and Stors Toreungen light. A flak ship and a merchantman were sunk.

On 28 September the Banff Wing Mosquitoes were at last modified to carry eight rocket-projectiles (RP) on Mk.IIIA projector rails beneath their wings just like the Beaufighters. The rails had to be set so that they were parallel with the airflow at correct diving speed, otherwise the RPs would weathercock and either under- or overshoot the target. They would also miss if the pilot dived at the wrong airspeed. At first the RPs were armed with 60lb semi-armour-piercing heads of the type used in the Western Desert for tank-busting. These did not however, penetrate shipping and caused little structural damage, so were soon replaced with 25lb solid armour-piercing warheads. Sometimes rockets would 'hang up' on the rails and fail to fire. If this happened, crews had to bail out because if they tried to land, the RPs were liable to explode.

When making an attack on shipping, the Mosquitoes normally commenced their dive of approximately 45 degrees at about 2,000 feet and then opened up with machine gun fire at 1,500-1,000 feet, before using the cannons and lastly, at about 500 feet, the RPs. The RPs were arranged to form a pattern spread on impact, so that if fired at the correct range and airspeed and angle of dive, four would hit the ship above the water-line and the other four would undershoot slightly to hit below the waterline. In the Norwegian fjords pilots usually had once chance, so they fired all eight rockets at once. After entering the ship's hull each would punch an 18-inch hole in the far side of the hull for the sea to flood in, while the remains of the cordite motor burned inside the hull to ignite fuel and ammunition in the ship. The Mosquitoes used the RPs for the first time on 26 October.

Only a few isolated vessels were found and sunk in early October because the enemy operated at night in the knowledge that the strike wing could not fly in tight formation at night. On 9 October the Banff Wing tried out a system that had been tried at North Coates during early August 1944. A Warwick laden with flame floats and markers took off at 0415 and 2 hours later, dropped them to form a circle 19 feet in diameter 100 yards from Stavanger. Half an hour later eight Mosquitoes on 235 Squadron followed by eighteen Beaufighters, traced the same course. At 0620 the first aircraft arrived and began to circle. As dawn appeared, the formation set off heading for Egrsund. Led by Wing Commander Tony Gadd on 144 Squadron, at 07.10 they sank a German merchantman and a submarine chaser, while a Norwegian vessel was badly damaged. When they had recovered from the surprise the enemy gunners put up a fierce flak barrage but this was smothered by cannon fire. Three aircraft were damaged but all returned.

On 19 October the flak alarm was raised by lookouts on three vessels at anchor at Askvoy at 13.30 as nineteen Mosquitoes streaked towards them. Flashes erupted from the nose of each Mosquito and spouts of water erupted in a line towards *U-5116*.

Rounds struck the bridge and more triggered a fire which the Tsetses fanned with their 57mm shells. Seven crew were injured. One said later that: '... they had been attacked by an aircraft carrying a big gun, emitting a long flame.' One 235 Squadron Mosquito was lost.

With the departure of the two Beaufighter squadrons on 22 October to Dallachy to form a wing with 455 and 489 Squadrons from Langham, 143 Beaufighter Squadron at North Coates moved north to join the Banff Strike Wing and convert to the Mosquito VI. On 24 October two Mosquitoes on 235 Squadron attacked three enemy aircraft, the first seen by the strike wing. Warrant Officer Cogswell dispatched one Bf 110, while Flight Lieutenant Jacques finished off the second Bf 110 hit by Cogswell, who had set an engine on fire. Jacques then destroyed the third aircraft, a Ju 88C. By the end of the month, five strikes had been made.

On 7 November 143 Squadron flew its first FB.VI operation when two aircraft carried out a search for enemy aircraft between Obrestad and Lindesnes. Frequent snow and hail was a feature of operations on 8 and 9 November when the Mosquitoes looked for shipping off Ytteriene, Marstein and Askvoll. The Banff Wing now began to operate in increasingly larger formations, including for the first time, on 13 November, a combined 'op' with the Dallachy Wing. The largest strike so far occurred on 21 November when New Zealander Wing Commander Bill Sise DSO DFC, who had taken over 248 Squadron on the death of Wing Commander Phillips led a formation of thirty-three Mosquitoes, accompanied by forty-two Beaufighters and twelve Mustang escorts, in a shipping strike at Ålesund on the Norwegian coast.

On 29 November in a diving attack on a U-boat off Lista Flying Officer Woodcock in a Tsetse fired eight 57mm shells, scoring two hits, while other XVIIIs attacked with depth charges and cannon. Tsetses were again in action on 5 December when Bill Sise led thirty-four Mosquitoes in an attack on merchantmen in Nord Gullen. On the 7th, twenty-one Mosquitoes and forty Beaufighters, escorted by twelve Mustangs, set out to attack a convoy in Ålesund harbour. Landfall was made as briefed but Squadron Leader Barnes DFC led them further up the coast, towards Gossen airfield, whereupon they were jumped by approximately twenty-five FW 190s and Bf 109Gs. They dived through the middle of the Mosquitoes and attacked singly and in pairs. Mustangs shot down four fighters and two more collided but two FB.VIs (flown by Bill Cosman and K. C. Wing), a Mustang and a Beaufighter, were lost. Seven enemy fighters were shot down.

On 12 December the Mosquitoes returned to Gossen but this time no fighters were seen. The following day Wing Commander Richard A. Atkinson DSO DFC* RAAF CO, 235 Squadron and his 20-year old navigator, Flying Officer Valentine 'Val' Upton, were killed when a cable across a fjord cut off the Australian's starboard wing during their attack on merchantmen at Ejdstjord. On the 16th the Mosquitoes came upon a merchantman and its escort between the steep cliffs of a fjord at Kraakhellesund. Despite intense flak from the escort and surrounding cliff sides, the Mosquitoes dived into the attack in line astern, because there was no space to manoeuvre. Two of the FB.VIs were shot down. On 19 December Mustangs escorted the Mosquitoes to Sulen, Norway but no fighters appeared.

On 26 December, twelve FB.VIs on 235 Squadron led by Squadron Leader Norman 'Jacko' Jackson-Smith, with two outriders from 333 Squadron, attacked two merchant ships at Leirvik harbour, about 70 miles up Sogne Fjord, with machine guns and cannon. A Mosquito crewed by Flying Officer Bill Clayton-Graham and Flying Officer 'Ginger'

Webster, was hit in the port engine during the second attack. Clayton-Graham climbed to 1,000 feet and tried to make his escape but twenty-four fighters high above sent about half their number to attack the wounded and badly smoking Mosquito. His cannons were empty but Clayton-Graham turned to meet them and fired his machine guns as the fighters raced towards and then past him. Incredibly, the Mosquito was not hit but several of the fighters were; one of them severely. Clayton-Graham was a sitting duck but they roared off and turned their attention on another aircraft, piloted by Flying Officer Jim Fletcher, which they shot down. Clayton-Graham and Webster came home hugging the wave tops escorted by an ASR Warwick and reached Scotland safely. One Mosquito crash-landed.

On 9 January 1945 eighteen FB.VIs on 235 Squadron returned to Leirvik with an escort of a dozen Mustangs and attacked eight merchant ships in the harbour. They left three ships burning and the Norwegian Underground later reported one ship sunk at its moorings. Two days later there was more success when Flight Lieutenant N. Russell DFC and another Mosquito pilot shot down a Bf 109 during an anti-shipping strike in Flekke fjord by fourteen Mosquitoes and eighteen Beaufighters. The Mosquitoes though, did not have it all their own way when a formation of thirteen strike Mosquitoes, one Tsetse and two 333 Squadron outriders, led by Wing Commander Geudj, now CO of 143 Squadron, returned to Leirvik again on 15 January. They completely surprised two merchantmen and an armed trawler and left them burning and sinking before they were jumped by about thirty FW 190s of III./JG5. Tsetse 'Z' fired four shells at a FW 190. Five enemy fighters were shot down but five Mosquitoes, including the one piloted by 'Maury' Geudj, were also lost. The rest fought their way back across the North Sea pursued for a time by nine fighters. This sudden rise in Banff Wing losses caused concern at Northwood and after this attack 248 Squadron's Tsetses were transferred south to North Coates.

On 11 February delayed action bombs were dropped in a narrow fjord off Midgulen to roll down the 3,000 feet cliffs to explode among the ships in the harbour below. On 21 February 235 Squadron carried RPs for the first time when a 5,000 ton ship in Askevold Fjord was attacked. Taking part for the first time were spare aircrew from 603 Squadron who had flown Beaufighters in the Middle East, led by Wing Commander Christopher N. Foxley-Norris DSO. Nearly all had joined 235 Squadron. In March, Mosquitoes began operating independently of the Beaufighters, seeking out specific targets in Norway. Over the first few days the installation of new, Mk.IB tiered RP projector rails, enabled long range drop tanks to be carried in addition to the RPs. 235 and 248 Squadrons were now able to operate at an increased range, but with a 50 or 100 gallon drop-tank and four RPs under each wing, the Mosquitoes tended to stagger on take-off!

On 7 March forty-four Mosquitoes led by Wing Commander Roy K. Orrock DFC, CO, 248 Squadron and escorted by twelve Mustangs, destroyed eight self-propelled barges in the Kattegat with machine guns, cannon and rocket fire. Two Mosquitoes collided shortly after the attack. No enemy fighters showed but a similar raid on 12 March by forty-four Mosquitoes and twelve Mustangs over the Skagerrak and Kattegat was met by a formation of Bf 109s. Two enemy fighters were shot down. On 17 March six ships at Ålesund harbour were repeatedly strafed by thirty-one FB.VIs on 235 Squadron after they had been led in by two Norwegian crews in 333 Squadron. Flak was heavy and two aircraft were lost but the Mosquitoes fired their cannon and RPs to deadly effect, leaving three of the ships sinking and the other three crippled. One ship was holed thirty-two times and another 37 times. All except twenty-four of the RPs hit below the waterline. On 21 March, 235 and 143 Squadrons made short work of another ship at Sandshavn and two days later a troopship, the 7,800-ton Rothenfels, at anchor in Dals fiord, was attacked by nine Mosquitoes. The strike leader, Squadron Leader Robbie Read and one other, was shot down. In the afternoon, Wing Commander Foxley-Norris led another strike, attacking a motor vessel at Tetgenaes. On 24 March some crews in 404 Squadron arrived to convert to Mosquitoes while the remainder attacked merchantmen at Egersund using Beaufighters. On 30 March Wing Commander Arthur H. Simmonds, CO of 235 Squadron led thirty-two rocket-firing FB.VIs, with eight more as escorts, in an attack on Porsgrunn-Skein harbour. No fighters troubled the formation and the eight FB.VIs detailed as escorts were able to fire against gun positions in the sides of the fjord. The attackers flew so low against the four merchantmen that they crested the wave tops. One merchantman was hit by 28 rockets, another by 39 rockets and a third by over sixty RPs. Two, Mosquitoes, one crewed by Flight Lieutenant Bill Knowles and Flight Sergeant L. Thomas, which struck an overhead electric cable and crashed, failed to return. Three of the four merchantmen were sunk and the fourth was badly damaged while a warehouse on Menstad quay full of chemicals was also destroyed.

On 5 April 37 Mosquitoes escorted by Mustangs flew across Denmark to attack a widely-spread out and heavily-armed convoy in the Kattegat. Every ship in the convoy was left on fire and sinking and an estimated 900 German soldiers were lost. One Sperrbrecher sank with all hands, 200 bodies being recovered by Swedish vessels. An escorting Mustang was shot down over Denmark and a Mosquito crash landed with the crew picked up by the Danish Underground. Four days later, on 9 April, thirty-one rocket-projectile FB.VIs on 248, 143 and 235 Squadrons with five others as fighter cover and DZ592, a 2nd TAF photo-Mosquito, returned to the area on the look-out for enemy shipping. Three U-boats - 804, 843 and 1065 - were spotted in line astern on the surface of the Kattegat coming from Denmark and heading for Norway. Squadron Leader Bert Gunnis DFC, who was leading the strike, ordered the nine FB.VIs on 143 Squadron near the rear of the formation being led by Squadron Leader David Pritchard to attack. The U-boats had not seen the Mosquitoes. Then they did, but it was too late. With the rest of the wing wheeling in behind, 143 Squadron attacked, their cannons blazing as they fired seventy RPs into the U-boats, now frantically trying to escape beneath the waves. All three were sunk, one of them taking the photo-Mosquito with it in an explosion. In fact the Mosquitoes were so low, three more suffered damaged engines when they were hit by flying debris and were forced to land in Sweden.

On 11 April another attack was made on Porsgrunn, by 35 Mosquitoes. Bf 109G-14s shot down two, although the remainder left four merchantmen sinking. Next day a FB.XVIII on 248 Squadron, one of five Tsetses sent on detachment to 254 Beaufighter Squadron at North Coates, attacked a U-boat in the North Sea. The Tsetse detachment was used primarily for operations against midget submarines and U-boats, with Spitfire XXIs for cover. Two Tsetses found five U-boats on the surface on 18 April. The XVIIIs got off just one round each before the submarines crash-dived. On 19 April the FB.VIs at Banff sank U-251 in the Kattegat. 150 miles off the Scottish coast on 21 April, 42 FB.VIs on 235, 248, 143 and 333 Squadrons, led by Wing Commander Foxley-Norris, CO, 143 Squadron, shot down five Ju 88A-17 and four Ju 188A-3 torpedo carrying aircraft of KG26. The German strike mission was inbound from Gardermoen, Denmark to attack convoy JW66 which had left the Clyde three days before. Twenty-four Mustang escorts missed the melee, having sought and gained permission to return early for a party at Peterhead!

On 22 April, 404 'Buffalo' Squadron flew its first operation from Banff since replacing its Beaufighter Xs with Mosquito VIs in March. They sank a Bv 138 flying boat at her moorings but the Squadron had little time left to make an impression as the war in Europe was now drawing to a close. However, on 2 May, a strike by twenty-seven Mosquitoes in the Kattegat resulted in the sinking of *U-2359*. On 4 May 48 Mosquitoes of 143, 235, 248, 333 and 404 Squadrons led by Wing Commander Christopher Foxley-Norris DSO, escorted by eighteen Mustangs, with three ASR Warwicks with airborne lifeboats along, sighted a very heavily armed convoy in the Kattegat, which they immediately attacked. Flight Lieutenant Thorburn DFC failed to return. Flight Lieutenant Gerry Yeates DFC* and Flight Lieutenant Tommy Scott on 248 Squadron were so low that when they attacked a destroyer they returned with the top of a mast-head complete with pennant embedded in the Mosquito's nose! This final, massive, battle was the end of the shooting war for the strike wing but patrols for U-boat crews who might be inclined to continue the fight went on until 24 May when four Mosquitoes on 143 and 248 Squadrons found only passive E-Boats.

The Banff Wing provided escorts for the King of Norway as he sailed back to his country under heavy naval escort. Days later a schnorkel was seen and attacked by a single Mosquito on 404 Squadron, by 25 May the rapid run down of the anti-shipping wing had begun.

Chapter 7

Free Lancing

From 1943 to 1945 Mosquito FB.VI and later NF.XII and NF.XIII squadrons in 100 Group and 2nd Tactical Air Force intruded over the Reich, bombing and strafing German lines of communication and Luftwaffe airfields. In 2nd TAF the FB.VI is probably best remembered for daylight precision operations, particularly pinpoint raids on Gestapo buildings in occupied Europe. On 1 June 1943 2 Group had been transferred to 2nd TAF. AVM Basil Embry DSO** DFC* AFC replaced AVM d'Albiac at HQ, Bylaugh Hall with the task of preparing 2 Group for invasion support in the run-up to Operation 'Overlord': the invasion of France. In Embry's opinion 'the Mosquito is the finest aeroplane, without exception that had ever been built in this country.' In 1942 Embry's request to convert eight of his Mosquito night fighters into 'Intruders' had been turned down. Finally, in July 1943 464 RAAF and 487 RNZAF Squadrons and 21 Squadron in 140 Wing got rid of their obsolete Venturas and they re-equipped with the Mosquito FB.VI, which was armed with four cannon for 'Night Intruder' operations.

William Richard Craig Sugden was a Flight Commander on 464 Squadron at that time, stationed at Sculthorpe. 'We had heard rumours that at last our Venturas ('Flying Pigs') were to be replaced, together with the Station Commander. Our AOC, Basil Embry insisted that we should now have Mosquito VIs and when Embry insisted then things started to happen - fast! And so Mossies started to arrive; plus a new Station Commander - Group Captain Pickard. Anyone meeting Charles Pickard for the first time, as I did in July 1943, could hardly fail to be impressed - very tall, 6 feet 3inch, blond, debonair, with an easy-going casual manner - plus three DSOs, a DFC, etc, a distinctive loping walk and invariably accompanied by his Old English sheep-dog, Ming. Most of us knew him by name since he had starred in the film *Target for Tonight,* flying a Wellington, 'F for Freddie'. We had heard about some of his 'cloak and dagger' operations, flown to the Continent from Tempsford - dropping and picking up agents by moonlight in Lysanders and the longer-range missions in Hudsons; we were familiar, too, with his ditching in the North Sea and the dropping of paratroops at Bruneval. We knew he would not be a chairborne CO - not many were in 2 Group as Embry insisted on almost everyone seeing a bit of the war - even the doctors and padres were encouraged to have a go! Pickard would certainly need no encouragement on that score.

'Our immediate role, once we had mastered the Mossie, was low-level daylight raids. Pick and his navigator [Flight Lieutenant J. A. 'Peter' Broadley DSO DFC DFM] joined in our practices with enthusiasm - almost too much enthusiasm, Pick's language over the R/T becoming more and more lurid. Afterwards, however, there would be light-hearted discussion and criticism, when even the lowliest could have his say. Inevitably there was the occasional accident, usually on take-offs or landings, as the Mossie tended to swing a bit and it was with some trepidation that we viewed a banner Pick had hung in the briefing room - in large letters: 'THE NEXT CLOT TO PRANG A MOSQUITO THROUGH FINGER TROUBLE WILL BE POSTED TO THE BLOODIEST JOB IN THE AIR FORCE.' The very next day a Mossie swerved off the runway and broke its tail wheel. Out of it stepped Pickard, smiling and as always fumbling for his pipe and matches, saying airily: 'There's always bloody something' - his favourite expression. After that we all felt better.

'Our Wing's first raid was on a power station in the Cherbourg area - three squadrons, led by Jack Meakin and essentially a try-out. Pick, of course, was participating, but as I was climbing aboard I was rather surprised to see Basil Embry and his SASO (Senior Air Staff Officer) , David Atcherley, one of the famous twins, also boarding an adjacent aircraft - with some difficulty as Atcherley's arm was encased in plaster, the result of a recent Mess party. It was these very senior officers' idea of a pleasant afternoon's outing! The raid was quite successful, no losses, but plenty of flak damage to Pick and others, so much so that he had to feather an engine and make an emergency landing at Predannack in Cornwall. However, he turned up at Sculthorpe a bit later, full of smiles. Everything had been under control; he said that if the other engine had failed he had earmarked a French trawler to ditch beside, then order the skipper at gunpoint to set course for England. Meanwhile Embry and Atcherley had returned safely, their only snag being that they had been unable to bomb as Atcherley's plaster had got in the way of the correct switches; otherwise most enjoyable.

'In January 1944 our 140 Wing moved to Hunsdon - much more pleasant and closer to London. The Officers' Mess was a large mansion where Pick installed himself on the top floor, leaving a few other bedrooms for some of the rest of us; all very cosy. The weather was often too bad for any serious flying so we had some good parties. After one particularly good one Pick was still fast asleep in his attic late next morning so we carried him and his bed down two flights of stairs and into the bar, where he finally awoke, calling loudly for healing draughts. He was essentially an outdoor man, his love of horse-riding dating back to his Kenya days and he was able to get in some rough shooting locally. At one of his previous stations he was nearly nabbed red-handed by a game-keeper, but managed to stuff the loot into the boot of his car, telling his wife Dorothy to lean on it and give one of her sweetest smiles.

'We guessed that something special was now coming up.'

Information had been received in London that over 100 loyal Frenchmen, among them Monsieur Vivant, a key Resistance leader in Abbeville, were being held in captivity in Amiens prison. Several attempts by the Resistance had been made to rescue them but had failed. Dominique Ponchardier the leader of the local Resistance requested an urgent air strike to break open the prison walls. The prison was built in the shape of a cross and surrounded by a wall 20 feet high and 3 feet thick. The plan was to breach this wall by using 11-second bombs dropped by five FB.VIs on 464 Squadron led by Wing Commander R. W. 'Bob' Iredale and six on 487 Squadron, led by Wing Commander Irving S. 'Black' Smith. The concussion from the bomb explosions should open the cell doors to give most of the prisoners a chance to escape. There would be casualties, but better to die from RAF bombs than be shot by a German firing squad.

'On 18 February, a vile, icy cold day with snow falling' continues Bill Sugden, 'we were called to an early briefing. Embry and Pickard were studying the model of a building which was apparently Amiens Gaol and which we were to break open at

12.30pm. The Free French were anxious to get some of their key men out before they were executed the next day.[89] Briefing was meticulous - 487 Squadron to breach the walls, 464 to destroy the guards' quarters and 21 to stand off close by. Pick would be circling around assessing results and would call in [six FB.VI crews on 21 Squadron led by Wing Commander I. G. 'Daddy' Dale] to flatten the whole place if the raid, so far, had been unsuccessful. Embry had been forbidden to take part, to his great fury.'

Pilot Officer N. Maxwell Sparkes, one of the pilots on 487 Squadron recalled: 'We were determined to give everything we could to this job. I remember Group Captain Pickard putting into words what we all were beginning to feel when he said, 'Well, boys, this is a death-or-glory show. If it succeeds it will be one of the most worthwhile ops of the war. If you never do anything else you can still count this as the finest job you could ever have done.' Wing Commander 'Black' Smith added. 'After four years of war just doing everything possible to destroy life, here we were going to use our skill to save it. It was a grand feeling and everybody left the briefing room prepared to fly into the walls rather than fail to breach them.'

'We went outside' continues Maxwell Sparkes 'and looked at the weather again. It was terrible! Snow was still falling, sweeping in gusts that every now and then hid the end of the runway from sight. If this had been an ordinary operation we were doing it would pretty certainly have been scrubbed-put off to another day. But this was not an ordinary job; every day, perhaps every hour, might be the last in the lives of those Frenchmen. We got into our aircraft warmed up the engines and sat there thinking it was no kind of weather to go flying in, but somehow knowing that we must. And when we saw the Group Captain drive up in his car and get out of it and into his own Mosquito [HX922, a 487 Squadron Mosquito which he flew in the 464 Squadron formation] we knew for certain that the show was 'on'.

Bill Sugden continues: 'It was still snowing thickly as we climbed aboard, but then came a slight lull. It still looked impossible to take off, but we saw Pick loping towards his F for Freddie, stuffing out his pipe and giving Ming a final pat. With his engines starting, we realised the game was on. Within minutes we were all airborne, visibility nil. I was flying No.2 to Bob Iredale but never saw him or anybody else; it was like flying in a blancmange. Suddenly, when we were (we hoped) over Littlehampton, the snow and murk cleared and there ahead was the sea, in bright sunlight, with another Mosquito in front swerving right across us. I yelled 'Get out of it you bastard,' which he obligingly did and I saw to my horror it was F for Freddie. I said to my navigator, Bunny Bridger, 'God, we'll be for it when we get home' - Pick had stressed complete radio silence at briefing, let alone being addressed like this. But at least we hadn't collided...'

Maxwell Sparkes adds: 'The 18 aircraft took off quickly, one after another, at about 11 in the morning - we were going to hit the prison when the guards were at lunch. By the time I got to 100 feet I could not see a thing except that grey soupy mist and snow and rain beating against the Perspex window. There was no hope of either getting into formation or staying in it and I headed straight for the Channel coast. Two miles out from the coast the weather was beautifully clear and it was only a matter of minutes before we were over France. [90]

We skimmed across the coast at deck level, swept round the north of Amiens and then split up for the attack.

89 A dozen prisoners were due to be executed on 19 February.
90 Two Mosquitoes on 21 Squadron and one on 487 Squadron and two Typhoons aborted.

'My own aircraft, with our Wing Commander's and one other, stayed together to make the first run-in; our job was to blast a hole in the eastern wall. We picked up the straight road that runs from Albert to Amiens and that led us straight to the prison. I shall never forget that road - long and straight and covered with snow. It was lined with tall poplars and the three of us were flying so low that I had to keep my aircraft tilted at an angle to avoid hitting the tops of the trees with my wing. It was then; as I flew with one eye on those poplars and the other watching the road ahead that I was reminded we had a fighter escort. A Typhoon came belting across right in front of us and I nearly jumped out of my seat.[91] The poplars suddenly petered out and there, a mile ahead, was the prison. It looked just like the briefing model and we were almost on top of it within a few seconds. We hugged the ground as low as we could and at the lowest possible speed; we pitched our bombs towards the base of the wall, fairly scraped over it-and our part of the job was over. There was not time to stay and watch the results. We had to get straight out and let the others come in; and when we turned away we could see the second New Zealand section make their attack and follow out behind us.'[92]

Wing Commander 'Black' Smith, leading that first Vic of Mosquitoes said afterwards: 'My section went right in for the corner of the east walls, while the others drew off a few miles and made their run-in on the north wall. Navigation was perfect and I've never done a better flight. It was like a Hendon demonstration. We flew as low and as slowly as possible, aiming to drop our bombs right at the foot of the wall. Even so, our bombs went across the first wall and across the courtyard, exploding on the wall at the other side. I dropped my own bombs from a height of ten feet, pulling hard on the stick. The air was thick with smoke but of all the bombs dropped by both my section and the other, only one went astray.'

The first bombs blew in almost all of the doors and the wall was breached. Wing Commander 'Bob' Iredale said later. 'I pinpointed the guards' quarters, let go my bombs so that they would skid right into the annex, with the sloping roof of the prison inches from the belly of my plane as I climbed over it.' Flight Lieutenant Tony Wickham in a specially equipped Film Photographic Unit Mosquito IV with a cameraman, Pilot Officer Leigh Howard, made three passes over the ruined jail, which was now disgorging smoke and flame and fleeing men and Howard filmed the flight of the prisoners. Wickham said later: 'We could see, the first time we flew over the objective, that the operation had been a complete success. Both ends of the prison had been completely demolished and the surrounding wall broken down in many places. We could see a large number of prisoners escaping along the road. The cameras fixed in the plane were steadily recording it all and Leigh Howard was crouched in the nose taking picture after picture, as fast as he could. He was so enthusiastic that he got us to stay over the objective longer than I considered healthy. After each run I would suggest to him that we about-turned and made for England and he would answer, 'Oh! no... do it again. Just once more'. But eventually he was satisfied and we headed for home.'

Bill Sugden continues: 'The gaol stood out like a sore thumb against the snowy ground. We collected a lot of flak over Glisy airfield, dropped our bombs on target and beat it for home. It was then that I heard Pick's voice on R/T shouting 'Red, Daddy, Red', which meant raid successful and so 'Daddy' Dale, leading 21, had to take the

91 Two Squadrons of Typhoon IBs flew escort on the operation.
92 Sparkes and his navigator Pilot Officer Arthur Dunlop suffered a flak hit in an engine and they were escorted home by 'Black' Smith. Sparkes put down safely at a south coast airfield in England.

squadron all the way back again. And that was the last we heard of poor Pick. Apparently he was then bounced by FW 190s, who shot his tail-plane off.' [93]

Pickard was the last over the prison and after dropping his bombs he circled the area at 500 feet to assess the results. Satisfied that the Mosquitoes had done their work, the success signal was radioed to Daddy Dale so that they could return home. Almost immediately Feldwebel Wilhelm Mayer of II/JG26 in a FW 190 shot F-Freddie down in flames and Pickard and Broadley were killed.[94] In March Dominique Ponchardier the leader of the local Resistance sent the following message to London. 'I thank you in the name of our comrades for the bombardment of the prison. We were not able to save all. Thanks to the admirable precision of the attack the first bomb blew in nearly all the doors and 150 prisoners escaped with the help of the civilian population. Of these, twelve were to have been shot on 19 February. In addition, 37 prisoners were killed; some of them by German machine guns. Fifty Germans were also killed.'

Early in 1944 85 (Base) Group was formed for the purpose of providing fighter cover over the continent leading up to and after, 'D-Day' by the transfer from Fighter Command to 2nd TAF of 29, 264, 409 'Nighthawk' RCAF, 410 'Cougar' Squadron RCAF, 488 RNZAF and 604 Squadrons. As part of the newfound offensive, the main work for the FB.VIs of 138 and 140 Wings was 'Day' and 'Night Ranger' operations and 'Intruder' sorties from England.[95]

In three months, 27 January-16 May, 27-year old pilot Flight Lieutenant Charlie Scherf DFC RAAF on 418 (City of Edmonton) Squadron RCAF racked up 23 destroyed; thirteen of them in the air. [96] Scherf was from Emmaville, New South Wales and had worked as a grazier on the family sheep ranch before joining the RAAF in September 1941. On 26 February Charlie Scherf and his navigator, Flying Officer Colin Finlayson and Flight Lieutenant 'Howie' Cleveland RCAF and Flight Sergeant Frank Day DFM flew an 'Intruder' to St-Yan, as Scherf recalled: 'Approaching St-Yan from the North we climbed to 500 feet, instantly seeing three aircraft on the airfield. As we crossed the north perimeter we passed over about 50 men in dark uniform, all walking in the same direction looking up at us. John, glancing at Cleveland going in for his attack saw black smoke pouring from his engines and believed that he had been hit. He was opening his mouth to yell at me to turn and get revenge by shooting up these Huns, when the smoke ceased and he realized that it had been caused by the extra boost necessary for the attack. I opened fire at range of 600 yards on the two E/A on the left side, both cannon and M/G, seeing strikes immediately on one of them. As I

93 *Charles Pickard Gaolbreaker* by W.R.C. Sugden, writing in *Thanks For The Memory: Unforgettable Characters in Air Warfare 1939-45* by Laddie Lucas (Stanley Paul & Co Ltd 1989).

94 Squadron Leader Ian McRitchie and Flight Lieutenant R. W. 'Sammy' Sampson on 464 Squadron RAAF were downed by flak. McRitchie, wounded in 26 places, crash-landed at over 200 mph near Poix. He survived and was taken prisoner but Sampson was dead. A Typhoon was shot down north of Amiens and the pilot was taken prisoner. Foul weather over the Channel claimed another Typhoon. Later Group Captain Peter Wykeham-Barnes DSO DFC* became the new 140 Wing commander.

95 Starting on 15 October 138 Wing at Lasham began operating FB.VIs when 613 (City of Manchester) Squadron joined 2 Group. In December 305 (Polish) Squadron converted from the Mitchell and in February 1944 107 Squadron converted from the Douglas Boston.

96 He was promoted Squadron Leader at the start of May and received a bar to his DFC with a DSO following in June. A month later he left the UK via the United States for his native Australia, where he instructed at 5 OTU Williamstown near Newcastle NSW, still on Mosquitoes.

closed, the other one burst into flames. Cleveland, who was behind, saw a petrol bowser go up in flames and the first E/A attacked also burst into flames. As we closed we had identified them as Ju 52s. The enemy aircraft on the right of the others was a Ju 86 and I left this to Cleveland and John saw this E/A go up in flames, as I was pulling up through the flames of the two Ju 52s.

'After setting course, I looked to see how much film had been used and found camera not switched on. We headed south for twenty miles, then set course for Dole/Tavaux having difficulty in finding the airfield as rivers appeared swollen (probably in flood) in comparison with their size. My observer, by excellent navigation, brought us to the town of Dole and we there encountered a Heinkel He 111Z [97] with its satellites. Owing to the low speed of the targets, I found it impossible in my climb to get into position to attack. I broke off and was delighted to see Cleveland knocking off the rear glider. I manoeuvred and came up behind the remaining glider and Heinkel I, taking cine-camera shots as I closed. When the glider filled the ring-sight I gave it a short burst (two seconds). Pieces blew off and I was very concerned in dodging the debris. I saw him going down out of control. I closed behind the Heinkel, opened fire and immediately saw strikes on two engines (3 to 4 seconds.). I broke off and Cleveland carried on the attack. When he had finished, I came in and gave him a burst of machine gun fire as he was slipping to earth. As I passed over him his starboard engines and fuselage were burning fiercely on the ground. It had crashed port wing down.'

As the Heinkel He 111Z consisted of two 'separate' Heinkels, it was requested that a claim of one He 111 destroyed each, be allowed to Scherf and Cleveland but each pilot received a half-share.[98]

More low-level pinpoint daylight raids, for which 140 and 138 Wings would become legendary, took place in 1944. On 18 March the last raid on Hengelo in Holland was flown when twelve Mosquitoes of 140 Wing at Hunsdon led by Wing Commander 'Bob' Iredale were detailed to attack the Hazemeyer Electrical Equipment factory at low level. Squadron Leader 'Dick' Sugden on 464 Squadron recalled: 'The navigation officer, Flight Lieutenant Webb, folded up his file, smiled and said: 'It's a very good route, chaps, there should be hardly any flak.' As we pushed out of the briefing room, I exchanged glances with Flying Officer 'Bunny' Bridger, my navigator. We had heard that one before.'

A Mosquito on 487 Squadron RNZAF aborted its sortie five miles SW of Lowestoft after an engine failure while another hit a tree when it took evasive action to avoid hitting another Mosquito. Three remaining aircrews bombed the target at 16.36 hours and very good results were claimed. Of 48 bombs dropped, forty were on target; twelve bombs hit the factory interior at 16.36 hours. Some bombs fell in the town centre, one

97 Basically, the He 111Z (the Z indicating Zwilling or twins) was two He 111H-6 airframes coupled by a new centre section fitted with a fifth engine. The He 111Z-1 was designed to tow the very large Messerschmitt Me 321 or up to three Gotha Go 242 transport gliders.

98 On 16 May 'Howie' Cleveland and Frank Day accompanied Scherf and Finlayson 'on just one last trip' to the Baltic. Cleveland destroyed a Do 217 on the ground and then forced a Heinkel He111 to crash into Kiel Bay without firing a shot but his own aircraft was hit in the engine by flak and he crashed in the sea 3 miles from Sweden. Rescue came in three hours, too late to save Frank Day. Cleveland was repatriated to England in June where his DFC had been awarded at the start of the month. After a spell in Canada in May 1945 he returned to 418 as their last wartime CO.

killing a German officer in the street. Two houses were damaged and two civilians were reported killed. The whole area was seen to have numerous fires. 464 Squadron bombed a minute ahead of 21 Squadron and crews succeeded in hitting the central part of the main building and setting it on fire. 'Dick' Sugden continues: 'As we opened our bomb doors, everything opened up as well; there was no chance of dodging the wall of tracer. I jabbed my bomb-release button several times to make sure the bombs had all gone and turned for home. It was then that Bridger said, 'Our starboard wing's on fire.' Monaghan, flying on my right, also noisily confirmed this on the R/T. I tried to feather the prop, no good; then the fire extinguisher, also no good. The wing was now well alight; there was nothing for it but to get down before it folded up. As we were flying right on the deck there was not much chance to pick and choose, but, fortunately, Holland is nice and flat. I shouted to Bridger to hold tight and tried to lose some speed, but we must still have been doing about 200 mph when we touched down. It was a very noisy 'landing run' as we slithered and swerved for half a mile, shedding bits and pieces on the way. Poor old Bridger was thrown clear (he broke his legs) and I managed to cut myself free of the tangle of wires and harness with a 'Boy Scout' knife which I carried. Some kind Dutch farmers picked us up and ran like mad towards their house. When I looked back I saw the reason for their speed. Our 'Mossie' was burning fiercely and scattered amongst the wreckage were three obscene-looking bombs. The release gear must have been hit before I pressed the bomb-return button. If I had known that three of the bombs were still aboard I would never have attempted a crash-landing, but would have climbed fast to give us a chance of bailing out. With our bulk and that tiny door, I don't think we'd have made it before the wing broke up.' [99]

On Tuesday 11 April six Mosquitoes on 613 Squadron at Lasham, led by the CO, Wing Commander R. N. 'Bob' Bateson DFC attacked the Huize Kleykamp in The Hague which was being used by the Gestapo. It housed the Dutch Central Population Registry and duplicates of all legally issued Dutch personal identity papers so that identity cards falsified by the Dutch Underground could be checked and recognized as false. The Gestapo building was completely destroyed and the majority of the identity papers destroyed. Buildings that surrounded the Kleycamp had suffered only slight damage but 61 civilians were killed, 24 seriously injured and 43 slightly injured. All six Mosquitoes got back safely, without a shot being fired at them. Five weeks later a report reached the RAF that the operation had been highly satisfactory. For his leadership of this operation Bateson was awarded the DSO and received the Dutch Flying Cross from Prince Bernhard of the Netherlands. An Air Ministry bulletin later described the raid as 'probably the most brilliant feat of low-level precision bombing of the war'.

One of the main proponents of 'Day Ranger' operations over France and the Low Countries was 418 Squadron RCAF, which had re-equipped with Mosquitoes in March 1943 and had flown 'Flower intruder operations out of RAF Ford, Sussex using AI.Mk.IV and Mk.VIII. 418 Squadron flew their first FB.VI operation on 7 May 1943. Since January 1944 the Canadians had reaped a rich harvest of victories on day and 'Night Rangers' and the high point came in April-May when they shot down 30 aircraft

---

99 Some Germans, who quickly arrived on the scene, took Sugden and Bridger prisoner. They were taken to hospital for a check up and three weeks later Sugden was sent by train to Amsterdam and from there with a group of American aircrew to Frankfurt. He ended up in Stalag Luft I Barth where he was reunited later with 'Bunny' and with his former commander, Squadron Leader Ian McRitchie DFC who had been shot down on the Amiens prison raid in February which Sugden and Bridger had also flown.

in the air and destroyed a further 38 on the ground. By May the Canadians, based at Holmsley South, had claimed 100 victories and would have the distinction of destroying more enemy aircraft both in the air and on the ground than any other Canadian squadron, in both night and daylight operations.

On 30 September two Mosquitoes crewed by Squadron Leader R. G. Gray RCAF and Flight Lieutenant Gibbons and Flight Lieutenant P. R. Brook RCAF and Flying Officer A. D. McLaren RCAF on 418 Squadron took off from Hunsdon at 12.00 hours on a 'Day Ranger' to Erding and Herding. Gray recalled: 'Flying about 3,000 feet about the hills en route to our first target, we were jumped from above and behind by two hostile fighters. We ran at full power for the mountains. The fighters closed range to about 1,000 yards, but we managed to shake them in a deep winding mountain pass after a five minutes' chase. A little later, about 50 miles SW of Munich, we saw two single engine aircraft approaching from the NW at 3,000 feet. Our immediate reaction was that they were fighters scrambled to intercept us. We kept our course and passed directly beneath the aircraft at deck level. The aircraft, which we now identified as Me 109s, continued straight on, so we turned and climbed to attack hoping to catch them by surprise.

'They probably saw us too for they climbed directly into the sun and were lost from our view. We resumed course for our first target - Erding, which was reached at 1357 hours. Approaching the airfield from the south-east, we spotted numerous aircraft all over the field. We selected two Me 110s parked close together at the western of the landing area. Attacking in a very shallow dive, I gave the nearest aircraft a very long burst of cannon and machine gun fire. A very great number of strikes were observed all over the engines, nose, port wing root and fuselage, large fragments of aircraft flying off in all directions as it disintegrated. Fire was held to approximately 50 yards. Although this aircraft did not catch fire, we are convinced that it can never be repaired and it is therefore claimed as destroyed. Some cannon strikes were observed on the adjacent Me 110 during the final part of the burst. This Me 110 is claimed as damaged. Proceeding on across the field, another aircraft was spotted at the northern boundary. It was given a 2-second burst of cannon and mg closing to about 40 yards. Many strikes were observed. This aircraft is claimed as damaged. During the run across the field we were met with a moderate amount of fairly accurate light flak.

'Our next call was Eferding which we approached from the north-east at 14.30 hours. Several FW 190s were seen flying above the aerodrome. We selected one which had its undercarriage down and attacked from its starboard beam. We opened fire with a 2-second burst of cannon and mg from 150 yards. The FW 190 burst into flames and spiralled into the ground just off the eastern perimeter. This is claimed as destroyed. Another FW 190 with its wheels down was seen and approached, but he must have seen us for he raised his undercarriage and climbed almost vertically. We fired a short burst from about 200 yards 40° angle-off (no strikes). Attempting to follow him in the climb, we stalled. The EA did a stall turn and dived to the deck and flew south-east. We resumed the chase and using maximum power slowly closed range. The 190's sole evasive action consisted of flying as low and as fast as possible together with a bit of porpoising. It was apparent that he was luring us right over Horsching. Hoping to bag him before we reached Horsching, we opened fire with several bursts at extreme range, mainly without effect, until finally a few strikes were observed and immediately my cannon ammunition was exhausted. By this time we were at the north edge of

Horsching aerodrome and broke off to the south-west. This FW 190 is claimed as damaged. At the SW corner of Horsching aerodrome we spotted what is believed to have been a Do 217, which we attacked with mg only. Some strikes were seen on the port wing root and this is claimed as damaged. By now we were well separated from Flight Lieutenant Brook, we had exhausted our cannon ammunition and in view of the CAVU [ceiling and visibility unlimited] weather and the great number of 190s, which by this time had doubtless recovered from their initial surprise, we dropped our tanks and quickly set course for home. The outstanding feature of the trip was the exceptional navigation of Flight Lieutenant Gibbons.'

Brook recalled: 'We went and attacked an FW 190 at Erding at 13.57 hours. It was parked on the south-east corner of the airfield. I fired about a 5-second burst of cannon and machine gun closing in from 200 yards to 40 yards. Strikes were seen and the EA disintegrated. Swinging off to port towards the centre of the airfield, we attacked another FW 190 with a two-second burst of cannon and mg, closing from 100 to 30 yards. We saw numerous strikes at the wing roots and claim this FW 190 as damaged. We pulled up slightly and saw a Me 110 parked in a dispersal to the north of the airfield. We attacked this aircraft with a 2½-second burst of cannon and mg from 300 to 50 yards. Strikes were observed on the fuselage behind the cockpit - claim damaged. At 1430 hours we were closing in to Eferding from the north-east and noticed a Me 109 on the east side of the airfield. I fired a 3½-second burst of cannon and mg and saw strikes all along the fuselage - claim damaged. We then set course for St-Dizier.'

On 27 January 1944 Flight Lieutenant James Johnson RCAF and Pilot Officer John Caine and Pilot Officer Earl Boal in FB.VIs attacked Clermont-Ferrand airfield. Johnson shot down a Ju 88 and damaged a Ju 86 and shared in the downing of two Ju W34s with Caine, who also destroyed a Ju 88. By 8 May Caine had destroyed 12 aircraft on the ground or water, with five more damaged on the ground or water. (In April-May 1945 Caine, now with 406 ('Lynx') Squadron RCAF and flying NF.XXXs, destroyed a Ju 88 on the ground and damaged four other aircraft on the ground). In the meantime, 418 (City of Edmonton) Squadron RCAF had also been busy. On 21 March American Lieutenant James F. Luma and Flying Officer Colin Finlayson and Flight Lieutenant Donald MacFadyen and 'Pinky' Wright flew a long-range 'Ranger' over France. Luma and Finlayson attacked Luxeuil airfield, where they shot down a JuW34 liaison aircraft and a Ju52/3m transport and damaged two Gotha Go 242 glider transports and two Bf 109s on the ground. MacFadyen and Wright shot down a Blohm und Voss Bv 141, which was coming into land. Moving on to Hagenau airfield MacFadyen proceeded to destroy nine Gotha Go 242 twin-boomed troop transports and a Do 217 on the ground. MacFadyen later operated in 406 ('Lynx') Squadron RCAF where he flew the NF.XXX on 'Night Intruders', finishing the war with seven aircraft and five V-1s destroyed and five aircraft destroyed and 17 damaged on the ground. Luma finished his tour in April and was awarded both a British and US DFC.

The main work for 138 and 140 Wings also was 'Day' and 'Night Ranger' operations and 'Intruder' sorties from England. FB.VIs of 2nd TAF continued their night fighting role and bombing of German targets in France and the Low Countries. On the night of 19/20 May when RAF Bomber Command carried out raids by 900 aircraft on five separate rail targets in France, Wing Commander Norman John 'Jack' Starr DFC and Pilot Officer J. Irvine on 605 Squadron in a FB.VI flew a successful 'Intruder' sortie over France. Starr and Irvine took off from Manston at 0100 hours for their patrol and they headed for the vicinity of Florennes where landing lights were obligingly switched on, as a twin-engined aircraft prepared to land. Starr and Irvine, whose Mosquito was at 2,000 feet were assisted further when a searchlight on the NW side of the airfield was switched on and began sweeping the area before it was switched off, the operators presumably satisfied that there no intruders following the landing aircraft. Starr dived to attack while his prey, oblivious to the Mosquito's presence, blinked its landing light on and off sufficiently for Starr to estimate his position on the runway. Just as he was about to open fire the German aircraft switched on its landing light again and appeared to be travelling at about 20 mph. Starr gave the aircraft a 1½-second burst of cannon only and strikes were seen in front of the machine and then strikes all over the aircraft. (Starr and Irvine were unable to identify their victim). By this time the Mosquito was very close to the ground in the dive and Starr had to pull out very sharply. As he pulled out Starr and Irvine saw the German machine catch fire and all the airfield lights were switched off. They orbited the airfield and saw a motor vehicle with powerful headlights on dash up to the now blazing aircraft, which the fire crew took about 12 minutes to extinguish the flames.

On the night of 5/6 June on the eve of 'D-Day', all six of 2nd TAF's FB.VI squadrons in 138 and 140 Wings carried out defensive operations over the invasion coast. In 85 Base Defence Group at this time were 264 and 410 Squadrons in 141 Wing at Hartford Bridge and 488 Squadron RNZAF and 604 Squadron in 147 Wing at Zeals. At West Malling were 29 and 409 Squadrons in 148 Group while in 11 Group ADGB in southern England were 605, 96, 125 (Newfoundland), 219, 456 Squadron RAAF and 418 Squadron RCAF.

Jack Meadows DFC AFC AE a pilot on 604 Squadron recalls: 'Newly arrived there was a USAAF Black Widow Squadron, recently re-equipped from the battered old Beaufighters with which at Scorton they had started UK familiarisation. One dusk on my way to dispersal I saw the entire Black Widow Squadron lining the taxi track as one aircraft taxied out. 'What's up?' I asked. 'It's the Major, he's gonna get a DFC for this; it's the first night fighter operational sortie in the European Theatre of Operations.' I thought wryly of the many of our crews on second, even third, tours who had bravely toiled on patrols night after night in all weathers, some in North Africa, usually without ever any enemy to have a go at and just a 1939-45 Star to show for it. A little later Ted Smith the CO was on patrol over the beach-head when he heard an American voice being directed onto a bogey. Plenty of unnecessary and undisciplined chatter ended up with, 'I see him, it's a Junkers 88, I'm gonna shoot the bastard down.' Next moment Ted saw tracers passing. 'Stop shooting, you fool,' he yelled on the R/T: 'It's me, a Mosquito, a friendly.' By then his port engine was on fire, he did some deft evasion, managed to put the fire out and crawled into Ford on one engine listening to the American voice saying, 'I got him, he's going down in flames, he's crashed into the sea, I got one destroyed.' It took the evidence of .5 calibre bullets in Ted's port engine to prove his point.

'This is not an anti-American statement. Like us they often had to learn the hard way, make their own mistakes. In France later the Black Widow squadrons in the US sector had enormous successes in both air interceptions and ground attack at night. In many cases we also, at times, were guilty of misidentification. I remember two cases particularly. As the first night fighter squadron into France after 'D-Day' 604 was operating out of a pierced steel planking runway airfield at Picauville in the US sector.

Canadian built Mosquitoes being
assembled at Downsview, Toronto. DH
Canada built a total of 1,076 Mosquitoes.
(National Aviation Museum of Canada)

Mosquito four 20mm cannon gun
arrangement used on the F.II fighter and
FB.VI fighter-bomber.
(BAe Hatfield via GMS)

The E0234 prototype being rolled out of the flight test shed at Hatfield on 21 November 1940. (DH)

Below: Mosquitoes on 128 Squadron at Wyton. (IWM)

Flying Officer Mike Gribbin DFM and Flight Lieutenant R. W. Griffiths RCAF on 627 Squadron were almost out of fuel and were forced to ditch B.IV DZ534 on the raid on the marshalling yards and junction at Givors on the night of 26 July 1944 after first jettisoning the bomb load in the sea. The first crew to survive a night ditching by a bomber Mosquito, they were picked up by a US destroyer and landed at Cherbourg, where they spent two or three days in the 12th Field Hospital. (via Andy Bird)

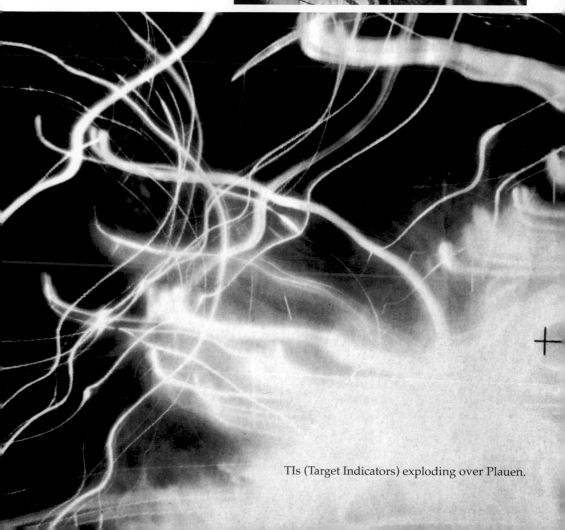

TIs (Target Indicators) exploding over Plauen.

B.IV DZ367 GB-J on 105 Squadron
which FTR from Berlin on 30 January
1943. (RAF Marham)

Michael H. A. T. Bayon DFC

Flight Lieutenant Norman
Spencer McPherson DFC and
Warrant Officer Deedman on 105
Squadron in 8 Group. (Ian
McPherson).

Armourers at work. (via
Andy Bird)

F.II Night Intruder crew
on 264 Squadron
discuss last minute
details before flying
another sortie.

Opposite and below: the
start of another 'op'

Above: Fitters on 684 Squadron carrying out an engine change on PR.XVI NS645/P at Dum Dum, Calcutta in 1944.Just visible in the background in silver dope is MM367/U.

Right: LAC Bennett adds the 141st lightning bolt on the nose of PR IX ML897 *Dorothy* which completed 161 sorties serving in 8 Group on bombing, marking and high and low recce, and Pampas on Met Flight at Wyton.

Fitters changing spark plugs on a PR.XVI on 140 Squadron, 2nd TAF of 34 PR Wing at Melsbroek, Belgium.

A long-focus camera being mounted into a PR Mosquito on 684 Squadron. (British Official)

Cameras being examined by LACs on 684 Squadron. (British Official)

The Mudon pagoda photographed by Wing Commander Lowry and Pilot Officer Stevens on 1 June 1945. (Gerald Stevens Coll)

Flight Lieutenant 'Hank' Cooper DSO DFC, navigator-radar operator and Flying Officer Kelt RNZAF, pilot, on 192 Squadron in 100 Group at Foulsham, Norfolk during the winter of 1944-45.

Right: 'Dicing Tonight'

Below: A NF.XXX on 85 Squadron in 100 Group taxies out at Swannington, Norfolk. (IWM)

Above: FB VI DM-H RF610 on 248 Squadron in the Banff Strike Wing, April 1945.

Right: Four 3-inch rocket projectiles (RP) with 60lb HE warheads under the wing of an FBVI fighter-bomber.

A FXVIII 'Tsetse' Mosquito showing the Mk four 20mm Hispano cannon and deadly Molins 57mm six-pounder gun.

An armourer loads up the .303 inch
Browning machine guns on an FB VI on 'B'
Flight on 333 Norwegian Squadron of the
Banff Strike Wing. (via Cato Guhnfeldt)

On 12 August 1944 FB.VIs on 235 and 248
Squadrons of the Portreath Strike Wing
flew to the Gironde Estuary near Bordeaux
and attacked enemy vessels with bombs
and rockets. Two German minesweepers,
the *M370* and the *Mari Therese*, were sunk.

A Banff Strike Wing Mosquito
attacking a U-boat on the surface.

FB.VI LR387 which was converted to Mk 33 prototype with folding wings and arrester hook.

FB.VI TA539/B on 4 Squadron landing at Celle, West Germany in 1949.

Canadian built FB.26, one of almost 180 FB.26s supplied to the Nationalist Chinese in 1947 and reassembled in Shanghai. Its delivery pilot is George Stewart, a WWII Canadian Intruder pilot who completed 50 ops on 23 Squadron in 100 Group at Little Snoring.

FB.VI of the 32nd Bomber Division of the JRV (Yugoslav Air Force) at Zagreb in 1951

G-AJZE (RG231) one of two
PR.34s that were used at
Cranfield by the BEA Gust
Research Unit 1948-49 for
investigating clear-air
turbulence. (British Airways
via ARP)

FB.VI NS993 that forced
landed in Switzerland on 30th
September 1944. The aircraft
was subserviently modified as
a test bed to the Swiss SM-1
turbofan version of the
Armstrong Siddeley Mamba
intended to power the Swiss-
designed N-20 jet fighter.

A.2 the second Vickers
rocket-propelled supersonic
model, in position under the
RAE Mosquito XVI (PF604)
at St. Eval in Cornwall in
October 1947. Squadron
Leader D. A. Hunt (left) and
Mr. G. B. Lochee Bayne pose
in front of the aircraft before
take-off on 8 October 1947.
(Aeroplane Monthly)

(Weren't US rations a wonderful change?!) My regular Radar Operator had been rested and pending a replacement I was flying with anyone available. One night it was Neb Elliot, who had a 'wooden' leg and boasted he could scramble quicker than the rest of us because one shoe was already on, laces tied. Neb was a bloodthirsty type. As we stooged around on patrol he kept muttering 'fifty thousand Huns in the brothels of Paris, come up and fight, you bastards, come up and fight'. Then control had a blip, a bogey and soon Neb picked it up and brought me in beautifully below and behind. Although I saw the twin exhausts earlier, it was only when we were in to about 300 feet that we saw the silhouette. It was as black a night as I can remember, no moon, not even any stars, just blackness and the silhouette was very vague. 'Looks like a Wimpy,' I said, 'only it seems a bit big.'

'It's a He 177' said Neb; 'shoot the bugger down.'

'No,' I said, 'I'm not sure it's not a He 177.' 'Yes it is, shoot the bugger down.'

'We argued for a while, swinging from side to side, looking up and ahead for about 100 feet in the intense dark, feeling rather vulnerable to tail guns. Finally I said, 'It's certainly no 177, I think it's a Warwick, one of those mysterious ones we saw at Hum; why would a 177 be flying west over the Cherbourg Peninsular out to sea, anyway?' he was still convinced it was a He 177, but in the end I was convinced it was a rare Warwick. As I had control of both stick and gun button we left it alone. As long as he lived he believed he was right - as I believe I was. What he reported to the R/O's union I dread to think!

'The second incident was shortly afterwards, soon after I took over a flight in 219. One of its most experienced teams returned from patrol saying they had shot down a Ju 88 over Belgium, at 2,000 feet. Both had positively identified it from several angles, the R/O also using night glasses. For some reason the intelligence officer was suspicious, showed them unmarked silhouettes of Ju 88s and Mosquitoes. Both unerringly picked out all the Ju88 silhouettes as the one they had shot down. Everyone then celebrated. 2 Group had reported a Mosquito missing. Its wreck was found where my crew had shot down the 'Ju 88'. That the green 2 Group NCO crew were in the wrong place at the wrong height, that no prior information of their activity had been given, that as a result ground control had mistakenly, unforgivably, given the target to my crew as a hostile, rather than - as they should - a bogey was no excuse for the terrible mistake made. My crew were posted away in disgrace, promotion was lost and perhaps worse retribution was avoided only because of the extenuating circumstances.

'So if an experienced crew like that could make such a mistake, perhaps we must be more sympathetic of a Black Widow tyro having a go at Ted Smith who happily survived.'[100]

Fewer than fifty enemy aircraft plots were made on 5/6 June. Then things hotted up. 264 Squadron flew jamming patrols before they went looking for enemy fighters. There was also another role for the Mosquitoes, as Bernard Job on 418 Squadron recalls. 'The squadron was stationed at Holmsley South near Bournemouth and six aircrews were detailed to act as 'Flak bait' to cover the paratroop and glider drops in the Cherbourg Peninsular, by drawing searchlights and flak away from these more vulnerable aircraft. So successful was this that two of the six were hit, one so badly that it crash landed near base and burnt up. The crew ran!'

100   Jack Meadows writing in *The Mossie* No.24 Spring 2000.

'When D-Day arrived', recalls Flight Lieutenant J. L. 'Les' Bulmer, a navigator on 21 Squadron, 'we were out whenever weather permitted patrolling behind the battlefront looking for anything that moved. The night of D-Day, the 6th, we were briefed to patrol the Caen-Lisieux-Boisney road to stop German reinforcements reaching the beachhead. We were told that there was a corridor across the Channel in which every aircraft must stay on outward and return flights. Our night-fighters were patrolling on either side of the corridor and were likely to regard any plane that was found outside the designated area as hostile. As we left the English coast a hail of flak went up from a ship in mid-Channel right where we were headed. Pretty shortly down went an aircraft in flames - it looked like one of our four-engined bombers. It seemed that one of our own ships (the Royal Navy got the blame) had parked itself right on the path that every aircraft going to and from the Continent that night would be following. And in true naval fashion, it let fly at everything that went over. We decided to risk the night-fighters rather than fly through that lot and did a wide detour.'

On the night of 6/7 June 'Stan' Cotterill and 'Pop' McKenna equalled the 418 Squadron RCAF record set by Robert Kipp during April [101] when they took off from Holmsley South at 22.18 hours to fly a 'Flower' patrol to Orléans and Châteaudun. They arrived at a pinpoint on the Loire at 23.44 hours and proceeded to skirt the town of Orléans. They then swung north to commence their east-to-west patrol of Orléans and Châteaudun airfields. On the first leg of their patrol they observed a large orange coloured fire at Terminiers and shortly afterwards saw an aircraft orbiting Châteaudun at 800 feet and burning navigation lights. They recognized it as a Ju 52 and Cotterill fired a two-second-burst of cannon and machine gun fire at an angle of 30 degrees astern and to port from 200 yards. Strikes were seen on the port wing and engine. A further four-second burst from 75 yards almost dead astern caused a small explosion and they broke to starboard. Cotterill and McKenna watched it crash and burst into flames two miles west of the airfield and then went down to photograph the burning wreckage.

They set course for Orléans using the fire at Terminiers as a pinpoint. When within five miles they noticed considerable activity at Orléans airfield. The V/L was on and the runway lighting but no beacon. One aircraft was landing and two more were circling preparatory to doing so. All were burning navigation lights. Cotterill attacked the second aircraft, a Ju 52, which was apparently going round again at 500 feet. He fired a three-second-burst of cannon and machine gun from 150 yards, 20 degrees astern and to starboard, the enemy aircraft blew up instantly and crashed 40 yards north of the east to west runway three-quarters of the way along. On breaking away to port the Mosquito crew observed the last of four aircraft break away from the circuit, douse all lights and head south. At once they took up the chase and overshot, as they were diving underneath trying to keep a visual. They noticed a series of 'dits' being flashed from three downward recognition lights in white and as they throttled back, managed to pull in behind, obtaining a clear silhouette of a Ju 188. The enemy aircraft took violent evasive action but Cotterill and McKenna managed to maintain contact and as he straightened out, fire a three-second-burst from 30 yards astern and slightly below. Strikes were seen on the port engine and fuselage and fire started in the belly. The

101   On 14 April Squadron Leader Robert Allan Kipp and Flight Lieutenant Peter Huletsky shot down two Ju 52/3mg6e minesweepers of the Minensuchgruppe fitted with de-gaussing rings. They also destroyed two Do 217s on the ground and they damaged a third.

Mosquito's windscreen was covered in oily liquid and debris started hitting their starboard wing. They broke to starboard and followed the enemy aircraft as it glided gently down into a field, the fire illuminating the terrain for several hundred yards. On impact, the whole aircraft burst into flames.

As they were now south of the town, Cotterill and McKenna returned to the airfield where they noticed that the V/L had been turned off but the runway was still lit. A large white floodlight had been installed on the left side and about 15 yards from the beginning of the runway. They then decided to bomb the runway in use and dropped two 500lb GP eleven seconds delay, from 500 feet. As they broke away to port, their bombs were seen to explode on the runway and a third of the way along. Immediately afterwards they noticed an aircraft with navigation lights on and a large landing light shining practically straight down from the nose, making an approach to land about 300 feet above and 1,000 yards away from the runway. They swung round to port and closed to 100 yards, recognizing the enemy aircraft as a Ju 52. Cotterill opened fire at this range with a four-second burst from an angle of 20 degrees astern and to port, strikes being seen on the port engine and fuselage. By this time the aircraft was only 100 yards from the perimeter track and 100 feet high. It crashed and blew up on the edge of the runway. As all their ammunition had been used up by that last burst they set course for home. [102]

In night operations on 7/8 June 70 Mosquitoes on 107, 305 and 613 Squadrons operating to the west on rail targets at Argentan, Domfort and Lisieux, sealed approaches to the bridgehead in Normandy. Night-fighter crews on 29, 307 (City of Lwow) Squadron, 406 ('Lynx') Squadron RCAF, 418 and 456 Squadrons made claims for ten enemy aircraft destroyed, one probably destroyed and three damaged. The Polish squadron had begun 'Night Rangers' on 16 May when one its Mosquito crews shot up a factory at Karlsruhe and then suffered an engine failure and home on one. Two nights later 307 shot up the German flying-boat base at Concarneau on the Brest Peninsular, leaving a flying-boat burning. Another 'Night Ranger' was flown to Bremen where a factory and a good yards were bombed and a train was stopped. Several trains were attacked by another Mosquito and four more locomotives, a signal box and three searchlights near Bremen were shot up. Five crews on 29 Squadron took the lion's share on 7/8 June with claims for five destroyed, one probably destroyed and two damaged. A Ju 52 and a UEA were claimed destroyed by Flight Lieutenant George E. Allison and Flying Officer R. G. 'Bob' Stainton and Flight Lieutenant John Barry and Guy Hopkins claimed two Ju 188s destroyed. Flying Officer Frank Pringle and his navigator Flying Officer Wain Eaton, flying a NF.XIII equipped with AI.Mk.VIII radar and armed with four 20mm cannon, took off from West Malling at 22.53 hours for an 'Intruder' patrol on German airfields at Evreux, St-André, Dreux and Chartres, just west of Paris.

Pringle recalls.'Intruding back in 1941 and '42 had been successfully carried out by both German and RAF crews, but radar-equipped RAF fighters were not permitted to cross the enemy coastline until 'Overlord'. In the build-up to the invasion, 29 Squadron had been working-up with low level night navigation at 240 mph in order to sharpen up rusty navigation skills, with the radar operators peering for hours into their PPIs (Plan and Position Indicators) guiding their pilots to make interceptions at all levels.

---

102   Stan Cotterill and John Finlayson were lost on 18 October 1944 when their Mosquito was shot down over Yugoslavia while on a sortie from Italy to Hunsdon.

Early 1941/42 Mk.IV airborne radar had height limitations due to obstructing ground returns, but this had now been replaced with the efficient and reliable Mk.VIII that could take on low level targets.

'The squadron had new aircraft and had been equipped with tents and motor transport with which they had 'shaken down' at Drem and had practiced night landings on grass with the minimum of lighting aids in preparation for full mobility when sent to Europe. Although a dim view was taken of the tents, morale was good.

'As we lined up on runway 23 Wain crouched beside me on his miserable hard seat, with his flight plan and computer handy and with only his knees as a worktop - inches away from the mask covering the PPI tube. It was all a very tight fit in Mae West and flying harness, while stuffed in his boot was a torch and in another pocket his emergency pouch containing a silk map of Europe, foreign currency, glucose tablets etc. - but no condoms. Sewn into his jacket and trousers were a couple of miniature compasses.

'Crossing out at the south coast over Beachy Head, I descended to below 500 feet to cross the Channel. Fifteen minutes later, I increased power for a quick climb to 3,000 feet before stuffing the nose down for maximum speed to nip over the French coast at Fécamp, north of the Seine, at 300 feet. We were now on the first leg to Evreux, which came up at 23.43 hours, the beacon flashing 'ZP'. There was no sign of activity at either Evreux or St-André.

'At 23.55 a Visual Lorenz was lit at Dreux. This was a long approach lighting aid, sometimes several kilometres in length, to make German pilots make a snappy approach and landing without having to wander around circuits. After a short while Wain obtained a contact at three-quarters of a mile, crossing fast at 90 degrees and descending through 1,500 feet. We turned hard to port, lost radar contact, but obtained a visual on a landing light from an aircraft touching down. I gave it a quick burst of fire, saw some strikes and claimed it as damaged.

'Bearing in mind that this was the first time I had fired my cannons at low level at night, I was scared of flying into the ground. On a previous occasion when I had fired cannon in daylight, at a practice target off the Clacton pier area, the Perspex radar dome in the nose of the Mosquito had disintegrated and a hunk of debris had pierced my leading edge radiator. All the port engine coolant went overboard. I had sweaty hands that it might happen again.

'We now climbed to 2,000 feet and stood off to watch down-wind, hoping for more contacts in the direction of Chartres to the south. Meanwhile the Visual Lorenz at Dreux stayed lit.

'At about 00.30 colours of the period were gently fired off from an aircraft nearby, but we failed to get a contact in spite of several orbits. Suddenly, south of Dreux, I saw an aircraft below - to my astonishment with a navigation light on! I made a quick beam attack down to low level with a five-second burst, again with numerous strikes. After breaking away there was a brilliant flash south of the airfield. We now observed a bright fire that had not been there before and in line with the runway. Bright objects were shooting off it in all directions. After emptying my remaining cannon rounds into this area, I made a couple of ciné camera runs over the site and claimed it destroyed, seeing inaccurate light flak coming up from a position south of the airfield. We set course for base via the Seine and crossed out north of Lillebonne at 00:55, making landfall at Beachy Head and we touched down at West Malling at 01.46

hours, ready for bacon and eggs.

'The weather over France had been good, with a slight ground haze and with cloud at 4,000 feet. All our cannon had fired, using 352 rounds of SAPI (semi-armour piercing incendiary) and 344 of HEI (high explosive incendiary). At 44 rounds per second this would take just fifteen seconds.'

Night-fighter operations over the Continent did not always end as successfully. A few weeks later a 'Night Intruder' to the Nachtjagd night-fighter training establishment near Stettin ended in a fruitless search for Wing Commander Karel Ranoszek, commanding 307 (City of Lwow) Squadron at Church Fenton. (It was not the first time he returned empty handed. It had happened when Ranoszek and Pilot Officer Krawiecki had flown the squadron's first night defensive sortie on 14 January 1943). As they turned for home his navigator was taken ill. Ranoszek had gained his 'wings' in the Polish Air Force in 1931 and had fought against the Luftwaffe in Poland and France before arriving in England 'with no English word in his vocabulary and no possessions save a toothbrush, a razor and just the suit he was wearing'.

'North of Kiel, we ran slap over a German flak ship which the navigator would normally have picked up on the AI screen and I could easily have avoided....I felt the Mark XII Mosquito being repeatedly hit amid the searchlight beams and coloured tracers. All hell had broken loose...' Ranoszek managed to get the Mosquito back across the North Sea to Coltishall, the forward base near the Norfolk coast albeit 'in a somewhat wobbly fashion'. As he made his approach it was obvious that the damage was severe.' As I lowered the flaps on the approach, the aircraft banked over to the left and nearly turned over onto its back. A quick retraction of the flaps saved us and I landed successfully without them at a very high speed. After taxiing in and switching off all was quiet except for some gentle hissing and gurgling in the pipes. The sick navigator was given immediate attention and then one of the ground crew, shining a torch underneath the wing, shouted out: 'Jesus bloody Christ! Come and look at this, sir.'

'The mess was unbelievable. A big shell had gone through the port wing, missing the main fuel tank by inches. The flap on that side only had a few ribs left. We finished counting the bullet holes in the aircraft at 300. But neither my navigator nor I had even a scratch - a clear case of 'more luck than brains'. The aeroplane was a write-off and another was sent to take us back to base. I doubt whether anything but a Mosquito could have stood up to that kind of punishment and still got us back... That's why I loved the Mosquito.'[103]

The opportunity for breakout and the eventual invasion of Germany was now within reach and 2nd TAF would go all the way with the ground forces. On 11 June six Mosquitoes on 464 and 487 Squadrons led by Wing Commander Bob Iredale and Flight Lieutenant McCaul attacked petrol tankers in a railway marshalling yard at Châtellerault at the request of the Army. Wing Commander Mike Pollard on 107 Squadron and his six Mosquitoes arrived at 22.44 hours to find fires burning in an area 300 x 200 yards with smoke rising to 4,000 feet. That night attacks continued on railway targets and 50 aircraft from 88, 98, 107, 180, 226 and 320 Squadrons bombed the railway junction at Le Haye, west of Carentan. Two nights later 42 Mosquitoes on 107, 305, 464 and 613 Squadrons strafed and bombed troop movements between Tours and Angers-

103 *Out of the Blue: The Role of Luck in Air Warfare 1917-1966,* edited by 'Laddie' Lucas (Hutchinson & Co 1985)

Vire, Dreux and Falaise and Evreux and Lisieux. The scene over France had changed completely. Whereas before 'D-Day' there had been almost total darkness, now there were lights everywhere and most of the Normandy towns burned for several nights. It made navigation much easier; pilots just flew 'from one fire to the next.'

On 14/15 June Mosquitoes wreaked havoc on the continent and eight enemy aircraft were shot down over the continent by 2nd TAF Mosquito crews. On 18/19 June the only ADGB success was achieved by 32-year old Wing Commander John Topham DFC* CO of 125 (Newfoundland) Squadron and Flight Lieutenant H. W. 'Wilber' Berridge DFC, who claimed two Ju 88s off the beachhead to take his score to thirteen. Topham, who had worked in the textile business in Manchester and Berridge, a 32-year old ex-printer and former air gunner, had crewed up on Beaufighters on 219 Squadron and they had shared in nine victories during 1941-42. Lieutenant Archie Harrington on 410 'Cougar' Squadron RCAF claimed a Ju 88 destroyed, as did Flying Officer G. E. Edwards.

On the night of 22/23 June 22-year old Flight Lieutenant the Honourable Mike Wedgewood Benn DFC, one of 21 Squadron's most experienced pilots, took off on his 31st Mosquito operation with his navigator, Flying Officer W. A. Roe, on a 'Night Ranger' from Thorney Island in FB.VI 'G-George'. On becoming airborne he found that his ASI (airspeed indicator) was not working and so he radioed Control that he had problems and was returning to base. Another Mosquito crew was able to formate with 'G-George' and led them into the approach to ensure that they were at the right speed but Benn's approach was such that he touched down too far down the runway. He overran the end of the runway and the Mosquito went over the low sea wall at the airfield boundary and bounced on the shingle strip. The undercarriage and wheels were torn off as they hit the barbed wire fence entanglement beyond the shingle and the tail dropped when it hit the mud flat. The fuselage snapped completely off art a near the tail fin and the aircraft's nose dropped and dug into the mud bringing the aircraft to a halt about thirty yards from the sea wall. Bill Roe survived but the sudden stop caused the armour plate behind the pilot's seat to hurl itself forward and this broke Mike Benn's back. They were in shallow water and Roe managed to keep Benn's head above water and carried him some way back to the airfield before the ambulance finally found them. Benn died later at St Richard's hospital in Chichester.

Tony Benn received a telegram reporting his brother's death at the airfield he was stationed at in North Africa. Writing later about his brother's death he says: 'Michael had planned to be with his family on the 7 June, his Mother's birthday. He had booked seats to see a West End show called the Lisbon Story which was playing at the Aldwych Theatre, but D-Day intervened to prevent him being there. A fortnight later Mother was at his bedside when he died. Father [104] who was also in the RAF was at that time with the Allied Control Commission in Italy and hurried home as soon as he heard the news.' The Squadron records stated, 'Michael was a favourite of the Squadron and his death is a great shock to us all.'

2nd TAF and ADGB destroyed at least 230 aircraft at night over the Channel, France, the Low Countries and Germany, June 1944-April 1945. In the run up to D-

104   William Wedgewood Benn DSO DFC Ld-H CdD, a WWI veteran pilot and prominent politician who was created Viscount Stansgate on 22 December 1940. Michael Benn was the eldest of three sons. Tony Benn, who rose to a senior position in the Labour Government, became Lord Stansgate on the death of his father.

Day, 29 Squadron of the ADGB had been the first Mosquito unit equipped with the superior AI.Mk.VIII radar to be released for intruding over the Continent. Whilst still equipped with Beaufighter VIFs, the unit had had its first taste of offensive night operations in spring 1943 when it began 'Night Rangers' over airfields in German-occupied France. After converting to the Mosquito in the summer 29 Squadron reverted to defensive operations in the ADGB, finally mounting its first 'Intruders' over France on the night of 14 May 1944. In July the six Mosquito fighter squadrons in 2nd TAF shot down 55 enemy aircraft and claimed two 'probables'. Until suitable airstrips could be made ready, the Mosquito wings flew operations from Thorney Island and Lasham. Some spectacular pinpoint daylight operations against specific buildings were flown.

On 14 July, Bastille Day, 18 Mosquitoes on 21, 464 and 487 Squadrons led by Group Captain Peter Wykeham-Barnes DSO DFC* and Flying Officer Chaplin carried out a daylight low-level attack on a Gestapo barracks at Bonneuil Matours, near Poitiers. The raid was to punish those responsible for the murder of some British prisoners of war who had been dubbed to death with rifle butts in a nearby village square. The target was a collection of six buildings inside a rectangle just 170 x 100 feet, close to the village, which had to be avoided. There was no model of the target for the crews because there had not been time to prepare one but the raid went quite smoothly. The Mosquitoes in shallow dives dropped nine tons of bombs fused for a 25-second delay on the barracks. Crews did not re-formate after bombing. It soon became dark and they returned independently. Three trains were attacked on the return flights for good measure. The rest of the trip was uneventful and all crews returned safely. [105]

On 23 July George Topliss and Ernest S. Gates on 613 Squadron at Lasham flew their first operation since arriving from the Mosquito OTU at Bicester where for three months they had spent most of their flying time speeding at low-level over the English countryside. 'Very few hours were devoted to night flying' recalls Gates 'and yet, on posting to 613 Squadron, all my operational hours except about four were spent on 'Night Intruder' flights. Learning on the job I think they call it! Although Lasham airfield during the summer of 1944 was similar to all other wartime stations in that there were several dispersed domestic sites and Nissen huts for the Messes, top-level administration compelled us to live under canvas. We were told that on eventual transfer to the Continent after 'D-Day' we should be required to take all our accommodation with us. The German scorched-earth policy would leave nothing of the airfields from which we were to operate in France. Therefore, experience of living in tents was 'vitally necessary'. So, for many months, we squelched about in rubber boots,

---

105 On 30 July the SAS learned that 2,000-3,000 Germans were massing for an anti-Maquis/SAS sweep and the majority were billeted in the Caserne des Dunes barracks at Poitiers. This resulted in a raid by 24 FB.VIs of 487 and 21 Squadrons escorted by Mustangs on 1 August. Meanwhile, the SAS learned that the survivors of the 158th Regiment were now in the Château de Fou, an SS police HQ south of Châtellerault. This and Château Maulny, a saboteur school was attacked by 23 FB.VIs on 107 and 305 Squadrons on Sunday 2 August. It is estimated that 80% of the regiment were killed. That same day, 613 Squadron attacked a château in Normandy, which was used as a rest home for German submariners. It appeared that Sunday was chosen because on Saturday nights the Germans had a dance, which went on rather late. The FB.VIs attacked early in the morning, with rather devastating results. AVM Embry under the alias 'Wing Commander Smith' and the Station Commander, Group Captain Bower, took part.

tried to shave in lukewarm, smoke-impregnated water and wore clothing that frequently got the mildew in our rather damp travelling cases. Needless to say, on arrival at Cambrai/Epinoy in the autumn of 1944 we found the aircrew quarters, recently vacated by the Luftwaffe, to be rather better that the average Nissen huts on the airfields back in Britain. Certainly, they were centrally heated and did not rely on temperamental coke stoves for warmth.

'I well remember my first operational flight with George Topliss. It might more fairly be described as the night operation that nearly never was. The task was to patrol a small area of northern France in the Amiens-Beauvais area. After meticulous flight planning and adopting all the techniques with which I had been drilled at OTU. I was ready to depart. George went through his pre-flight checks with more than usual care and eventually we were airborne. Crossing the Channel was peaceful enough and then we saw the French coast darkly outlined against the sea ahead of us. Acting as he had been instructed, George commenced evasive action to confuse the enemy aircraft and flak. Unfortunately, his action confused us more than the enemy. My pilot later admitted that he scared himself to death as he nearly lost control with his over-violent manoeuvres. Busy in my endeavours to maintain checks on our directions, I was unaware of the situation. Ever after that we simply took no evasive action whatsoever on crossing the enemy coast and on no occasion did enemy guns open fire as we entered their territory. We certainly have lived to tell the tale which nearly was never told because of my pilot's enthusiasm to follow his flying instructors.'

On 18 August at Lasham 613 Squadron crews, like those in 305 (Polish) and 107 Squadron,[106] had been granted a 24-hour stand down by Group to celebrate 138 Wing's thousandth sortie since 'D-Day' and no-one was expecting to fly again until the 19th as Ernest Gates recalls: 'A great party developed, officers bringing their wives and 'popsies' from all corners of the country. On the understanding that there would be no operations task given to the squadron on the morrow, everyone had a thoroughly good time, eventually seeking rest in the early hours either in damp beds out on the airfield or with human hot-water bottles in hotels in nearby Alton. To everyone's horror Steve, the squadron adjutant, came round about mid-morning on the following day trying to rouse heavy-headed aircrews who were expected to be airborne by two o'clock in the afternoon. After much searching and the making of many telephone calls, the adjutant found the required number of personnel to man six aircraft. In my case, as both my pilot George Topliss and I were bachelors sharing the same tent, we were able to fly together on this low-level daylight raid on Egletons 50 miles SE of Limoges in central France. A number of the other aircraft had very mixed crews. The only common feature about us all was the alcoholic haze which

106   On 26 August 219 Squadron joined 147 Wing, 85 (Base) Group, 2nd TAF and on 3 September 264 Squadron made a move to Caen/Carpiquet with the first patrols flown over the Paris area and later over Brussels. 138 Wing received incoming reports on 25/26 August of a concentration of troops and vehicles in the Rouen area and off attempts to retreat across the Seine. This now seemed to be a critical area and could well be a pivot to the successful advance of Allied troops into Belgium and Germany. 2nd TAF received the highest possible commendation for the attacks on 25/26 August and this support continued on 26/27 August when an all-out attack was carried out. On 31 August a huge petrol dump at Nomency near Nancy was destroyed and twelve FB.VIs on 464 Squadron attacked a dozen petrol trains near Chagney from between 20 and 200 feet and caused widespread destruction. The Panzer divisions in the Battle of Normandy were deprived of millions of gallons of much needed fuel. Wing Commander G. Panitz the CO, failed to return.

threatened to reduce our vision and perception. Slowly we collected our thoughts and struggled through briefing. Eventually we became airborne about two hours late. However, merely to prove that aircrew did not require boisterous good health for the success of a flying mission, the result of our raid on a French technical school, currently believed to be in use as an SS troops barracks, was a tremendous success. Only one aircraft was shot down and its crew reached the safety of the Allied lines on the north side of the river Loire. [107]

John Conlin, a Canadian pilot would fly a total of 53 sorties on 107 Squadron before VE Day but he had fantastic imaginings of what to expect on the occasion of his first operation from Lasham on 26 August.

'Being a new boy going out to strike the German Army pulling out across the Seine (as per our briefing) I expected to see German troops crossing that stream by every conceivable means, from swimming to paddling bath-tubs and upon arrival found nothing. In fact, I had great difficulty in finding the river for it was as black as seven yards up a chimney and after I had used up both flares without any success I was thoroughly lost. Not with-standing a strict admonition at briefing to stay away from Rouen, I approached it unhesitatingly for I did not know where I was and flew around the biggest bonfire I have ever seen in my life, ultimately dropping two fairly ineffective 500lb bombs and returning to base. On another occasion, early in my career with the squadron, being unable to find any suitable target in ten-tenths cloud down to 300 feet, I brought back my bombs and landed with them, much to the chagrin of the ground crew who came up to help with parking in the dispersal and then disappeared pell-mell as soon as they found the aircraft armed. I always thought that was proper when you could fly well for the cost of running the war was high and I felt that aircrew should not be wasteful.

'From August 1944 until the end of the war, 107 Squadron was comprised of the most homogeneous mix of personnel I have ever had the pleasure of meeting. Most of the navigators were RAF of English stock, but the pilots were a mixture of RAF, Canadians in the RCAF, Americans in the RCAF, an American in the USAAC, a Norwegian Lieutenant Commander in the Norwegian Navy, a Norwegian Captain in the Norwegian Army Air Corps, New Zealanders and even a South African Air Force captain, ultimately a Major. Wing Commander W. J. Scott, who had command of the squadron just before I joined it, was an Irishman who enjoyed sending the boys to South Ireland on leave if he could possibly entice them there in civvies. This crowd operated happily together.'

Mid-afternoon in late August 1944 Flight Sergeant Terry Ridout, a navigator on 107 Squadron and his pilot Flight Lieutenant Tony Rippon DFC were briefed for a low-level strike on the marshalling yards outside Chalon-sur-Saone in Central France. 'The local Resistance fighters knew these were vital to the German retreat from the south' recalled Ridout 'and, on hearing from rail workers that the yards held trainloads of munitions and demolition explosive, had signalled our Intelligence that same

---

107   Fifteen FB.VI crews on 613 Squadron led by Squadron Leader Charles Newman carried out the daring low level attack on the school building at Egletons. AVM Basil Embry and Group Captain Bower, as usual, went along. Fourteen of the Mosquitoes located and bombed the target, scoring at least 20 direct hits and the target was almost completely destroyed. One Mosquito, crewed by Flight Lieutenant House and Flying Officer Savill, was hit in the starboard engine over the target area and FTR but the crew survived and returned to the squadron just five days later.

morning for urgent action. Bar a fighter scare, all went smoothly up to the target. Then Tony, being unhappy with our first pass, came in low for a second. As we finished it, bombs and ammunition gone, flak knocked out the port motor. Some flames licked below the throttle quadrant and Tony made a brief R/T call to say we'd had it. So far as memory serves me, abandoning a FB.VI entails either feathering the starboard prop to ease slipstream pressure on the hatch or, half-rolling the aircraft, blowing the canopy off and dodging the fin and rudder (did it pass between the pilot and the navigator I wonder?). Neither option being open to us I braced myself half across the floor against the hatch and using leg leverage, shot with it into space before I could unplug my helmet, then all went blank. I came to on a straw bed in a barn, unable to move my head. I had no recollection of my descent or arrival there, not could I grasp why two men were replacing my uniform with civilian clothing, a process I was in no state either to help or hinder anyway. I couldn't interpret their French vernacular, but a young girl with them - I blushed to think she'd seen me debagged - made clear I must walk or be carried, as the Germans were coming. I think I walked. An hour later a local doctor had improved my mobility and passed me to a Resistance lieutenant and his small company, who drove me surreptitiously at bicycle speed along narrow lanes to their hide-out. I asked about Tony but learned he'd not left the aircraft, which had abruptly plunged into a nearby wood and burnt. (A Resistance spotter assured me that we had flown right across the flak tower that hit us. What followed was one of the biggest explosions of WW2 in the European theatre, involving bogie wagons carrying 70 tonnes of gelignite and 800 munitions trucks and killing hundreds of German soldiers. Baldly quantified, it shifted 400,000 cubic metres of soil, leaving a crater 15 metres deep and blasting a Chalon suburb flat).

'Having been kept out of German hands by the Resistance, I could scarcely quibble about joining them. Thus I found myself re-mustered overnight from flying duties to supernumerary rural guerrilla from then on. As the weeks passed, both our routine and our vigilance relaxed as the Germans withdrew. I was driven north as soon as roads could be cleared of booby traps and transport devised. Conveyed to Paris (then about half liberated) and the totally unwelcoming arms of the temporary RAF HQ, where a secretarial type curtly told me to look after myself! I did better on asking help from a US colonel crossing my path as I left. Unlike my fellow countrymen he proved a man of action. One hour later I was kitted out in a GI uniform. Yet another found me seated in a Blackbushe-bound Dakota explaining to an incredulous RAF checker that although I was admittedly from central France, with a French name but speaking English and having no documentation but wearing American uniform, I was like himself an RAF navigator.' [108]

Ernest Gates grew very fond of the Mosquito in which he and his pilot George Topliss carried out most of their first tour operations. 'The two ground crew were also very proud of the aircraft and did everything in their power to maintain it, in near-perfect state, often under appalling conditions on the dispersal. As each operation was successfully accomplished, I felt that I owed something more to the machine itself, rather than to the men who serviced it and a kind of dependence on it for survival developed in my mind. Each time as we thundered down the runway at the start of another trip, I settled into my seat with a complete sense of security and

I accepted that 'K for King' would see us through another mission. Looking back on it now I become rather embarrassed at my naivety of thought but, at the time, it felt reassuring as one placed one's faith blindly in a complicated mass of machinery. The persistent, powerful drone of the engines, a steady vibration through the warm, snug cockpit, the pale opalescent glow of the instrument panel and the green flickering haze from the 'Gee' set all created a special tiny microcosmic world of their own. We seemed completely separated from the reality of the earth below and the war in which we were engaged. I suppose I was subconsciously recreating the security of the womb. However, I never had the same feelings in other aircraft and I can only conclude that it was the neat efficiency of the Mosquito and its cockpit layout which led me to this secure state of mind.

'It really never occurred to me that I was flying in a wooden box with all the associated frailties of plywood. As the aircraft roared across the enemy countryside, our small secure and powerful world seemed detached and immune from the worst terrors that the enemy could produce. Nevertheless, this is not to say that I was not afraid. Every time George dived towards our target into the midst of the colourful streams of anti-aircraft fire, I sat immobile, anxiously counting out the altimeter readings and suddenly realising that my heart was thudding heavily against my ribs. There was the natural excitement of the situation, but there was also the fear. Does any man knowingly place himself in a position where the possibility of death in its most horrifying form is there before him and not feel some kind of fear? A number of incidents still vividly stand out in my mind and the following typify my feelings at the time. One pitch dark night we were patrolling in western Germany and spotted a small light immediately ahead of us. Working on the principle that any light in blacked-out Germany was always worth attacking, George immediately pushed the nose down and lined up to make a cannon attack. In actual fact we were unfavourably placed to make this attack, being too near the target and too low in altitude. Steeply we rushed in, the altimeter lagging dangerously. Suddenly .the reading dropped dramatically to 500 feet, which was the height of the ground in these parts. Clapping George on the back, I yelled at him to pull out. He did so and as we levelled off and then quickly commenced to climb, the dark silhouettes of trees rushed past the aircraft on the starboard side. We must have been merely a split second from disaster and oblivion on that occasion. For the remainder of that 'Intruder' trip our actions were far from enthusiastic and daring.

'On another occasion we decided to work as a pair of 'Intruders' with another aircraft in the squadron, piloted by Frankie Read. He was to drop the flare over the town of Venlo when we were favourably placed to take advantage of the illumination. Thoughtlessly we forgot that we too would be lit up and that we would present a splendid near-daylight target to the enemy gunners. There we were at about 1,500 feet above Venlo, naked under the yellow light of Frankie Read's flare and nearly blinded by its brilliance. Not so blinded were the German light AA gunners and almost immediately we were engulfed by a tangle trellis of coloured tracer shells. Identifying nothing and with the instinct of self-preservation uppermost in our minds, we dived rapidly away from the light of the flare into the comparative safety of the stygian blackness of night beyond the town. Once again we trembled to ourselves· and decided to use greater prudence in any future combined attacks.

'One night we were called upon to patrol an area in eastern Holland. The 'Intruder' trip itself was uneventful and we saw nothing worthy of serious attack. So, dropping our bombs on a secondary target-a railway marshalling yard-we set off for home at the end of the hour-long patrol. Rather than flyover enemy-held Belgium and France as we made our way back to Lasham, we decided to cross the Dutch coast near Ijmuiden and seek the relative safety of the open North Sea route. Passing over the coastline we suddenly found ourselves enveloped in heavy cumulo-nimbus cloud. One minute we had been sailing across calm untroubled skies and then the next we were immersed in apparently endless masses of black turbulent cloud. As the aircraft writhed and creaked in the terrifyingly violent air currents, George wrestled with the controls' to maintain the aircraft on an even keel. He dared not attempt to turn to escape the way back we had come through fear of the aircraft being thrown on its back; so he first tried to climb out of the storm. The rain and hail spun off the propellers, the inherent charges of static electricity making them glow like huge Catherine wheels. Then we heard the clatter of ice against the fuselage as chunks broke off the blades. Down - went the nose as George tried a second plan to fly beneath the storm. However, the up-currents were so powerful that the aircraft continued to go upward all the time.

'After what seemed an interminable period of terror, we suddenly broke out of the cloud at about 16,000 feet. The tortured groaning of our sturdy little Mosquito ceased as she found herself flying once more through untroubled air. My own memory of that moment of peace after the anguish and strain of the previous ten minutes will forever live in my mind. We were now flying down a huge valley of sky between mountains of cumulo-nimbus. A half-moon illuminated the turret tops and massive towers of cloud in a cold, pale glow. Black, fearful shadows were cast in the depths beneath us. It was a Himalayan fairyland. We had just escaped from the dark, terrifying dungeon of the ogre's castle and were now sailing serenely away on the wings of our gallant wooden saviour.

'On this occasion I, as navigator, swallowed my pride and permitted George to call up Manston for a QDM. After quarter of an hour when it was nearly impossible to keep any kind of air plot, I thought it prudent to accept outside aid. In actual fact the course I had given my pilot after our ordeal was almost identical with that obtained from Manston control.

'A less terrifying but nonetheless apprehensive moment occurred when we were told to patrol the railway systems running into Hanover. The night was very dark with low cloud scudding across the sky in a strong westerly wind. I faintly discerned certain landmarks which enabled us to locate a marshalling yard somewhere on the west side of the city. We dropped a flare at about 1,500 feet just below the cloud base and made a turn to port trying to identify something worth attacking. We had not allowed sufficiently for the strong wind and by the time we had completed the circuit and were coming up to the flare, it had drifted a considerable distance towards the east. Peering ahead searching for the target, we were in fact skimming over the roof tops of the centre of Hanover. Apprehensively we waited for the trigger-happy Germans to let fly at us, a naked sitting target in the light of the flare. Miraculously not a gun was fired and as we climbed rapidly into the thick cloud, we heaved a sigh of relief. I rather think we dropped our second flare with greater care that night.

'In the Mosquito two-man crews the relationship grew very close; not like the larger crews where the situation in a bomber aircraft did not encourage the same growth of intimate friendship. We on 613 Squadron (and no doubt on other Mosquito units) worked, flew and enjoyed our leisure together and naturally, a close friendship grew up between certain crews. In addition, the camaraderie usually divided up again into pilot and navigator associates.

'The happier side of squadron life included many humorous episodes. There was the time we tried to 'borrow' the parrot from a pub in Odiham; trying to help George Topliss, a great hulk of a chap, into bed after his getting blotto on champagne, losing my Service Dress hat and finding it a fortnight later under the mattress of his bed. On stand-down periods we usually collected together in the Mess bar. Life on the squadron was one of some strain and the only release for one's tension and pent-up feelings was to seek refuge behind a pint of beer, a game of darts and conversation. Sometimes we would gather with the other fellows of the squadron and slowly a party would develop quite spontaneously. They were tremendous fun on account of this spontaneity, quite unlike the rigid present-day guest nights when one is expected to be in a party spirit to order.

There was an air traffic controller, whose name now escapes me, who was a wonderful pianist. Prime him with pints of beer and he would lead us in a sing-song. It may sound rather tame but the songs were far from subdued. *Salome, Eskimo Nell, The Ball of Kirriemuir* - all came in for regular treatment and I blush now to think of the obscenities which I sang so gustily with all the others. As we tired of this kind of entertainment some enthusiasts would challenge the rest to party games. 'High Cockalorum' was popular and forward rolls over the Mess furniture required a skill which one apparently possessed only after several jugs of ale. In the cold, sober light afterwards we wondered why no one had broken his neck. Other activities centred around a pile of Mess chairs up which crews were compelled to climb in order to write their last successful operational exploit on the roof of the Nissen hut. Slowly one scaled the furniture and then, precariously perched at the top of the pyramid, pilot and navigator would daub a picture of a train or similar enemy target on the ceiling with the date of the action. Immediately on successful completion of this acrobatic exercise, well-intentioned fellows below assisted you down by pulling away the chairs at the bottom. About 11 o'clock after such evening beer parties, we healthy young aircrew by this time were fairly hungry. Someone would suggest a night-flying supper so off we'd dash to the Airmen's Mess where a 24-hour service appeared to be arranged for flying crews. I well remember a flight commander on 107 Squadron - another Mosquito squadron on 138 Wing - going off on his own for such a supper on a perishing cold winter night. He never made the Mess and was eventually discovered the following morning curled up fast asleep in a snow-drift. Needless to say, he spent many days in hospital recovering from pneumonia.

'The reality of life was often brought home to us at the termination of an operation. Frequently, fellows with whom one had shared the previous evening's entertainment were posted missing. For me the thought of being shot down never entered my head. I suppose it was inevitable that one thought 'it's not going to be me'. If one had not thought this way, one could not have carried on. Every crew member in a Mosquito squadron was known to the others and each time one aircraft went missing, we all felt the loss. Nevertheless, one carried on and left it to the Commanding Officer and his adjutant to write the usual letters to bereaved parents and wives. However, I was seriously disturbed by the loss of Ronnie Elvin, a navigator. He and his pilot went missing on a patrol over Germany in the autumn of 1944. Ronnie and I were great buddies and we had a lot of similar interests. Very often we would walk out into the countryside and chat about home, life before joining the RAF and what we intended to do 'after the war'. On such excursions when we were stationed at Epinoy, we would end up at a small estaminet on the road to Cambrai. There we practised our schoolboy French and helped the patron to drink some pre-war vintage champagne which he had hidden successfully from the Germans for four years. Afterwards, with fuzzy heads and full of bonhomie, we would stagger back to our billet, arms locked together and singing all the popular choruses from Vera Lynn's latest hits. Then suddenly it was all over. A gap appeared in my routine and for the first time in my life I realised what it meant to lose for ever a true friend.

'It might not be inappropriate to conclude these reminiscences with a story that concerned neither death nor glory. George Topliss and I were on a night-flying test from Lasham one day early in 1944 and therefore only expected to be airborne for a few minutes whilst we tested the Mosquito and its equipment. Consequently, I did not take a map or list of call-signs for other flying stations in the vicinity. Unfortunately, as we made our final approach to the runway, a rain squall came across the airfield. Hastily, the air traffic controller sent us away to another airfield. He gave us a course to steer, a distance to fly and the call-sign of the diversionary airfield. Turning on to the heading according to the directional indicator, we flew off calling up the airfield, the name and location of which were unknown to us because I had no list of call-signs with me. We could not compromise the airfield over the R/T by asking for its name in plain language. We flew for a period of time to cover the distance quoted and saw no airfield ahead. Only then did George realise that he had set his directional indicator to zero as he had lined up on the runway for landing at Lasham and we had flown off in a direction which took us anywhere but along the route given by the controller. Correcting this error, George called base again for a QDM, only to be told that the weather had closed in and we were diverted to yet another airfield, of which we were given the call-sign. We did as we were told and eventually flew out of the rainstorms to see an airfield ahead. We eventually landed there and you can imagine our shame as we stepped out of the Mosquito to ask the ground crew at what aerodrome had we landed. It turned out to be Dunsfold and we found ourselves having to spend the night in the Mess in battle-dress and flying boots. We looked a sorry, unshaven sight on the following day when we finally returned to Lasham after a 'short' night-flying test which lasted 24 hours. On all future flights, whatever their duration, I took everything in my navigation bag, including a shaving kit.'

Though V-1 patrols had occupied most of 418 Squadron's time in July and August they were interspersed with other types of activity, 418 reverting, in September, to 'Rangers' and abortive 'Big Ben' patrols (trying to 'jam' V-2 rockets). They flew 'Flowers', harassing enemy bases in support of the invasion or of bombers and 'Day Rangers' hunting in pairs. These were carried out at low level and ideally with cloud cover at 1,000 feet or more, to facilitate evasion if attacked. By the end of the war Wing Commander Russ Bannock DFC* and Flying Officer Bob Bruce would be credited with nine enemy aircraft and 19 V-1s destroyed. 'The V-1 patrols occupied most of our time in July and August' recalls Bob Bruce. 'We did 18 of them. Interspersed were other types of activity; 'Flowers' harassing enemy bases in support of the invasion or of bombers and 'Day Rangers', hunting in pairs. There were carried out at low level and ideally with cloud cover at 1,000 feet or more, to facilitate evasion if attacked. Our first of these was on 28 June led by Flight Lieutenant C. M. Jasper (Long Beach, California) and his navigator Archie Martin. Jas was one of several American pilots who joined the RCAF. Crossing Denmark at treetop height, we found a Ju 88 crossing the Baltic, close to a fair sized vessel. Jasper destroyed the Junkers in the air, but was caught by the ship's fire. I vividly recall his blazing tailfin above the seemingly static ship. The damage was limited and he flew home successfully.

'We did two other 'Day Rangers', one to Copenhagen with Sid Seid (another Californian) and Dave McIntosh with gratifying result, the other alone arriving at Parow on the Baltic coast at sunrise. We found an OTU in full operation. After destroying two Me 108s in the circuit we were attacked by another older type Me 109. We broke off at treetop height but our port engine caught fire (due to debris holing the radiator). We feathered and returned on one engine landing back at Hunsdon after 7 hours 15 minutes. 'We were lucky sometimes and Russ's shooting was deadly' recalls Bob Bruce. Typical of their sorties was one on the night of 12/13 September when they took off from Hunsdon airfield on a 'Flower' sortie in support of Bomber Command.

Bannock recalled: 'We crossed the French coast at Coxyde at 22.54 hours and proceeded directly to the target area (Illesheim). After patrolling in the target area from 00.44 hours to 02.12 hours, we set course homeward. While passing just south of Kitzingen at 02.20 hours we saw this aerodrome lit with double flare-path and east/west V/L. The right-hand bar of the outer and inner horizons was not lit. We commenced to prowl around the airfield at about 400 feet and almost immediately observed an aircraft with navigation lights on coming towards us, doing a steep climbing turn towards the aerodrome. I did a 180° turn to port and followed the aircraft which was climbing very steeply over the airfield. I positioned myself at about 125 yards behind and slightly below and fired a 1½-second burst of cannon and machine gun at about 5° angle-off to starboard. There were numerous strikes on the starboard side of the fuselage and along the starboard wing. Almost immediately I fired another 1½ -second burst of both cannon and machine gun fire from the same position. Numerous strikes were again observed along the starboard wing and fuselage and the starboard engine exploded. The aircraft immediately dropped straight down and as we passed over it I started a turn to the right to observe the results. During the turn there was a large flash on the ground below us, but as we completed the turn we would not see any fire on the ground. Since there was not a fire, we are claiming this aircraft as only probably destroyed, but as the starboard engine was seen to explode and the subsequent flash seen from an explosion on the ground, we are almost certain that it crashed and request that the claim be raised to destroyed.'

It was. For a higher success rate AI was needed, with which 406 ('Lynx') Squadron RCAF was equipped. Even so, 418 would finish the war with the distinction of destroying more enemy aircraft both in the air and on the ground, than any other Canadian squadron, in both night and daylight operations. The following month Bannock was appointed Commanding Officer of 418 Squadron but not before he and Bob Bruce flew another unique trip when they and another Mosquito crew flew to Toulouse to escort back to Farnborough a captured He 177. 'Toulouse had only just been liberated' recalls Bruce 'and we found a very highly charged atmosphere in the town. We were entertained by a colonel of the Maquis. I remember in a cafe, a local man stood to sing solo the Marseillaise. No one spoke; none joined in. It was as vivid a display of patriotism as I ever knew.' [109]

Early in September the focus of the war changed dramatically. On 17 September Operation 'Market-Garden' took place. 'Market-Garden' has been described in an official report as 'by far the biggest and most ambitious airborne operation ever carried out by any nation or nations.' Thirty-two FB.VIs on 107 and 613 Squadrons attacked a German barracks at Arnhem, while 21 Squadron at Thorney Island bombed three school buildings in the centre of Nijmegen, which were being used by the German garrison. On 18 September the Germans counter-attacked and forestalled an American attempt to capture the bridge at Nijmegen. Altogether, nine Mosquito bomber squadrons now equipped 2nd TAF. In September 1944, following the outbreak from the Normandy beachhead, plans were in progress to move them to airfields in France. As part of the newfound offensive, Mosquito squadrons outside 2nd TAF also made daylight 'Rangers' from France and 'Intruder' sorties over the Continent. In September-October 2nd TAF Mosquito night-fighters destroyed 43 enemy aircraft. On 31 October 25 FB.VIs, each carrying 11-second delayed action bombs, destroyed Aarhus University, the HQ for the Gestapo in the whole of Jutland, Denmark and its incriminating records were destroyed.

'Early in October 107 Squadron had a most successful strike destroying many trains and road transport' recalls John Conlin. 'We had moved into Nissen huts at Lasham and since we were stood down the next night, we had a big party to celebrate the event and lord it over our sister squadrons in the wing. Johnny McClurg, one of the Canadian flight commanders at the time (who was later killed in Canada in a flying mishap) decided that the whole episode should be recorded for posterity on the ceiling of the Nissen hut in paint. In order to reach it he had to erect a precarious trestle starting with a ping-pong table, upon the top of which he loaded two other tables of successively smaller size, topping the whole thing off with a chair which formed a platform from which his artistic efforts were carried on. While he was painting locomotives, trucks etc, on the ceiling, black paint dripping down his arm to the elbow, E. G. Smith poured a tankard of beer into his rubber boot (these were necessary in the mud) and McClurg lashed out a kick at him, promptly stepping off perch and hurtling down to shove his foot through the ping-pong table up to the hip. This table, being made of plywood, impaled him and we had to dismantle the whole thing with saws to get him out. This was one of our more successful Mess parties. In like vein were the steeple chases organised by Jock McLeod, the group captain's navigator. Jock was a short man with an enormous walrus moustache. He delighted in getting the entire wing organised in a steeplechase, using all the chairs and chesterfields in the Mess as hurdles and the cushions to pad the fall on the other side. Being short, Jock felt that there should be some form of handicap for taller fellows who could clear a high obstacle, so he used to buy gallons of beer all poured into pint glasses which he would line up along the back

109   When near the end of November 418 were posted to 2nd TAF, Russ Bannock went to take command of 406 Squadron, equipped with Mk.XXX Mosquitoes with AI at Manston. They had been on home night fighter duties for some time. I went along as Navigation Officer, non-operational and Squadron Leader Don MacFadyen as Operations Officer. We set up a lively ops room with all the intelligence available. The squadron had considerable success with the use of AI but with 418 tactics and morale rose beyond all possible expectation.'

of a chesterfield. Following one successful circuit of the 'course' by all contestants, Jock would call a halt until he had brought more beer to pile on top of the last row, continuing this process until a tall and shaky barricade of glass filled with beer confronted the runners. The whole thing generally ended up in a shambles of broken glass, with uniforms and cushions sopping and reeking of beer.

'Our squadron navigation officer, Flight Lieutenant Arthur Little, was generally a source of music whose piano playing was almost a religion with him; once at the keyboard it took a lot to disturb him. On one occasion the Mess members had made a pile of furniture and perched the piano on top. At the piano was Arthur Little playing happily away. Suddenly he smelt burning and on looking down saw that he was 'playing' Joan of Arc as well.

'Flight Lieutenant E. G. Smith and I had identical Service careers on 107 Squadron. About the time we had reached 48 trips, a directive came down from headquarters that the tour would be extended from 50 trips (as it then was) to 85 trips, 300 hours or nine months service on the squadron, whichever should first elapse. We were given one month's leave at the end of 50 trips which we spent in England, returning to do three more trips before the expiry of our nine months' service and the termination of the war coincided.'

By this stage of the war the Panzers and other German troops were being given no respite in the daylight raids by Mitchells and Bostons and the nightly visits by Mosquitoes. In November 14 enemy aircraft were shot down by 2nd TAF Mosquitoes but in December the weather and other factors limited night-fighter activity over the Reich. Only three Ju 88s and two Bf 110s were destroyed 4-18/19 December. [110]

By now 107, 305 (Polish) and 613 Squadrons of 138 Wing finally arrived in France, to be based at Epinoy near Cambrai and 464 RAAF and 487 RNZAF Squadrons sent advance detachments to Rosières-en-Santerre. Late in November, 136 Wing had been created within 2nd TAF by the arrival, from Fighter Command, of 418 Squadron RCAF and 605 Squadron, which transferred to Hartford Bridge, as Gordon Allen, a navigator on 605, recalls. 'In typical RAF style, December was spent practising those things we had been doing, e.g. night attacks. Operations resumed on New Year's Eve. Support for the Americans in the Bulge by bombing a tank laager at St-Vith in Belgium. Snow covered the ground, low stratus the target area. With a large target and 'Gee' coming in strongly we used it for bombing from 1,000-1,500 feet. Not perhaps precision stuff, but hopefully annoying to the invaders. We returned to St-Vith a few nights later to bomb (visually this time) an MT concentration. From then onwards it was patrolling on anti-movement duties. In other words we went after anything that moved or was foolish enough to show a light. Our attacks on trains, barges, MT and factories continued. Perhaps surprisingly and despite the blackout, one could see quite a lot on the ground, sometimes aided by firing illuminating cartridges from a Very pistol from the cockpit canopy. Only rarely did one see a 'flamer' from MT and only twice see an exploding engine on a train, but occasionally we were rewarded by lines of exploding or burning railway wagons. Consequently many of our reports were of 'damaged' or 'NRO' (no results observed). Any target would do. Once again a marshalling yard was bombed - could hardly miss something that size!

---

110   From June 1944 to April 1945 2nd TAF and ADGB (Air Defence of Great Britain) Mosquitoes destroyed
       at least 230 aircraft at night over the Channel, France, the Low Countries and Germany.

'Twice we attacked airfields with bombs and cannon fire. On the second occasion we were perhaps a bit 'flak happy' as end of tour was approaching. We had been patrolling Celle-Berlin and on the way back we saw, over to port, the runways at Wessendorf in bright moonlight. Still had our bombs so went on for 2-3 miles, turned, opened bomb doors and dived to about 50 feet towards the main runway. By this time Jerry was awake. Coming over the hedge we had light flak, white searchlights, blue radar controlled master searchlights - the 'bloody lot'! Flak wrapped around us and yet not a round touched us. My pilot, with his head down watching instruments, had missed most of the display, now claims it was because the Mossie was so fast. Probably doing 330-350 over the hedge.

'Once we managed to get into an Air Ministry bulletin. It recorded that whilst attacking a train at Zarrentin we spotted a factory and made three attacks upon it with bombs and cannon. It quoted our report that the subsequent flames were visible after 40 miles of our flight home.'

Flying Officer Bob Kirkpatrick RCAF, an American from Cleveland, Ohio and a pilot on 21 Squadron who 'truly loved the Mossie', recalled that 'Christmas Eve, at Thorney Island, the weather was not very good. Ops were delayed but started about 23.00. Flight Lieutenant Undrill and I took off about 02.30-02.45. The weather in the target area was about 500 feet, thin scattered cloud, 2,500 feet broken, 4,000 feet overcast; pretty good night visibility because of snow on the ground. This area was about 40 miles east of the 'Bulge' area and instructions were to interfere with transportation in any way possible. We had 4 x 250lb bombs. Not seeing anything moving we picked out a R/R bridge over a small river. We couldn't dive bomb because of the 1,500 feet height restrictions on instantaneous bombing. Flying along the R/R we figured if we missed the bridge we'd at least damage the R/R. I overshot the bridge by 200 or 300 yards. As we released two bombs we were surprised by light flak from woods south of the R/R and a parallel road. With nothing better to do we circled and lobbed the other two bombs into the woods. We got lucky and started a couple of fires. From the light of the fires we could see some MT and men running around. Flak a little heavier but not alarming so we made a strafing pass with cannon and machine guns. Undrill started shouting 'pull up, pull up' and having broken our own rule of 'never go back', I pulled up into the overcast and we returned to Thorney about 05.30 Christmas morning. Squadron Leader Carlisle and Rex Ingram spotted the fires and added their bombs and guns to Jerry's Christmas stocking.'

The Luftwaffe was powerless to stop the inexorable advance westwards but there was one last attempt to try to halt the allies. Since 20 December many Jagdgeschwader had been transferred to airfields in the west for Operation Bodenplatte, when approximately 850 Luftwaffe fighters took off at 0745 hours on Sunday morning 1 January 1945 to attack 27 airfields in northern France, Belgium and southern Holland. The four-hour operation succeeded in destroying about 100 Allied aircraft, but it cost the Luftwaffe 300 aircraft, most of which were shot down by Allied anti-aircraft guns deployed primarily against the V-1s. Beginning with the shooting down on 1/2 January of three Ju 88s, 2nd TAF Mosquitoes exacted a measure of revenge. By the end of the month the Mosquito night fighters had shot down 17 enemy aircraft.

The Luftwaffe's air launched 'Diver' offensive had tailed off considerably in December 1944 and for the first two weeks of the month interceptions were nonexistent. The air-launch Heinkel He 111H-22s carried out their last major raid on

England on the night of 3/4 January 1945 when 45 'Divers' were launched. RAF night-fighter crews made no claims but three Heinkels failed to return. On the night of 5/6 January Wing Commander Russ Bannock, now CO of 406 ('Lynx') Squadron RCAF, scored his seventh victory. Bannock reported: 'I spent many hours trying to catch some of these fellows but they were really far too smart. Many times my radar operator would say, 'We've got a fix at 400 yards. He's dead ahead and 20 degrees below.' I would look down and see the wave tops right below me and not dare go any lower. [On this night] we made landfall at Pellworm at 20.10 and proceeded towards Husum aerodrome, which was lit with outer perimeter lights and double flare path. We immediately commenced to do a right-hand circuit at about 400 feet and obtained a head-on contact on an aircraft. We turned hard about and picked up the contact again at 4,000 feet, almost dead ahead and followed it across the aerodrome, obtaining a visual at 1,000 feet. As I closed in to identify, I interrogated with a 'waggle your wings, bogey', with no response. From dead below and slightly behind we identified the aircraft as a He 111. The aircraft was burning a blue resin light inboard of the starboard engine. I dropped back to 600 feet and fired a one-second burst. The e/a immediately burst into flames and spun down into a wooded dispersal area at the south-west corner of the aerodrome. The airfield immediately doused so we flew towards Schleswig, which had a searchlight navigational marker over it. At approximately 20.35, I heard a 'waggle your wings, bogey', which seemed very close, causing me to waggle violently. However, I soon found I wasn't the intended victim for an aircraft immediately went down in flames, crashing approximately four miles north-west of Schleswig.' [111]

The final air-launched flying-bomb attack on England took place on 13/14 January when 25 Divers were launched but only seven got through. By the end of the V-1 offensive on 29 March 1945 approximately 10,500 flying-bombs had been launched against England, including about 1,500 V-1s air-launched from He 111s, of which 5,890 crossed the coast. KG 53 Legion Kondor ceased operations having lost 77 Heinkels, 16 of them claimed by Mosquitoes.

Meanwhile, 'Intruder' operations continued. On the night of 28 January Canadians Flying Officer A. T. Sherrett and Flight Lieutenant K. MacKenzie on 406 Squadron took off from Manston at 17.40 hours on a high level 'Intruder' sortie in support of a Bomber Command raid on Stuttgart. Sherrett recalled: 'We left the English coast at Manston, striking directly to target area by DR, 'Gee' being poor at 15,000 feet. En route, at 18.45 hours, a V-2 was seen about 30 miles past Brussels, travelling up very fast in a course of 250 degrees. Patrol was begun in target position at 19.25 hours at 15,000 feet ENE and WSW in relation to beacon Otto. Weather was cloudy below 15,000 feet with haze up to 18,000 feet. At 20.05 hours, the navigator made a contact at 5 miles range, 80 degrees to port and 45° above. Target was followed in an easterly vector for ten minutes then in a 270° port turn southwards. Fighter was climbing all the time at full bore without gaining. After another ten minutes a course of 280° was followed and the aircraft began to gain shortening range to 3,000 yards. At this point we obtained another contact, head-on and to starboard and turned off starboard at 2,000 feet. I saw his vapour trails from our target's engines and obtained an outline at 15,000 feet. Closing to 200 feet I obtained a clear visual, identifying quarry as a Ju 188 by the pointed wings and

111   Bannock's victims were Hauptmann Siegfried Jessen and crew of A1+HT of 9/KG 53.

tail plane and exhausts. Target was interrogated and a 'Waggle your wings bogey' challenge, both without response. We were then at 27,000 feet. I fell back to between 200 and 250 yards and gave a short burst but observed no strikes. A second burst however caused a large explosion in the port engine and fuselage. I was just starting to layoff deflection for another burst when the enemy aircraft started to roll, went over on its back and spun straight down. We pulled out at 15,000 and did a port orbit to watch him going in, the target hitting the ground and bursting into flames at 2050 hours. This was confirmed by Flight Lieutenant Honeyman on 151 Squadron ('Sneezy 44') who immediately took the fix.

'The chase had lasted 45 minutes at full bore, the speed on closing in for the visual at 27,000 was 265 mph indicated. After the chase we discovered we had only 60 gallons of petrol left, about 20 minutes flying time, so I throttled back to minimum revs and boost. I gave a 'Mayday' on Channel C, asking for fix and homing. We were answered by 'Baggage', an American sector GCI who took a fix and gave us a vector of 140°. We challenged this and received the wrong answer, but as it was in a decidedly American voice and little else could be done we obeyed and were brought into Croix-de-Metz aerodrome at 2135 hours. All fuel gauges registered zero. 'Baggage' did an excellent job of getting us in and every available comfort was extended to us at the aerodrome. We returned to base at 13.25 hours on the 29th.

After flying in Beaufighters Bob Morgan and his pilot Jim Cattanach converted to Mosquitoes and in January 1945 they were posted to 604 Squadron at Vendeville in France. Morgan recalled: 'We sailed from Tilbury to Ostend, glad to get away from London and V-2 rockets. We lived in a moated chateau near Lille which had recently been evacuated by the Germans, two of whom had been buried just inside the gates. Three British soldiers were buried alongside their wrecked tank in the village behind the chateau. 604 Squadron had originally been a weekend auxiliary squadron whose motto was 'If you want peace be prepared for war', but this had been modernised to 'Not to worry, it may never happen'. As new corners to the operational scene we found these sentiments rather reassuring, as we were yet to fly into the unknown. On our first operational flight we took off at 11 that night and flew on until we reached our heavy ack-ack barrage, which stretched from side to side and was intended to shoot down V-1s and enemy planes with no questions asked. This meant that we followed the path of three vertical searchlights through the barrage. It took us to the front line and what remained of the Battle of the Bulge, which from our point of view was a circle surrounded by hundreds of guns and searchlights directing their fire into its centre. Our ground controller gave us various courses to fly, with the ultimate intention of directing us in pursuit of enemy aircraft in the area. The navigator peered into the radar screen visor. This gadget had a range of 100 miles for navigating purposes and 10 miles for aircraft interception. On making radar contact the navigator had to interpret the blips on the screen and direct the pilot towards the enemy aircraft so that our plane was aimed up its stern and hopefully shoot it down with our four 20mm cannons. Most of our trips lasted about three hours, but later we ranged as far as Berlin. We operated on a two nights on and two nights off basis. A tour generally lasted 18 months and we were flown to England every six weeks for 10 days' leave.

'To sum up, from the time I started flying in October 1943, I had flown 175 daylight hours and 50 hours night flying to January 1945. Operational flying to May

1945 only totalled 19 hours day and 33 hours night and not a shot fired in anger. This seemed to be a very mediocre result for all the time and effort over the years. However, Jim and I were proud to have been chosen to fly such a good looking, efficient and versatile aircraft as the Mosquito and to have filled some small place on the giant chessboard of war.' [112]

On 6 February 21, 464 and 487 Squadrons in 140 Wing left southern England and moved to Amiens and Rosières-en-Santerre. On 13 February the squadrons had a break from operations to practice for a daylight formation operation ('Clarion'). On 16 February two Mosquitoes of the Fighter Experimental Flight at Tangmere left at 10.15 hours for an advanced base in France on a 'Day Ranger' to the Vienna area. Crews were Flight Lieutenant P. S. Compton and Flying Officer S. F. Melloy in the lead Mosquito, with Flying Officer K. V. Panter and Flying Officer J. D. Sharples DFC RCAF in the second aircraft. Landing at Juvincourt at 1125 hours, they took off again at 1445 hours for the sortie. This was altered to a 'Ranger' in the Linz area, taking in Bad Aibling, Wels, Eferding and Straubing, as there had been trouble with long-range drop tanks. Just south of Munich, at 16.30 hours, Compton attacked and probably destroyed a truck carrying a large packing case and a camouflaged staff car which was seen to turn turtle. Compton's report continues.

'On approaching Bad Aibling aerodrome at zero feet we warned Panter that we were now getting near the target area. After receiving his OK, Melloy sighted an FW 190 in the air at 10 o'clock at approximately 1,500 feet altitude. We passed this information to Panter and told him to follow us. We made a medium 180° port turn ending up about one mile behind and below the enemy aircraft. At about 1,000 yards range the enemy aircraft started a steep turn to port. We also turned port to attack, closing to about 300 yards and at an angle of about 45° ahead. We fired approximately 3-second burst, seeing strikes on cockpit just below Perspex. The enemy aircraft dived down in a port turn. We also turned port and dived after him. The enemy aircraft continued port turn and turned in towards us apparently after sighting Panter. We got a 45° astern shot from approximately 200 yards range and at 300 feet height giving him approximately 2-3 seconds burst. My navigator saw strikes on the side of the fuselage and the enemy aircraft rolled on to its back and dived into the ground and burst into flames. We proceeded to set course when told by Panter that he was over the airfield and that there was 'bags of joy'. We made a run towards the airfield from south to north and Melloy saw a Me 410 (camouflaged blue-grey and dark. green) on the ground slightly to port. We gave it a 1-2 second burst of cannon from 100 yards range, strikes being seen on port wing and on the ground and afterwards the aircraft was seen to emit much grey smoke. In the meanwhile Panter had made a similar run on a Me 109 to the port of us, which was also observed to emit clouds of smoke after attack. We both made a second run on these same aircraft. Our burst struck the ground and then pulled up through the fuselage of the 410. The area was then left and both the aircraft were seen to be smoking. There was slight inaccurate flak (self-destroying) from the east side of the aerodrome.

'A course was then set for Linz area at 17.08 hours and we crossed Wels marshalling yards where we observed six goods trains. We passed east of the town and observing a number of aircraft parked around the perimeter track. There was no flying here, so we continued to the Straubling area. At 17.27 hours Panter reported two Me 109s to port over Landau airfield at 2,000 feet. We turned towards them, Panter taking the nearest and ourselves the farthest enemy aircraft. At about 1½-miles range our Me 109 turned hard to port and we followed and at about 250 yards gave him a 90° deflection shot, strikes seen on rear of fuselage, also using .303 when cannon ammunition had run out. The enemy aircraft continued to turn port and dived over the top of us, so we did a steep diving turn to port and saw Panter at 45° to our enemy aircraft, which then hit the ground bursting into flames just to the east of Landau airfield. It is believed that Panter had also attacked this aircraft. Meanwhile my navigator saw the first Me 109 (Panter's quarry) burning on the ground half a mile west of the airfield. Panter then turned to starboard and warned us that two Me 109s were overhead at 2,500 feet. At the same time he received a burst of light flak from the airfield (time 1730 hours approximately). Panter then called us up and said that he thought he was on fire. We told him that this was so, as we could see black smoke coming from the belly of the aircraft and told him that he should bail out. He immediately climbed to 1,500 feet and both he and Sharples were seen to jump by Melloy and to land safely 6 miles west of Landau. The aircraft was then in flames and seen to crash. We then set course for Juvincourt. Neither of the other Me 109s made any attempt to attack. Juvincourt was reached at 1930 hours.'

Doug Mault and John Bulmer, as a new Mosquito crew, pilot and navigator respectively, joined 613 (City of Manchester) Squadron at Cambrai/Epinoy in February. The airfield was the base for the three Squadrons of 138 Wing, 2nd TAF comprising 107, 305 (Polish) and 613.

'The routine' recalls Mault 'started with rising not too early, piling into the 3 tonner and off to breakfast about 1½-miles away. Return to the Nest, by which time the Battle Order would be on the notice board if there were operations that night. The Battle Order showed our names, which aircraft was allocated to us and what time to attend briefing. It was up to us then to get to the dispersal points to do our NFT, usually early afternoon. Briefing was held in the cellar of the Nest and was done usually by the CO along with the Met Officer and our Army Liaison Officer. Our destination was revealed, along with the route, time of take-off, bomb load, anything special to look out for, the expected position of the 'bomb line', which showed the front line of friendly troops and which we had to cross before taking aggressive action. Later, this occasionally became a problem and operations were cancelled because our troops were moving so rapidly it was impossible to define exactly where they were. Our patrol area was either the roads and railways between two defined places or a triangular area within which we arranged our own patrol route along roads and railways selected from the map. The purpose of our efforts was to deny the enemy the use of any transport route usually not far behind his front line for movement of troops or supplies. We did this by shooting at any light or other evidence of movement we could see. This was difficult on very dark nights and we sometimes dropped flares to help - not always with any result because what night vision we had acquired was destroyed temporarily by the bright light. It also led to us being shot at by AA fire on one occasion when another aircraft dropped a flare above us and standing out brilliantly, there we were - a sitting target. We were not hit but it was unpleasant. In fact, it was unusual for two of us to be in the area at the same time, but our presence was more or less continuous for the time the Squadron was responsible - one aircraft taking over from the previous one about every 30 minutes.

Occasionally (and this never happened to us), somebody early in the night might spot, say, a concentration of troops and a 'strike' would be laid on. All previous arrangements were cancelled and everybody took off as quickly as possible to unload everything on one defined position.

'The journey back was an anti-climax and it was with relief that one announced ones imminent arrival to 'Josephine', our ground station at Epinoy, to receive landing instruction. Then look out for the 'pundit' - a light flashing two Morse characters to define our home base. So one could say we had about an hour of intense activity every two or three days, with periods of dull straight and level flight in between and little else to do. This could lead to bouts of serious boozing on off nights, but in general, we were a fairly responsible crowd! The 'better' trips were just behind enemy lines - about 2 hours and the others were deeper penetrations, say to Hanover and Magdeburg of nearly four hours. We avoided the cities themselves because of their hostile intentions and concentrated on the miles in-between.' [113]

On the day of the 'Clarion' operation, Thursday 22 February, it was a maximum effort and all crews and serviceable aircraft were to be involved. 'Clarion' was intended to be the 'coup de grace' for the German transport system with 9,000 Allied aircraft taking part in attacks on enemy railway stations, trains and engines, cross roads, bridges, ships and barges on canals and rivers, stores and other targets. It was to be the last time that the Mosquitoes operated in daylight in such numbers. Wing Commander S. Grodzicki DFC led 305 Squadron and Squadron Leader P. Hanburg led the British Flight. For half an hour the Mosquitoes of 305 Squadron wreaked havoc in the Bremen-Hamburg-Kiel region. The German ground defences were strong. Ten aircraft suffered damage and one with a British crew was lost; the pilot was killed and the navigator taken prisoner. Gordon Allen on 605 recalls.

'My only daylight op was with a strange pilot on Operation 'Clarion', with every available Mosquito wandering about over Holland and North Germany. My pilot was unfit and our flight commander asked me to fly with this new pilot, who had been shot up on each of his three trips to date. Our target was pathetic, a small bridge and railway line over a canal at Hoogesand in north Holland. Don't know if our bombs hit the target but we certainly hit the station - with our aircraft! Lost the starboard aileron, wing tip and flap and damaged a prop and tailplane. As we were still airborne, I decided it was too far to walk home. We came out over the Frisian Islands, turning very(!) gently to port. Back over the North Sea at no more than 50 feet and then overland to Hartford Bridge.' [114]

2 Group lost twenty-one Mosquitoes on Clarion with forty damaged. The Mosquito was not, after all, invulnerable. Bill Brittain, a navigator on 418 Squadron would probably agree. He and his Canadian pilot, Guy Hackett, were forced to ditch on a sandbank at about 13.45 hours one and a half miles from shore off the Dutch coast. 'After mild panic we made our way to the coast using dinghies and walking across sandbanks. Dutchmen in a punt picked us up but the Huns were waiting on the coast. The sea water was very cold and I mean cold. We were whipped off to Leeuwarden at 18.00 hours and put in solitary confinement. The guards were decent enough to dry our clothes. I had a straw palliasse and two blankets. Next day I was

113   *My Private War* by Doug Mault writing in *The Mossie* No.32 September 2002.
114   *The Mossie* No.37 January 2005.

given a bowl of soup at midday. I nearly cried over it, I was so hungry. I had gone 30 hours without food. At 17.00 hours we went in a charcoal driven bus to Enschede, which appeared to be a central Luftwaffe PoW prison. I had a few slices of Jerry bread and butter in transit. I could not get a liking for that bread. I arrived at 22.00 hours and more solitary which continued all day, Saturday. It was very cold and I wish I had worn my 'long johns'. Solitary was hellish. I began to worry about my wife and parents. There was nothing to do but sit and think. The menu consisted of two slices of bread and butter at 08.00, two bowls (lucky) of soup at lunch, two slices of bread and butter at 17.00 with a cup of ersatz tea or coffee; certainly peculiar stuff. Bed at 18.00 but it was not easy to sleep.

'On Sunday I woke early, cold and stiff and had the usual breakfast. There was a mild interrogation at 100 and then I was put into a compound wired off inside a large factory where I joined Guy and three other chaps. I thought that I was in heaven. We were taken to an 'erks' mess for lunch. Plenty of spuds and sauerkraut. We built a coke fire and toasted the bread. It was infinitely better. Very homely. Monday was similar. At 17.00 the five of us were taken on a bus to Gronau on the German side of the border to entrain for our journey to Dulag Luft interrogation centre at Oberusel near Frankfurt. What a journey it transpired to be. The railways were in a chaotic state and we would journey for a few hours and then get held up for a longer period and only travel during the hours of darkness. On Tuesday we spent the day in a waiting room at Hagen. We travelled on at 17.00 and repeated the previous night's erratic moving, passing through Essen and the Ruhr during the night. On Wednesday we spent the day in a boiler room at Giessen. There was much bomb damage there - in fact it was colossal. Many engines and wagons had 'gone for a Burton'. People were none to friendly - hence our staying in the boiler room. I guess their antagonism was warrantable, knowing that we were RAF. This journey of less than 150 miles took two days and five hours! Men en route: six slices of b+b and a small portion of meat loaf per day. 'Must be a war on!' But we got by. The German public didn't seem much better fed - except for potatoes. Meat seemed a non entity and folks back home grumbled at minor things. We arrived at Oberusel at 22.00 hours and we were shoved into a dirty room to spend the night on the floorboards, without blankets. But the room was quite warm. Later we were transported to Stalag Luft III.' [115]

On 12 March Wing Commander Victor Oates the CO of 21 Squadron and navigator F. C. Gubbings were lost during an attack on the railway line in the Siegen-Dillenburg-Wetzlar-Lahn area between Frankfurt to the south and Marburg to the north. Oates noticed a fire on the ground, around which could he see people moving. The fire was a result of a US attack from the late evening which set fire to the railway station buildings at Frankenberg. Oates dived and started to strafe the station. The strikes prevented the fire brigade from putting the fire out and set fire to an adjacent building. When the Mosquito passed over the building it was hit by 20mm shells by the local defence at the station. The aircraft pulled up and flew on in the direction of Willersdorf when suddenly the nose dipped and the Mosquito hit the ground at Linnerberg Hill. The following morning the villagers of the small village of Bottendorf nearby were ordered to recover the dead aircrew.

Three nights' later Flight Lieutenant Allott L. 'Al' Gabitas and Flying Officer Phil

---

Bryers on 488 Squadron RNZAF at Amiens-Glisy took off in a lone Mosquito for a night patrol to the Remagen bridgehead, as Gabitas, who trained as a pilot in New Zealand and arrived in the UK in 1941, recalls: 'Early in March 1945 the 9th Armoured Division managed to cross the Rhine at Remagen and the importance of this bridgehead became immediately apparent. Air cover around the clock in all weather was called for and 488 Squadron drew the night shift on several occasions. The flying weather that winter was appalling with the freezing level at zero feet for weeks on end. Frequently great fronts swept across the continent from the North Atlantic and in the worst conditions air operations were almost completely suspended. But radar-equipped Mosquitoes were expected to fill the role of all-weather fighters and battle the elements, even when all other aircraft were firmly grounded. On 15 March the Met reports indicated a rapidly deteriorating picture. The whole of the British Isles, the North Sea and the NW areas of continental Europe were already enveloped in a wall of icy cloud which extended from the highest levels down to the ground. The low cloud which preceded this wall of weather had not yet reached Amiens and while the air armadas based in Britain and the German Air Force defenders were all stood down for the night, a lone Mosquito (MT461) took off from Amiens to patrol the bridgehead. As I climbed on course for Remagen there wasn't a great deal of conversation between my navigator and myself, but I can remember him remarking that for one night we were the spearhead of the great Allied invasion of Germany. In a brief moment of glory we were alone in carrying the air war to the enemy!

'We arrived at the patrol line at 10,000 feet to be greeted by a display of 'friendly' light flak. Ground defences were firing blindly towards the noise of the aircraft but fortunately the fireworks fizzled out at about 7,000 feet. We could distinguish the bridgehead through the ground fog by a concentration of floodlights, flares and tracer; and we kept a respectful distance from this hive of ground activity. Not a sausage on our radar. The ground controller sounded a trifle lethargic when eventually he gave us a heading in the general direction of the Third Reich. Although things were relatively quiet, these long sorties were not exactly boring. Phil was entirely absorbed in tuning his radar and scanning the tube for green-white blips, which would indicate the presence of another aircraft ahead. And flying with no auto-pilot meant a total concentration on the flight and engine instruments with an ear cocked to the beat of the Merlins for any sign of roughness or irregularity. A flash-light from the cockpit was the only means of checking any build up of ice on the wings.

'We were flying totally blind in pitch darkness when we turned back somewhere between Hannover and Hamburg. We climbed and headed once more for Remagen. I must have felt a wave of home-sickness and levelled off at 12,500 feet on a sensitive altimeter. The altitude would have cleared the top of Mount Cook by precisely one foot. Still no sign of air activity. By this time the bridgehead was merely a faint glow through the thickening cloud. No flak this time. The petrol gauges looked low but not dangerously so. The ground controller sounded more cheerful and as a gesture gave us a heading to the north. No doubt he felt that a sweep over the German night fighter airfields which protected the Ruhr might provoke some activity from the Luftwaffe.

'At low levels the turbulence was shocking and the aircraft positively vibrated as it rode the bumps. But the response from the enemy was nil and we rather envied their night fighter pilots cosseted with schnapps and kummel in their messes. Fuel supplies were now running low and over Venlo we turned south with the thought of diverting to the Allied airfield at Lille rather than facing the longer haul to base at Amiens. In due course we picked up the radar beacon at Lille but the weather had clamped down completely and from the air there wasn't a glimmer of light to be seen. And what's more, ground control knew of nowhere else to go, but thought Amiens might still be open. We had no option but to head for our home base some 70 miles to the south and hope for the best. The sky certainly looked lighter in that direction and the low cloud took the form of fog patches on the ground as we approached the beacon. I called the ground controller and after a pause his familiar voice came back loudly in the earphones, 'Sorry, old man, we're closed. Go to Lille'.

'As I orbited the beacon with all petrol gauges looking decidedly sick and trying to think of a suitable reply, a patch of fog lifted and I glimpsed a flare path under one wing. 'Hallelujah, I'm coming in'. Wheels and flaps seemed to take ages to come down. I completed the cockpit drill without taking my eyes off the lights and we stood on one wing to line up for approach. Even this was better than trying to bail out which in any case was considered to be almost impossible from a Mosquito at this altitude. The airspeed came down beautifully and we settled down to a normal approach. As the wheels touched a brilliant red Very light flashed under the port wing, but there was no time to grasp its significance as the aircraft was already settling into the landing attitude. Then all hell broke loose as the aeroplane leapt into the air again and then stalled sharply back on to the flare path with a sickening crunch. Incredibly, we burst through a thicket of young trees which created an alarming racket as their bare branches whipped against the propellers and cockpit. The undercarriage held up through all this hammering but shortly afterwards the port wheel sank deeply into a patch of soft ground and collapsed. The effect of this was immediate as the nose of the aircraft buried itself into the hallowed soil of France and the tail rose high. For a moment it seemed as if the machine would be completely overturned. The bewildered crew of two were thrown violently against the instrument panels. But the safety harness held. The Merlins cut themselves as the propellers bit into the soft ground and the silence that followed was eerie. But there was no fire, probably because the tanks were virtually dry.

'My first reaction was one of entire disbelief. This turned to rage as I couldn't think where I had gone wrong. There was simply no explanation in my mind for this incredible landing. By this time Phil had managed to get the lower escape door open and was lying doubled up on the ground. I crawled out after him, in some pain as a knob on the instrument panel had smashed into my knee-cap. But Phil seemed to be in a bad way so I climbed back into the cockpit to see if I could raise the ambulance on the radio. This came to life as I plugged in again and a voice said, 'Where are you?' Still completely nonplussed I replied, 'On the aerodrome,' thus adding to the general confusion. We heard afterwards that all hands were called out in the thick fog to mount a shoulder to shoulder search which was called off only when the true situation was known. In due course the ambulance arrived and after a check-up in the sick bay we were just in time to stop a casualty report being sent off to HQ and then, presumably, to our next-of-kin. It turned out that Phil, who had a long-standing cartilage problem in his right knees from too much rugby in his youth, had received a painful bang on his other knee with crippling results.

'We had landed on a dummy flare path about 3 miles from our airfield, virtually on the south bank of the River Somme. The existence of the 'Q-site' as it was called was explained to me as I had earlier missed a vital briefing on the subject while on a gunnery leader's course in England. Next day we took a ride out to the crash scene and hobbled around the site. The aeroplane made a striking picture with its tail high in the air and odd pieces of cowling strewn around. It was a strange feeling to be treading on ground which less than thirty years earlier had been the scene of some of the most bitter carnage in WWI. One could almost sense the ghostly presence of long-departed heroes. But it was unhealthy to allow one's imagination too much reign as further battles still lay ahead. Soon our minds were occupied with other matters when our replacement aircraft arrived from de Havilland's factory.'

Wing Commander Peter Kleboe DSO DFC AFC had taken command of 21 Squadron after the loss of Wing Commander Oates and it was he who would lead the squadron on the next momentous operation. Special Operations Executive (SOE) in London had received intelligence that various Resistance and political prisoners held captive in the Gestapo HQ in the Shellhaus building in Copenhagen were to be shot on 21 March. The Free Danish Resistance movement had made repeated requests that the RAF should attack the building even though most of the prisoners were held in the attic to thwart any attempt to bomb the HQ. CIC 2 Group, AVM Basil Embry DSO** DFC* AFC considered the implications. He decided to send the low level experts in 140 Wing, some of whom had flown on the Amiens prison raid and the attack on the Gestapo HQ in The Hague, to make a daring pinpoint attack on the Shellhaus. On 20 March 18 FB.VIs of 140 Wing plus two FPU (Film Production Unit) specially modified Mosquito B.IVs were detached from their base at Rosiéres-en-Santerre to RAF Fersfield in Norfolk. The move was made so that the route over the North Sea to Denmark would avoid flying over enemy-held territory with all the attendant risk of flak and radar detection. However, this stretched the Mosquitoes' range to the limit of endurance, a total flight time of over five hours.

Next day the Mosquitoes led by Group Captain 'Bob' Bateson DSO DFC AFC and Squadron Leader Ted Sismore DSO DFC, the leading tactical navigator, escorted by 28 Mustangs bombed the 'Shell House' building in Copenhagen The operation, code-named 'Carthage', was successful. Of the 26 prisoners on the sixth floor, eighteen escaped. Some of those that had survived the attack were injured or killed by jumping from the fifth floor into the street below. The remaining prisoners died in the building. The Gestapo lost their precious archive material and their Headquarters. The total number of dead was 72, with 26 members of the Gestapo and 30 being Danish collaborators. The remainder were innocent Danes. Four Mosquitoes and two Mustangs failed to return for the loss of nine air crew. One of them was Wing Commander Peter Kleboe, whose Mosquito collided with a light projector tower over the marshalling yards about a mile from the target and then clipped the roof of an apartment building and the bomb load fell into a building on the opposite side of the street killing twelve people. The aircraft was observed to be 'waggling' its wings before it crashed into a garage adjacent to the Jeanne d'Arc School in Frederiksberg. Kleboe died instantly. Reg Hall his Canadian navigator was flung out of the aircraft in the impact and his body fell through the roof of the Frederiksberg Theatre. The second wave was misled by the smoke from Kleboe's aircraft. In the confusion, the wave was split in two. It appears that two Mosquitoes then bombed the Jeanne d'Arc School by mistake. The third wave was also misled by the smoke. Only one aircraft realized the mistake and did not bomb. Before the schoolchildren and their teachers could take refuge the Mosquito's bombs had begun exploding. Eighty-six children were killed and 67 wounded, 16 adults also lost their lives with 35 more injured. [116]

Flight Lieutenant Reg Everson, an ex-railway policeman who was a pilot on 305 (Polish) Squadron, still had a tour to finish: 'After all the excitement of 'Clarion', night operations resumed and on 5 March, on return from patrol, we found the base covered with 10/10 cloud. This time we took the offered diversion to Brussels, a wise move; owing to the adverse weather conditions we had to stay in Brussels, enjoying an enforced 48-hour 'leave'. By this time our patrol areas were moving further into Germany, making a longer trip there and back, which cut down the time we could spend in the patrol areas, due to fuel capacity. On these operations we used 'drop tanks' and carried flares in the bomb bay instead of bombs. On sighting anything suspicious we would climb to 4,000 feet, drop a flare and circle below it to give Tony [Flight Lieutenant Tony Rudd, a University graduate and Everson's navigator] a chance to inspect the ground more thoroughly. We then attacked using machine guns and cannon.

'On 8 April, for operation No. 436 (the squadron's, not mine), 12 aircraft were briefed to patrol and attack enemy movements on railways and roads in the Leipzig-Berlin-Magdeburg-Brunswick region. It all started prosaically. My aircraft was u/s so I borrowed my friend 'Duke' Earle's brand new aircraft. He was on leave and he didn't need it that night. The weather was cloudless, visibility good. At first all went well, we completed a low level night patrol on the outskirts of Berlin on the Berlin-Magdeburg road and made an attack on enemy troop and transport movements by dropping two clusters of flares from about 3,000 feet and then attacking with machine guns and cannon by diving under the flares until my navigator advised me 'politely' to pull up before I hit the ground. Lights on the transport were extinguished and movement stopped but the flares went out so we could not assess fully the extent of the damage. A dark moonless night and not much enemy activity. We then climbed to 4,000 feet at about 02.00 hours to return to base for our eggs and bacon.

'We were flying along on the leg from Warburg to Cologne approaching the Ruhr, minding our own business thinking of breakfast and a warm bed when suddenly there came the sound of machine gun fire, most unfriendly. It was directed at and hit our port engine. Port engines don't appreciate that sort of treatment and promptly caught fire. Tony operated the fire extinguisher and I feathered the engine. Whilst we were trying to extinguish the fire another burst of gunfire gave our starboard engine the same treatment. I think the starboard engine must have been in the same union as the port engine as it decided to 'come out in sympathy' with the same result. I throttled back and operated the fire extinguisher, but the fire did not go out. Now a Mosquito mainly made of wood burns like a well built bonfire and since it is not designed to fly like a glider with no engines I decided it was better to test Mr. Irvine's invention of the parachute and I ordered Tony to abandon the aircraft. He clipped on his parachute. Bearing in mind the tradition that the captain is the last to leave the ship, I instructed Tony Rudd to jettison the escape door and 'hit the silk'. This he did with alacrity.

116   On 17 April six FB.VIs of 140 Wing, led by Bob Bateson and Ted Sismore taxied out for a daylight strike on a school building on the outskirts of Odense, which was being used by the Gestapo as a HQ. AVM Basil Embry went along, as usual. The six Mosquitoes destroyed the Gestapo HQ and 18 days later Denmark was free. Right up until the German surrender, 2 Group continued operations against rail and road targets. On the night of 2 May, for instance, 42 aircraft attacked troop transports with 500lb bombs, flares and cannon and machine gun fire, leaving nine trains burning furiously.

Actually of course 1 had no choice; the escape door was on his side of the aircraft and I couldn't get out until he had left even if I had wanted to! I was left with the problem of struggling out of my seat with no one to hold the controls and making for the door myself. The only means of exit from a Mark 6 Mosquito was through the door on the starboard side. Meanwhile Isaac Newton had taken over and the 'plane with no power was rapidly making its way back to earth. During this manoeuvre the aircraft was losing height rapidly. I struggled out of the seat, at the same time trying to keep the aircraft on an even keel. With some difficulty I reached the doorway and dived head first through the opening.

'As I left the aircraft I remembered vaguely being told to count to ten before pulling the ripcord. Fortunately I am not one to do what I am told and I pulled the cord to open the 'chute immediately I was clear of the doorway. I hit the ground just as the parachute opened which only goes to show that doing what one is told does not always pay, if I had I would not be here today. Later it was calculated from evidence of time taken to reach the ground that I must have left my cosy cockpit to seek cooler air outside at about 400 feet above the ground. I had joined the most exclusive club in the world, 'The Caterpillar Club' - the only club no-one wants to join - but is glad when accepted as a member - qualification for membership is to have saved one's life in an emergency by parachute. Strictly speaking we should be called 'worms' since our lives were saved by the silkworm, which provided the silk for the parachute, but poetic licence prevailed and the caterpillar was adopted as our emblem. It is strange to think that such a little creature could save so many lives. Thank you Mr. Irvine for your invention. On arrival on German soil I was greeted warmly with 'unfriendly fire' by German infantry and was then introduced to a welcoming party of the Gestapo.'

Reg Everson was taken for interrogation later, at Gestapo Headquarters in Gummerbach, where his interrogator, a former insurance agent in the Purley area before the war, questioned him at length before having him sent to Stalag VIG, a PoW camp near Olpe. After a short stay the prisoners were marched under armed guard to another camp, at Enbach. During the forced march the prisoners were quite often attacked by American fighter-bombers, who, thinking they were German troop columns, opened fire, but fortunately there were no casualties among the prisoners. Finally, on 12 April at 1400 hours, the 78th US Infantry Division liberated the camp. Reg was reunited with Tony Rudd and later they discovered that the aircraft that had shot them down on 8 April had been a P-61 Black Widow whose pilot had claimed a Ju 88 destroyed!' [117]

Kel Purdie's experience as a navigator/radar operator was limited to an uncompleted tour of 19 operations in 1945 with his pilot, Jack Flanagan. Both were New Zealanders and at the conclusion of four months OTU at Charter Hall in December 1944 they went on leave with the expectation that they would be posted to 488 (New Zealand) Night Fighter Squadron in France. 'It was not to be however' says Purdie 'and we were disappointed to receive telegrams to report to 1692 Bomber Support Training Unit at Great Massingham. It was obvious that a posting to a 100 Group Squadron would follow but first of all we had to spend two more weeks learning to operate a new type of AI radar - Mk.XV or ASH as it was commonly called. More training when we were keen to become operational. After two weeks we were transported a few miles to

117   Black Widows of the 422nd NFS were by this time based at Strassfeldt, Germany and P-61s of the 425th NFS were at Etain, France.

Little Snoring to join 515 Squadron. Their Mk.VI fighter bombers were equipped with ASH AI, 'Monica' rear scanning radar, 'Gee', infrared light type F and type Z shining fore and aft and radio altimeters. After a week or two settling into the Squadron routine we were listed to do our first operation, the so called 'Freshman'. A clamp frustrated us for a further day and then it was briefing with the older hands giving us assistance and advice as I prepared our flight plan. Our appointed task was to do a circuit of the Zuider Zee - a simple exercise with little risk involved to get us used to flying over enemy territory. We saw bursts of tracer from time to time but they were obviously not directed at us and perhaps the most exciting part of the trip was seeing the tail flare of a V-2 rocket heading for the stars not too far away from us.

'It was very satisfying to have completed our first op and the second followed the next night. This was the real thing with two German night fighter airfields at Malmsheim and Sachsenheim near Stuttgart to be patrolled for one hour. It seems that low level radar contacts were starting to dry up at this stage in the war and frustrated pilots were attacking more trains and ground targets. Station CO Sammy Hoare must have suspected that crews were doing too much of this during patrol time and at briefing he made it very clear that there was to be no attacking of trains etc during patrol time but at the end of the patrol - 'Go for it'. Of course, we found no activity at either airfield during our one hour patrol but a number of trains chugged by on a nearby line. It goes without saying that at the end of our patrol there was not a train to be seen. However, Jack was keen to give his cannons some work so we went searching and soon found some tell-tale smoke on another line nearby. Down we swooped with me calling out the altitude at each 100 feet. I could feel the movements of the plane as Jack lined up his sights then the cannons thudded beneath us. A slight pause and we saw the strikes straddling the engine which we left belching forth large quantities of steam as we went looking for further prey. Back near Malmsheim airfield we found another train and gave it the treatment but, much to our surprise, the airfield defences opened up on us. After checking from a safe distance that this second train was stationary and steaming profusely we decided to call it a night and headed for base. This was exciting stuff for two raw crew members on their second operation.

'There was an interesting interlude in the March full moon period when German intruders were expected to attack heavy bombers returning from raids on the Continent. Some crews, after being briefed, were waiting at readiness with flying gear donned, flight plans prepared and engines warmed up for sorties to the German airfields to which the intruders were expected to return. They did not arrive however, but a few did come over in April when we were not at readiness!

'More variety was to follow and our third operation was a 'Night Ranger' to an area north of Berlin. The main force was not out that night and after checking out several airfields and finding no activity we cruised to the outskirts of Berlin and watched the activity there as 8 Group carried out their nightly attack. Op.6 required some real navigation as we were to escort some minelayers to the Heligoland Bight and had to meet them at dusk at a specified place and time over the North Sea. Our altitude was to be 1,000 feet and theirs 500 but cloud base was 900 feet as we reached the rendezvous and started a circuit. They appeared almost below us and with a waggling of wings we fell in behind them and dropped to their altitude to facilitate tracking them on our radar as it became darker. As planned, we later turned to starboard to place ourselves between them and the German coast. We patrolled uneventfully for the appointed time before heading for base. There were no bomber losses. Op.7 was to be a standard one hour patrol of Fritzlar airfield but we found that the fuel in our drop tanks would not transfer into the wing tanks. We made it to the airfield, however and had the satisfaction of dropping our load of incendiaries. We repeated the trip the following night with no problems. Op.9 was to Lista airfield on the south-west coast of Norway where we were greeted on arrival with a spectacular curtain of multi-coloured flak. We completed our one hour radar patrol by circling the airfield at a safe distance and were rather thankful we had no bombs to drop! Then followed the 424 mile return flight across the boring North Sea. Op.10 was also to Norway but was anything but boring. It was an anti-flak patrol to Oslo Fjord in support of more mine-laying. Intense anti-aircraft fire signalled the arrival of the bombers and this was our cue. With throttles at plus 12 we moved in and sprayed the ground defences repeatedly with cannon fire. I doubt if we silenced any but at least we distracted their attention from the bombers for the next twenty minutes or so. They all returned safely but an unescorted force of 15 planes mining the nearby Kattegat lost three.

'Op.13 was a one hour patrol of Lübeck airfield in north Germany and it was on Friday 13 April - anyone superstitious? We had 2 x 500HE and two cans of incendiaries to dispose of, but alas low cloud from the Baltic extended from about 1,000' to ground level. We circled down into it as far as we dared so the next question was what to do with those HEs and IBs? I suggested to Jack that I do some calculations and use our ASH to fix our position from a nearby lake before making a timed run to a dropping point. The calculations included finding the square root of 128,000 and with some minor adjustments to ground speed and altitude we were ready to go. I gave Jack the signal for bombs away and after a pause we felt the blast. Alas we shall never know how close we were but it was an interesting exercise. I had done Stage 1 applied mathematics at university and was able to recall the necessary formulas. More variety followed with mass attacks becoming the rule rather than the exception. From mid April we were involved in four - Munich Schleiszheim, Munich-Riem, Flensburg and Jägel. For the Riem raid we refuelled and bombed up at Juvincourt in France with extra bombs in place of the usual drop tanks. It was a fiery do and our total flying time was 6 hours 50 minutes.'

There remained one more task in the wide-ranging activities of 100 Group, which operated under the code-name 'Firebash'. This involved dropping 'bombs' (100-gallon drop tanks) containing napalmgel (petrol thickened with a compound made from aluminium, naphthenic and palmitie acids to which white phosphorous was added for ignition). Several 'Firebash' raids were flown against night-fighter airfields in April with devastating results but not without losses.

Leutnant Wolfhard Galinsky was a night-fighter pilot flying Me 110G aircraft with III./NJG6 at München/Neubiberg airfield. On the night of 18/19 April Galinsky and his crewman were tasked with a night strike against US Army ground forces in Eastern France. They departed the base at 20.53 hours and after attacking truck convoys with GP bombs and 20mm and 30mm cannon fire they returned at 23.45 hours. After debriefing they remained at the Command Post chatting with duty personnel. Between 01.00 and 02.00 hours the next morning, ground crew reported that the airfield was under attack by two enemy aircraft. The personnel had run from their anti-aircraft gun pits to the shelter of the Command Post. Galinsky took the initiative and left with several others to man the anti-aircraft guns. Clambering onto a staff car driven by the Gruppenkommanduer, the party was proceeding to the gun pits when it came under attack from one of the enemy aircraft. As it passed overhead it was illuminated by light from a huge fire in one of the hangars. Galinsky recognised it as a Mosquito by the typical characteristics of wing mounted oil coolers between the engines and the fuselage. It was 'Winball 7'; one of seven 141 Squadron Mosquitoes carrying two 100-gallon drop tanks filled with napalm for a 'Firebash' raid on München/Neubiberg airfield and was being flown by Warrant Officer Ronald G. Dawson and Flying Officer Charles P. D. Childs, an all New Zealand crew. The 24-year old pilot and his 32-year old navigator/radar operator had joined the Squadron on 22 January and this was their tenth op.

After the Mosquito passed, the Germans resumed their journey in the staff car. Near the Officers' Club, Galinsky jumped off the vehicle and leapt a fence to man an anti-aircraft gun post. This post had a twin machine gun mounted on a wooden pole. He pulled the covers off and armed the guns. He fired a quick burst in the general direction of the attacking aircraft to let the crews know the airfield defences were now in action. One of his colleagues manned a single machine gun in the adjacent gun pit. A Mosquito was heard approaching at full speed. Galinsky recalled: 'We were not afraid because as pilots we knew that in such a situation a single man is not in danger. Then both gunners shot out almost at the same time in a certain direction. Suddenly the Mosquito had been hit by one of the first shells from our cannons. One of its wings immediately caught fire - we knew it was made of balsa wood and we fired all the shells in our weapons, but had no further success. We shouted out our victory and were very glad to have put up such a good defence. We felt elated but understood that only one aircraft had been fighting against us, as the attacking Mosquito had not shot again - not even after our defensive shooting.

'The Mosquito pilot lifted his plane immediately as it flew in a bend towards Munich. Rather soon after this we heard a big bang as the aircraft hit the ground. Everything was over and we walked back to our staff car position while heavy anti-aircraft artillery around Munich was still in operation - as it had been for many nights.' Back at the Command Post, reports came in indicating only minor damage to the airfield. The German aircrews were full of admiration for the Mosquito crews in locating their airfield at night. However, they could not understand why the second aircraft had not continued its attack with such light resistance from the German defenders. Galinsky and two other officers, Leutnants Kamprath and Kogler, took a staff car to see where the Mosquito crashed. They wanted to bring survivors back to the airfield for an interview before handing the prisoners over. After an hour's drive they located the Mosquito in the garden of a large housing estate.

'The fire in the Mosquito aircraft had almost been extinguished by civilian firemen,' recalled Galinsky. 'It was only between one and three yards away from one of the detached houses in the garden where it had crashed in a belly-flop landing position. The pilot was killed when the plane landed and had been burnt in his seat. The firemen had already taken him out of the aircraft. The radio operator had jumped out of the aircraft before it crashed, but the altitude had been too low and his parachute had not opened. He had crashed through a barrack's roof and wooden floor onto the ground floor in a foreign worker's living room. He had been killed instantly. Now our minds were quite different to immediately after the aircraft had been shot down and we had been filled with enthusiasm. None of us could see any sense in such action anymore, so shortly before the expected end of this terrible war. We felt the senseless loss of these victims.' Dawson and Childs were the last casualties on 141 Squadron in WW2. They were laid to rest in the Durnbach War Cemetery.

The last attack on the 'Big City' by Mosquitoes took place on the night of 20/21 April when 76 Mosquitoes made six separate attacks on the German capital. Flying Officers A. C. Austin and P. Moorhead flying XVI ML929 claimed the last bombs dropped on the 'Big City' when they released four 500 pounders at 02.14 British Time. All the aircraft returned safely. Two Mosquitoes were lost on 21/22 April when 107 Mosquitoes bombed Kiel. On 23/24 April sixty Mosquitoes carried out another attack on Kiel and returned without loss. On Sunday 25 April 482 aircraft raided coastal batteries on the Friesian Island of Wangerooge and in a fitting climax to bomber operations, on Hitler's mountain retreat at Berchtesgaden in the southeast corner of Germany. The Obersalzberg, a beautiful mountainous region close to the Austrian border was one that had long appealed to Hitler. Following the Munich Putsch and his imprisonment, Hitler had stayed in the Obersalzberg, writing part of Mien Kampf there. Royalties from the book's sale had enabled the German dictator to buy a house called the 'Berghof'. After coming to power the building had been rebuilt on a lavish scale the best known addition was the dramatically named 'Eagle's Nest', a tea-house that had been built on Kehlshein mountain apparently as an isolated conference building. Hitler's home, referred to as the 'Chalet' by the RAF, was the target for 359 Lancaster heavy bombers and fourteen 'Oboe' Mosquito and 24 Lancaster marker aircraft. Included in the mighty force were thirty-three Lancasters on 9 Squadron and 617 the 'Dam Busters', each carrying a potentially devastating 12,000lb 'Tallboy' bomb in their long, rakish bomb bay. For once, the BBC was permitted to announce the raid while it was in progress. At least 126 Mustangs of 11 Group RAF and 98 P-51s from two American fighter groups provided escort relays along the route, a round trip of 1,400 miles.[118]

One of the 'Oboe' Mosquito markers was crewed by Flight Lieutenant Derek James DFC and Flight Lieutenant John C. Sampson on 105 Squadron. Sampson recalls. 'We took off at 07.25 and the flight was 4 hours 15 minutes. We carried four red TIs to mark for the heavies. We flew at 36,000 feet because of the Alps and since 'Oboe' signals went line of sight and did not follow the curvature of the earth, the further the target, the higher one needed to be. (Following the Normandy invasion, 'Oboe' ground stations were located on the continent thus increasing the effective range of the system). I heard the first two dots of the release signal and then nothing more. We were unable to drop and brought the markers back to base. On investigation, it was established that a mountain peak between the ground station and the aircraft had blocked out the signal. No 'Oboe' Mosquito was successful this day.'

Those who bombed the 'Chalet' mostly missed but the Berghof sustained much blast damage as a result of the bombs and the 'Tallboy's. Only 53 bombers attacked their primary target but at the SS barracks, one building and several others were damaged. Six of the 3,500 who had sheltered in the air raid tunnels were killed. Soon after the raid the US 3rd Infantry Division won the race to occupy Berchtesgaden and share in the spoils of victory.

118   *Barnes Wallis' Bombs: 'Tallboy', Dambuster & Grand Slam* by Stephen Flower (Tempus 2004).

Bomber Command's last heavy bombing operations were flown that night when 119 Lancasters and Mosquitoes directed by the master bomber, Wing Commander Maurice A. Smith DFC attacked oil storage depots at Tonsberg in Southern Norway and U-boat fuel storage tanks at Vallo in Oslo Fjord. Operation orders for attacks on Heligoland on the 26th and 27th were each cancelled in turn.

Freedom now beckoned for thousands of captured airmen who had been languishing in PoW camps, some of them for years. On 25/26 April twelve Mosquitoes dropped leaflets over PoW camps in Germany telling Allied prisoners the war was almost over. For men like Bill Brittain and Guy Hackett, captivity had thankfully been short and liberation by General Patton's 3rd Army was at hand, as Brittain recalled on notes made on toilet paper and later transcribed into a Red Cross notebook.

29 April 1945, Sunday: Prospects of a bright day. BBC's news last night contained a message from SHAEF direct to us. A tonic. A few prunes, a couple of fried sardines on toast for brekker. Jake Jessop came around to our fire so I climbed through the window to chew the bull with him over a cup of tea. Then we were really bucked by the sight of two Mustangs giving us the old reccon and did they take their time, really 'shooting us up'. Small arms fire uncomfortably close followed and I dived indoors. Convinced that our infantry are fighting on all sides of us. The rat-tat of machine guns is incessant. Maybe today is the day. Let's hope. More and more news, really official poop from group keeps coming in and it's all wizard. Bang on. I'm coming home soon sweetheart. More light arms fire, with Kriegies scrambling madly for cover and anything that would suffice as a foxhole. A stray bullet actually did ricochet off our block, so I'm told and a Medic got one in the leg. Folks this is the day: 12.00 hours - tanks were purported to have been seen in the factory area outside the camp; 12.37 hours - the 'Stars and Stripes' seen to be hoisted over Moosburg town; 13.00 – 'Stars and Stripes', Union Jack and flags of numerous other nations hoisted over Stalag VIIB, i.e. we took over; 14.03 hours - Liberation - two tanks and another armoured vehicle rolled into our compound.'

With the Germans at the brink of defeat, thousands of people in the western and north-western provinces of the Netherlands, which were still in German hands, were without food. Parts of the country had been under German blockade and 20,000 men, women and children had died of starvation during a very short period and the survivors were in a desperate plight. Dutch railway-men had gone on strike in protest against German demands and as a result there was no distribution of food. Townsfolk went foraging in the country and thousands camped in fields in search of food. Five slung panniers, each capable of carrying 70 sacks containing flour, yeast, powdered egg, dried milk, peas, beans, tins of meat and bacon, tea, sugar, pepper and special vitamin chocolate were fitted into the Lancaster bomb bays. Orders were issued for each squadron to drop the panniers in their allotted area, which they would find 'marked' by PFF Mosquitoes after liaison with the Dutch authorities and the underground movement. [119] Only the bedridden appeared to be confined to their homes as the Lancasters flew over to drop their loads and there was a sea of hands waving handkerchiefs and flags to greet the RAF bombers while even some German gunners standing by their anti-aircraft guns waved solemnly in acquiescence.

The authorities tried to keep the drop zones clear but there were a few incidents. A Lancaster on 186 Squadron, which were briefed to drop five large panniers each on

119   PFF Mosquitoes made 124 sorties to 'mark' the dropping zones.

Waalhaven aerodrome near Rotterdam, dropped three packages, by which time crowds had swarmed across the field and they could not risk dropping the others. Another Lancaster could not get all its packages away because the bomb doors had been damaged by small arms fire. Back over Stradishall the pilot found that he could not lower the undercarriage. While 'jinking' his aircraft to jolt the wheels down, a package fell, strewing tea, sugar and tins over the countryside to the north of Stradishall which caused something of a race between villagers and the RAF recovery party. Finally the pilot flew to Woodbridge and landed safely on the long runway. Next day one of this squadron's Lancasters was hit by two bags from an aircraft above, fortunately without causing damage. The drops continued for several days. Crews reported that on a number of houses messages had been whitewashed - 'THANKS RAF' and 'GOOD LUCK TOMMY'. Many crews gave their own sweet rations and their aircrew issue, wrapped up and tied by string to handkerchiefs or pieces of linen to make a parachute. They flung them from the open windows of their Lancasters with notes saying, Ver Het Kinde - 'For The Children'. The sweets became a free for all! Stones marked out 'TABAC' and a whip round of the cigarette ration was organized and it was dropped at the location the next day. A target indicator in the Rotterdam area fell by a house and set it on fire. One pannier dropped in a lake, but later crews reported rowing boats going out to salvage the contents. During the operation one Lancaster, after dropping 284 sacks, got into trouble over the North Sea on the return journey. A short in a microphone heater caused a fire in the rear turret and exploded rounds of ammunition. The pilot was able to land at Oulton without injury to any of the crew. During Operation 'Manna' from 29 April to 7 May a total of 6,684 tons of food were dropped in 3,156 sorties by Lancasters and 145 flown in Mosquitoes.

It was feared that the enemy might stage a last stand in Norway when ships laden with troops began assembling at Kiel so on the night of 2/3 May three final raids by Mosquitoes of eight squadrons in 8 Group and 37 Mosquitoes of 100 Group were organized. There were unseasonal snow showers in the morning and there was a possibility of thundery activity in the afternoon and early evening but close to take-off time the weather improved and the raids went ahead. In the first raid, a record 126 aircraft on 23, 169, 141 and 515 Squadrons in 100 Group led by sixteen 'Oboe' Mosquitoes attacked airfields at Flensburg, Hohn, Westerland/Sylt and Schleswig/Jägel with Napalm and incendiaries directed by a Master Bomber. In the second and third attacks, one hour apart, 126 Mosquitoes of 8 Group bombed through thick cloud using H_2X (the US development of H2S) and 'Oboe'. There was no opposition at all on the way to Kiel and even the searchlights were very few and far between. At the targets things were different, as Kel Purdie on 515 Squadron recalls. 'Jägel was more hair-raising than anything that had gone before and having regard to the state of the war, seemed to us to be rather pointless and fraught with danger which we did not want at that stage. From recent experience we knew that German ground defences had been concentrated in the small area of northern Germany still held by the Germans, with all the airfields bristling with AA defences. This was to be a mass attack by three squadrons. Jack Flanagan and I circled in our holding position waiting for our call from the master bomber. At one stage there was a large oily explosion on the airfield, which looked like a plane going in and this did nothing to calm the jitters. In due course we received our call and Jack carried out his usual dive bombing routine, going in at plus-12 boost. As we approached the perimeter the flak ahead was intense and suddenly Jack pulled away and told the master bomber that he would make a second run. He remarked to me that with so much flak coming up ahead of us he did not like our chances, so on his next call he opened up through the gate to plus 18 from a slightly higher altitude and in we went. This time most of the flak was coming up behind us and we made it through without a scratch - and so we began the long haul home across the North Sea. I could not help but wonder if Jack's action in aborting the first run had kept us off the casualty list. In fact, one plane was lost, two came home on one engine and others were damaged.'

On 142 Squadron, Flying Officer Ted Jenner, Flight Lieutenant Mike Young's navigator, who had flown their first op, on Berlin, on 11 April, recalled: 'We discovered, after the event, that this was the last raid carried out by the LNSF of Path Finder Group. The trip was uneventful but extremely colourful, with assorted air and ground route markers and d TIs in great profusion in all directions! One doubted if the enemy appreciated the 'show'; maybe some squadrons were 'in the know' and were inclined to celebrate!'

At 0800 hours on 8 May the cease-fire came into effect and VE Day was declared.

Chapter 8

Post War

In the Far East, PoWs like Cliff Emeny, who had been shot down over Meiktila, Burma while leading 'B' Flight on 45 Squadron Mosquitoes on 9 November 1944, had to wait a little longer for their liberation. With the port engine on fire and the starboard engine losing coolant fast, he was eventually shot down by two Oscars, after quite a hectic battle. Emeny, who as an NCO gunner/observer on Defiants on 225 Squadron destroyed a German bomber attacking Hull on 9 May 1941, was saved at the last moment by his Aussie room mates who drove the Oscars off his tail and enabled him to make a controlled crash landing in the jungle. Being already on fire the Mosquito exploded on impact and cut a swath through the trees at ground level. Luckily Emeny carried a special axe with a very short handle and he was able to cut himself free of the wreckage before being burnt too badly. He and his navigator were captured by the Japanese, being classified as 'Missing believed killed'. After very brutal interrogation they were imprisoned in Rangoon where Cliff managed to persuade the Japanese to let him run a hospital of sorts, with very little help from the Japanese. He had done a first aid course in his teens in New Zealand's Territorial Army and he succeeded in completely stopping the awful death toll. Cliff took part in the prisoners 'take-over' of Rangoon and lead a force of Indian ex-British troops to take over Mingaladon airfield, Rangoon, where the invasion troops found the 'dead' pilot, weighing just 6 stone 10lbs, with a rifle over his shoulder, commanding the field. With the runway de-mined, huge bomb holes filled and RAF landing signals laid out the runway was operational again.

The war in the Far East proved the bitterest campaign of all that Mosquito crews fought in. This was a war far from home, with no home leave, against an implacable foe, pursued without pause despite the very hostile and uncomfortable climatic conditions. Keeping the aircraft flying was no mean feat. To reach the operational area, the Chin Hills rising to 9,000 feet had to be negotiated first. The clouds over the mountains were just one of the hazards, as Squadron Leader C. L. Gotch on 82 Squadron at Kumbhirgram in northern Assam recalls: 'On the night of 10 February I took off on an operational sortie at 20.00 hours. At briefing we had been warned by the Met Officer that the weather was not good and that on no account was it safe to enter cloud. Knowing that I had to climb to approximately 15,000 feet to climb over the cloud tops, I decided to make height over base to at least 10,000 feet. It was a dark night with no moon, but seeing some broken patches above, I tried to find a gap through which to climb. At 8,000 feet while heading for a gap I found myself in cloud without warning. The bumpy conditions were immediately so severe that I had no apparent control of the aircraft. Relying solely upon instruments I saw that the artificial horizon was showing the aircraft upside down. I carried out the normal correction as best I could. The aircraft then stalled, ASI showing 80 mph and the rate of dive 4,000 feet per minute. What happened next is extremely confused, but after being in the cloud for not more than two minutes I found myself in a gap at 13,000 feet, the cloud top continuous above to at least 16,000 feet. Seeing the airfield lights below, I dived immediately and landed straight away. I consider myself extraordinary lucky to have come out of the incident alive. Just before coming out of the cloud I had told my navigator to prepare to bail out as I had no control of the aircraft at all.'

At the end of April 1945 82 Squadron and 45 Squadron withdrew from Kumbhirgram to support the planned invasion of Rangoon from the sea to be followed by the invasion of Malaya. At Kinmagon, a 2,000 yard strip on the central Burma plain occupied by 47 Squadron and 110 'Hyderabad' Squadron from April-August 1945, Mosquito FB.VIs flew daily sorties against Japanese road, railway and river communications and gave close support for the XIV Army advancing to Rangoon and beyond. The strip, originally rolled out by the Japanese, was situated about 60 miles south-west of Mandalay, a few miles from the Irrawaddy and subject to severe flash floods as the Monsoon struck. Every facility had to be flown in. The local water was contaminated. There were no hangars, very limited shelter except the small ridge tents as illustrated, plus two or three marquees. It was hot with ground crew stripped to the waist servicing the aircraft. Mosquito nets at night plus mepacrin to keep malaria at bay.

The FB.VI squadrons moved into central Burma proper in direct support of the 14th Army in its dash to Rangoon before the monsoon brought all movement of heavy guns and tanks to a halt. In July Paul Hunt, a navigator had left England and had arrived in Karachi in a BOAC Dakota on the 22nd. It was 8 August before he started the next stage of his journey to Calcutta, again with BOAC but this time he enjoyed the luxury of a 'C' Class Empire Flying Boat. There were two stops on the way, at Rajsamand and Gwalior and one involved landing on a lake. The journey to Calcutta was completed in the day and he then found himself resident in the Grand Hotel on Chowringee Street. While in Calcutta it was left to him to find air transport to join 110 'Hyderabad' Squadron at Hmawbi north of Rangoon. Finally, in mid-August just as the war in the Far East ended with the dropping of two atomic bombs on Japan, he got a lift to Rangoon and then he went by road to the airstrip. They passed, going in the opposite direction, a convoy of vehicles with a number of Japanese officers. It was later understood that this was connected with the arrangements for surrender.

'Joining the Squadron, I found out why we had 'Hyderabad' in the name. When the Squadron was first formed during the 1914-1918 War the Nizam of Hyderabad had met the cost of the aircraft as a contribution to the war effort. It was said that if any member of the Squadron was in the vicinity of the Nizam's palace, there was a welcome awaiting him with lavish hospitality. Regrettably, I never had the opportunity to claim this privilege. The full Japanese surrender was announced while I was in camp at Hmawbi and it followed the dropping of the atom bomb on Hiroshima and Nagasaki. In spite of the horrors attendant upon the dropping of the bomb, the general consensus in camp was that it was justified to hasten the end of the war. Official surrender did not put an immediate end to the fighting everywhere and pockets of resistance remained in the jungle. On several occasions grenades were lobbed into the camp at night, but without injury while I was there. The most unnerving part was when a visit to the toilet was necessary in the dark, because the toilets were situated near the camp perimeter. Fortunately, we were well protected in the camp by a company of Ghurkhas who won our admiration, not least by their daily parade and vigorous exercise in the sticky heat.

Several times I ventured out with fellow officers into the jungle. We saw to it that we had our revolvers with us in readiness, but the most we saw of Jap presence was one or two vacated 'fox-holes'.'

Warrant Officer Jimmy Gibson, a Mosquito pilot on 47 Squadron recalls: 'On the night of 16 August some Japanese forces decided that the war for them was not yet over despite the unconditional surrender announced by the Emperor on 15 August. Pete Rostance my navigator and I were fast asleep on our charpoys when all hell broke loose. Coming from the officers lines was the sound of gunfire and explosives. We just thought some of the crazy officers were celebrating victory a little too enthusiastically. Not to be, the officers' lines were under attack from approximately 80 Japanese who had no intention of surrendering. From a hail of hand grenades and Molotov cocktails six officers on 47 Squadron and two on 110 Squadron received minor injuries and were taken to hospital. Fortunately most of the officers were still celebrating VJ Day in the Officers Mess which escaped attack. One Mosquito was written off and much personal baggage destroyed. From that night a considerable increase in security was imposed by squadron personnel and the RAF Regiment.'

Squadron Leader C. L. 'Twitch' Turner AFC 'B' Flight Commander on 110 (Hyderabad) Squadron at Hmawbi, who was settling in at their tented camp area, adds. 'Our Squadron doctor, Flight Lieutenant A. R. Harbinson, a very close friend, was 'established' in the next tent to mine and on this particular night he decided to have a party in his tent and accordingly invited me to join him, which included, the two flight commanders on 47 Squadron. Having already over-imbibed most of the day in celebration, I decided I had had enough and took a 'rain check'. I had not long been stretched out on the charpoy under the mosquito net when I heard, literally, the patter of feet, then 'bang, bang' as the bullets flew. Since our side arms had been handed over on the Jap surrender and being no hero under such circumstances, I dived (starkers!) out of the back of the tent into the conveniently dug monsoon trench at the rear, just as there was a mighty explosion in Doe's tent. Needless to say I was quite stunned and shattered and took some time to recover; the full memory is hazy. However, as far as I can recall, the grenade imploded and one casualty was the Doc's pet collie which suffered head cuts and lost an eye and two of the lads suffered burst ear drums. The Doc thereafter suffered 'the shakes' quite a bit, noticeably when holding a glass! - or that's what he put it down to. The next day I heard that Ghurkhas had caught some Jap infiltrators and a bit later I met up with a Ghurkha officer (British) and asked him about it. His reply - 'What Japs?'

'Soon after this incident, on 20 August, out of the blue came an SOS for help from a section of our Guerrilla force 136 who were being attacked by Japs, who could nay accept surrender. I led the raid which put paid to the problem. It was established later that on this raid the last bomb of the war was dropped by the RAF. (110 Squadron also dropped the first bomb of the war when Blenheims attacked Wilhelmshaven).' Although Warrant Officer Alan Rendell was 'credited' with dropping the last bombs on the Japanese in Burma by the RAF he never regarded that there was any credit involved. 'The reason why I was last was because when I took off with the Squadron on this sortie the undercarriage of my aircraft failed to retract. As we were above maximum landing weight I decided to drop the bombs in the sea but halfway to the coat the undercarriage retracted so I decided to follow the Squadron although I did not catch them up. The approach to the target was down a valley and because of the monsoon weather the tops of the hills on each side were in cloud but the valley was wide enough so that the Squadron was able to maintain formation. I met them as they were returning to base obliging me to dive beneath the formation on my way to the target area. In the briefing we were told that the enemy was concealed in 'elephant grass' and accordingly would be difficult to see from the air. However, we were given a good description of their location. The briefing was correct but we could not see anything of the Japs although we could see the result of the attention given by the Squadron. I added my contribution to and followed the Squadron back to base when I was relieved to find that my undercarriage locked down.' [120]

'Before the Japanese surrender,' continues Paul Hunt, 'Mountbatten had planned extensive combined operations for the invasion of Malaya and Singapore, operations 'Zipper' and 'Tiderace': It was decided that the logistics of the plan should be carried through for the occupation of these areas, even though the war was officially over. 110 Squadron would fly direct to Singapore. The Squadron had already played a part in the surrender arrangements: by good fortune the CO, Wing Commander Saunders had been in the right place at the right time. Flying over Rangoon he saw what he understood to be an indication that the Japanese commander there was ready to surrender, so he landed and accepted the surrender of the enemy forces in the immediate area! This was regarded on the Squadron as good one-upmanship and a feather in the Squadron's cap.'

After the surrender ceremony, on 12 September, 110 Squadron, now at Seletar, Singapore prepared to leave Burma but the local inhabitants of Java were flexing their muscles for revolt against the return of Dutch colonial rule, having been armed by the Japanese. The Squadron was requested to fly south and make a show of force, especially over Batavia (now Jakarta). 'The request' continues Paul Hunt 'was taken up with a fair degree of enthusiasm as life was getting a little boring. The Squadron of 'Mossies' took off on the morning of 29 September from Seletar. Bob Hummel, the pilot I had teamed up with and I had a most enjoyable flight in brilliant sunshine out over the many islands south of Singapore and then close to the coast of Sumatra on the way to Batavia. The sea was a deep blue in contrast to the white sand of the beaches and the dark green of the jungle inland. On our way we passed near to the large island of Bangka where we witnessed a strange sight. Below us and to the left, not far inland, there was an airfield where a plane was taking off. We were flying quite low and could clearly see a row of Japanese officers standing to attention along the side of the runway. As the twin engined plane gathered speed and passed the officers they bowed and we could see the light catch the sheaths of their swords as they swung behind them. Typically Japanese, we thought.

'On arrival over Batavia a good deal of fun was had by all. We were expected to 'show the flag' and this was done with some verve. It was line astern for 'B' Flight and Squadron Leader 'Twitch' Turner led the way, twisting and turning over the town. Not many could keep on his tail but, somehow, Bob Hummel managed it being second in the line. Then it was a case of each doing his own thing and I recall diving low over a sampan and causing utter confusion on board until the occupants jumped overboard in terror. Soon it was all over and we were on our way home, but we made our presence known without a shadow of a doubt.'

Squadron Leader 'Twitch' Turner's navigator was Tom Easton, who recalled: 'We had an uneventful trip down; 'didn't even feel the bump as we flew over the Equator, flew around Batavia to show the flag and set course for Singapore. As we were approaching Sumatra Squadron Leader Turner reported that we had a fuel leak and had insufficient fuel to reach Singapore. We looked around and came on a Japanese airfield at Palembang in south east Sumatra and prepared to land. At this time it was not known whether these remote outposts had been informed of the surrender, or whether or not they would be friendly. As we landed, we saw a Japanese officer running towards us and we taxied to him. He ran up tripping over his sword and saluting. I would have liked to have his sword as a memento, but he would probably give it to me in the neck! So with a deep breath, down I went through the exit door. I knew no Japanese and he obviously did not understand English particularly with my Scottish accent. So I descended to arm waving, head shaking and pointing, the gist of which was that he had no fuel but kept pointing in a north-westerly direction. So we decided to take off NW. First of all I had to start the engines. This was a first for me, as ground crew were always available on home bases. The engines started all right and the slip stream just about blew me over, but we were off and away. About five minutes later we came to another Japanese airfield. This time we were in luck. They had no fuel either but they had a Dakota either crashed or shot down. The Japanese were very willing to help, obtained a manual pump and hose and soon had our tanks filled. We took off and arrived safely back at Seletar.'

Paul Hunt on 110 Squadron concludes: 'We made our way back separately. Off the coast of Sumatra the drama commenced and the trouble started when we tried to switch petrol tanks. Soon Bob asked for a course to the nearest airfield, saying that we did not have sufficient fuel to reach Seletar. So we arrived at Palembang, where we were welcomed by Dutchmen who had very recently been released from internment. We ended up staying until 2 October and it was quite an experience. It transpired that Sumatra and Palembang in particular was still teeming with Japanese, all fully armed! The Allies, having at that time been unable to send occupying forces following the Japanese surrender, had agreed to leave the Japanese army in charge 'to keep law and order'. I must say it was somewhat disconcerting to walk the streets at close quarters with Japs who were armed to the teeth and we felt somewhat vulnerable. For our short stay we found a hotel where most of the residents seemed to be Japanese officers; they were polite but eyed us rather suspiciously from time to time. Eventually, we managed to leave Palembang in much the same way as Tom Easton left his airfield for Singapore. Another Dakota saved the day and our Dutch friends on the airfield helped us to siphon off petrol into our Mosquito; whereupon Bob decided it would be a good idea to demonstrate the manoeuvrability of the Mossie as a farewell gesture. Climbing high we dived on the airfield and Bob then proceeded to give an impressive display which resulted in much arm waving from below by the Dutch. We were not to return to Palembang but, at the end of the month, we were again on our way to Batavia where we were to be based for several weeks.

'During October the situation in Java had worsened and the Squadron was asked to send a detachment to be based, temporarily, at Batavia. We flew down on 31 October and remained there for most of the following month. It was a dangerous situation which could easily escalate unless checked. The Indonesians had been incited to rebellion, many had accepted Japanese arms and they were out to prevent the Dutch re-asserting sovereignty over their islands. Even heavy artillery had fallen into the hands of the' rebels' and it was rumoured that they had control of at least one airfield. Possibly, Japs were staying behind to help them. Our task proved to be mainly reconnaissance but, initially, there were some leaflets to drop, aiming to placate the local inhabitants and tell them what nice friendly people we were. Unfortunately, the Mosquito proved to be a most unsuitable aircraft from which to scatter leaflets, especially if thrown by the navigator out of his side window. This was just above the air intake for the starboard engine and at least one embarrassed crew returned from a sortie on one engine, the other stopped because it had overheated when the air intake became stuffed with leaflets.

'One particularly strong centre of resistance to Allied occupation was Surabaya, a town towards the eastern end of the island of Java. Here the Indonesians had some heavy armour and sorties over Surabaya met anti-aircraft fire which, although somewhat erratic, caused some damage. There was one most unfortunate incident when one of the squadron aircraft was attacking an anti-aircraft gun at Surabaya. The pilot was Warrant Officer Alan Rendell and the navigator was Flying Officer Joe Wynne. They were both injured by a cannon shell exploding in the cockpit and Joe suffered serious and permanent injury to his left hand. Nevertheless, they returned safely to base.

'The Indonesian resistance in the island lacked co-ordination and much of it around Batavia took the form of terrorist activities. Sometimes at night the urban area was infiltrated and sporadic attacks were made on buildings occupied by members of the Allied forces, or on installations which appeared of importance to the Allied cause. It could be a little unnerving, as hand grenades were thrown indiscriminately. We devised our own 'defences' for the house in which we were living, piling sandbags on the veranda facing the road and arranging for one of our number to be on guard throughout the night. Probably, the greatest risk was for anyone to go out and return late, because any shadowy figure was liable to be shot at with the minimum of warning by the officer on guard behind the sandbags. We were much safer on the airstrip in Burma. Batavia was the only place where I slept with a loaded revolver under my pillow. On 22 November we returned to Seletar and although I did not realise it at the time, this was to be the last time I would enjoy the exhilaration of flying as a navigator in a Mosquito.' Jimmy Gibson on 47 Squadron adds: 'The security situation in the old Dutch East Indies was chaotic with thousands of Dutch citizens, mainly women and children who had suffered very badly in internment camps, awaiting repatriation home in a very hostile atmosphere. Many of the native population of Java were far from friendly to any occupying power. Batavia, later renamed Jakarta, was in a political turmoil. Much unrest was being created by two radio stations which the Allied Command decided should be destroyed. This task was given to a 47 Squadron detachment of four Mosquitoes led by Flight Lieutenant Peter Jacomb Hood. During 20-21 November as one of the four crews, I flew with Peter from Hmawbi to Butterworth in Malaya and then to the airfield at Batavia in FB.VI RF946 equipped with rocket rails. Our prime purpose was to protect convoys of Dutch women and children coming down from the hills under British Army protection. These convoys were being harassed by local insurgents, with the British Army having some difficulty in preventing casualties. There were several tragic incidents of women and children killed by Indonesian extremists. This 'messy little war' was not over until early 1946. In the meantime, on 25 November Mosquitoes on 47 and

84 Squadrons destroyed by rockets the W/T stations at Surakarta and Jogjakarta. Prior to these attacks and to avoid civilian casualties, we flew over the target area to make sure we could identify and subsequently hit the target and not civilian homes. A Beaufighter one hour before the attack dropped leaflets giving forewarning of the attack to come. The radio stations were taken off the air and never returned.'

'Soon after our return to Seletar' continues Paul Hunt 'all Mosquitoes in the Far East were grounded: the heat and the dampness of the climate had taken its toll on their wooden construction. There had been several fatal accidents and after our return from Java, one aircraft flying over Seletar had plunged to the ground after a wing had parted company from the fuselage. Investigations on other aircraft revealed serious weaknesses and flying was stopped while experts were sent out by de Havilland to see what could be done to safeguard Mosquito flying in the future. It was, to say the least, disturbing to think of the way in which 'Mossies' had been flown with this potential hazard, as one recalls the flamboyant manner in which squadron pilots such as 'Dizzy' Addicott had demonstrated to VIPs the aerobatic capabilities of the aircraft.' [121]

Early in 1945, 45, 82, 47 and 110 Squadrons had received new replacement aircraft after several Mosquitoes had been involved in fatal crashes after breaking up in flight, although this was blamed on the glue and the large scale re-equipping of squadrons never took place. Cyril Norridge, a Fitter II (airframe) on 45 Squadron recalled: 'Many and varied targets were attacked with great effect and the aircraft sometimes returned with bricks and other debris wedged in the radiators and leading edges, keeping ground crews well occupied. It was at this time that the Mosquito's vulnerability began to show itself, with alarming cracks appearing at vital joints in spars and main members and we lost good aircraft, which just broke up in the air. One of the main areas of failure was in the area of the rear hatch on the starboard side. It was possible to pull off literally yards of ply and the disintegrated glue would fly up in clouds, almost like 'French chalk'. Evidence was shown of severe shrinkage in joints in the wood. Main spar joints had, in several cases, opened up to one eighth of an inch and under carriage attachments were pulling loose from their anchorages. There was also evidence of fracture of metal attachments thought to be due to excessive play. This marked the end of our operations and for many months the unit was virtually shut down, whilst special tropical finishes were tested, seemingly with no great success.'

Incidents of the Mosquito's glue coming unstuck occurred in Germany with BAFO too as Squadron Leader Ian R. Dick, a pilot on 4 Squadron at Celle in 1949-50 recalls. 'The first concerned an FB.VI when the pilot flying with a ground crew airman on a dive/steep glide bombing sortie to Noordhorn had the wings fold up on pulling out with fatal results to both occupants. The second occasion happened to me. The Squadron PAI (Pilot Attack Instructor) Flying Officer Les de Garis had a 'personal' aircraft (UP-D, TA539) to which had been fitted a second gun-sight - to show us plebs where to aim in air-to-air combat. He liked finger-like aileron control and had the ailerons dropped a little. When the aircraft went in for maintenance, the ailerons were returned to their correct angle. On the re-issue air test she flew 'like a ruddy bus' - 'droop the ailerons again!' This down and up game went on for some time and may or may not have been responsible for what happened to me. Nav.3 Readings and I were briefed for a night

121 'From Seletar I began my journey back to England in a Short Sunderland (V) flying boat on 8 March 1946.' Paul Hunt writing in The Mossie No.31 May 2002.

cross-country in Les' beastie. It was a glorious night, clear sky, half moon and not a breath of wind. When airborne it felt as though we were sitting in a darkened hangar with the engines running! NOT A TREMOR! The trip itself was uneventful until it came to landing. On 'Finals'; lined up nicely with the runway, speed and height spot on. 'This is going to be THE LANDING of the year! Ooze over the hedge with a whisper, ease back on the pole sweetly ... when WHAM. The pole flew out of my hand into the far left corner of the cockpit. Making a grab for it, it bruised my thumb badly as it shot back to the right rear. So busy was I chasing the dammed thing all over the cockpit that the landing took care of itself. The aircraft thumped down on the runway threshold and veered to the left by which time I had caught the stick and slammed on the brakes to come to a stop on the grass just behind the caravan! It was the shortest landing that I ever made. Tower called '26 where are you? You've not passed us on the runway yet!' I told them where I was and taxied back to the line VERY gingerly. The only 'damage' to the aircraft was a fractured u/c bolt which was soon replaced. The OC Engineer, after a lengthy de-brief, contacted the Ministry for permission to investigate - which meant destroying the whole wing. He got the OK and when the skin was peeled off it was found that the entire rear spar had come unstuck... Roll on Araldite!'

In Europe, meanwhile, 540 Squadron had ended the war making a complete photo reconnaissance of the whole of France, starting in March 1945 and finishing in November that year, when the squadron returned to Benson, disbanding there on 30 September 1946. After 'VE Day' 400 Squadron remained in Germany with BAFO until it disbanded at Lüneburg on 7 August 1945. In February 1945, 680 Squadron's PR.XVIs at Deversoir in the Egyptian Canal Zone finished the mapping of Italy and began work solely as a survey squadron. During late 1944 to August 1946 detachments were sent to Habbaniya and Tehran in Iraq and Aqir in Palestine. The Squadron moved to Ein Shemer in Palestine in July 1946 and disbanded that September prior to re-forming as 13 Squadron at Fayid.

Following operational duties on 692 and 128 Squadrons, Bomber Command Peter Ketley was posted on 28 August 1945 to 313 FTU at North Bay, Ontario, Canada for instruction in advanced astro navigation in order to fly Canadian built Mosquitoes to the Far East, which were to be used in operational duties against the Japanese. 'As the Japanese armistice was signed soon after our arrival' says Ketley '313 FTU was disbanded. I returned to the UK and was posted to 1409 Met Flight at Lyneham on 13 December. Following the end of hostilities in the Middle and Far Eastern theatres of war the main duties of the RAF Transport and Bomber Commands was to transport personnel from all those areas back to the UK for demobilisation or re-posting. The vast majority of these transport flights would be during the daylight hours, through the Mediterranean as far as Marseilles and then up through the centre of France in a direct line to Lyneham. Therefore, the main duties on 1409 Met Flight at that time was to ensure that all the aircrews of the aircraft concerned in carrying returning personnel to the UK would have the knowledge of the base and height of types of cloud en route in order to fly at the height to avoid any inclement conditions; and therefore have the safest of flights back to the UK. Each flight made by 1409 was known as a 'Pampa'.

Another navigator on 1409 at this time was Alan Shufflebottom, who recalls: '1409 was an extremely happy unit with aircrews and ground staff making a great team. At Lyneham we were an independent unit immediately responsible to the Air Ministry, all orders coming from them by telephone on an 'Immediate take-off basis'. Our operational HQ was a derelict old hut equipped with a map table, telephones and assorted chairs in various stages of decay adjacent to our hanger in a corner of the airfield. The crews lived in Dugdale House about two miles away. It had belonged to a pre-war big game hunter and its walls were festooned with animal heads, hence it nickname 'The Lion House'! It was late Georgian with a semi-circular drive way, several bathrooms and bedrooms some of the latter being shared. My skipper, Roy Pigden, was living in rented accommodation with his wife Beryl. Dugdale was only used for sleeping and drinking as our meals were taken in the Mess at Lyneham the catering being just first rate. At the time the CO was Squadron Leader Johnnie Johnson DFC AFC. We had some superb parties, Johnnie's demob being the most memorable one; we flew with hangovers for days afterwards!

'Whilst on 1409 we completed a total of 27 'Pampa's. Our equipment was basic. I carried a plywood 18-inches square map board with clips, rubber on a string, 2 pencils sharpened at each end. We also had a torch, camera 5" x 5", thermometer, barometer and diversion kit. On 10 January 1946 when we were on a 'Pampa' to 16 West over the Atlantic, we went out low climbing to 36,000 feet at 15W so as to take advantage of the prevailing west wind for the return journey when the starboard engine packed up completely due to an oil leak. Unfortunately the generator was on the starboard engine and so by the time we arrived back at Lyneham the batteries had run flat, toppling the gyroscope and most of the instruments. The whole country was covered in dense fog and although GCA (Ground Control Approach) had just been installed at Lyneham they wouldn't risk talking us in and suggested Graveley near Cambridge, as a diversion. Fortunately I was carrying a torch so Roy flew with me holding it on the instruments that were working, through the fog we saw what appeared to be an airfield but got no response to our distress flares, the fog swept in and everything disappeared. We knew we were near Graveley but despite 'blipping an engine' could not attract their attention, by then we only had 10 minutes fuel left so Roy told me to bail out. Meanwhile the Air Ministry had phoned the Wing Commander Flying at Graveley enquiring why we hadn't answered, whereupon he ordered a 'Sandra' searchlight to be lit and I spotted the shaft of light just as I was about to open the door prior to jumping, we dived in on the beam and Roy made a superb one engine landing on to the grass at the end of the runway as we ran out of fuel.

'Besides routine 'Pampa' Met flights there were specials when Prime Minister Clement Attlee and Foreign Secretary, Ernest Bevin, were going abroad and one of our aircraft was 'Scrambled' to check the weather conditions no matter what base conditions were like; i.e. fog etc. The reports were phoned through to an Air Ministry contact as soon as we landed; top priority wherever we were. I learnt respect for the elements whilst on a trip with Flying Officer 'Percy' Vere covering Ernest Bevin's flight to Berlin (he was en route to Moscow but the Russians would not allow our Mossies behind Berlin), there were two aircraft involved one taking the northern route and the other the southern, ours was the latter. Flying low over the Rhine near Karlsruhe we were 'sucked up' in a cumulo-nimbus thunder cloud reaching 30,000 feet in seconds! If ever a test of the strength of a Mossie was needed it was more than proved on that day 27 February 1946. Once again thanks to great piloting we survived to tell the tale.' [122]

---

122 Alan Shufflebottom writing in *The Mossie*.

There was a 'milk run' round France every morning with reports by code (when required) to French VHF stations and there was a duty crew roster for emergency take-off requirements day and night. At about 0200 hours on 14 March 1946 Peter Ketley and Nick Carter were briefed for a flight to Bordeaux and return with take-off time set for 03.05 hours. This was in order to arrive over Marseilles at sunrise and would gradually alter according to the time of year and the time of sunrise; and of course, the winds affecting the aircraft. The route for the 'Pampa' flight was Base - Marseilles - Toulouse - Bordeaux - Base. Total flying time 5 hours 25 minutes.

'The first leg to Marseilles was uneventful' recalls Alan Ketley 'and little was required to be noted regarding weather conditions experienced. On the return flight at approximately 15minute intervals, I would note the latitude and longitudinal positions and request the pilot to climb to the cloud tops and descend to the cloud base and would then record time - type - base and height of all cloud experienced. The flight back to base was also uneventful until just south of Paris, when one engine started to give trouble. Nick Carter decided to feather the troublesome engine and we continued on one engine back to base. At this stage Nick and I were unconcerned as the Mosquito was known to fly well on one engine. Pilots were required to carry out single engine landings during training, but they were told to avoid, if possible going round again. We eventually arrived back at Lyneham a little later than ETA and requested permission to carry out a single engine landing. The Control Tower gave us permission to land and everything appeared to be in order, so Nick lowered the undercarriage and made a final approach. The direction of the wind was not directly down the runway, so with a crosswind a little more speed and slight amount of 'crabbing' was necessary, which made it difficult for Nick to put down at the approach end of the runway. In fact we did eventually touch down near to half way down the runway. No going round again on one engine! So when we came to the far end of the runway we still had 'many miles on the clock' and ran out of runway. We went through the perimeter fence and hedge into the field beyond, before coming to a standstill at 08.40. The overshoot caused the undercarriage to crumple, which in turn caused the escape hatch to buckle and lose shape, so when the jettison handle was pulled the release hatch would not come away from its surroundings. Nick and I stood on our parachutes placed on our seats and attempted to force it open with our shoulders, but it would not budge. By this time some of the ground staff who had witnessed the crash, ran over, broke the Perspex of the escape hatch and pulled Nick and I out to safety. Neither of us had so much as a scratch on our hands, face or bodies. I guess after 5 hours 25 minutes of flying there was very little petrol left in the tanks, so the threat of fire in a wooden aircraft was minimal. May I at this stage say 'Thank You' to those very brave ground staff who acted so quickly.

'We were eventually picked up by the transport awaiting for us should we have completed a normal landing and I was then able to make my report to the RAF Meteorological Office at the Air Ministry, the information being of vital importance to the transporting aircraft flying over France on 14 March. Nick Carter and I flew our next 'Pampa' on 20 March, six days after our crash. Later we were reposted when 1409 was disbanded in April 1946.'

In the immediate aftermath of WWII the Mosquito continued to serve the RAF at both home and overseas and new models were even introduced, at a time when other wartime aircraft had already ended their development. The Royal Navy had wanted to have Mosquitoes for carrier operations in WWII, but it did not begin to operate Mosquitoes until 1946, long after the Pacific War had ended. Admiralty Specification N15/44 had been issued in 1944 for a twin-engined aircraft that was capable of operating from carriers and de Havillands had responded with the Sea Mosquito. The first prototype was actually a converted Mk.VI (LR359) with an arrester hook added, the rear fuselage strengthened on either side by reinforced longeron ribs, Merlin 25s boosted up to +18lbs boost and non-feathering four-bladed de Havilland airscrews.

Boscombe Down test pilot, Lieutenant Commander Eric 'Winkle' Brown OBE DSC was asked in January 1944, 'Do you think you could land a Mosquito on an aircraft carrier?' With all the 'brash arrogance of youth', he said 'Yes!' As he later confessed; 'When I reconsidered it I wasn't so sure, but I'd burnt my boats by this time, because as a form of entertainment, deck landing is probably on a parallel with Russian roulette.'

Early in March 1944 deck landing trials with LR359 were ready to take place aboard the 766 feet long flight-deck of HMS *Indefatigable*. The deck was 95 feet wide but this diminished to 80 feet at the island and the Mosquito had a span of 54 feet - not much margin for error! Lieutenant Commander Brown recalls: 'The first landing occurred on 25 March, so we hadn't really had much time between getting the aircraft to making the actual first landing. In 1944 the arrester gear on an aircraft carrier had limitations in that it could only absorb an entry speed of about 65 knots and that for an aircraft of 10,000lbs or so weight. Here we were talking about an aircraft that, in the pilots' notes, said the approach speed was 125mph and the weight for the first landings we were going to make was 16,000lbs. Another problem was would the undercarriage, which had not been modified, take the vertical velocities which are normally extremely high in deck landing? Or would it collapse under the strain?). The aircraft, strangely enough, behaved extremely well on the approach and the actual touchdown speed was believe it not, 78 mph. There were about 8-10 wires on HMS *Indefatigable* and I caught the second wire. Then we carried on the landings mounting up the weight. All went well until the eighth landing, which was at the weight of 18,000lbs and when at touchdown I felt the deceleration start, which is normal when you catch a wire, then suddenly it stopped and the aircraft began to move forward again. Well, I had to make a lightning assessment - one of two things could have happened: either the hook had broken, in which case we had to go on (there was no crash barrier) and take off again. If the wire had broken however, then if opened up again too early I might cause another disaster and pull the hook out, because I had to give it sufficient time to get to at least one more wire. We did get to this position, when I realized that something had gone wrong that was not going to arrest us. So I had to give it the full gun, irrespective of the swing and the torque caused. What actually happened was that the claw of the arrester hook had rotated and the wire thrown clear of the claw because the forward bolt, one of two which held the frame of the hook to the claw had sheared off. Hatfield very rapidly modified it for the second series of landings and all told, the whole thing was a very successful exercise.'

Hereward de Havilland agreed: 'On 9/10 May Mosquito trials were completed on HMS *Indefatigable* near Ailsa Craig. Starting at 18,000lb the all-up weight was progressively increased to 22,000lb for take-off and 20,000lb for landing on; the reduction for landing was made by dropping four live 500lb bombs into the sea unpleasantly close to a small fishing boat the pilot hadn't seen. All take-offs and landings were successful; on one full load landing the arrester hook locked 'up' after hitting the deck without picking up a wire; the pilot, Commander Lans, jammed his brakes on and pulled up with 160 feet of deck to spare, which inspired a lot of confidence after the excitement died down. One's general impression of these trials was that considerable skill is required to land a Mosquito on a carrier under average conditions.'

Production of the TR.33 Sea Mosquito began at Leavesden late in 1945. When folding wings were introduced from the fourteenth Sea Mosquito on, the folded width, at 27 feet 3 inches, was greater than the 20 feet folded width for the lifts of the Navy's new carriers then coming into service! Manual folding was used too as power folding would have meant a complete redesign of the hydraulic system. The original undercarriage using rubber blocks in compression though was later changed by the installation of a Lockheed oleo-pneumatic undercarriage with slightly smaller wheels. In August 1946 the first of fifty Sea Mosquito TR.33s began equipping 811 Squadron at HMS *Peregrine* at Ford replacing the Mk.VIs, which had arrived in September 1945. Nos. 771 and 772 Training Squadrons also used TR.33s. 811 Squadron disbanded at RNAS Brawdy in July 1947. Only 14 Chester-built TR.37 models which followed the TR.33 were built and just six saw service with 703 Squadron.

Bob Henderson worked at RA Short Aviation at Lossiemouth (HMS *Fulmer*) from 1953-1955 where about 20 Mosquitoes were prepared for dispatch to Israel. Amongst this batch of Mosquitoes were a few Sea Mosquito TR.33s previously used by the Royal Navy.

'The fifty or so aircraft at 'Lossie' included possibly up to twenty of the aircraft carrier versions of the Mossie. These varied considerably from all the land based versions (and there were many of them) in as much as they had folding wings which were hinged and locked but had to be folded with a long beam with hooks and catches. They required several strong 'Matelots' to lift and lever the wings up and over to finish, almost wing tip to wing tip, just above and behind the cockpit cover and above the emergency dinghy box, used for any emergency ditching situation. These TR33s were fitted with the fairly basic Merlin 25 engines, but more importantly, with de Havilland's own four bladed propellers which, being narrower revved up much faster and were much quicker to respond to the engine throttles, both on and off. The usual three, almost paddle bladed Hamilton props, seemed sometimes only to reach their maximum revs half way down the runway. On an aircraft carrier any such delay would almost always be fatal!' [123]

Civil Mosquitoes also operated throughout the world and RAF record-breaking attempts saw many more Mosquito achievements in the late 1940s. On 6 September 1945 Wing Commander J. R. H. Merrifield DSO DFC and Flight Lieutenant J. H. Spires DFC DFM made the east-west crossing of the Atlantic from St. Mawgan to Gander in a PR.34 in 7 hours, returning on 23 October in 5 hours 10 minutes. In April 1947 two PR.34As (one a reserve) were prepared by RAF Transport Command for an attempt on the London to Cape Town record, set in 1947 by a de Havilland DH.88 Comet. On 30 April Squadron Leader H. B. 'Micky' Martin DSO DFC and Squadron Leader Ted Sismore DSO DFC took off from Heathrow Airport for the 6,717 mile flight with stops at El Adem, in Libya and Kisumu in Kenya. They easily broke the record, landing at Cape Town's Brooklyn Airport on 1 May after 21 hours 31 minutes at an average speed of 279 mph.

123 *The Mossie* No.37 January 2005.

PR.34s were operated for a number of years by RAF home and overseas commands. 540 Squadron, which had disbanded at Benson on 30 September 1946, reformed there on 1 December 1947 with PR.34 aircraft. Frank Baylis, a wartime 544 Squadron PR navigator, who had just finished an overseas tour on 13 Squadron, joined 540 in June 1949: 'Early one Saturday evening in September, I was 'mooching' around the parade ground at Benson, when I was accosted by Wing Commander Hal Bufton. He ordered me to collect my overnight gear and report to the briefing room. Much mystified, I did. Flying Officer Mike Whitworth-Jones and I were briefed for a flight to Leuchars. We were told that some 'boffins' from Harwell were fixing a filter to the belly of a PR.34. It meant nothing to us. Off we went to bonny Scotland. Next day we had to fly along a pre-arranged bearing to PLE (Prudent Limit of Endurance). It was a long and boring flight over the sea all the way. Next day we did another trip to PLE, this time around the eastern coast of Iceland and back. Each time we landed, the filter was removed and flown immediately to Harwell. A few days later, the Government announced that the Russians had exploded their own atomic bomb. The New Year's Honours List showed Mike Whitworth-Jones and me with King's Commendations - for two straightforward flights!'

540's PR.34s were used on PR and survey duties until December 1952 when Canberra PR.3s took over. Meanwhile, 58 Squadron had reformed at Benson on 1 October 1946 in the PR role and its first task was involvement in the Ordnance Survey of Great Britain, using Ansons and PR.34s. In 1953 both types were replaced by English Electric Canberras. At Wyton that winter, 58 Squadron's PR.34 and PR.35 aircraft (including four in 'B' Flight converted for night photo reconnaissance using flashlights) and 540 Squadron's PR.34s at Benson, were used to photograph the terrible floods which hit Britain's east coast in February 1953. For eight days they photographed the devastation, taking over 100,000 photographs which were used to help aid the rescue and repair efforts. In mid-1953 58 Squadron's PR.34s were replaced by Canberra PR.3s, 540 having begun re-equipment with the jet in December 1952.

In the Far and Middle East, Mosquitoes still had a role to play. After VJ Day 684 Squadron's PR.34s were used as a high-speed courier service throughout the Far East before moving to Bangkok in January 1946 to take up survey duties. This continued until 1 September when 684 disbanded at Seletar by renumbering as 81 Squadron. On 1 August 1947 Spitfires of 34 Squadron were added to the strength and 81 Squadron became the only PR unit in FEAF (Far Eastern Air Forces), responsible for long-range PR and survey over the East Indian area. 13 Squadron reformed on 13 September 1946 vice 680 Squadron, which disbanded at Ein Shemer and using PR.IXs and XVIs carried out PR and photo-survey work in Palestine and the Canal Zone until February 1952.

NF.36s fitted with AI Mk X radar provided night defence for the Canal Zone from bases at Fayid and Kabrit, 1949-53. Forty NF.36s also equipped 23, 25, 29, 85, 141 and 264 Squadrons at home. [124] Nos. 39 and 219 Squadrons, both of which reformed at Kabrit, in May 1949 and early in 1951 respectively, were the last two squadrons to be re-equipped with NF.36s. Peter Verney, a navigator who was posted to 39 Squadron in February 1952, recalls: '39 Squadron was reformed in May 1949 at Fayid in the Suez Canal Zone equipped with Mosquito NF 36. The first CO was Squadron Leader Richard Doleman

---

124   They represented Fighter Command's only all-weather fighters until replacement by Vampire NF.10s and Meteor F.11s in 1951-52.

DSO DFC. The Squadron moved to Kabrit on the Great Bitter Lake in February 1951 and was joined by a reformed 219 Squadron, also flying NF.36, resurrecting a famous wartime night fighter squadron number. We joined 13 Squadron, which was equipped with the Mosquito PR.34 and which used this Mark until replaced by the Meteor PR.10, over the period January-March 1952 and so for a while Kabrit was home to three Mosquito squadrons. In October 1951 the Egyptian parliament abrogated the treaty by which British Forces were stationed in the Canal Zone. They sent in a force of tanks, guns and infantry to throw us out and a very unpleasant situation arose. A 39 Squadron aircraft discovered this force some 20 miles from Kabrit and the GOC arranged for a Lancaster to drop a message urging them to return home or face the consequences. This they very sensibly did but a very tense period followed. Squadron Leader J. C. 'Fungus' (or 'Coggers') Cogill DSO DFC took over from Squadron Leader Doleman at this very inopportune moment. With my pilot, Flight Sergeant Joe Halkiew, I and another crew joined 39 as normal replacements in February 1952.

'The first attempt by the Egyptians to remove us was inspired by the notorious King Farouk in a desperate attempt to gain some popularity. When he was deposed by General Neguib in July 1952 there was another half hearted attempt and an increase in the so-called 'terrorist' activity. Eventually Neguib was replaced by Colonel Nasser in mid 1953 which led to yet another stand-off. It was rumoured that General Festing of Berlin Blockade fame, who was then GOC, had personally spoken to Nasser by telephone and told him that 'If your tanks are not back across the Nile in 48 hours we will attack you'. This produced the desired result.

'In the meantime we had been to the Armament Practice School at Nicosia in Cyprus for the annual concentrated gunnery practice for the pilots. Apart from the APS, considerable attention was paid to gunnery, especially air to ground. We had a range at Shallufa, 15 miles from Kabrit where we would regularly go firing both by day and at night. The night air to ground was very interesting and navigators had to fly to read off the altimeter to persuade the pilots to break off at a briefed 400 feet. The targets, a ten foot canvas square, were marked at night by three gooseneck flares, one each side and one at such a distance to the rear to be invisible if the dive angle was less than the briefed 30°. Most of our time was spent on practice interceptions under GCI control, doing the odd cross-country, much cine gun work and single engine practice. The pilots were required to do one single engine landing and two single-engine-overshoots per month so that they could cope when the real emergency arose. Luckily for Joe and me it never did. These were fun at night when a decision to land had to be made while at 800 feet when on one engine.

'All told, I did 230 hours on the Mosquito and feel privileged to have done so. We had a few alarms and excursions but low level during the Egyptian summer was not enjoyable with cockpit temperatures reaching 160°F [70°C]. It was also very easy to boil an engine while waiting to take off and Kabrit was one of the few stations where piston-engined aircraft had precedence over jets, 13 Squadron, who we shared the airfield with having exchanged their PR.34s for the Meteor PR.10 early in 1952.

'We were to be re-equipped at the start of 1953 with the Meteor NF 13 (a tropicalised NF 11), but there was some delay in producing them. The Mosquito had a 'glue joint' inspection at set intervals and if an aircraft failed to meet the required tolerance it was scrapped. So eventually we ran short of Mosquitoes and in late 1952 219 was temporarily re-equipped with the Meteor NFI1. A technical conference was held and the 'glue joint' tolerance was increased to allow us to continue with the Mosquito. In due course we ran short again and another technical conference decided that perhaps this glue joint problem was not important and could be ignored!

'Eventually the Meteors arrived in March 1953, the ferry pilots who brought them out taking back our Mosquitoes. Squadron Leader Cogill appropriated the very last one, RL141 and he took me with him. We ferried back to Benson via Luqa and Istres on 24/25 July 1953 and as far as I know, this was the last occasion that an RAF crew flew the night-fighter version of this famous aircraft.'

The last RAF Mosquitoes to see RAF service anywhere were the PR.34As of 81 Squadron at Seletar. In 1946-47 81 Squadron had carried out an aerial survey of the country. A state of emergency in Malaya was declared on 17 June 1948 when a full-scale Communist uprising began and 81 Squadron Mosquitoes reverted to their PR role as part of Operation 'Firedog', which began in July 1949. By the end of 1952 81 Squadron had made over 4,000 sorties and had photographed 34,000 square miles. 81 Squadron flew no less than 6,619 sorties during eight years of operations in Malaya. The honour of flying the very last Mosquito sortie went to RG314, when Flying Officer A. J. 'Collie' Knox and Flying Officer 'Tommy' Thompson returned from a 'Firedog' reconnaissance sortie against two terrorist camps in Malaya on 15 December 1955. Incredibly, fourteen years and three months had passed since the first ever Mosquito operation on 17 September 1941 when another PR machine (W5055) had photographed Brest and the Spanish-French border. In 1955-56 a number of PR.34As were converted for civil use at Hatfield and many were subsequently operated in the United States, Canada, Africa and South America on photo-survey work.

Percival Aircraft Ltd built its last PR.34 in July 1946. Post-war production of Mosquitoes though, was centred on the plants at Hatfield and Leavesden. Standard Motors Ltd had built the last of its 1,065 FB.VIs in December 1945, while Airspeed Ltd built its last B.35 in February 1946. In Germany, three squadrons in BAFO (British Air Forces of Occupation) operated B.35 aircraft, the last in February 1951 when they were replaced by Vampire FB.5s.

Chester built Sea Mosquito TR.37s and most of the 101 NF.38s, including the 7,781st and final Mosquito to be built, NF.38 VX916, on 15 November 1950. The NF.38 never entered service with Fighter Command because it was too heavy and too slow to reach the altitudes flown by the Soviet Tupolev Tu-2 and Tu-4 bombers so NF36s fitted with AI.Mk.X remained in front-line service until January 1952 when they converted to the Meteor NF.11. The last NF.36s in front-line service were a few operated on RCM duties and at Kabrit in the Canal Zone.

In the early fifties the NF.38s and many more Mosquitoes, simply became surplus to requirements and hundreds were refurbished for use by foreign air forces, some being supplied under the terms of the Mutual Defence Aid Programme (MDAP). In February 1951 the French sold 59 Mosquitoes to the new state of Israel, which, in 1948-49, had just fought a bitter War of Independence. Once the British arms embargo to Israel was lifted, a number of surplus Mosquitoes were flown to Israel after overhaul and de-navalization by Eagle Aviation (later British Eagle International Airlines) between October 1954 and August 1955 where they equipped two squadrons. Late in 1955 these were disbanded because of re-equipment with jets and in June 1956 they were placed in storage. However, by October they were needed again, when war with Egypt broke out. The Mosquitoes were taken out of store and used in the interceptor, bomber and photo reconnaissance roles before and during the Sinai (Suez) campaign, 29 October to 2 November, fought jointly with Anglo-French forces. Although many of the Mosquitoes received combat damage and a few had to crash-land, none were lost in combat and serviceability of the elderly aircraft remained high. The Mk.VI was the main variant, its rocket rails and bomb racks being used to good effect, while some escorted the two surviving Israeli B-17s on bombing missions over Egypt, but the larger-nosed NF.XXXs were difficult to master and in the heat their overall black finish contributed greatly to rapid deterioration of the airframes.

In 1963, in Britain, the last operational Mosquitoes - of No 3 Civil Anti-Aircraft Co-Operation Unit (CAACU) at Exeter Airport - made their final bow, when that unit's seven TT.35s and two T.IIIs were finally retired. Shortly afterwards the Mosquitoes were used in flying and ground sequences in the film *633 Squadron* and again in 1968, for the filming of *Mosquito Squadron*.

Index